Enabling Technologies for Effective Planning and Management in Sustainable Smart Cities

Mohd Abdul Ahad • Gabriella Casalino
Bharat Bhushan

Editors

Enabling Technologies for Effective Planning and Management in Sustainable Smart Cities

 Springer

Editors
Mohd Abdul Ahad
Department of Computer Science
and Engineering
Jamia Hamdard
New Delhi, Delhi, India

Gabriella Casalino ⓘ
CILAB Laboratory
Department of Computer Science
University of Bari "Aldo Moro"
Via E. Orabona, Bari, Italy

Bharat Bhushan
Department of Computer Science and
Engineering
School of Engineering and
Technology (SET)
Sharda University
Greater Noida, India

ISBN 978-3-031-22924-4   ISBN 978-3-031-22922-0   (eBook)
https://doi.org/10.1007/978-3-031-22922-0

This Springer imprint is published by the registered company Springer Nature Switzerland AG
The registered company address is: Gewerbestrasse 11, 6330 Cham, Switzerland

Preface

With the rapid penetration of technology in varied application domains, existing cities are getting connected more seamlessly. Cities become smart by inducing ICT in the classical city infrastructure for their management. According to McKenzie Report, about 68% of the world population will migrate towards urban settlements in near future. This migration is largely because of the improved quality of life (QoL) and livelihood in urban settlements. In light of urbanization, climate change, democratic flaws, and rising urban welfare expenditures, smart cities have emerged as an important approach for society's future development. Smart cities have achieved enhanced QoL by giving smart information to people regarding healthcare, transportation, smart parking, smart traffic structure, smart home, smart agronomy, and community security. Typically, in smart cities, data is sensed by the sensor devices and provided to end users for further use. The sensitive data is transferred with the help of the Internet, creating higher chances for adversaries to breach the data. Considering privacy and security as the area of prime focus, this book covers the most prominent security vulnerabilities associated with varied application areas like healthcare, manufacturing, transportation, education, and agriculture. Furthermore, the massive amount of data being generated through ubiquitous sensors placed across the smart cities needs to be handled in an effective, efficient, secured, and privacy-preserved manner. Since a typical smart city ecosystem is data driven, it is imperative to manage this data in an optimal manner. Enabling technologies like Internet of Things (IoT), natural language processing (NLP), blockchain technology, deep learning, machine learning, computer vision, big data analytics, next generation networks, and software-defined networks (SDNs) provide exemplary benefits if they are integrated in the classical city ecosystem in an effective manner. The application of artificial intelligence (AI) is expanding across many domains in the smart city, such as infrastructure, transportation, environmental protection, power and energy, privacy and security, governance, data management, healthcare, and more. AI has the potential to improve human health, prosperity, and happiness by reducing our reliance on manual labor and accelerating our progress in the sciences and technologies. NLP is an extensive domain of AI and is used in collaboration with machine learning and deep learning algorithms for clinical informatics and data processing. In modern smart cities, blockchain provides a complete framework that controls the city operations and ensures that they are managed as effectively as possible. Besides having an impact on our daily lives, it also facilitates many areas of city management. This book provides the basic knowledge about smart cities and their components and challenges in their effective realization. It sheds light on the know-how about the role of enabling technologies in effective management of smart cities to make them a better abode for the inhabitants. The book explores various enabling technologies like information communication technology (ICT), edge computing, AI, NLP, IoT, blockchain, cloud computing, 5G, 6G, and SDN.

New Delhi, Delhi, India   Mohd Abdul Ahad
Via E. Orabona, Bari, Italy   Gabriella Casalino
Greater Noida, India   Bharat Bhushan

Contents

List of Contributors

Mubasshir Ahmed Department of Electrical and Computer Engineering, North South University, Dhaka, Bangladesh

Manpreet Kaur Aiden Computer Science and Engineering, Sharda University, Greater Noida, Uttar Pradesh, India

Nujood Al Haddabi Independent Researcher, Muscat, Oman

Mustafa Al-Asadi Faculty of Engineering and Natural Sciences, Computer Engineering Department, KTO Karatay University (KTO Karatay Üniversitesi), Konya, Turkey

Duaa Alhusein Department of Computer Science, University of Babylon, Babylon, Iraq

Azad I. Ali School of Computer and Information Sciences, University of the Cumberlands, Williamsburg, KY, USA

Abdullah Mohammed Alshukaili University of Nizwa, Nizwa, Oman

A. K. M. Bahalul Haque LUT University, Lappeenranta, Finland

Rasmeet Singh Bali Department of CSE, Chandigarh University, Mohali, Punjab, India

Shambhavi Bashishth Kalinga Institute of Industrial Technology, Bhubaneswar, India

Bharat Bhushan School of Engineering and Technology (SET), Sharda University, Greater Noida, India

Korhan Cengiz Department of Computer Engineering, Istinye University, Istanbul, Turkey

Abhilasha Chauhan DIT, Dehradun, India

Sonia Chhabra Computer Science and Engineering, Sharda University, Greater Noida, Uttar Pradesh, India

Bhawna Choudhary School of Business Studies, Sharda University, Greater Noida, India

Raisa Nusrat Chowdhury North South University, Dhaka, Bangladesh

Tamanna Dalwai Department of Business and Accounting, Muscat College, Muscat, Oman

Bibhu Dash School of Computer and Information Sciences, University of the Cumberlands, Williamsburg, KY, USA

T. T. Dhivyaprabha Centre for Machine Learning and Intelligence, Avinashilingam Institute for Home Science and Higher Education for Women, Coimbatore, Tamil Nadu, India

Deepanshu Garg Department of CSE, Chandigarh University, Mohali, Punjab, India

Manisha Gupta School of Business Studies, Sharda University, Greater Noida, India

Shaurya Gupta School of Computer Science, UPES, Dehradun, Uttarakhand, India

Rakibul Hasan Department of Electrical and Computer Engineering, North South University, Dhaka, Bangladesh

Kazi Tamzid Akhter Md Hasib Department of Electrical and Computer Engineering, North South University, Dhaka, Bangladesh

Ali Kadhum Idrees Department of Computer Science, University of Babylon, Babylon, Iraq

Menila James Department of Computing, Muscat College, Muscat, Oman

M. B. Jennyfer Susan Department of Computer Science, Centre for Machine Learning and Intelligence, Avinashilingam Institute for Home Science and Higher Education for Women, Coimbatore, Tamil Nadu, India

Lamia Karim National School of Applied Sciences of Berrechid (ENSA), Hassan 1st University, Settat, Morocco

M. Krishnaveni Department of Computer Science, Centre for Machine Learning and Intelligence, Avinashilingam Institute for Home Science and Higher Education for Women, Coimbatore, Tamil Nadu, India

Ayasha Malik Delhi Technical Campus (DTC), GGSIPU, Greater Noida, India

Shilpi Mittal University Institute of Computing, Chandigarh University, Mohali, Punjab, India

Sachi Nandan Mohanty School of Computer Science & Engineering (SCOPE), VIT-AP University, Amaravati, Andhra Pradesh, India

Pradyumna Kumar Mohapatra Department of Electronics & Communication Engineering, Vedang Institute of Technology, Bhubaneswar, Odisha, India

Anjoom Nur North South University, Dhaka, Bangladesh

Nikunj Pansari Computer Science and Engineering, Indian Institute of Technology, Dharwad, Karnataka, India

Veena Parihar KIET Group of Institutions, Ghaziabad, India

Chittaranjan Pradhan Kalinga Institute of Industrial Technology, Bhubaneswar, India

Aniket Rathi Kalinga Institute of Industrial Technology, Bhubaneswar, India

Saroja Kumar Rout Department of Information Technology, Vardhaman College of Engineering (Autonomous), Hyderabad, India

Sanghamitra Roy Kalinga Institute of Industrial Technology, Bhubaneswar, India

Shweta Mayor Sabharwal Computer Science and Engineering, Sharda University, Greater Noida, Uttar Pradesh, India

Antara Sahoo Kalinga Institute of Industrial Technology, Bhubaneswar, India

Bibhuprasad Sahu Department of Artificial Intelligence and Data Science, Vardhaman College of Engineering, Hyderabad, India

Sameeka Saini Dev Bhoomi Uttarakhand University, Dehradun, India

Rishit Saiya Computer Science and Engineering, Indian Institute of Technology, Dharwad, Karnataka, India

Luxmi Sapra Graphic Era Hill University, Dehradun, Uttarakhand, India

Anu Sharma Department of CSE, Chandigarh University, Mohali, Punjab, India

Ashish K. Sharma Department of Computer Science Engineering, Bajaj Institute of Technology (BIT), Wardha, India

Deergha Sharma NorthCap University, Gurugram, Haryana, India

Vinod Kumar Shukla School of Engineering and Architecture, Amity University, Dubai, UAE

Arockiasamy Soosaimanickam University of Nizwa, Nizwa, Oman

P. Subashini Department of Computer Science, Centre for Machine Learning and Intelligence, Avinashilingam Institute for Home Science and Higher Education for Women, Coimbatore, Tamil Nadu, India

Swati Swayamsiddha School of Electronics Engineering, KIIT University, Bhubaneswar, India

Gesu Thakur University of Engineering & Technology, Roorkee, Roorkee, Uttarakhand, India

Nemika Tyagi School of Engineering and Technology, Sharda University, Greater Noida, Uttar Pradesh, India

Sonali Vyas School of Computer Science, UPES, Dehradun, Uttarakhand, India

William Webster University of Stirling, Stirling, UK

About the Editors

Mohd Abdul Ahad is currently working in the Department of Computer Science and Engineering, School of Engineering Sciences and Technology, Jamia Hamdard, New Delhi, India. He has a rich experience of more than 14 years in the field of computer science and engineering. He obtained his PhD degree in the field of big data architecture. His research areas include big data architecture, distributed computing, IoT, and sustainable computing. He has published several research papers in various international journals of repute in Q1 and Q2 categories. His cumulative impact factor for the last 3 years is 49.8 (As per Clarivate/JCR). He has chaired several sessions at international conferences of Springer, Elsevier, etc. He is a certified Microsoft Innovative Educator and a certified Google Educator. He is a life member of the Indian Society of Technical Education (ISTE) as well as an active senior member of IEEE. Apart from that, he is also on the review board of several prestigious journals such as the *Journal of Networks and Computer Applications*, Elsevier; *Sustainable Cities and Society*, Elsevier; the *Journal of Ambient Intelligence and Humanized Computing (JAIHC)*, Springer; and *Computers in Biology*, Elsevier.

Gabriella Casalino is currently an assistant professor at the CILab laboratory in the Department of Informatics, University of Bari, working on machine learning techniques applied to Web economy domain. This position has been funded by the Italian Ministry of Education, University and Research (MIUR) through the European funding project AIM (Attraction and International Mobility). Her research interests span in the field of data analysis. Her works cover different domains such as text mining, hyperspectral imaging, e-health, bioinformatics, anomaly detection, and educational data mining. She is currently working on stream data mining algorithms. Gabriella Casalino obtained her PhD in computer science from the Doctoral School in Computer Science in the Department of Informatics at the University of Bari "A. Moro." She defended her thesis "Non-negative factorization methods for extracting semantically relevant features in Intelligent Data Analysis." She was awarded by the Italian Ministry of Education, University and Research (MIUR) with a grant covering the 3-year period of her PhD. In 2008, she obtained a BSc in computer science from the University of Bari, and in 2011 she obtained an MSc in computer science from the same university.

Bharat Bhushan is an assistant professor in the Department of Computer Science and Engineering (CSE) in the School of Engineering and Technology, Sharda University, Greater Noida, India. He received his undergraduate degree (BTech in Computer Science and Engineering) with distinction in 2012, received his post-graduate Degree (MTech in Information Security) with distinction in 2015, and doctoral degree (PhD in Computer Science and Engineering) in 2021 from Birla Institute of Technology, Mesra, India. In the year 2021, Stanford University (USA) listed Dr. Bharat Bhushan in the top 2% scientists list. He has earned numerous international certifications such as CCNA, MCTS, MCITP, RHCE, and CCNP. Bharat has published more than 150 research papers in various renowned international conferences and SCI-indexed journals including the *Journal of Network and Computer Applications* (Elsevier), *Wireless Networks* (Springer), *Wireless Personal Communications* (Springer), *Sustainable Cities and Society* (Elsevier), and *Emerging Transactions on Telecommunications* (Wiley). He has contributed more than 30 book chapters in various books and has edited 20 books by reputed publishers such as Elsevier, Springer, Wiley, IOP Press, IGI Global, and CRC Press. He has served as keynote speaker (resource person) in numerous reputed faculty development programs and international conferences held in different countries including India, Iraq, Morocco, China, Belgium, and Bangladesh. Bharat has served as a reviewer/editorial board member for several reputed international journals. In the past, he worked as an assistant professor at HMR Institute of Technology and Management, New Delhi, and as a network engineer at HCL Infosystems Ltd., Noida. In addition to being a senior member of IEEE, he is also a member of numerous renowned bodies including IAENG, CSTA, SCIEI, IAE, and UACEE.

Chapter 1
Challenges and Opportunities in Secure Smart Cities for Enhancing the Security and Privacy

Sameeka Saini, Abhilasha Chauhan, Gesu Thakur, and Luxmi Sapra

Abstract Internet of Things is providing concept of connectivity with internet as well as interconnectivity between devices which has laid foundation for the smart cities. Smart cities have provided substantial enhancement in quality of life while considering environment impact also by giving smart information to people regarding healthcare, transportation, smart parking, smart traffic structure, smart home, smart agronomy, community security etc. In smart cities data is sensed by the sensor devices and provided to end users for further use. The sensitive data is transferred to and fro with the help of internet creating numerous chances for attackers to breach the data and invade the privacy and security of people. So, it's important to recognize the attacks, privacy and security concerns and there countermeasures while implementing the devices in smart cities. A number of research effort has been carried out on this aspect and several efforts have been made to assure the security and privacy of sensed sensitive data. The chapter focuses mainly on privacy and security tangled in the smart cities. This chapter highlights about smart cities, what make them smart and how, challenges in making cities smart, the numerous kinds of attacks and threats in smart city, the current resolutions working to make smart cities more secure and opportunities for improvement in smart cities.

Keywords Attacks · IoT · Information security · Privacy · Smart cities · Security · Security breaches

S. Saini (✉)
Dev Bhoomi Uttarakhand University, Dehradun, India

A. Chauhan
DIT, Dehradun, India

G. Thakur
University of Engineering & Technology, Roorkee, India

L. Sapra
Graphic Era Hill University, Dehradun, India

© The Author(s), under exclusive license to Springer Nature Switzerland AG 2023
M. A. Ahad et al. (eds.), *Enabling Technologies for Effective Planning and Management in Sustainable Smart Cities*, https://doi.org/10.1007/978-3-031-22922-0_1

1.1 Introduction

The rapid and continuous advancement of Computers and Information technology is impacting human lives in various manners. Daily individuals are moving from ruler to urban areas in exploration of enhanced and easy life. The modern urban areas are converting rapidly into smart cities just to give people quality life and comfort. All together the main aim is to make life comfortable. As per UNPF (United Nations Population Fund), more than half of world's populace have been moved to urban zones and by 2050 this number will be increased and approx. 68% population will live in urban regions [1] which will directly and indirectly going to affect climate, environment, energy and living surroundings. IoT i.e. internet of things is the foundation for commencement of future smart cities. With continuous progress in area of IoT devices are becoming smart and their efficiency is scattering in several applications like smart buildings, smart vehicle system, smart agriculture, smart hospitals, smart city etc. Devices are called smart because they are equipped with microcontrollers that can transmit and receive data. It assimilates ubiquitous sensing devices, network infrastructures and prevailing computing components. The data is sensed through sensors, RFID (Radio frequency identification) devices or other wearables that provides real time monitoring from house to public areas, traffic roads to environments etc. Later this information is transmitted to central controller or computing systems such as cloud, servers and so on [2]. The Fig. 1.1 shows the basic working of IoT environment.

The smart city provides modern services such as: smart buildings that autonomously manages temperature, lighting, energy consumption, self-automation of doors/windows and locks for large constructions; smart energy for optimized generation, monitor and usage of clean and green energy; smart transportation of vehicles; street traffic and pedestrian management; smart healthcare that promotes wellness, health observing and diagnostics; smart technology; smart governance and to facilitate smart educational system; smart security for ensuring the better and safe place to live [3].

The quick evolution in size of populations creates a varied range difficulties such as air pollution, congestion due to heavy traffic, disposal of waste problem, more consumption of energy, and increase in crime rate [4]. These difficulties can be hard

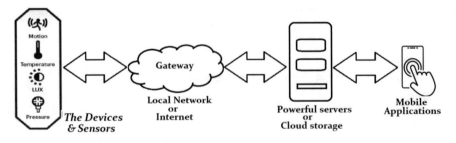

Fig. 1.1 Basic working of IoT (Internet of Things) network

to hold if the city or the governance is not prepared for it. As the population grows the demands and expectation for a better life also increases. Providing comfort and latest services to citizen in keeping the environment clean and less harmful can be a big challenge. Many countries are working and researching constantly related to smart city and are investing a huge amount of money to provide their population a better life. The enhancement of cities to smart city includes distribution of numerous sensors nodes to offer real-time information to individuals regarding diverse amenities like public transference, traffic drifts, eminence of water and air, energy consumption rate etc. The cities can have the capability to be smart in some major regions included as environment, governance, public individuals, economy, living and movement.

The chapter is categorized into 6 sections, each section have its own specification and contribution related to the topic of the chapter. Section 1.1, introduces IoT technologies, working of IoT network, applications of IoT, smart city etc. In Sect. 1.2 basic definitions, components, history, architecture, pillar, features, components, characteristics, applications, examples of smart city and why smart city is gaining popularity is discussed. In Sect. 1.3, the security requirements are covered such as privacy, confidentiality, authentication etc. In Sect. 1.4 the security and privacy issues/risks in smart city, threats and attacks in smart city are discussed. In Sect. 1.5 various opportunities and solutions that are currently existing related to security and privacy of smart city are highlighted. Finally the chapter is concluded in Sect. 1.6.

1.2 Smart City

1.2.1 Basic Definitions

Smart city doesn't have any specific definition and it can be defined in various aspects. City is made smart and smart is defined in terms of intelligence in urban life that provides safety and comfort to its citizens while keeping environment clean and green. The main objective of smart city includes promoting sustainability in city by providing decent quality of services and lifestyle to that city people. The other primary objective is to provide core infrastructure and to keep clean environment and find alternative ways in promoting smart solutions to the existing problems of the city.

The objectives also includes effective allocation of resources to yield productivity while keeping in mind that these resources will not be wasted. Staying competitive against the competitors is last but not the least one in list. Skilled cities compete with each other in terms of cleaner environment, resources utilization, recent technologies, investments etc. The following Table 1.1 shows the various definition of smart city explained by various sources.

Although different authors/researchers and organizations defines smart city in their terms but the common thing is the main idea of using recent technologies that

Table 1.1 Smart city definitions

Source	Definition
[3]	A city is called smart if it is sustainable & innovative city having ICT beside with other technologies to increase the effectiveness of facilities and life's quality while keeping in mind the future generations
[4]	It is technology that modern urban city uses electronics, voice activation and sensors to accumulate data which is used to achieve and improve the assets, services, resources etc. The smart city incorporates IoT devices and ICT technologies to optimize efficiency of city services and operations
[5]	Smart city is combination of ICT and IoT technologies that optimizes the services and operation which enhances the lifestyle of citizens of the city
[6]	A city that concentrates on environment, commercial and social phases of urban lifestyle for gaining the quality in life with the help of intelligent and sustainable technologies is called as smart city
[7]	As per IBM, a smart city is the one that makes optimal utilization interconnected info that is available today to make understanding better and to make effective and efficient utilization of resources available
[8]	Smart city aims at managing various sectors i.e. urbanization, green environment, consumption of energy, life style of citizens etc. It aims at increasing the capability of the people to use and adapt the growing advancements in ICT
[9]	Smart city can also be defined from data management perspective as, A city that contains data from collection, processing and distributing technologies to promote overall quality of life and covers wide areas of applications such as health, utilities, transport, education, governmental services etc.

provides comfort, security and improves the quality of life of humans living in that city makes a city smart keeping future generation and sustainability for clean and green environment. The smart city application is not limited to smart card that are used for authentication in case of online payment, but also for smart resource management of marine and power, smart motion application for traffic management and CO_2 emanations etc. The devices used in smart city include Sensors, PLC (programmable logic controller), Smart meter, Smart streetlights, CCTV etc., the systems in a smart city includes smart server, smart database, HMI (Human machine interface) etc. and the network in smart city incudes WiFi, Zigbee, TCP/IP, LoRa etc. The following Fig. 1.2 depicts the smart city overview.

1.2.2 Components of Smart City

The main six components of smart city includes economy, living, environment, individuals, transport and government [10]. The element economy comprises innovation & entrepreneurship such as innovative start-ups, Research and development, employment levels etc., productivity i.e. GRP per capita & local and global connections. The element living embraces culture, wellbeing, safety, security & health of individuals. The element environment includes smart homes or buildings, utilization of resources such as smart energy consumption, air quality, waste management,

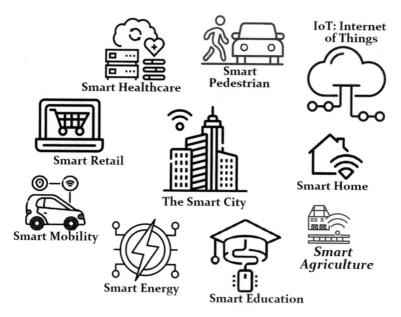

Fig. 1.2 Overview of a smart city

water consumption etc. and urban sustainable scheduling such as climate resilience planning. The element people or individual, comprises of education such as secondary and higher education with smart classrooms, security, creativity etc. The element transport or mobility includes effective smart transportation such as clean-green vehicles emitting less pollutants to the atmosphere, multimodal access, of public vehicles, infrastructure technology enabled and smart traffic system. The Element government embraces online services, open government, infrastructure such as Wi-Fi coverage, broadband coverage, sensor coverage, integrated health and safety functions etc.

1.2.3   History of Smart City

The term Smart city was initial casted in 1990s and the main emphasis was at importance of ICT with regards of infrastructure. California Institute of Smart Communities was first one to research on cities to implement ICT on them [11]. There are 3 key ideas for smart cities i.e. Digital city, ICT city and Compound city [12]. The very first version was referred as smart city with digital instrumentation for modifying the urban infrastructure. The city was smart because it contained CCTvs, Smart meters, sensors and software controlled devices. They produced huge amount of data after sensing it from various surrounding devices that was used to control real time situations such as transportation systems, energy supplies, security services etc. [14].

The second version of smart city basically focused on economy and e-government. The city plans to develop and advance urban policies by implementing ICT advancements to recreate human creativity, capital and innovation to make smart citizens and workers. Also it considered utilization of ICT in educational area.

The third version considers both digital technologies and ICT that results in advancement of social justice, innovation and transparent governance. For developing countries the smart city is the city that manages the economic and urban transitions, advancing modernization, development of nation and managing population growth. Whereas the developed countries promotes efficiency of services and sustainability [12].

1.2.4   Architecture of Smart City

The smart city is an assembly of smart sensors and processors that sense and collects the data from various sources and that data is further used by citizens and government. As such there is no fixed architecture and several authors have defined the architecture in their researches in different ways. Sookhak et al. [12] proposed 4 layer architecture of smart city. The sensing layer comprised of devices that collects data after being sensed from devices. This layer consists of sensors, actuators and cameras. The data collection layer contains storage devices. The data processing layer collects the stored data and derive meaningful information from it. The smart processing and application layer is responsible for exchanging data and smart applications.

Cui et al. [17] has described a layer architecture of smart city that contains the perception layer, Network layer, Support layer and Application layer. The perception layer also knows as sensing layer or edge layer or recognition layer and it is responsible for data collection from real world. The network layer is also called as core layer because it depends on internet and is responsible for transmitting the data between devices. The support layer close to application layer provides support to computing technologies. The application layer being the top layer is responsible for personalized requirements application for end users.

As per Gaur et al. [19] the architecture of Smart city is divided into four levels. Level 1 consist of data collection that comprises of sensors of various types, level 2 consist of data processing, level 3 consists of data integration and reasoning and the last level is device control and alerts that communicates services to the customized users.

Al-Turjman et al. [20] proposed IoT based architecture that consists of 6 layers mainly physical layer, network layer, database layer, virtualization layer, Data analytics and mining layer and application layer. The physical layer consists of wearables devices, sensing devices and control components. This layer is called as perception layer that comprises heterogeneous devices for sensing and gathering the data. Network layer being second also called as communication layer responsible for communicating the collected data. The layer consists of wireless sensor networks, cellular networks and other types of WLAN. The third layer is called as Database layer which entails of cloud servers, database and control centres. This layer is also called as support layer and its main responsibility is to provide support for application requests through intelligent computing methodologies. The virtualization layer provides mechanism to collectively integrate hardware software and networks into a logical single software entity. The Data analytics and mining layer converts raw data into meaningful information. This layer comprises of data analytics and machine learning algorithms. The application layer is the top most layer of architecture held accountable for giving application and services to the individuals founded on their requirements.

As per Butt and Afzaal [21] the design of smart city comprises of Perception, Integration, Cloud, Application and Business layers. The perception layer is responsible for sensing the environment and identifying objects/things for collecting data. The layer comprises RFID tags, wearables, smart devices, and other sensors. The second layer is Integration layer that takes input data from perception layer and integrate heterogeneous networks to next layer. The protocol in this layer includes Bluetooth, ZigBee, 4G, 6LowPAN etc. The cloud layer includes the storage components that are managed by Big-data technologies. The application layer provides services to the end users. The Business layer helps to produce diverse models created on services delivered by smart city system. From the literature survey of various available architecture, we have proposed a simple model or architecture of smart city. The architecture can be broadly divided into 3 main layers, namely

- Physical data sensing,
- Data storing & processing, and
- Network & application layer.

The Physical data sensing layer consist of the smart IoT devices which helps in collecting data from humans or surroundings with the help of smart sensors or mini devices such as wearables, body sensors, monitoring systems etc. The key aim of this layer is to collect raw and lots of data. Now this data is to be stored further for processing. The next layer is data storing and processing layer. This layer acts as a database or cloud central server storage that stores and collects the data gathered by the physical layer. This layer contains smart devices such as cloud storage, databases, servers etc. The collected data is also processed here by using ML/AI algorithms and meaningful information is extracted out from these data. The third and top most layer is the application and network layer. As the name suggest this contains smart networks that are used to connect the users with these databases. The networks can be wireless or wired, can be virtual or cellular. The following Fig. 1.3 shows the proposed architecture of smart city.

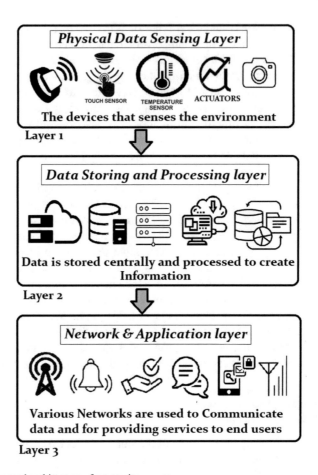

Fig. 1.3 Proposed architecture of smart city

1.2.5 Pillars of Smart City

There are four broad categories of infrastructure or pillar of smart city that includes Institutional, Physical, Social and Economic Infrastructure. The essential events such as governance, management and planning of city aiming decision making process of citizens, efficiency, accountability and transparency is known as Institutional pillar. The Physical Pillar consists of ICT applicable infrastructure and services such as waste management, urban mobility, smart transportation etc. The social infrastructure contains mechanism to endorse human development, social capital, citizen services, inclusive planning, environment and healthcare. The economic infrastructure refers to main services to promote process of construction, circulation of financial activities and improve proper organization to produce employment chances and fascinate investments. Such as market growth, GDP, job creation etc. The following Fig. 1.4 shows the 4 pillars of smart city.

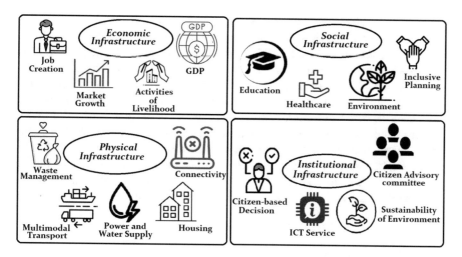

Fig. 1.4 Four basic pillars of any smart city

1.2.6 Features of Smart City

Smart city includes following features:

- Smart city endorse use of technology, data and information to encourage and improve the infrastructure and its services. This means access to water and electricity, providing homes to all, proper education, health services and IT connectivity.
- The governmental services are made reachable to the normal citizens. The services are both online and offline.
- A rise in access to public transportation such as smart parking, smart pedestrian, smart modal transport and intelligent management mobility system etc.
- A smart city redevelops the poor slum areas in order to make cities safer and bring every citizen to equal level. With the use of CCTvs and surveillance cameras, criminal activities will be tracked and crime can be controlled.
- Living areas will be made comfortable and all services will be accommodated to the population of the city. Such as maintaining parks, playgrounds, smart homes etc. that will enrich the standard of living.
- The surroundings will be made sustainable and environmental friendly by implementing smart energy, smart industries, smart vehicles and waste management.

1.2.7 Components of Smart City

Smart city is the assembly of smart devices and networks. The technologies are connected like a web of spider and the appearance of city changes from each other based on the technologies the city consist of [5]. We can classify the modules of a smart city basically into the devices it connects, the system it uses and the networks it created. The main devices in a smart city can be sensors that collects data based on what they can sense, PLC (programmable logic controller) that helps to operates and monitors the transmitted information, Smart meters for measuring electricity, water, gas etc., Smart streetlights that are LED equipped which not only consumes less electricity but also keeps the environment protected from harmful radiations, and CCTV devices that captures day to day activities of the city.

The systems are smart city management that overall manages the whole city, the smart servers that provides all time anywhere information of city, the smart city database DB, and HMI (human machine interface) that is used to display on-site and off-site information. The network component of smart city helps in communicating between devices with the help of Wi-Fi, Bluetooth, Zigbee, LoRa, TCP/IP etc.

1.2.8 Requirements of Smart City

Being the new and recent topic in concept of urbanization, a smart is interconnected and sustainable. The various sectors included are [13].

- Smart human capital: Effective, competent, educated human resource having social learning and critical thinking.
- Smart infrastructure: For better QoL (Quality of life) the infrastructure of smart city needs smart buildings that protect environment, lowers the energy consumption and provides better performance to citizens.
- Smart services: The important smart city services includes smart healthcare advancements, smart education, smart online banking etc.
- Security and privacy: The data plays a crucial role here. A lot of data is being sensed and collected by various sensor devices and smart wearables. This data needs to be protected from being breached and attacked by the attackers.
- QoL and sustainable environment: Smart government is required for increasing the QoL for healthy living of people.

1.2.9 Applications, Characteristics and Examples of Smart City

The application of smart cities involves smart street light that enables and disable by sensing the light surrounding, smart traffic management that includes the traffic light control and handling fast drivers and also issuing penalty in case of any rule violation, smart hospitals that are equipped with full automated machines that senses data from the patient's body and helps in diagnosing the disease and curing them, smart classrooms with smart boards with the help of which students get a good idea about any difficult concept easily, smart parking system that tell the drivers about the vacant space in the area, smart emergency system that detects and predicts any disaster and can guide the citizen about what to do and what not to at that situation, smart grids that saves the over usage and wastage of electricity by the consumers of the city etc.

The characteristics of smart city includes heterogeneity, which means that the system are independent, distributed, used and managed by different types of users. Resources constraints means that smart city devices are battery operated and have limited memory. To be specific they are inexpensive, smaller yet energy effective embedded devices. Mobility refers to the flexible mobility of people and goods both from one place to another. Connectivity and Scalability features the smart city to be connected to world all the time with regards of handling small and large population both effectively and efficiently. User involvement means the city is made smart just for the comfort of citizen, so citizen's involvement enhances the smart city. The following Fig. 1.5 shows the basic characteristics of smart city [17].

Some common examples of smart city includes Seattle in USA, Helsinki in Finland, Barcelona in Spain, The Island city state of Singapore, Songdo of South Korea, Milton Keyes in UK etc. [18]. They are smart cities because they have following features:

- They don't create harm to nature as they have reduced carbon emission.
- They have implemented RainWatch that monitors and alerts in case of flood.
- They have adapted smart traffic transportation system, that changes light in whether and road conditions.
- They have implemented CCTV on roads and other important areas.
- They have car charging facilities within parking.

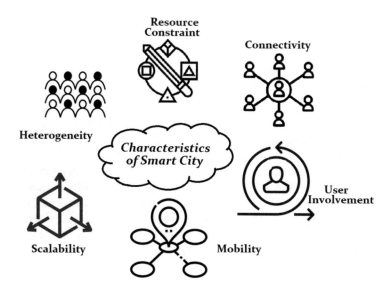

Fig. 1.5 Characteristics of smart city

- They have garbage trucks for smart waste management system purpose.
- They have smart grids and real-time energy saver systems.
- They have implemented smart LED streetlights which reacts to the movement.
- They have smart work centres with teleconferencing which helps the government to work and normal people to access fully equipped sensor networks.
- Smart devices and medical equipment are also implemented in hospital for better and fast treatment of diseases.

1.2.10 Why Smart Cities Are Popular and Its Benefits

The smart city is gaining popularity because it aims at providing comfort to the people while considering good to the environment. As people are migrating from rural to urban areas the smart cities needs to be more efficient and should welcome the large population effectively. It also focuses on growing the economic rate of the country. Smart city gives the solutions to the challenges the cities that are facing today and will face in future. The benefits of a smart includes:

- Better planning and development of any city.
- E-government services that can be provided to the citizens faster and at low expenses.
- The local economic development which endorses usage of technology in handling economic resources to upsurge productivity.
- Productivity is improved and the services are made best.
- The wastage is controlled and alternative way is find out to re-use the wastes.
- The energy is used wisely by making green buildings and using renewable resources of energy.

1.3 Security Requirements

Smart cities are made smart because of the smart devices it incorporates. The use of IoT based technologies enables a city in becoming smarter. The smart city influence everything from personal to various application areas such as education, healthcare, living style and national security. The implementation and adaptation of this smart city concept have become a major aim for majority of governments to monitors water, energy, healthcare, transportation, waste management, surveillance, security and privacy. Since smart city aims at making lives comfortable and easy they also brings some complexities, vulnerabilities and challenges related to security and privacy. The following Fig. 1.6 shows some requirements related to smart city [17].

Fig. 1.6 Security requirements of smart city

1.3.1 Authentication

Authentication is the technique to authenticate or proves one identity. It is considered to be the most basic requirement. This is required to ensure that only authorized users or clients can get admittance to the facilities provided by the heterogeneous devices of a smart city. It is highly recommended to get real-time and precise authentication mechanism for smart cities as the network and devices need to be examined and authenticate first to avoid any type of unauthorized access.

1.3.2 Confidentiality

It means that only the sender and receiver or the only authorized user will get the information. The main aim here is to prevent the sensitive information from attacks or being exposed to unauthorized users or attackers. For this purpose various encryption algorithms are used.

1.3.3 Integrity

Yet another security requirement is to achieve proper and full integrity in the communication. Integrity refers to the originality if the message that is not tampered or altered by any third person or attacker. Because a lot of data is being sensed, exchanged and stored between IoT devices in network, these data needs to be protected from attackers. The data will be tempered during transmission if not properly managed and encrypted.

1.3.4 Availability

The term availability means that the devices in network should be always available and the services should be provided to the users anytime and anywhere. If any Attack is performed on the network than also it should be properly working and effectively functional. In case of any attack or abnormal conditions the network or devices should be able to detect that and should stop for any further damage.

1.3.5 Intrusion Detection

An intruder is someone who wants to gain access to the system forcefully. Intruder can be external or internal. IDS or intrusion detection system is the system that monitors or scans the networks and network traffic for suspicious activities or any issues and then should alerts or stop the system when such activities are discovered. The IDS is used in 3 main methodologies namely mis-use detection, anomaly detection and specification based detection system.

1.3.6 Privacy Protection

The privacy and security are diligently related to each other. In smart cities the personal data collected from citizens are processed and stored at databases. These data are sensitive and personal, so that data needs to be protected from data breaches and sensitive data leakage intentionally or unintentionally. To prevent misuse of data by unauthorized user effective and adequate countermeasures should be use such as encryption methods etc.

1.3.7 Access Control

The authorization and access control are closely related to each other. Access control allows users to restrict the access of resources and data. This will help in ensuring security and privacy on user's sensitive and private data.

1.3.8 Data Security

As already discussed, the data is the main core of smart city. This data needs to be secure from the attackers and hackers. Various encryption and security algorithms are implemented on these data to achieve security of sensitive data.

The above stated security requirements needs to be considered and implemented in the smart city to avoid any malicious attacks. The other challenges that are faced during creating a smart city includes mainly 3 broad challenges: Infrastructures, resources and Skillset challenges [18]. The infrastructure for smart city is one of the major challenge as it includes public transports, healthcare, education and other public and private utilities. The city needs good and vast infrastructure that will incorporates all devices, sensors and databases along keeping in mind safety and security of them and data. Another challenge is of resources. The smart devices and smart solution implementation requires a lot of cost and money. Some projects are still not fully implemented because of insufficient funds. From these recent technologies and innovation a new challenge arises that is not having proper knowledge or skill of recent technologies. This is also a challenge to make people or worker aware about the technology and provide them training to improve their skills. Other challenges may include lack of planning and framing the success factor of smart city, lack of vision oriented policy makers, lack of good private partnership, lack of awareness regarding resource management, lack of smart people etc.

The security function for smart city includes mechanism that prevents data leakage, falsification of data and prevention of device tampering. FIWARE is a suite of software that supports development and distribution of apps supporting next gen internet technology. It was developed in Europe and it contains several components called as Generic Enablers. Data falsification means altering the novel data with the intension of providing false impression. Encryption is used to prevent from this but in case of IoT devices sometimes it's impossible to implement as the devices are small and lightweight having low memory capacity. TWINE is a lightweight encryption specially developed by NEC for IoT devices. For tampering detection in IoT devices a lightweight TrsutZOne, memory function of ARM Cortex-M is used [16].

1.4 Security and Privacy Issues in Smart City

The smart wearables collects the physical and medical data of users or patients. The smart mobility application collects data like vehicles details, vehicle owner's detail and location of drivers or users. The smart homes collects the data of person living in that house. All these information are sensitive and needs to be more secure and private. Various attacks and threats exists in a smart city in which the attacker mainly aims to:

- Gain access on private information after breaking confidentiality of message.
- Modify or alter the data to break integrity of the original sensitive message.

- Make the system and resources unavailable to the authorized users.
- Gain the access rights after breaking the authorized devices.

1.4.1 Threats to Smart City

Threats are the possible illegal or harmful chances or activities that are carried out by the malicious users to gain access on the sensitive data. The threats can be classified in 3 major areas namely threats against security, threats against system and threats against networks [5].

The threats against systems may have alteration and destruction of sensitive information by unauthorized users, access to the sensitive information by attackers and hackers, bypassing control means attackers can access to the access rights and can change the administrator bypassing the firewall, staff's mistake is an internal intruder threat where an inside authenticated can leak the confidential data. The security threats against networks includes wiretapping or sniffing the packets of confidential information during communication, Man-in-the-middle attack, Traffic analysis, message forgery and tempering of data. The following Fig. 1.7 shows the threats against some of the counter measures of the respective threats [15].

1.4.2 Attacks on Smart City

Attacks are the thoughtful attempts that are made on any system, resource or data to evade the security and privacy. Some of the major attacks that needs attention includes Jamming attack, Denial-of-service, spoofing, cryptanalysis attack,

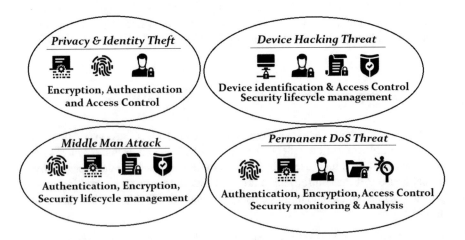

Fig. 1.7 Some common threats and their countermeasures on smart city

Table 1.2 Smart city definitions

Attack	Definition
DoS	The DoS attack or Denial of Service attack prevents the authorized users to gain access on the services provided to them. The attackers tries to gain access on monitoring and control activities of the central data storage network by consuming computing resources and bandwidths. For example a person with voice recognition or other smart locking system implemented wants to access his/her own house but can't
Delay	Some information of message are so crucial that they need to be communicated within short range of time between 3 and 500 ms. The attackers delay these messages to have the effect of DoS attack. For example the data of a patient needs to be transmitted on time to the doctor for urgent treatment but is not because of this attack
Spoofing	Spoofing is the attack performed by the attackers to gain access of private information. Attacker impersonates the device and steals the data. As example when a fraud calls you and pretends to be a bank officer that warns you, threats you or asks from you to change your password or other account details
Distort message	The attacker will try to change the original message and will try to evade the integrity of the message. For example the attacker will send an incorrect control message to various devices in smart city to make the devices work abnormally
Eavesdropping	Eavesdropping the sensitive information by attacker lead to evade of privacy. For example if customer is purchasing online and entering his/her confidential card details there the attacker can gain access on that information and can misuse it
Forging the identity	The attacker can interrupt and can false the identity of authorized users to gain control on monitoring or storage devices. For example the attacker can gain intelligent electronic monitor devices and can misuse it by sending fake and wrong messages to the users
Jamming	The attacker here intestinally interfere and inserts some noisy signals on a wireless network to stop it working properly. For example the radio jamming attack and collision attack
Spyware	Spyware is a malware that invades device security and steals the sensitive information of users. It monitors the activity of user for example credit card numbers, banking information of user etc.
Botnet	Botnet is comprised of two words network and robot. It is a malicious infected device controlled by an attacker or group of attackers. It sometimes pronounced as zombie also. For example Zeus, Methbot, Mirai etc. these botnets are used for fraudulent, data theft, money stealing phishing fraud etc.

eavesdropping attack, spywares etc. [22]. The following Table 1.2 describes the possible attacks that can be performed on smart cities to evade the security and privacy.

The categories of attacks can be classified into Availability attacks that either deny some services to be accessed by the users or completely brings the system down, Confidentiality attacks that are related to gaining access on the information, Integrity attack that seeks to break the system and alter the information or configuration settings on systems [21]. The following Fig. 1.8 shows the common cyber security attacks on smart city.

Fig. 1.8 Some common cyber security attacks on smart city

1.4.3 Motivation for Attacks

In smart city the attackers can get access to CCTV cameras, sensors, databases, mobile phones or even to the whole network. This is possible because the following activities are performed on these devices that make them vulnerable to attacks:

- Privacy breach,
- Extortion from users,
- Cyber- warfare,
- DDoS attack on data or resources, etc.

As the importance of smart city is increasing and people are moving towards urbanization to get better life, so the attackers are also getting motivation for attacking and hacking the smart city. Following are some of the motivational reasons that attracts attackers and motivate them to attack [23]:

- As the devices require continuously connection with internet it attracts the attacker.
- Lack of having basic security protocols implemented on network.
- Easily crack able and exploitable passwords.
- Cyber warfares between countries motivates the hacker to do cyber-crime.
- Business Rivalry can invite and give opportunities to attacker.
- Financial benefits i.e. for money an attacker can attack and hack any system or city.
- Political motivations are also one of the factors for attackers to do attack on sensitive data.
- No-security updates against more updated attacks.
- Inabilities to reset or make authorization process more secure.
- Intellectual challenges.
- Cost-effectiveness to applications.

1.4.4 Privacy Risks

Privacy is considered as a major and challenging issue of smart city. Privacy is defined as the basic human right that make sure that no sensitive or private information of any person should be disclosed or misused by the third person or the outsider. The privacy can be stated in following dimensions [21]:

- Identity privacy that stated the personal data of any individual should be remained private.
- Territorial privacy focuses and protects personal property of a person.
- Mobility privacy aims securing location related details of individuals against tracking.
- Communication privacy deals protecting communication channels being eavesdropped by third person on wired or wireless communication.
- Transaction privacy aiming to protect queries, responses and transitions done by any individual.

The following Fig. 1.9 shows the five types of privacy [24].

The location privacy focuses on spatiotemporal information. The violation of this privacy not only considers the location of an individual but also for how many time and for how long the place was visited. The privacy of state, body and mind concentrates on characteristic of body of individuals including biometrics, genome, mental conditions, sentiments, views, thoughts, their health etc. The privacy of social life includes the personal and social lives of individuals for example the social media apps such as whats app, Facebook, twitter, Instagram etc. The privacy of

Fig. 1.9 Type of privacy attacks on smart city

behaviour and action comprises a person's habits, actions and purchase history. For example purchasing online and using credit card information are shared by the retailers that can exploit privacy. The privacy of media includes privacy or private images, audio, video and other stuff of an individual uploaded on media or social media platforms.

The following Table 1.3 shows the security and privacy concerns in various sectors, their threats and its countermeasures [44].

1.5 Opportunities and Proposed Solutions

The smart city provides us a lots of possible solutions that we can implement to protect the data from attackers and their theft meanwhile making our city smarter. The development of smart city serves two main purposes namely smart infrastructure and improving environmental sustainability. Smart infrastructure includes smart electricity and water meters, smart energy consumption, smart doors etc. which reduces the over wastage. For instance, in Mumbai, earlier about half of water was wasted but after smart infrastructure the buildings and pipes are made so that they reduced almost that half wastage and also rain water harvesting was emphasised [25]. The smart infrastructure also improves city and environmental sustainability and affordability. After the smart vehicles were introduced the harmful emission of carbon and soot has also been reduced which increased the good health rate in humans. A safe and secure environment has been made available to citizens. Due to the smart classroom infrastructure higher education rate has also been increased. Some smart city opportunities such as TMS (smart Traffic Monitoring System) that can sense the data from heterogenous traffic and can be used to find out type of traffic on a particular road, the parking space, the condition of road, alternative route in case of heavy traffic etc. [26].

The existing security and privacy solution for smart city environment contains technologies such as:

- **Blockchain:** Blockchain is one of the latest and amazing technology that is introduced to increase the security of IoT devices implemented in smart city [27]. The decentralized nature of Blockchain provides reliability and efficiency to the system. It is been used in smart homes to prevent the data loss and chances of robbery in the house. Lie Ao et al. [29] developed a secure mechanism to protect vehicles using Blockchain technology. Dorri Ali et al. [30] proposed a Blockchain based smart home solution. They developed the framework using Blockchain that provided integrity, confidentiality and availability. Authors discussed various previous and latest work in securing IoT communication using Blockchain technologies [31].
- **Cryptography:** The data is made in unreadable or cipher form to prevent from attack over a network. The stronger is cryptographic algorithm the stronger will be the system against the attacks. Traditional encryption algorithms are strong

Table 1.3 Types of Attacks/Threats as per division of different IoT based smart city along with countermeasure

Segment	Threats/Attacks	Countermeasures
Smart building	Fire system controlling, Infected by malware, System failure, Smart meter modifying, Parking gates opening and closing, Start/stop irrigation water system, Stopping RES (renewable energy systems), Opening/closing smart doors & lifts	Threat and risk modelling IoT forensics DigiCertiIoT PKI sol Data backup & recovery Two factor authentication One time passwords for stronger authentication Comodo security solu
Smart transportation	Vehicle's braking system upsetting, Sending false emergency messages, Stopping/altering vehicle's engine, Prompting false displays dashboard of vehicle, Disrupting emergency system of vehicles, GPS signals altering	PKI, digital certificate (ECDSA), ECIES & AES data encryption solution Misbehaviour detection solutions Pseudorandom identities
Government	Individual identity threat, Financial fraud, Changed files, Infrastructure disrupting	Symantec, Fortinet- data leakage prevention Risk valuation (MEHARI, EBIOS) Insider threat investigation Awareness training
Smart healthcare	Jamming attacks, Emergency alert transmitting, Eavesdropping info, Transmitting wrong info, Disrupting monitoring & emergency system, Changing record of patients	AirTight networks solution Aerohive security solutions Rapid7 solutions Health security solutions Intel healthcare security solutions Stanley security solutions SafeNet's data security solutions
Financial sector	Privacy loss, DoS attack, Trojan, Phishing. SQL injection attack, Defacing websites, Accessing confidential information of customers & company, Mobile banking exploitation	Antimalware sol such as McAfee, Symantec Encrypted files Fraud detection & prevention technique- NICE Actimize, Signifyd etc. Risk assessment- MEHARI, EBIOS Cybercrime intelligence (RSA Cybercrime intelligence service, IBM enterprise, ThreatMetrix Cybercrime prevention, SurfWatch vC-Suite
Smart energy	Zero day attack Botnets Dos and DDoS attack Unauthorized access Spoofing address	MEHARI, EBIOS risk assessment Cybercrime intelligence IDS- Intrusion detection system Radiflow and snort

but are not appropriate for resource restriction devices as the energy consumption is increased and complexity is also increased [32]. The light-weight encryption algorithms were researched by various authors. Mahmood Zahid et al. [28] developed a light weight encryption algorithm for end users to get protection from DDoS attacks. Li Nan et al. [33] proposed a novel public key encryption algorithm for securing various applications of smart city.

- **Biometrics:** The biometric technique is used to identify and authenticate ones identity. Various methods such as handwritten, fingerprints, voices, signatures, faces, retina scan etc. were used to recognize person by unique biological or physical characteristics. Amini Ruhul et al. [34] proposed a key negotiation and mutual authentication protocol for achieving confidentiality. Natgunanathan Iynkaran et al. [35] proposed a biometric developed for privacy-preserving PPBSs.
- **Machine learning:** This recent technology is used to improve the IDS intrusion detection system which plays an important role in securing smart city. Luo Xiong et al. [36] proposed a scheme based on machines to secure sensor devices. The WSNs are the key component of smart city and it need to be secure to secure overall city. Biggio Batista et al. [37] reviewed existing situation of biometric security system from the viewpoint of ML.
- **Data Mining:** Researchers surveyed in this field to regulate that the data collected by the devices is used to mine new regulations to provide better services to the users. More privacy and security is require in the data because it consists of personal information of users such as location, patient's history, tourist's history etc. To protect this researchers are continuously working in this field [38–40].
- **Game theory and ontology:** Game theory is the new mathematical powerful technique recently gaining popularity because it provides cybersecurity a privacy protection in smart cities [40]. Do Cuong T. et al. [41] suggested advantages and characteristics of game theory such as proven mathematics, reliable defence, timely action, distributed solutions. Ontology is a branch of philosophy which is to understand better, describe better and reuse better some knowledge and to search for new knowledge [42, 43].

The privacy and security is a very serious concern for all the researchers as it is very challenging to protect the sensitive data from hackers all the time. Some live examples are as in Hong Kong there are more than 600 locations where free Wi-Fi access is given to citizens and government has full access on the data gathered this time when any citizen uses this Wi-Fi, where any attacker can hack and attack on this data. Same Estonia and Chicago also provides free Wi-Fi to citizens indirectly motivating hackers. Similarly the citizen card of Zaragoza in Spain, MyKad card in Malaysia and Octopus card in Hong Kong have all information of a citizen that is used to pay bills, parking, shopping etc. Observing such cases give importance to security and privacy issues in smart city. The policy regarding securing IoT devices in smart cities to achieve security and privacy includes:

- Removal of default and weak passwords. The passwords should be strong and should be kept secret to avoid any interference of attackers.

- The security related software and applications should be updated time to time to keep it strong against strong attacks.
- Allow plug and play after proper authentication only.
- Only predefined services in the network should be allowed only.
- Filter in firewall should be implemented to avoid attacks.
- Strong cryptographic algorithms should be used in order to prevent information leak at the time of communication.

The following Table 1.4 shows some of technology or solution been proposed by different authors recently for security and privacy enhancing in smart IoT based cities.

Table 1.4 Example of privacy enhancing solutions invented for IoT based smart city

Work of authors	Proposed solutions	Outcomes
[45]	SM-EAPOL authentication based method on EAP over LAN for TLS datagram	Basically proposed to provide authentication and access control for IoT based devices in smart city. The EAPOL protocol was necessary for this to be installed in IoT devices for working
[46]	DCapBAC a distributed authorization approach using CoAP, 6LoWPAN, ECC data interchange format and JSON	Basically proposed to provide authentication and access control for IoT based devices in smart city. It fails to provide trust in making decision related to access control
[47]	It provides users a mechanism to protect their privacy by allowing users to consider real info, anonymized info or terminate execution	Basically proposed to provide privacy threat control in IoT based devices. It fails to handle control flows
[48]	Access control privilege applications that access user's private and sensitive info through cloud computing	Basically proposed to provide privacy threat control in IoT based devices. It creates overhead on CPS and end users along with high computation overhead
[49]	Author proposed a PrivySHaring Blockchain based framework for handling security and privacy	They proposed PrivyCoin reward for owners of sharing data about their health to third party using smart contracts
[50]	ISA- Identified security attributes framework was developed by authors for IoHT	Patient's data that is collected by sensors attached on his/her body can be attacked during transmission. The framework was designed to protect the sensitive data of patient
[51]	A lightweight IoT based security assessment framework for wireless sensor networks	The inventory automation requires IoT and hence requires security, authentication, integrity, authorization, confidentiality etc.

1.6   Conclusion

The concept of smart city is derived from the IoT technologies. IoT and smart city has become reality in modern world and has demonized the gap between reality and Sci-fi. Smart cities can enhance and advance the urban environments and enhance the quality of lives of citizens. In this chapter we have discussed about the smart city, applications, services, elements or components, architecture, features, pillars, applications, benefits and examples of smart cities. We have proposed a novel architecture for smart city defining each layers, its components and its working mechanisms. The security requirements and the main issues of smart city were also discussed. The security and privacy issues including types of attacks, types of threats and privacy were also discussed. The potential solutions for addressing security and privacy in smart city was also addressed. As the technology is advancing so the attacker's approach and mechanisms. The development of more secure advance protection models and frameworks are essential and much needed for both industrial and academic fields. Various protection mechanisms for gaining security from unauthorized access or attackers are developing rapidly these days. However still there is a long way to go to satisfy all security requirements and making smart city smarter and secure in all aspects.

References

1. World cities report 2020: The value of sustainable urbanization, 2020 [online] https://unhabitat.org/sites/default/files/2020/10/wcr_2020_report.pdf
2. Zhang, K., Ni, J., Yang, K., Liang, X., Ren, J., & Shen, X. S. (2017). Security and privacy in smart city applications: Challenges and solutions. *IEEE Communications Magazine, 55*(1), 122–129.
3. Lea, R. J. (2017). Smart cities: An overview of the technology trends driving smart cities. Working Paper. IEEE. https://doi.org/10.13140/RG.2.2.15303.39840
4. [online] https://en.wikipedia.org/wiki/Smart_city
5. Lee, J., Kim, J., & Seo, J. (2019, January). Cyber attack scenarios on smart city and their ripple effects. In *2019 International Conference on Platform Technology and Service (PlatCon)* (pp. 1–5). IEEE.
6. Kumar, N. M., Goel, S., & Mallick, P. K. (2018). Smart cities in India: Features, policies, current status, and challenges. In *2018 Technologies for Smart-City Energy Security and Power (ICSESP)*, pp. 1–4.
7. [online] IBM: https://www.ibm.com/in-en/industries/government/infrastructure-citizen-services
8. Mehta, S., Bhushan, B., & Kumar, R. (2022). Machine learning approaches for smart city applications: Emergence, challenges and opportunities. In *Recent advances in Internet of Things and machine learning*. Intelligent Systems Reference Library, vol. 215. (pp. 147–163). Springer, Cham. https://doi.org/10.1007/978-3-030-90119-6_12
9. Gharaibeh, A., Salahuddin, M. A., Hussini, S. J., Khreishah, A., Khalil, I., Guizani, M., & Al-Fuqaha, A. (2017). Smart cities: A survey on data management, security, and enabling technologies. *IEEE Communications Surveys & Tutorials, 19*(4), 2456–2501.
10. Pira, M. (2021). A novel taxonomy of smart sustainable city indicators. *Humanities and Social Sciences Communications, 8*(1), 1–10.

11. Ati, M., & Basmaji, T. (2018, April). Framework for managing smart cities security and privacy applications. In *2018 IEEE Symposium on Computer Applications & Industrial Electronics (ISCAIE)* (pp. 191–194). IEEE.
12. Sookhak, M., Tang, H., He, Y., & Yu, F. R. (2018). Security and privacy of smart cities: A survey, research issues and challenges. *IEEE Communications Surveys & Tutorials, 21*(2), 1718–1743.
13. Haque, A. B., Bhushan, B., & Dhiman, G. (2022). Conceptualizing smart city applications: Requirements, architecture, security issues, and emerging trends. *Expert Systems, 39*(5), e12753.
14. Schaffers, H., Komninos, N., Pallot, M., Trousse, B., Nilsson, M., & Oliveira, A. (2011, May). Smart cities and the future internet: Towards cooperation frameworks for open innovation. In *The future internet assembly* (pp. 431–446). Springer.
15. Manchanda, C., Sharma, N., Rathi, R., Bhushan, B., & Grover, M. (2020, April). Neoteric security and privacy sanctuary technologies in smart cities. In *2020 IEEE 9th International Conference on Communication Systems and Network Technologies (CSNT)* (pp. 236–241). IEEE.
16. Sasaki, T., Morita, Y., & Kobayashi, T. (2018). Security requirements and technologies for smart city IoT. *NEC Technical Journal, 13*(1), 54–57.
17. Cui, L., Xie, G., Qu, Y., Gao, L., & Yang, Y. (2018). Security and privacy in smart cities: Challenges and opportunities. *IEEE Access, 6*, 46134–46145.
18. Okai, E., Feng, X., & Sant, P. (2018, June). Smart cities survey. In *2018 IEEE 20th international conference on High Performance Computing and Communications; IEEE 16th international conference on Smart City; IEEE 4th international conference on Data Science and Systems (HPCC/SmartCity/DSS)* (pp. 1726–1730). IEEE.
19. Gaur, A., Scotney, B., Parr, G., & McClean, S. (2015). Smart city architecture and its applications based on IoT. *Procedia Computer Science, 52*, 1089–1094.
20. Al-Turjman, F., Zahmatkesh, H., & Shahroze, R. (2022). An overview of security and privacy in smart cities' IoT communications. *Transactions on Emerging Telecommunications Technologies, 33*(3), e3677.
21. Butt, T. A., & Afzaal, M. (2019). Security and privacy in smart cities: Issues and current solutions. In *Smart technologies and innovation for a sustainable future* (pp. 317–323). Springer.
22. Hamid, B., Jhanjhi, N. Z., Humayun, M., Khan, A., & Alsayat, A. (2019, December). Cyber security issues and challenges for smart cities: A survey. In *2019 13th International Conference on Mathematics, Actuarial Science, Computer Science and Statistics (MACS)* (pp. 1–7). IEEE.
23. Gupta, S. K., Vanjale, S., Rasal, S., & Vanjale, M. (2020, March). Securing IoT devices in smart city environments. In *2020 International Conference on Emerging Smart Computing and Informatics (ESCI)* (pp. 119–123). IEEE.
24. Eckhoff, D., & Wagner, I. (2017). Privacy in the smart city—Applications, technologies, challenges, and solutions. *IEEE Communications Surveys & Tutorials, 20*(1), 489–516.
25. [online] https://www.datainnovation.org/2015/02/how-to-finance-a-smart-city/
26. Arroub, A., Zahi, B., Sabir, E., & Sadik, M. (2016, October). A literature review on smart cities: Paradigms, opportunities and open problems. In *2016 international conference on Wireless Networks and Mobile Communications (WINCOM)* (pp. 180–186). IEEE.
27. Saini, S., Maithani, A., Dhiman, D., Rohilla, A., Chaube, N., & Bisht, A. (2021, April). Blockchain technology: A smart and efficient way for securing IoT communication. In *2021 2nd International Conference on Intelligent Engineering and Management (ICIEM)* (pp. 567–571). IEEE.
28. Mahmood, Z., Ning, H., & Ghafoor, A. (2016, December). Lightweight two-level session key management for end user authentication in Internet of Things. In *2016 IEEE international conference on Internet of Things (iThings) and IEEE Green Computing and Communications (GreenCom) and IEEE Cyber, Physical and Social Computing (CPSCom) and IEEE Smart Data (SmartData)* (pp. 323–327). IEEE.

29. Lei, A., Cruickshank, H., Cao, Y., Asuquo, P., Ogah, C. P. A., & Sun, Z. (2017). Blockchain-based dynamic key management for heterogeneous intelligent transportation systems. *IEEE Internet of Things Journal, 4*(6), 1832–1843.
30. Dorri, A., Kanhere, S. S., Jurdak, R., & Gauravaram, P. (2017, March). Blockchain for IoT security and privacy: The case study of a smart home. In *2017 IEEE international conference on Pervasive Computing and Communications workshops (PerCom workshops)* (pp. 618–623). IEEE.
31. Bhushan, B., Khamparia, A., Sagayam, K. M., Sharma, S. K., Ahad, M. A., & Debnath, N. C. (2020). Blockchain for smart cities: A review of architectures, integration trends and future research directions. *Sustainable Cities and Society, 61*, 102360.
32. Davies, A. R., & Mullin, S. J. (2011). Greening the economy: Interrogating sustainability innovations beyond the mainstream. *Journal of Economic Geography, 11*(5), 793–816.
33. Li, N., Liu, D., & Nepal, S. (2017). Lightweight mutual authentication for IoT and its applications. *IEEE Transactions on Sustainable Computing, 2*(4), 359–370.
34. Amin, R., Sherratt, R. S., Giri, D., Islam, S. H., & Khan, M. K. (2017). A software agent enabled biometric security algorithm for secure file access in consumer storage devices. *IEEE Transactions on Consumer Electronics, 63*(1), 53–61.
35. Natgunanathan, I., Mehmood, A., Xiang, Y., Beliakov, G., & Yearwood, J. (2016). Protection of privacy in biometric data. *IEEE Access, 4*, 880–892.
36. Luo, X., Zhang, D., Yang, L. T., Liu, J., Chang, X., & Ning, H. (2016). A kernel machine-based secure data sensing and fusion scheme in wireless sensor networks for the cyber-physical systems. *Future Generation Computer Systems, 61*, 85–96.
37. Biggio, B., Russu, P., Didaci, L., & Roli, F. (2015). Adversarial biometric recognition: A review on biometric system security from the adversarial machine-learning perspective. *IEEE Signal Processing Magazine, 32*(5), 31–41.
38. Xing, K., Hu, C., Yu, J., Cheng, X., & Zhang, F. (2017). Mutual privacy preserving k-means clustering in social participatory sensing. *IEEE Transactions on Industrial Informatics, 13*(4), 2066–2076.
39. Tsai, C. W., Lai, C. F., Chiang, M. C., & Yang, L. T. (2013). Data mining for internet of things: A survey. *IEEE Communications Surveys & Tutorials, 16*(1), 77–97.
40. Li, L., Lu, R., Choo, K. K. R., Datta, A., & Shao, J. (2016). Privacy-preserving-outsourced association rule mining on vertically partitioned databases. *IEEE Transactions on Information Forensics and Security, 11*(8), 1847–1861.
41. Do, C. T., Tran, N. H., Hong, C., Kamhoua, C. A., Kwiat, K. A., Blasch, E., et al. (2017). Game theory for cyber security and privacy. *ACM Computing Surveys (CSUR), 50*(2), 1–37.
42. Tao, M., Zuo, J., Liu, Z., Castiglione, A., & Palmieri, F. (2018). Multi-layer cloud architectural model and ontology-based security service framework for IoT-based smart homes. *Future Generation Computer Systems, 78*, 1040–1051.
43. Mohsin, M., Anwar, Z., Zaman, F., & Al-Shaer, E. (2017). IoTChecker: A data-driven framework for security analytics of Internet of Things configurations. *Computers & Security, 70*, 199–223.
44. Khatoun, R., & Zeadally, S. (2017). Cybersecurity and privacy solutions in smart cities. *IEEE Communications Magazine, 55*(3), 51–59.
45. Hernandez-Ramos, J. L., Pawlowski, M. P., Jara, A. J., Skarmeta, A. F., & Ladid, L. (2015). Toward a lightweight authentication and authorization framework for smart objects. *IEEE Journal on Selected Areas in Communications, 33*(4), 690–702.
46. Hernández-Ramos, J. L., Jara, A. J., Marín, L., & Skarmeta Gómez, A. F. (2016). DCapBAC: Embedding authorization logic into smart things through ECC optimizations. *International Journal of Computer Mathematics, 93*(2), 345–366.
47. Xiao, X., Tillmann, N., Fahndrich, M., De Halleux, J., Moskal, M., & Xie, T. (2015). User-aware privacy control via extended static-information-flow analysis. *Automated Software Engineering, 22*(3), 333–366.

48. Li, Y., Dai, W., Ming, Z., & Qiu, M. (2015). Privacy protection for preventing data over-collection in smart city. *IEEE Transactions on Computers, 65*(5), 1339–1350.
49. Makhdoom, I., Zhou, I., Abolhasan, M., Lipman, J., & Ni, W. (2020). PrivySharing: A blockchain-based framework for privacy-preserving and secure data sharing in smart cities. *Computers & Security, 88*, 101653.
50. Wang, L., Ali, Y., Nazir, S., & Niazi, M. (2020). ISA evaluation framework for security of internet of health things system using AHP-TOPSIS methods. *IEEE Access, 8*, 152316–152332.
51. Batra, I., Verma, S., & Alazab, M. (2020). A lightweight IoT-based security framework for inventory automation using wireless sensor network. *International Journal of Communication Systems, 33*(4), e4228.

Chapter 2
Reliability and Security of Edge Computing Devices for Smart Cities

Nikunj Pansari and Rishit Saiya

Abstract In today's modern and developing world, security and privacy are essential ingredients for ensuring data safety and the legitimate access of one's information for most of the real-time applications they utilize, be it using smartphones, laptops, tablets, or electronic gadgets which are connected through the Internet thus making it an easy target to leverage the security of that device, resulting in enabling the attackers getting access to the sensitive and confidential data of the individual or organization. With the progression of technology at such a rapid pace, it may be frequent to conclude that drones will be delivering goods and merchandise, thus catering to the accessibility of mobile hotspots and ensuring the security & surveillance of smart cities. Considering the long-term utility of drones for smart cities, there also comes the threat of cyber-attacks like Deauthentication Attacks, GPS Spoofing, etc., which will lead to the disclosure of sensitive information. The smart devices consist of various embedded SoCs (System-On-Chip), which are integrated to sustain a large amount of user data by focusing primarily on avoiding the trade-off between the complexity of the machine learning implemented model and the available compatible edge devices (Hardware SoCs). Thus, it is essential to enhance the security of edge devices on a large scale, specifically from the perspective of smart cities. Several researchers have also proposed methodologies to improve and sustain the security of smart devices using optimized blockchain-based security frameworks using physical parameters like temperature, light, etc. This chapter defines an insight towards ensuring the security (focuses majorly on the Edge computing devices) of the smart devices, which are the prime source to enhance and maximize privacy, thus enabling the smart cities to be more secure from any cyberattack.

N. Pansari (✉) · R. Saiya
Computer Science and Engineering, Indian Institute of Technology,
Dharwad, Karnataka, India

M. A. Ahad et al. (eds.), *Enabling Technologies for Effective Planning and Management in Sustainable Smart Cities*, https://doi.org/10.1007/978-3-031-22922-0_2

Keywords Smart City · Edge computing · Security · Privacy · Cyber attacks ·
Adversarial attacks · IoT security · Robustness level · Deep Neural
Networks (DNNs)

2.1   Introduction

Security is the defining pillar of the smart cities' effective functioning to ensure a
threat-free environment for the continuous flow of information and communication
among different components. The adversaries or attackers look for small loopholes
to leverage the security of electronic or smart devices connected through the same
network (necessarily to ensure easy integration and interaction among several components). The evolution of modern technologies has increased to such an extent that
drones would be employed to deliver the necessities and ensure hassle-free production of lightweight goods. It could also be very useful to deliver the medicines in an
emergency to the corresponding person. Since it acts as an asset to the smart city's
essential functionality by ensuring surveillance and security by employing the sensors, threats like Global Positioning System (GPS) spoofing attacks and
De-Authentication attacks [1] also arise and would serve as bait for attackers to
capture sensitive and confidential information. Another important asset in smart cities would be the deployment of the edge computing-based infrastructure for the IoT
devices, which ensures the interaction between the cyber-physical system and the
IoT. Its applications include smart transportation, smart grid, and state-of-the-art
healthcare facilities [2]. Researchers have also defined PASH (Privacy-aware
s-health access control system), which partially hides the access information (health
information attribute values) through strong encryption methodologies. It defines
the standard model for a large set of health records, thus making it more secure than
usual storage and analysis [3].

Nowadays, cloud storage of data is very important to avoid the over-collection
of data. Previous works have shown different frameworks employed to improve the
security of users' data [4]. Management of large-scale data is quite important in the
perspective of smart cities to ensure consistency, granularity, reusability, and
interoperability of the available data to ensure secure and reliable access to information for the users [5]. While implementing security methodologies of real-time
data, there are a lot of constraints and assumptions to ensure optimum privacy [6]
and security. An Support Vector Machine (SVM) training scheme known as
'SecureSVM' was proposed that ensured preserving privacy and emphasized
increasing the confidentiality between the data provider and model parameters of
the SVM, making it easy to analyze for data analysts [7]. Identifying the correct
SoCs for ML-based model analysis is important to ensure the optimum performance and reliability of the system deployed in smart cities.

Researchers have defined blockchain-based frameworks [8] for analyzing smart devices considering different parameters like temperature, light, etc., giving a good insight for maintaining and integrating the security with new modifications into the system [9]. Integrating blockchain to ensure data authentication [10] and improving CCTV surveillance is also substantial for smart cities [11]. Data should be secured at every level of system functioning; for instance, researchers define this concept in the case of a smart grid system consisting of different levels [12], namely data storage, data acquisition, data processing, and data generation, which is strongly encrypted against the security threats in the real-time system [13]. Furthermore, optimum and efficient defensive strategies should be adopted to ensure and enhance the security and privacy of the system in smart cities [14].

This chapter aims to explain and cover some of the known attacks & threats which disrupt the smart cities' functionality. To begin with, it illustrates the IoT-based attacks and their prime source of occurrence. Then, it covers the countermeasures or defensive mechanisms against those known IoT attacks. Analysis of the threats to the operating systems have been discussed to give an insight into the in-system vulnerabilities also. Then, we provide a detailed analysis of the security threats in edge computing in a tabular manner. Next, we performed reliability & performance analysis of a common task of fire detection on an Intel processor to give a glimpse of its utilization in terms of energy, power, and temperature. Lastly, we have shown the impact of adversarial attacks like FGSM-T (targeted) & FGSM-U (Untargeted) attacks for seven different DNNs on the Intel processor to illustrate the robustness of these models on different noise values.

Section 2.2 defines different IoT-based challenges and countermeasures applicable to various systems in smart cities. While Sect. 2.3 covers different cyber-attacks possible in systems that may be vulnerable, Sect. 2.4 defines the security threats of employing edge computing and the possible defense mechanism for the corresponding threats. Then, Sect. 2.5 broadly illustrates the fire detection application's performance and reliability analysis on an Intel-based processor. Section 2.6 highlights the adversarial attack analysis for different DNNs, which may provide a glimpse of the adversarial attack effect (level of robustness) in the real-time system in smart cities. The conclusion highlights and summarizes the need for the security and reliability of edge devices in smart cities.

2.2   IoT-Based Attacks

IoT (Internet of things) is a useful innovation of modern technology wherein the data or information integrated from several connected devices will be processed, modified, and gathered to input into the new modules and services within the same network. Various IoT-based applications have been defined for smart cities, smart installation [15] of devices, smart parking assistance, etc., which would be sustainable solutions for the future. Utilizing IoT has certain drawbacks in the applicability of parameters like adverse weather conditions, energy consumption, and power dissipation. Now, the heterogeneous nature of the IoT can help improve security, and researchers have also carried out works integrating it with blockchain [10]. IoT deployment can also cause some security loopholes in the system, like employing heavyweight cryptographic algorithms in the system will lead the system to become computationally and memory intensive. Secondly, if standard protocols are not employed, it would increase the number of exchanges between nodes for the information or data [16].

2.2.1 IoT-Security Challenges

There are numerous security challenges (Fig. 2.1) in the different layers of IoT, and researchers are continuously working to ensure a safe and secure real-time system involving IoT.

Hardware attacks are the most prominent source of a security vulnerability in the IoT system. Now, most of them are linked with wireless sensor networks (WSNs) or sensors like RFID, which can be quite vulnerable to physical attacks. Attackers or adversaries exploit sensitive information from IoT-based devices like smart TVs, smart watches, or smart appliances to get the victim's ransom. Security threats in IoT can be explored in different layers of network architecture like the Physical layer, network layer, and application layer.

In the physical layer, security threats consist of timing, replay, and eavesdropping. When the attacker tries to get the sensitive or confidential information of the victim transmitted by the source device, it is defined as sniffing, spoofing, or eavesdropping attack. An insecure channel of communication is the primary reason for the attack. Now, when the intruder modifies the communication or conversation between the sender and the corresponding receiving medium by monitoring the

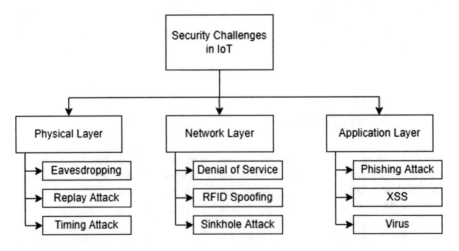

Fig. 2.1 Various security challenges in IoT

authentic information of the sender, it illustrates the replay attack. While, in a replay attack, the intruder modifies or alters the communication between the sender and the receiver by capturing personal or sensitive information, i.e., the authentic information from the sender. They breach the communication medium protocols to discard the existence of a Certificate of validity ensuring security. The devices with computational abilities are most vulnerable to attacks as the attackers analyze the cryptographic algorithms and access the encryption key.

Considering the network layer, which bridges the physical and application layer, acts as the medium of transmission of the information integrated from different sensors into the communication channel. Data privacy, confidentiality, and availability are the major security challenges. Some threats are RFID spoofing, Sinkhole attacks, and the Denial of Service (DoS) attack when the attackers try to disrupt the user's services by continuously flooding many requests (including redundant requests) to the IoT device to a DDoS attack. When the attacker is malicious data into the IoT system, getting access to the system leads to RFID spoofing. Lastly, the attached node will function as the full node for sinkhole attacks. The devices and the other neighboring node utilize this full node for communication, acting as a forwarding node within the routing functionality.

Finally, the application layer comes into action when the application utilizes IoT technology. Software attacks like cross-site scripting, phishing attacks, and malicious worms/viruses are the ones that affect the most. When the attackers try to spoof the victim's users' data like passwords, confidential information like bank account details could be significant enough for attacks, leading to phishing attacks. The attacker carries this out by tricking the victim into logging into the false or illegitimate website and capturing their sensitive information. In injection attacks like cross-site scripting (XSS), the attackers insert some client-side script (usually javascript) into the trusted website to view & modify the contents of the application. Self-propagation attacks like worms/viruses alter the users' information and can be significantly challenging to secure users' confidential data in IoT devices. Firewalls & virus detection methodologies can be a suitable defense against these attacks.

2.2.2 IoT-Security Countermeasures

IoT Security Countermeasures (Fig. 2.2) are quite substantial in defending or safeguarding against the security threats at three different layers discussed above, ensuring confidentiality at the application layer, forwarding & transmitting at the network layer, and gathering information at the physical layer.

Protective defense mechanisms are important to safeguard the physical layer from security threats. Some possible defense countermeasures include PKI protocol, hashed-based encryption, and lightweight cryptography. When the message is encrypted into cipher text, hashes are used for it, which defines the concept of hashed-based encryption. The length of the generated key to encrypt the message is usually twice the length of the message; thus, decrypting by the attacker or intruder

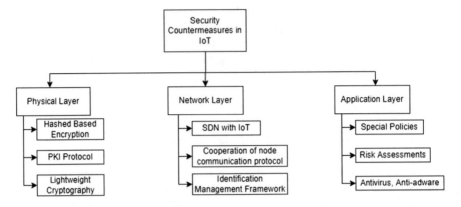

Fig. 2.2 Different countermeasures for security threats in IoT

won't be easy. PKI protocol defines integrating several mechanisms like authorization, authentication, and Intrusion Detection. Lightweight cryptography is preferable for devices with certain constraints for real-time implementation of security solutions. Symmetric-key encryption proves to be quite useful for communication security.

For the network layer, security defense mechanisms include identity management framework, Cooperation of node communication protocols, and defining an SDN with IoT. To check the authenticity of the devices, authentication in an identity management framework (IMF) is crucial before communicating the data. It consists of four components: sensors, environment, Network, and the receiver. Sensors are responsible for capturing information from objects. Considering the node communication protocols, the possible threat inside the Network is defended to detect the nodes that might affect the full Network by their behavior by the security-conscious ad-hoc protocol. It also consists of four components: trail manager, trust manager, reputation system, and monitor. The trust manager gets the suspicious behavior of any nodes within the Network. Subsequently, the trust manager signaled the ALERT message to notify the other nodes within that range.

Appropriate defense measures should be ensured to safeguard the appliance layer from security threats or attacks. Possible defense mechanisms include certain policies and permissions to improve security using strong cryptographic algorithms, risk assessment techniques, and anti-virus software. By defining some special policies and permissions, control over the access of the IoT structure could be defined. Protection, consistency, confidentiality, and reliability within the IoT landscape could be ensured using the anti-virus or anti-spyware software or tools. Thus, the application layer can be assured of optimum security by monitoring the updates regarding the systems' firmware.

Table 2.1 summarizes the security challenges and countermeasures for attacks or threats in IoT for the different layers of attack occurrence, i.e., Physical, Network, and application layer.

Table 2.1 Security challenges & countermeasures in IoT

Security challenges in IoT	Attack occurrence	Description	Countermeasures
Physical layer	Eavesdropping	Passively intercepting network to gain access in future	Using Personal Firewall and Virtual Private Network
	Replay attack	Passively intercepting network and exploits by fraudulently delaying traffic	Establish a random session, capture and resend with message-key
	Timing attack	Detecting vulnerabilities based on different input response times	Prevent timing attacks to make the computation independent of the input
Network layer	Denial of service	Huge load of packets included. Exploited protocols are SYN, HTTP, etc	Framework investigation, Cloudfare protections, ML-based filtering of packets
	RFID spoofing	RFID tags are hacked to gain access to location, authorization and authentication	Separating identification details
	Sinkhole attack	Creating network traffic to collapse network communication	Distributed detection procedure
Application layer	Phishing attack	Install and access IoT devices with malicious software	Antivirus that schedules signature updates, monitor antivirus status
	XSS	Usage of the malicious script to a benign website	Validating URLs and CSS, preventing DOM-based XSS
	Virus	Infect all unsecured device in IoT and corrupt them	Antivirus, signature-based detection

2.3   Analysis of Cyberattacks in Smart Cities

Utilizing the three D's, i.e., data, design thinking, and digital technology, can significantly improve the lifestyle and services in smart cities. Subsequently, the security attacks also come into action with the evolution of new technologies, specifically in smart cities [17]. Cyber attacks can be lethal in real-time systems focusing on physical assets and confidential information. The existence of smart cities will provide a direction to ensure sustainability in terms of environmental changes and expanding population, too. Some of the severe consequences may result in financial theft, reputational damage risks, or the system's sensitive data loss, which can subsequently affect other services and infrastructure of the smart cities like transportation, healthcare, sports, etc. Thus, at times, smart cities' ever-evolving digitalization and hyperconnectivity can be a boon for their benefit [15]. Section 2.3.1 explores the reasons behind the security threats in the smart cities landscape and strategies to mitigate the risks.

2.3.1 Security Vulnerabilities and Threats in Smart Cities

There are primarily two security vulnerabilities that affect the smart cities' function-alities: the security associated with the integrated technology with its regular updates for the systems and the security of the data stored and shared among the different technologies and the system. Now, the security of the data is interlinked with the unauthorized access of the data, as the sensitive data is gathered from the compo-nents of the system using its operations & architecture. Similarly, operational secu-rity (ensuring reliability in real-time) and information security (protecting the data) can be integrated to output important insights. The most vulnerable part could be the loopholes in municipal infrastructures and systems that may compromise the entire security system. Attackers may aim to alter, damage, or disrupt the contents of the victim's network, application, or system within the city landscape. Figure 2.3 illus-trates some possible security threats to the system deployed in smart cities: confidentiality-based, availability-based, and integrity-based attacks.

Adversaries or attackers try to accumulate the advantages of breaching the secu-rity of smart cities in different ways. One such loophole is encrypted software secu-rity. This can happen due to the weak encryption algorithms employed while designing the software for smart cities. Also, the smart city network system would be quite diverse and complex, leading to several interdependencies on internal com-ponents resulting in vulnerable attack surfaces. Confirming end-to-end security would be difficult to mitigate live risks and ensure the security of all the compo-nents. Independent systems are a threat to attack, and inter-linking them to other systems increases the risk of a breach by the security only held by a thin line.

For instance, power infrastructure affected by a cyber attack may also affect some essential and emergency services, like water, healthcare, etc. Several other factors also exaggerate the security vulnerabilities in smart cities, and it is the responsibility of the authorities of the city native council to ensure the timely moni-toring & maintenance of the city's system. The third-party vendors offering their

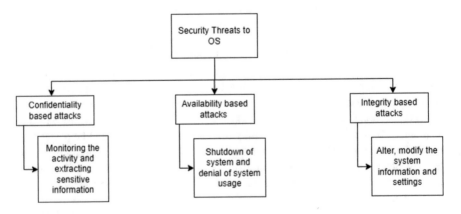

Fig. 2.3 Operational systems security threats

services in smart cities can be vulnerable. Thus, they should be provided with limited access to maintain and improve the cities' overall security. Further, some cities are unwilling to employ a strong and efficient security control system to save the cost of services, again sensing a security threat to the overall system.

2.4   Security Threats to Edge Computing

This section defines the major security threats in Edge computing (Fig. 2.4) that have predominantly been manifested from design, manufacturing, and functionality flaws. It then transitions over possible defense mechanisms to defend against the attack occurrence. Finally, the motive is to understand the reasons behind such vulnerabilities and essentially try to come up with a defense in response. Moving towards safeguarding the landscape for smart cities, creating awareness of privacy and security threats is very important to avoid victims of social engineering attacks.

Table 2.2 shows a detailed analysis of the threats/vulnerabilities to Edge Computing and their corresponding defenses or mitigation strategies which might be useful in real-time scenarios. The Security threats range from DDoS-based attacks to malware-injection attacks followed by leveraging the authentication & authorization protocols, which can prove to be substantially critical for the edge devices.

2.5   Performance and Reliability Analysis

We analyzed the performance & reliability of the fire detection application (which may be possible in smart cities, also) obtained from the Kaggle dataset [18] for mobilenet_v1 with weights referred from the inferno module [19] for a different set of the test images to understand the impact of model inference on the Intel processor

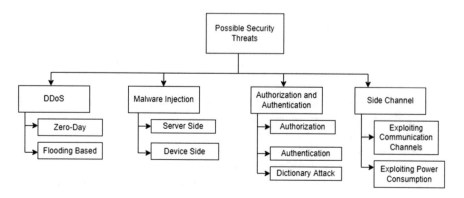

Fig. 2.4 Different countermeasures for security threats in IoT

Table 2.2 Security threats & mitigation strategies for edge computing

Security threats to edge computing	Sub attacks type occurrence	Description	Mitigation techniques/ tools
DDoS based attacks	Flooding-based attacks	A huge load of packets included. Exploited protocols are SYN, HTTP, etc	Framework investigation, Cloudflare protections, ML-based filtering of packets
	Zero day attack	Lethal, and take more time to acknowledge. Sleeping cells of cyber world	
Malware-injection based attacks	Server-side injections	Malicious combination of strings to render logic of backend null	Deploying proxy filters, instruction set randomization (ISRs)
	Device-side injections	Insinuates malware into IoT-based devices	Automatic binary structure randomization (ABSR), ISRs
Authentication and authorisation	Dictionary attacks	Due to the stored credentials to target unsecured credentials	Biometric systems, password support system
	Exploiting weaknesses in authentication protocols	Exploited protocols include WPA	Secure cryptographic algorithms, safe communication protocols
	Exploiting weaknesses in authorisation protocols	OAuth and other deprecated versions are exploited	Static code analysis, OAuth manager framework
Side-Channel attacks	Exploiting communication channels	Leveraging the system's security and privacy, attackers use the publicly shared information that is not often sensitive (also defined as side-channel information)	Communication channels should be strongly encrypted to avoid the leakage of any kind of information.
	Exploiting power consumption	Edge device power consumption & its trace is analyzed to infer the model architecture prediction of the deployed model on the edge device	Power line filtering and conditioning

(Fig. 2.5), using Keras-based implementation [20] (part of TensorFlow [21]) for three different parameters namely accuracy, average inference time and average pre-processing time.

The test image set has been divided into five sets, each consisting of a certain no of fire and non-fire images defined in Table 2.3.

Figure 2.6 gives a good insight about the accuracy in the classification of fire images across large sets of images, which could also be useful in smart cities for a

> **Hardware Setup for Experimental Analysis**
> 11th Gen Intel® Core™ i7-11700
> 16 CPUs, 2.5GHz, 8 cores
> Mesa Intel® Graphics (RKL GT1)
> 32GB RAM

Fig. 2.5 Hardware details of Intel processor

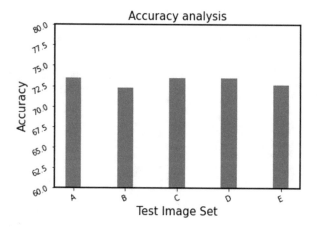

Fig. 2.6 Accuracy analysis on the different test set

Table 2.3 Test set image classification

Input set	Fire images	Non-fire images	Total no. of images
A	151	49	200
B	302	98	400
C	453	147	600
D	604	196	800
E	755	245	1000

real-time system. This approach could also be significantly adopted in smart cities in case of emergency fire detection. Hence, the most accurate fire detection model could be adopted for real-time scenarios considering that it is flexible enough to accommodate any modifications when deployed on a system integrated with different edge devices.

Figure 2.7a depicts that the average inference time is decreasing marginally because since more images are included in different sets for analysis, it is normalized for a single image as a whole. Considering the average pre-processing time, Fig. 2.7b again shows a negligible difference collectively, as total pre-processing time doesn't change much. However, the average pre-processing time for one image

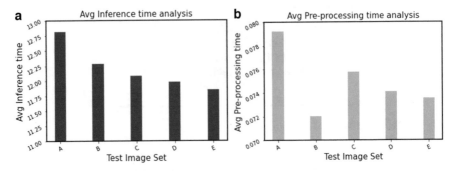

Fig. 2.7 (**a**) Avg inference time analysis (**b**) Avg pre-processing time analysis

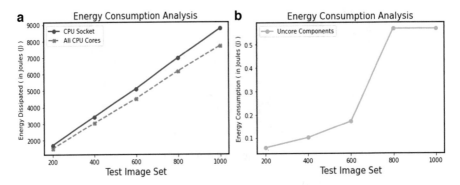

Fig. 2.8 (**a**) Energy Consumption analysis (**b**) Energy consumption analysis (Uncore components)

changes only slightly but won't matter much in the computation of the prediction results.

We analyzed the reliability of this fire detection model on certain parameters like power, energy, and temperature, and the results were interesting. Figure 2.8a shows the energy [22] consumption analysis on the Intel processor for CPU sockets (per package domain) and all the CPU Cores (per core domain), which defines that the energy increases almost linearly for the different test sets. While analyzing the energy consumption for uncore components (Fig. 2.8b), like some integrated graphics on the processor, it shows increasing behavior for the range of different data sets, except for the fact that from 600 images to 800 images, energy consumption increases a bit sharply. This behavior is assumed to be due to loading the new images each time on uncore components. The uncore component consumes different individual energy for each image processing, resulting in a slightly higher cumulative energy consumption than in other cases.

While we consider the power dissipation as a metric, Fig. 2.9 shows that the power [23] increases slightly as we move from set A to B but decreases slightly at C and increases further. This may be because while test set B was executed on Intel processors, most sets of images in set C were loaded, which might be a possible reason for the power decrease. Since the number of the images in each set is

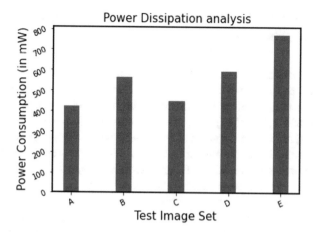

Fig. 2.9 Power dissipation analysis

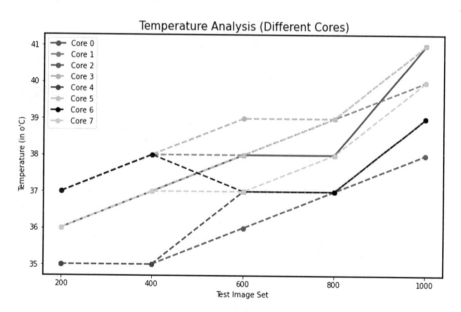

Fig. 2.10 Temperature analysis of different cores for different test sets

random, i.e., there is no guarantee that each test set will contain the same set of images in its first half, it ascertains that test set D also may not necessarily contain its first half, i.e., 400 images within the previous test sets.

Figure 2.10 shows the cores' temperature [24] variations for the different test sets. It is generalized and uses only one particular core for computation throughout. Also, it shows for a particular test set how each core temperature varies between 35° and 41°, which is logically high for high-end inference cases of 1000 images (Case E).

2.6 Edge Device Implementation in Autonomous Driving System

Autonomous driving tasks are implemented using edge devices that are considered good in terms of performance and, at the same time, more secure than other hardware. Now the main challenge which comes up in the implementation of different autonomous driving tasks [25] like traffic sign classification, lane detection, parking assistance, or road scene understanding arises from its execution on different resource constraint hardware consisting of state-of-the-art accelerators like NVIDIA GPUs (Tegra or Jetson family), NPUs and few others, whose main aim is to reduce the latency and improve the accuracy at the same time.

To deploy neural network-based algorithms like CNNs (Convolutional Neural Networks) on resource-constraint hardware, some embedding or optimization strategies are utilized to reduce the model network's overall size, making it less computationally expensive to execute on different hardware. Some prominent embedding strategies include network weight quantization, pruning, layer fusion, etc. The researchers have proposed optimized and effective architectures for the autonomous driving system functionality, which can improve the real-time system [26].

B. Yu et al. defined the SoV (System on a vehicle) hardware architecture using Xilinx Ultrascalae+ FPGA, which is more effective than some modern accelerators implementation, including NVIDIA TX2 SoCs for some of the perception layer tasks like depth estimation, localization, etc. While from the energy consumption point of view, it consumes the least energy for these different tasks compared to other processors involving Intel Coffee Lake CPU, NVIDIA GTX 1060 GPU, and SoCs boards like NVIDIA TX2 [27].

Hence, there is a tradeoff between the hardware on which the computation model for autonomous driving tasks is implemented and the model itself. So, the main aim would be to reduce this tradeoff to ensure optimum performance in terms of good speed (high fps) and high accuracy. Thus, performance and security should go hand in hand when implementing autonomous driving tasks on different hardware in a real-time driving system.

2.6.1 Security of Autonomous Driving System

Security plays a significant role in autonomous driving systems as it is pretty substantial to ensure the safety of the drivers as well as the people not only inside the vehicle but also outside the vehicle due to any mishap, accidents, or security attacks from adversaries, which can be catastrophic at times. Now, security challenges in the autonomous driving system are majorly defined as per the mode of its attack, i.e., physical/sensor-based attacks, cyber-based attacks [28, 29], and lastly and the most critical adversarial attacks (Fig. 2.11). In this section, the main emphasis would be only on adversarial attacks.

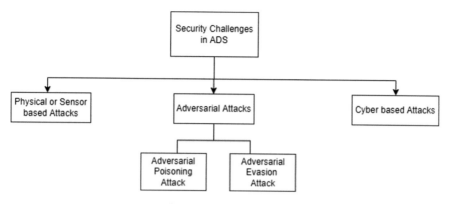

Fig. 2.11 Security threats in the autonomous driving system [30]

Physical or sensor-based attacks occur through hardware sensors where the sensor captures incorrect or false data, which will then be misclassified [30] since the autonomous system would be connected through the network for some synchronization services like real-time traffic estimation from the map on a given route and regularly updating the surrounding information of the vehicle, resulting in the possibility of a cyber-attack [31]. Adversarial attacks can be classified into two primary categories, i.e., adversarial poisoning attacks, [30] which occur during the model training time, and adversarial evasion attacks, which occur during model inference time. These attacks can cause severe damage to the autonomous system in real-time scenarios. Hence, appropriate defenses should be adopted like adversarial training, defensive distillation, etc., to reduce the impact of these attacks.

2.6.2 Level of Robustness in Adversarial Attacks

A certain level of robustness (Fig. 2.12) can be defined for implementing adversarial attacks for autonomous driving tasks. This could be analyzed from the experimental analysis defined below for two sets of adversarial attacks, i.e., targeted and untargeted attacks [32].

Targeted adversarial attacks occur when the adversaries know the target class of the model network to misclassify, while in untargeted attacks, adversaries have no access to the model architecture; hence, it is unknown to adversaries which target class to attack.

The main aim is to provide a perspective regarding the effect of adversarial attacks with a focus on their robustness against several DNNs in the real-time system. The metric employed here for classification and analysis is the confidence score that illustrates a number between 0 and 1, depicting the likelihood or probability that the DNN output is correct or not while corresponding to an attack. *Now, these three levels of robustness are stated as **R1, R2, and R3.***

Fig. 2.12 Level of
robustness in adversarial
attacks

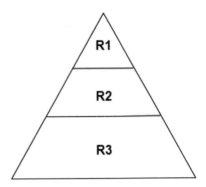

R1 – DNNs are highly robust or less vulnerable against adversarial attacks
R2 – DNNs are moderately robust & vulnerable against adversarial attacks
R3 – DNNs are least robust or most vulnerable against adversarial attacks

The metric used for classification can vary according to the model network used. It is not always true that model network size will affect the confidence score or that the metric used for defining the robustness level would always be only the confidence score. Thus, the classification for the level of robustness is not standardized as this can be done specific to any attack with various sets of DNNs, to classify while researching or analyzing.

We employ Pytorch-based implementation [33] of adversarial attacks for the targeted fast gradient sign method (FGSM-T) and the untargeted fast gradient sign method (FGSM-U). The Intel processor's experimental analysis has been performed (Fig. 2.5). The adversarial attacks, namely FGSM-T & FGSM-U, are carried out on Intel CPUs for different DNNs (deep neural networks). For ease and clarity, we use the pre-trained models with weights trained on imagenet [34] dataset consisting of 1000 classes for different DNNs namely squeezenet [35], shufflenet [36], mobilenet_v2 [37], resnet18 [38], densenet [39], alexnet [40] and vgg16 [41]. Analysis was carried out for different perturbation or noise values like 0.05, 0.10, 0.40, 0.60, 0.80, and 0.95, respectively. These noise values were taken randomly from almost minimum to maximum within 0 to 1.

2.6.3   *Experimental Results*

We analyzed the **FGSM -T** (Fast Gradient Sign Method – targeted) adversarial attack for seven different DNNs, namely squeezenet, shufflenet, mobilenet_V2, resnet18, densenet, alexnet, and VGG16 (from lighter DNN model to heavier DNN model – model size) and focused on metrics like confidence score, inference time and pre-processing time. Using the imagenet dataset for targeted attacks, the original class of the image used was 919 (street night), and the target defined class was 675 (moving van).

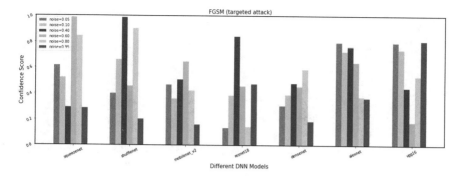

Fig. 2.13 Confidence Score variations of different DNNs for FGSM-T attack

From the analysis shown (Fig. 2.13) for different noise values, it is evident that it is difficult to conclude which model is highly robust regarding all the perturbations (noise) values. Like, for some values, alexnet performs well, and for some shufflenet and squeezenet perform well. An instance of it can be defined as when the attack intensity is about 0.10, then alexnet and vgg16 incur the maximum confidence score (highly robust). In contrast, mobilenet_v2, resnet18, and densenet least confidence score being most vulnerable to adversarial attack (least robust), and other models like squeezenet and shufflenet have mid-range confidence scores (moderately robust). Another instance shows that when the attack intensity is fixed at a noise of 0.60, the squeezenet has the highest confidence score (highly robust). In contrast, VGG16 has the least confidence score being highly vulnerable to adversarial attack (least robust), and other models like shufflenet, mobilenet_v2, resnet18, densenet, and alexnet have mid-range confidence score (moderately robust). Hence, we can define the level of robustness only by fixing some constraints (here, noise factor) and then only infer the robustness of models.

Figure 2.14 shows the confidence variations for different models under the FGSM-T attack. For most of the models' midway noise values (0.40–0.80), the confidence score is the maximum, except for vgg16, for which the confidence score is highest in peak noise value, i.e., 0.95. Thus, for FGSM targeted attack, Fig. 2.14 depicts the variations in attack intensity affecting the confidence score of different DNN models.

Figure 2.15 shows the effect of perturbations/noise on the inference time of the DNN models for the FGSM-T attack. As the value of noise increases and reaches close to 1, inference time tends to be slightly higher than the usual cases.

Figure 2.16 shows the pre-processing time of the different DNN models for the FGSM-T attack against different noise values. There is a very negligible difference in the pre-processing time for the models.

Then, we also analyzed FGSM -U (Fast Gradient Sign Method – Untargeted) adversarial attack for the same 7 DNNs against metrics like confidence score, inference time, and pre-processing time. Using the imagenet dataset for targeted attacks, the original class of the image used is 919 (street night), and the target class will be different for all DNNs. (can be considered as a random target class assignment).

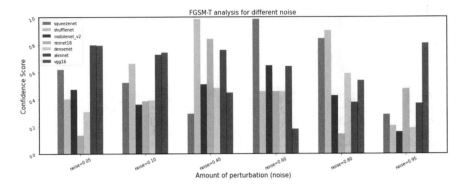

Fig. 2.14 Confidence score variations for different noise values employing FGSM-T attack

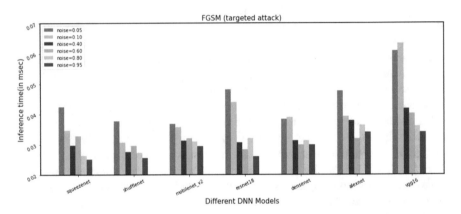

Fig. 2.15 FGSM-T attack average inference time analysis for different DNNs

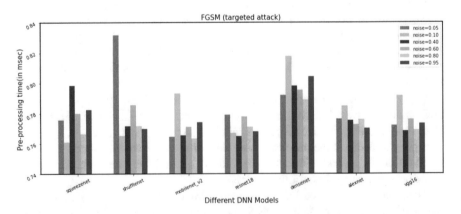

Fig. 2.16 FGSM-T attack pre-processing time analysis for different DNNs

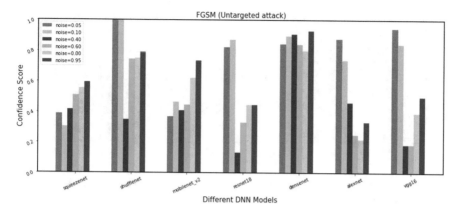

Fig. 2.17 FGSM-U (Untargeted) attack confidence score analysis for different DNNs

From the analysis for FGSM- U attacks shown above (Fig. 2.17) for different noise values, it is evident that it is difficult to infer the overall model robustness for various noise values. It can still be seen that densenet performs slightly better than other DNNs for many noise values except for noise as 0.05 and 0.10, for which shufflenet and vgg16 perform better. An instance of it can be defined as when the attack intensity is about 0.10, then shufflenet incur the maximum confidence score (highly robust), while squeezenet & mobilenet_v2 least confidence score being more vulnerable to adversarial attack (least robust) and other models like resnet18, densenet, alexnet and VGG16 have mid-range confidence score (moderately robust). Another instance shows that when the attack intensity is fixed at a noise/perturbation factor of 0.60, the densenet & shufflenet have the maximum confidence score (highly robust). In contrast, resnet18, alexnet, and VGG16 have the least confidence score being highly vulnerable to adversarial attack (least robust). In contrast, squeezenet and mobilenet_v2 have mid-range confidence scores (moderately robust). Hence, again for FGSM-U attacks, it is difficult to define the robustness level and can be inferred only by fixing some constraints (here, noise factor).

Figure 2.18 depicts the confidence variations model-wise for different noise values under the FGSM-U attack. For some models like shufflenet, resnet18, densenet, alexnet, and VGG16, the confidence score is maximum at values of perturbation/ noise close to 0, i.e. (0.05–0.10). While for some other models like squeezenet and mobilenet_v2, it has a maximum confidence score at high values of the noise factor, i.e., close to 1 (0.80–0.95). The above figure describes how variations in attack intensity (noise/perturbation factor) affect the confidence score of different DNN models for FGSM-U attacks.

Figure 2.19 shows the effect of perturbations/noise on the inference time of the DNN models for the FGMS-U attack. As the value of noise increases and reaches close to 1, inference time tends to be slightly higher than usual.

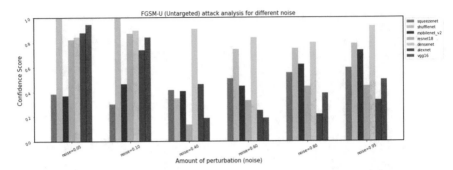

Fig. 2.18 Confidence Score variations for different noise values employing FGSM-U (Untargeted) attack

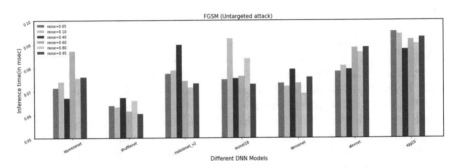

Fig. 2.19 FGSM-U (Untargeted) attack average inference time analysis for different DNNs

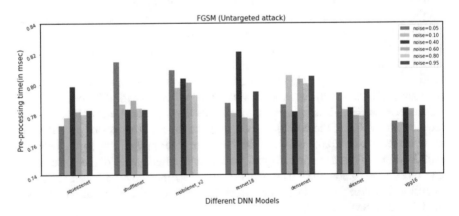

Fig. 2.20 FGSM-U (Untargeted) attack pre-processing time analysis for different DNNs

Figure 2.20 shows the pre-processing time of the different DNN models for FGMS-U attack against different noise values. There is a very negligible difference in the pre-processing time for the models (Table 2.4).

Figures 2.21, 2.22, 2.23 and 2.24 shows a few examples of perturbation added to the traffic sign for FGSM-T and FGSM-U attacks for resnet18 and mobilenet_v2 DNN models.

Table 2.4 Identified target class for FGSM-U (untargeted) attack

Models	Perturbation/noise value					
	0.05	0.10	0.40	0.60	0.80	0.95
Squeezenet	455	117	806	806	806	806
Shufflenet	455	455	506	506	506	506
mobilenet_v2	737	746	746	646	646	646
resnet18	455	455	528	506	506	506
Densenet	455	455	455	455	539	539
Alexnet	455	455	806	806	109	109
vgg16	455	455	712	646	646	646

 +  =

Fig. 2.21 FGSM-T (Targeted) attack for **resnet18** at noise 0.10

 +  =

Fig. 2.22 FGSM-T (Targeted) attack for **mobilenet_V2** at noise 0.10

 +  =

Fig. 2.23 FGSM-U (Untargeted) attack for **mobilenet_V2** at noise 0.10 and target class 746

 +  =

Fig. 2.24 FGSM-U (Untargeted) attack for **mobilenet_V2** at noise 0.10 and target class 455

2.7   Conclusion

In today's pragmatic technological medium, where many smart devices are being integrated within the systems to ease and enable the functionalities of day-to-day tasks, edge devices should be performance-optimized and highly secure at the same time from any attacks. This chapter covers the security threats in IoT systems, a brief survey of the state-of-the-art cyber-attacks possible in smart cities, and its possible defense mechanism. Then it highlighted the performance and reliability analysis of fire detection tasks on intel processors as a study to understand the model network analysis and its parameter-like accuracy for different test sets. Finally, it focused on the detailed experimental analysis of adversarial attacks for different DNNs against various perturbation or noise values for FGSM-T (fast gradient sign method – targeted) and FGSM-U (fast gradient sign method – untargeted) attacks.

References

1. Vattapparamban, E., Gven, A., Yurekli, K. A., & Uluaa, S. (2016). Drones for smart cities: Issues in cybersecurity, privacy, and public safety. In *2016 International Wireless Communications and Mobile Computing Conference (IWCMC)* (pp. 216–221).
2. Lin, J., Yu, W., Zhang, N., Yang, X., Zhang, H., & Zhao, W. (2017). A survey on internet of things: Architecture, enabling technologies, security and privacy, and applications. *IEEE Internet of Things Journal, 4*(5), 1125–1142.
3. Zhang, Y., Zheng, D., & Deng, R. H. (2018). Security and privacy in smart health: Efficient policy-hiding attribute-based access control. *IEEE Internet of Things Journal, 5*(3), 2130–2145.
4. Li, Y., Dai, W., Ming, Z., & Qiu, M. (2016). Privacy protection for preventing data over-collection in smart city. *IEEE Transactions on Computers, 65*(5), 1339–1350.
5. Gharaibeh, A., Salahuddin, M. A., Hussini, S. J., Khreishah, A., Khalil, I., Guizani, M., & Al-Fuqaha, A. (2017). Smart cities: A survey on data management, security, and enabling technologies. *IEEE Communications Surveys Tutorials, 19*(4), 2456–2501.
6. Eckhoff, D., & Wagner, I. (2018). Privacy in the smart city applications, technologies, challenges, and solutions. *IEEE Communications Surveys Tutorials, 20*(1), 489–516.
7. Shen, M., Tang, X., Zhu, L., Du, X., & Guizani, M. (2019). Privacy-preserving support vector machine training over blockchain-based encrypted iot data in smart cities. *IEEE Internet of Things Journal, 6*(5), 7702–7712.
8. Rahman, M. A., Rashid, M. M., Hossain, M. S., Hassanain, E., Alhamid, M. F., & Guizani, M. (2019). Blockchain and iot-based cognitive edge framework for sharing economy services in a smart city. *IEEE Access, 7*, 18611–18621.
9. Jose, A. C., & Malekian, R. (2017, July 1). Improving smart home security: Integrating logical sensing into smart home. *IEEE Sensors Journal, 17*(13), 4269–4286.
10. Biswas, K., & Muthukkumarasamy, V. (2016). Securing smart cities using blockchain technology. In *2016 IEEE 18th international conference on high performance computing and communications; IEEE 14th international conference on Smart City; IEEE 2nd International Conference on Data Science and Systems (HPCC/SmartCity/DSS)* (pp. 1392–1393).
11. Khan, P. W., Byun, Y.-C., & Park, N. (2020). A data verification system for CCTV surveillance cameras using blockchain technology in smart cities. *Electronics, 9*(3), 484.

12. Khan, L. U., Yaqoob, I., Tran, N. H., Kazmi, S. M. A., Dang, T. N., & Hong, C. S. (2020). Edge-computing-enabled smart cities: A comprehensive survey. *IEEE Internet of Things Journal, 7*(10), 10200–10232.
13. Tan, S., De, D., Song, W.-Z., Yang, J., & Das, S. K. (2017). Survey of security advances in smart grid: A data driven approach. *IEEE Communications Surveys & Tutorials, 19*(1), 397–422.
14. Cui, L., Xie, G., Qu, Y., Gao, L., & Yang, Y. (2018). Security and privacy in smart cities: Challenges and opportunities. *IEEE Access, 6*, 46134–46145.
15. Podder, P., Mondal, M. R. H., Bharati, S., & Paul, P. K. (2020, July). Review on the security threats of internet of things. *International Journal of Computer Applications, 176*, 37–45.
16. Husamuddin, M., & Qayyum, M. (2017). Internet of things: A study on security and privacy threats. In *2017 2nd International Conference on Anti-Cyber Crimes (ICACC)* (pp. 93–97).
17. Toh, C. K. (2020, July). Security for smart cities. *IET Smart Cities, 2*(9), 95–104.
18. https://www.kaggle.com/datasets/elikplim/forest-fires-data-set
19. Mukhopadhyay, D., Iyer, R., Kadam, S., & Koli, R. (2019). Fpga deployable fire detection model for real-time video surveillance systems using convolutional neural networks. In *2019 Global Conference for Advancement in Technology (GCAT)* (pp. 1–7).
20. Chollet, F. et al. (2015). Keras. https://keras.io
21. Abadi, M., Agarwal, A., Barham, P., Brevdo, E., Chen, Z., Citro, C., Corrado, G. S., Davis, A., Dean, J., Devin, M., Ghemawat, S., Goodfellow, I., Harp, A., Irving, G., Isard, M., Jia, Y., Jozefowicz, R., Kaiser, L., Kudlur, M., Levenberg, J., Mane, D., Monga, R., Moore, S., Murray, D., Olah, C., Schuster, M., Shlens, J., Steiner, B., Sutskever, I., Talwar, K., Tucker, P., Vanhoucke, V., Vasudevan, V., Viegas, F., Vinyals, O., Warden, P., Wattenberg, M., Wicke, M., Yu, Y., & Zheng, X. (2015). *TensorFlow: Large-scale machine learning on heterogeneous systems*. Software available from tensorflow.org.
22. https://github.com/sosy-lab/cpu-energy-meter
23. https://github.com/fenrus75/powertop
24. https://github.com/opcm/pcm
25. Moujahid, A., ElAraki Tantaoui, M., Hina, M. D., Soukane, A., Ortalda, A., ElKhadimi, A., & Ramdane-Cherif, A. (2018). Machine learning techniques in ADAS: A review. In *2018 International Conference on Advances in Computing and Communication Engineering (ICACCE)* (pp. 235–242).
26. Borrego-Carazo, J., Castells-Rufas, D., Biempica, E., & Carrabina, J. (2020). Resource-constrained machine learning for ADAS: A systematic review. *IEEE Access, 8*, 40573–40598.
27. Yu, B., Hu, W., Xu, L., Tang, J., Liu, S., & Zhu, Y. (2020). Building the computing system for autonomous micromobility vehicles: Design constraints and architectural optimizations. In *2020 53rd Annual IEEE/ACM International Symposium on Microarchitecture (MICRO)* (pp. 1067–1081).
28. Pansari, N., & Agarwal, A. (2020). A comparative study of analysis and investigation using digital forensics. *International Journal of Linguistics and Computational Applications (IJLCA), 7*(2), 16–20.
29. Pansari, N., & Kushwaha, D. (2018). Advancement in robust cyber attacks-an overview. *International Journal of Research in Engineering, IT and Social Sciences, 8*(Special Issue), 113–119.
30. Deng, Y., Zhang, T., Lou, G., Zheng, X., Jin, J., & Han, Q.-L. (2021). Deep learning-based autonomous driving systems: A survey of attacks and defenses. *IEEE Transactions on Industrial Informatics, 17*(12), 7897–7912.
31. Pansari, N., & Kushwaha, D. (2019). Forensic analysis and investigation using digital forensics-an overview. *International Journal of Advance Research, Ideas and Innovations in Technology, 5*, 191.
32. Goodfellow, I. J., Shlens, J., & Szegedy, C. (2014). Explaining and harnessing adversarial examples. *arXiv preprint arXiv*, 1412.6572.

33. Paszke, A., Gross, S., Massa, F., Lerer, A., Bradbury, J., Chanan, G., Killeen, T., Lin, Z., Gimelshein, N., Antiga, L., et al. (2019). Pytorch: An imperative style, high-performance deep learning library. *Advances in Neural Information Processing Systems, 32*, 8024–8035.
34. Deng, J., Dong, W., Socher, R., Li, L.-J., Li, K., & Fei-Fei, L. (2009). Imagenet: A large scale hierarchical image database. In *2009 IEEE conference on computer vision and pattern recognition* (pp. 248–255).
35. Iandola, F. N., Han, S., Moskewicz, M. W., Ashraf, K., Dally, W. J., & Keutzer, K. (2016). Squeezenet: Alexnet-level accuracy with 50x fewer parameters and¡ 0.5 mb model size. *arXiv preprint arXiv*, 1602.07360.
36. Zhang, X., Zhou, X., Lin, M., & Sun, J. (2018). Shufflenet: An extremely efficient convolutional neural network for mobile devices. In *Proceedings of the IEEE conference on computer vision and pattern recognition* (pp. 6848–6856).
37. Sandler, M., Howard, A., Zhu, M., Zhmoginov, A., & Chen, L.-C. (2018). Mobilenetv2: Inverted residuals and linear bottlenecks. In *Proceedings of the IEEE conference on computer vision and pattern recognition* (pp. 4510–4520).
38. He, K., Zhang, X., Ren, S., & Sun, J. (2016). Deep residual learning for image recognition. In *Proceedings of the IEEE conference on computer vision and pattern recognition* (pp. 770–778).
39. Huang, G., Liu, Z., Van Der Maaten, L., & Weinberger, K. Q. (2017). Densely connected convolutional networks. In *Proceedings of the IEEE conference on computer vision and pattern recognition* (pp. 4700–4708).
40. Krizhevsky, A., Sutskever, I., & Hinton, G. E. (2012). Imagenet classification with deep convolutional neural networks. In F. Pereira, C. Burges, L. Bottou, & K. Weinberger (Eds.), *Advances in neural information processing systems* (Vol. 25). Curran Associates, Inc..
41. Simonyan, K., & Zisserman, A. (2014). Very deep convolutional networks for large-scale image recognition. *arXiv preprint arXiv*, 1409.1556.

Chapter 3
Artificial Intelligence in Smart City-Systematic Literature Review of Current Knowledge and Future Research Avenues

A. K. M. Bahalul Haque, Anjoom Nur, and Raisa Nusrat Chowdhury

Abstract Artificial intelligence (AI) is gaining acceptance and applicability all over the world rapidly. AI has the ability to revolutionaize our cities and society due to its advanced capabilities. Major technical, economic, and environmental developments have piqued mankind's interest in building a society that is technologically smarter and safer to live in. AI is prevalent in multiple sectors of smart city such as infrastructure, transportation, environmental protection, power and energy, privacy and security, governance, Data Management, Healthcare etc. and the rising usage is anticipated to expand. In this systematic literature review (SLR) on artificial intelligence in smart cities, an attempt is being made to examine and critically assess the findings related to recent development. It provides insights into developing urban artificial intelligence and the possibility for a smart city- AI symbiosis. In terms of approach, this SLR employs a detailed analysis of the current state of AI and smart city literature, research, advancements, patterns, and applications. As a result, it adds to ongoing scholarly discussions in the disciplines of smart cities and artificial intelligence. We performed thematic analysis over 100 papers, categorized them into themes and sub themes and identified the research gaps. To conclude we present our recommendations to address the research gaps as future research avenue.

Keyword Smart city · IOT · Artificial intelligence · Applications · Sustainability

A. K. M. B. Haque (✉)
LUT University, Lappeenranta, Finland
e-mail: bahalul.haque@lut.fi

A. Nur · R. N. Chowdhury
North South University, Dhaka, Bangladesh
e-mail: anjoom.nur@northsouth.edu; raisa.chowdhury@northsouth.edu

© The Author(s), under exclusive license to Springer Nature Switzerland AG 2023   53
M. A. Ahad et al. (eds.), *Enabling Technologies for Effective Planning and Management in Sustainable Smart Cities*, https://doi.org/10.1007/978-3-031-22922-0_3

3.1   Introduction

During the last decade smart cities have evolved significantly and spread across various part of our life. The facilities inside smart city ecosystem are the fruitful outcome of significant socioeconomic digitization. Cloud computing, IoT, and cyber-physical systems, etc. are the building block of state-of-the-art smart city facilities. The application of smart cities is multidisciplinary and those range from living, governance, intelligent citizen management, traffic and transportation system, financial and economic growth, cyber security and intelligent infrastructure [1–3].

Smart cities have become an actual pick-up term for a variety of technologies, not only by introducing new applications but also by making existing services more accessible to citizens. In the light of urbanization, climate change, democratic flaws, and rising urban welfare expenditures, smart cities have emerged as an important approach for society's future development [4, 5]. "Smart cities" is a broad phenomenon that has been described variously by many experts. However, being a smart city necessitates accomplishing long-term social, environmental, and economic growth, as well as enhancing society living standards through the use of ICT and AI [6].

AI has the ability to usher in a new era of technological advancement. AI is defined as "the ability of a system to accurately receive external input, learn from it, and use that learning to accomplish particular objectives and activities through balancing" [7]. Rapid growth in AI's popularity and practicality is a global phenomenon. The foundation of artificial intelligence is the development of self-guided agents that can articulate their goals and plan their actions independently of external data [8]. AI has the potential to improve human health, prosperity, and happiness by reducing our reliance on manual labor and accelerating our progress in the sciences and technologies [9]. However, AI has the ability to drastically alter our urban areas and culture. Humanity's ambition in building a more technologically advanced and secure society has been fueled by major scientific, economic, and environmental breakthroughs. Artificial intelligence (AI) has already significantly changed our daily lives in numerous ways such as; from semi-autonomous vehicles on the roads to robotic systems in our homes, and it will continue to do so in the years to come [10, 11], attempting to permeate all facets of society. The application of AI is expanding across many domains in the smart city, such as infrastructure, transportation, environmental protection, power and energy, privacy and security, governance, data management, healthcare, and more.

Various studies on AI in smart cities have been conducted in recent years. This article attempts to address the use of artificial intelligence in smart cities is an attempt to review and critically analyze previous discoveries. It offers insights on the development of urban artificial intelligences as well as the possibilities of a smart city-AI symbiotic relationship. This viewpoint provides a thorough analysis of the state of the literature, research, advances, patterns, and applications related to AI and smart cities at the time. As a result, it contributes to ongoing scholarly debates in the fields of smart cities and artificial intelligence. An exhaustive literature evaluation is carried out between 2014 and 2021 to determine the depth of AI in smart cities. The following is a list of the paper's major contributions:

- Analyze the findings of previous research and identify research gaps of AI use in smart cities.
- This Paper will allow us to have a better understanding of the significance of various technologies and their use in the development of smart cities.
- Identify the recent scholarly contribution trend in various smart city domains.

The structure of this paper is as follows. First, we'll go through the background of smart city (Sect. 3.2). Second, we will go through the research methodology (Sect. 3.3). Section 3.4 will next go through thematic analysis. Finally, we will review the important findings and set some future goals to ensure that AI produces the greatest results for smart cities.

3.2 Background

A smart city is one that has sophisticated modern technology, new applications, and creations that make life simpler, more efficient, and easier. City residents' lifestyles are becoming more suitable for quality living and efficiency as a result of smart cities. Transparency, reliability, optimization, and monitoring are also necessary for successful deployment [12].

3.2.1 Smart City Infrastructure

The establishment of the overall smart city framework and architecture begins with smart city infrastructure [13]. Some essential smart city infrastructures are:

3.2.1.1 Physical Infrastructure

Information and communication technology (ICT) enable smart city to integrate cost-effective and smart socio technical, physical and virtual infrastructure. However, physical infrastructure tends to have a solid role on the basic infrastructure of smart city. Physical infrastructure of smart city provides different types of social and municipal benefits. For example, (i) solid waste management refers to waste generation, prevention, characterization, monitoring, handling, reuse, and disposal; and (ii) urban mobility refers to the quality of urban walking, cycling, and smart transportation systems.

3.2.1.2   Institutional Infrastructure

The basic functions of activity, such as management, governance and planning with the goal of including inhabitants in decision-making processes. The institutional infrastructure collaborates with both the central and regional administrations to get the most out of the smart city. It is critical to process information in real time under complete Service Level Agreements to ensure that such judgments are made without arbitrariness or discrimination (SLA). Furthermore, ICT aids in the creation of an effective, responsible and transparent citizen-centered system.

3.2.1.3   Social Infrastructure

It includes a variety of frameworks for the development and progress of individual and societal resources, as well as intelligent and transparent, integrated infrastructure to meet people's diverse social demand and services. In addition, it includes a variety of frameworks for the development and progress of individual and societal resources.

3.2.1.4   Economic Infrastructure

It is a term that pertains to the fundamental establishments and conveniences that contribute to the growth and allocation of funds to build appropriate infrastructure in order to generate employment opportunities and entice industry [14]. Even while this kind of activity does not directly produce goods or services, it does have an impact on external economies by encouraging agriculture, manufacturing, and commerce to produce more goods and services. This, in turn, has a knock-on effect on the global economy. It is possible that the idea of a smart city will have an effect on every facet of contemporary culture. As a consequence of this, creating smart cities and improving the circumstances for networking and communication are absolutely necessary in order to successfully capture and interpret massive volumes of data.

3.2.2   Smart City Layered Architecture

The data that is acquired from the physical world, the data that is transferred in the communication world, and the data that is processed in the information world are all manipulated by the smart city in order to achieve comprehensive sensing and smart city management. As can be seen in Fig. 3.1, the incorporation of this system includes not only control and operational elements but also processing units, sensing elements, and heterogeneous network infrastructure.

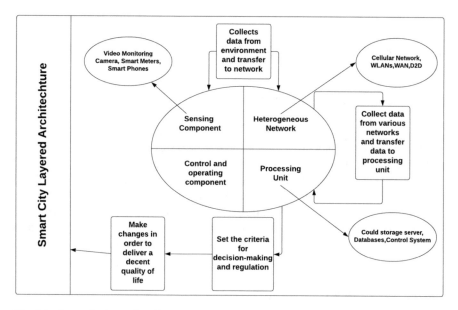

Fig. 3.1 Smart city layered architecture

3.2.2.1 Sensing Components

To put it another way, sensing elements act as a bridge between the realm of physics and the world of knowledge [15]. As was previously mentioned, the sensing devices can be placed by the government, organizations, and businesses; alternatively, customers can carry them with them. Additionally included are mobile devices, sensors for industrial use, and wearable technology.

3.2.2.2 Heterogeneous Networks

The sensing information is gathered in a variety of ways due to the cohabitation of big sensing instruments and numerous applications and the heterogeneous network design plays an important role in aiding the smart city. Heterogeneous networks include cellular networks, wireless local area networks (WLANs), large area networks (WANs), device-to-device (D2D) communications, millimeter-wave communications, sensor networks, and other forms of networks to allow smooth switching.

3.2.2.3 The Processing Unit

It interprets and processes the collected sensory input from the real environment for decision-making using efficient cloud storage, smart and efficient processing and control system. The processing unit in a smart city is in charge of the information world. The information can be used by certain companies with a view to analyzing the data for citizens wellbeing. However, smart city authorities should establish standards or policies for smart city decision-making and regulation.

3.2.2.4 Control and Operating Components

In order to give a fair quality of life in a smart city, this control and running aspects refine the real environment and make modifications. They also explain how smart cities work in both directions (i.e., sensory and administration). It can track and operate any system for making the smart city smarter and intelligent by learning knowledge about the physical environment from its two-way flow.

The demand for smart cities is surprisingly enormous in today's world. In today's world, it is the next ground-breaking technical development. The advantages or contributions that smart cities will bring are mentioned further down.

3.2.2.5 Sustainability

One of the most crucial characteristics of a smart city is its ability to be sustainable. A smart city focuses on establishing smart and sustainable healthcare, a sustainable energy consumption framework, and assisting in the preservation of a more environmentally friendly lifestyle [16]. Another important component in the development of smart cities is the intelligent use of natural resources, waste and pollution management, climate change and social difficulties. Humans will be prioritized when technology is adapted to improve people's quality of life as a result of smart cities.

3.2.2.6 Security

When it comes to smart cities, security is the most import factor. Each component to fa smart city is linked via the internet to the rest of the network. Thanks to blockchain technology, which serves as the smart city's security provider, smart city infrastructure, which is state-of-the-art technology, aids in strengthening physical architecture and cybersecurity [17]. Blockchain technology's pseudo-anonymity ensures the secure transmission of massive data in the smart city. Because blockchain prohibits the use of any third-party solution in any of its processes, it ensures that the entire operation is free of fraudulent activity. Cyber-attacks on numerous infrastructures are inescapable when technology, namely the internet, is involved. Smart cities typically use co variety of sensor networks and IoT devices to build context-aware apps and sensor networks are more vulnerable to cyber-attacks due to their infrastructure [18]. Devices may be out of reach as a result of infrastructure attacks, or data may be lost; as a result, smart city residents may experience a privacy breach or malicious codes may be injected to spread false information that has a catastrophic impact on the overall environment and living standard and thus infect smart city infrastructure. To avoid this smart city always use cutting-edge security attack counter measures whenever an attack occurs [19–21].

3.2.2.7 Connectivity

It is such a vital aspect that a smart city would be impossible to imagine without it. Connectivity is essential in a smart city and it can be wired or wireless. The easier it is for data to flow in smart cities while offering real-time application and security services to residents, the smoother the connection is.

3.2.3 Decentralization

When it comes to smart city development, decentralization is the primary goal. A smart city's major goal is to decentralize governance, healthcare, education, and other services. This is done so that consumers can receive whatever service they want at any time and from any location. Transparency and immutability will prohibit any type of fraud if individual records are saved using blockchain technology. On an individual and company level, we can always employ digital identification elements for authentication.

3.3 Research Methodology

The SLR is an approach that allows for a thorough assessment of the state-of-the-art in any given research field while also identifying research gaps to encourage further exploration and knowledge expansion [22–24]. We use an inductive technique to develop concepts of influencing aspects of algorithm aversion in order to execute SLR. This SLR reviewed the prior research in the following order: identification, selection of those that were relevant, information retrieval, data summarization, and finally, delivery of the findings. To assure the consistency and accuracy of our findings, we used standard method sand followed the steps below:

- **Step I:** Design the assessment by defining the research criteria that will be used to find relevant papers.
- **Step II:** Characterizing study selection-inclusion and exclusion criteria
- **Step III:** Review past research and collect data while using several screening levels to analyze content and extract data.
- **Step IV:** Executing data by combining the results of the study. Synthesize from extracted data and analysis.

Table 3.1 Characterizing criteria

Inclusion criteria	Exclusion criteria
Article focusing on AI in Smart City	Article that fails to address AI in smart cities.
English-language articles with peer review	Articles not written in English
Journal articles published before November, 2021	Workpapers, conference papers, project reports, and white papers.
	Articles that covered the same subject twice.

3.4 Review Designing/Planning

The creation of a research protocol is the initial step in conducting an SLR. The creation of a research topic, which will direct the report's succeeding phases, is the first step in the search technique. Choosing a search strategy, locating relevant studies, creating inclusion and exclusion criteria, and selecting a synthesis approach are all parts of these processes. We started by getting the RQs ready for this SLR. We looked at a well-known database—Scopus—to address these RQs. In order to explore databases and further define and improve the comprehensive keywords that would be used as search strings, we first chose the main term "AI and smart city." Our search included all relevant studies and was not restricted to any one-time frame.

3.4.1 Characterizing Study Selection

The unit of analysis for our SLR was determined to be academic research papers. Then, in order to identify the particular study papers, we specified the inclusion and exclusion criteria. We identify inclusion, exclusion, and the area of the re-view in order to base our evaluation on high-quality evidence. Only those papers are chosen for evaluation that precisely satisfy all of the requirements. The inclusion and exclusion criteria are outlined in Table 3.1.

3.5 Data Extraction and Analysis

Initially, we used Google Scholar to look for publications using the phrase 'Smart city and AI.' By analyzing the titles, abstracts, and keywords from the papers obtained in this initial search, we created a comprehensive list of terms and established the final search strings. The subsequent search was eventually generated using this method.: (AI and Smart City) OR ('Artificial Intelligence and Smart City'). Scopus yielded a total of 2042 studies. We did not limit our study's election to a certain time period. However, a main examination of earlier studies found that smart cities have sparked academic interest since 2014. However, we focused at the

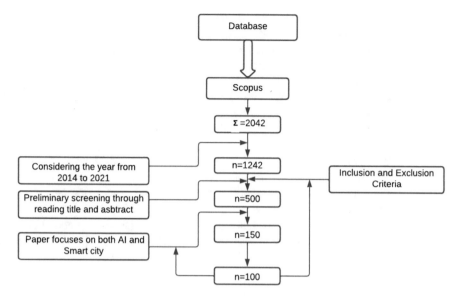

Fig. 3.2 Data extraction

latest seven years of paper from 2014 to 2021. The filtering criteria were increased beyond the fundamental bibliographic details, such as journal title, author and year to include each article's abstract. The screening procedure was carried out in four steps. This procedure was carried out independently by the two authors, and at the end of each step, a conversation was held to establish a decision on moving on to the next level.

First, we evaluate the papers from 2014 to 2021, which totaled 1242. Second, after applying the previously outlined inclusion and exclusion criteria to these 1242 investigations, we were left with 500 studies. Third, we excluded papers that focused on either AI or Smart city but did not clearly cover AI deployment in Smart city. Following this phase, 150 studies remained. Finally, we reviewed the remaining 150 studies and selected those that covered AI applications in smart cities. This left us with 100 studies and we chose these 100 publications for our next research to fulfill our requirements. Figure 3.2 shows all the steps for data extraction.

3.6 Data Execution

Based on descriptive statistics, we created a research profile for the 100 selected studies, which included the publishing origin, publication year, geographic scope and methodology utilized, in accordance with previous studies. The small number of researches published previous to 2016 is highlighted by categorizing them by year, with a rapid growth from 2019 to 2021. There are 52 publications linked to smart cities and AI among the 100 research, while the rest are conference papers. Springer Science and Business Media DeutschlandGmbH publishes the majority of articles and conference papers. A large number of studies were carried out in the India (15 articles), China (13 articles), Australia (7articles), United States (5articles), Italy (5articles) and United Kingdom (3articles). Based on descriptive statistics, we created a research profile for the 100 selected studies, which included the publishing origin, publication year, geographic scope and methodology utilized, in accordance with previous studies. The small number of researches published previous to 2016 is highlighted by categorizing them by year, with a rapid growth from 2019 to 2021. There are 52 publications linked to smart cities and AI among the 100 research, while the rest are conference papers. Springer Science and Business Media DeutschlandGmbH publishes the majority of articles and conference papers. A large number of studies were carried out in the India (15 articles), China (13 articles), Australia (7 articles), United States (5 articles), Italy (5 articles) and United Kingdom (3 articles). Figure 3.3 represents number of selected publications from each year.

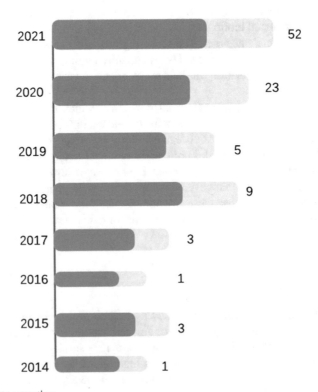

Fig. 3.3 Data execution

3.7 Thematic Analysis

We started by reading the Excel data file containing major findings from primary research, and then we gave each study a descriptive description based on what we had read and our overall experiences. This stage allowed us to have a better understanding of the research. Second, because we were interested in investigating themes Smart city and AI, the excel data file which is the list of articles were analyzed. We have coded the excel file data into broad thematic categories [25].

3.7.1 *Environmental Protection*

3.7.1.1 Air Quality

Because it studies the possibility of explicitly integrating emission sources through into prediction model, it is significant in the field of air quality forecasting (AQ prediction). In earlier research [26], the process of prediction relied solely on context information. Other researchers, on the other hand, have recently improved the existing prediction algorithms by taking feature extraction from time series into account. These time series contained fair pollutant concentrations and weather factors. Long-term series and short-term pollution sources generate low frequency high peak pollution, which is extremely challenging to anticipate while also comprehending the significance of a reliable machine learning prediction method. Long-term series and short-term pollution sources generate low frequency high peak pollution. Additional research is necessary before implementing these solutions [27].

3.7.1.2 Water Leakage

The problem of water leakage has spawned a slew of innovative solutions. However, a step toward smart cities may be seen in the detection and localization of water Leaks in water Nets with the use of an ICT system using artificial intelligence techniques. As a result, many precautions are taken to assure this. These include developing a hydraulic model for the water supply network, calibrating the model, running the hydraulic model through several computations for simulated leaks, choosing a neural classifier for leak location, and identifying water leaks. The problem of water leakage has spawned as Lew of innovative solutions. However, Finding and Locating Water Leaks in Water Nets with the Help of an ICT.

System and Artificial Intelligence Techniques: A Step Toward Smart Cities. As a result, several safe guard shaves been implemented to ensure this. Planning a SCADA monitoring system for the water supply network, trying to formulate a hydraulic model for the water supply network adjusting the hydraulic model, execute multiple calculations of the hydraulic model for simulated leaks, determining a neural classifier for leak location, and detecting water leaks are some of the setbacks [28]. The analysis revealed that the MLP network is better suited for handling this kind of issue. Additionally, the calculation of neural networks model shows that it may be a valuable and practical tool for finding and discovering concealed leaks in the water supply network. This indicates that when it comes to finding leaks, a simpler network performs better than a more complicated network. Three components of an IT system must be disposable to handle the challenge of detecting and localizing water leaks in Water Nets: an appropriately built monitoring system, a precisely calibrated water net model, and a neural failures classifier. The hydraulic model of the network may be calibrated using data from the monitoring system, and the failures classifier can be built using this model. The identification of suspected water leaks may then be documented using the monitoring system, and the subsequent usage of the neural classifier will result in the leaks localization be unrecognized.

3.7.1.3 Environmental Intelligence

To enhance the standard of living of their populations, smart cities implement cutting-edge technologies such as 5G and other forms of advanced wireless communication. Because of the uprise in the prevalence of IoE technology and the volume of data that this generates, a cutting-edge architecture is necessary to handle a wide range of application types in order to provide efficient and intelligent resource management in smart cities. As a result of this, an original proposal was made (6G) [29] for the development of a conventional resource distribution and task off-loading infrastructure for Internet of Everything devices within the context of a smart city framework. Based on the suggested intelligent model, an enhanced multi-layer intelligence architecture for 6G networks is provided for Internet of Everything devices to use in smart city environments. In addition to particular study subjects for the purpose of designing and assessing the functionality of each item in the recommended traditional and smart architectures.

3.7.2   Healthcare

3.7.2.1 IoT Healthcare System

In the field of medicine, it has become clear that intelligent solutions built on AI and the IoT can be highly advantageous. It is possible that the Internet of Things (IoT) with edge computing capabilities will revolutionize the healthcare sector by enabling a huge proportion of embedded sensors and IoT devices to communicate with one another and deliver a variety of services to communities for the benefit of the residents of those communities. In the current COVID-19 environment, interconnected IoT devices produce a vast stream of IoT data, which is amplified by the presence of chronic illnesses and an aging population [30–32]. Because of the lightning-fast rate at which the environment is changing, health-care organizations are having a hard time keeping up. In order to ensure that patients receive treatment as quickly as possible, it is essential to diagnose and detect illnesses at an early stage [33]. Because of this, there is a corresponding decrease in the cost of medical care. In order to accomplish this objective, the combination of edge AI and IoT possesses the capability to classify and cluster the enormous volume of data produced by IoT devices, as well as to develop predictions and supply early insights. It is possible that this will assist in resolving various problems related with the pandemic as well as the global challenge posed by the epidemic. The current research presents a cutting-edge artificial intelligence (AI)-enabled internet of things (IoT) healthcare monitoring system for a smart city. This system has the potential to significantly improve medical structures and infrastructure while also ensuring patients receive prompt treatment. In the event that a pandemic occurs, this might prove to be quite helpful in terms of shoring up the health care system. A concept known as an end-to-end network slice is also provided for the provision of health care services. This concept offers both decreased latency and increased scalability.

3.7.2.2 Corona Virus Outbreak and Smart City

Due to the pandemic outbreak, various smart city infrastructures and administrators around the globe had to take protective and precautionary measures [33]. Surveillance systems have been placed in most of these institutions, which are largely located in metropolitan areas, to guarantee the safety and isolation of any person showing symptoms [34]. In these situations, anonymizing medical data is essential, as it appears to be in the current publication, to ensure that utilization of the technology in question does not run afoul of data privacy and security laws in various countries. New technologies, such quantum cryptography and blockchain, can be made to operate with data collection techniques in this situation and can aid in the conversation. Despite the undeniable functions that implanted devices play in giving valuable health information, the data transmission component of their operation has to be examined. First, communications are seen to be geography-bound (limited to a certain spot), with the result that they seldom extend or communicate with their counter parts installed outside of their restricted locations. Second, these devices are frequently obtained and installed by independent companies who have their own set of rules for data processing and exchange, thereby linking cities to their product [35]. Furthermore, in the event of an emergency, such as the present COVID-19 epidemic or any other adherence to regulatory norms and international healthcare recommendations is critical. This would guarantee that both healthcare providers and the general public are kept informed, safe and within the law.

3.7.2.3 Hospitals Equipped with Smart Systems

The city's political system, traffic and transit, medical resources, educational information, and tourism conditions all use modern information technology. All activity in the city, every landmark, and every detail are under data tracking and surveillance, and big data collects all of the city's information. When the Internet is used to transport data, the city becomes transparent, palpable, visible, measurable, and quantifiable. This configuration operates well and meets test requirements. It can help patients find medical facilities based on scientific data, guide them to acceptable therapy, and utilize fewer resources [36]. Long-term free healthcare service patients can access large hospitals instantly. Preference causes disorganized access to medical care, as well as systemic and implementation inefficiency. Hierarchical policies govern diagnosis and therapy. This article [37] analyzes how patients pick medical facilities, both individually and as a group, and how to support their decision-making.

3.7.3 Transportation

3.7.3.1 Smart Mobility

As the researchers have shown, KB included information on the environment, transportation, buildings, cars and town planning. These topics are also proven to be significant in the context of self-driving automobiles. Experimentation with a Scribbler robot was done to perform a prototype system that creates a transportation knowledge base that may be used for a variety of applications, including autonomous cars in a smart city setting. The experiment's first phase consists primarily of image gathering. This portion was [38] a success since they were able to create a program that could perform image analysis using Common Sense Knowledge. On a local scale, the prototype for automatic driving works well, but on a larger scale, it shows computing issues in gathering and processing photos while reasoning using the knowledge base. Even though energy and mobility are not correlated but as electric vehicles are reawakened, we need to think about the balance in both. So far, we have found a charging optimization component [39] that contributes to local grid load stabilization. Recent studies have shown the application of artificial intelligence for Smarter mobility. For example, collecting weather sensor data to detect the useful data of the environment, transportation networks, etc. while making a journey plan [40]. We see the usage of NLP to interpret the raw data, Data normalization, discarding the unreliable data are also done to get high-level concepts. Additional data sources are compared with the data from social networks in order to filter out noisy information, ensure dependability, offer event explanations, validate the findings reached by the detection system, and identify disruptive occurrences.

3.7.3.2 Smart Parking

Sensors, real-time data collecting and analytics, and automated payment systems constitute a smart parking system that lets people discover parking and pay in advance. Traffic causes pollution and noise in people's neighborhoods. Intelligent parking helps [41]. Smart Mobility has created a predictive forecasting system based on street parking occupancy. Researchers have produced reliable short-term parking space occupancy estimates to ease cities' parking problems (for the next few hours). To increase forecast performance, Kalman filter, MSTARMA, LASSO, multi-layer Long Short-Term Memory (LSTM) and multiple information sources were merged, including traffic scenarios, meteorological data, and customer transactions. A clever, efficient, and reliable edge computing surveillance system identifies parking space occupancy. This system dealt with limited network capacity in real-time video analytics by keeping data transfer volume modest. To identify in strong illumination and occlusion, it used background subtraction and SSD detection. The design [42] emphasized stability, scalability, and the balance between computational load and data transfer volume.

3.7.3.3 Autonomous/Electric Vehicle

Focusing on autonomous cars, or those that conduct automated driving and must make autonomous or independent, judgments, a method based on commonsense knowledge (CSK) from global repositories has been proposed to imitate intuitive human like decision-making in autonomous vehicles. The repository under consideration is Web-Child, which has a large number of CSK ideas, attributes, and relationships and researchers looked into it as well as related domain-specific knowledgebases [43] (domain KBs) to see if they could use them in their suggested strategy. As a result, a transportation domain KB is created, which incorporates CSK as well as the requirements of autonomous cars. This would be important in directing automated driving and bringing systems closer to human cognition's limits.

3.7.3.4 License Plate Recognition

The system's algorithm is more impervious to tough scenarios such as photographs acquired in inclement weather, tilted plates, more information supplied to the plate, and plate alignment concerning the brightness because it extracts character/number characteristics and cluttered backdrop features. The vehicle image is transformed to grayscale and canny edge detection is utilized to sharpen it, resulting in a feed for the first CNN's detection phase. CNN models classify the region of interest in license-plate/non-license plate photos by filtering, localizing, and selecting features. This Visual Saliency map uses feature detection. Visual Saliency map feature detection extracts the license plate. Detecting license plate variants that include surroundings might be difficult. Plate location in the image, numerous plates in the image, plate orientation towards brightness, wear and tear distortion, cleanliness, and additional information (stickers) on the plate [44]. To verify the algorithm's robustness, a new data set containing hard issues is provided. The LPDS system's performance and accuracy indicate the applicability of the proposed strategies.

3.7.3.5 Traffic Management

A generic neuro-inspired framework for the control of complex systems applied to smart city challenges, with a proof of concept focusing on urban transportation as one of the city's primary integrative subsystems. The perception function of the framework helped it to function better. More specifically, it is addressed how traffic data can be used and analyzed so that the system can be reconfigured in proportion to the number of vehicles. The framework also dealt with forecasting short and long-term changes in car flow. The decisional basis for reconfiguring the traffic management architecture is based on predicted traffic values [45]. In order to avoid junction congestion, local junction controllers set the traffic light length of the associated traffic signal based on the projected car flow. Validity was determined by selecting an approach to urban traffic control architecture that had previously been established and largely implemented had been tested on real data and had been upgraded specifically for this purpose. Adaptation to the traffic context was accomplished by varying the duration of each light while maintaining the cycle's sequence and duration, which was referred to as a light scenario. The major part [46] of the problem was solved at the supervisory level by correctly identifying the traffic structure that necessitates a change of light scenario, as the functional requirement for the control architecture appropriately apply learned behavior which necessitates continuous monitoring. Different traffic scenarios might be imagined based on the expected traffic information. The use of computer vision technology to categorize pedestrian traffic signals efficiently solves the problem of traffic monitoring and surveillance. Data augmentation, as well as photo classification utilizing transfer learning, were employed to address the issue of limited data (DNN). In this context [47], the employment of the pretrained model MobileNetV2 has also been seen. As a classifier for picture detection an artificial neural network and arrange of other machine learning approaches are used to evaluate the implementation of a 3Dcolortexturefeature for traffic sign detection [48, 49].

3.7.4 Safety

3.7.4.1 Privacy

Data safety and privacy are a worry for society as more networked systems share information without a solid auditing process before going live [50]. A technique [51] ensures that each system or device utilized in smart city operations follows basic norms and standards, lowering the likelihood of information being handled incorrectly. This model extends the state of the art by combining an AI- and cognitive-powered Audit Process Framework. This research assessed the IoT security of numerous application technologies. LoRa, a novel wireless technology, is used to secure IoT signals. LoRa signal sources [52] expand with the network, guaranteeing that conflict signals can monitor and identify information and preventing hostile signal source assaults from endangering network security. REBEB, a novel back-off algorithm, is more equitable than BEB in LoRa networks with varying numbers of nodes. The REBEB algorithm improves security and satisfies the throughput protocol's communication needs. An IoT system based on LoRa communication technology increased smart city security and signal transmission security.

3.7.4.2 Security

From an AI standpoint, I-VEmoSYS, an integrated virtual emotion system, has been introduced. It was divided into two subsystems. IoT gadgets power smart cities. They're structured to construct a physical environment that gives residents what they need. Cyberattacks like bogus sensor data or data injection might ruin the whole system if not monitored. For an automated reaction, harmful behavior and assaults must be carefully analyzed. For the IoT device to perform this analysis and deliver a response, the system must be scalable. A system can be used to eliminate suspicious behavior. The system must disable, temporarily separate, or remove problematic IoT device parts. In addition to other monitoring tactics, companies in a smart city must also monitor suspicious activity, service stability, anomalous behavior, and other system-threatening actions [53].

3.7.5 Power and Energy

3.7.5.1 Intelligent Energy Optimization

Smart city uses various Ai based techniques to optimize the energy usage. Now a days a green energy and green economy progress, the usage of electric vehicles has increased to a greater extent. In addition, seamless energy providing is also a requirement for the smart city citizens. Use of renewable energy production have also increased. More and more countries are also being aware of it. Combinations of all these energy sources, nowadays there is an increasing demand for energy optimization. Moreover, sustainability is also a motto for today's smart societies. Therefore, optimized energy production and distribution is one of the impactful additions of smart city [54–57].

3.7.5.2 Smart Monitoring

Real-time IoT-enabled person detection is introduced. The built system employs an internet connection to process high-resolution pictures in the cloud [58]. Real-time IoT-enabled person detection is introduced. The device leverages an internet connection to process high-resolution photographs in the cloud, reducing computing expenses. Pre-trained Cascade RCNN is utilized for human detection. It's an object detection architecture developed to boost IoU thresholds. Because the structure has already been pre-trained using the COCO data set, extra training is needed to enhance detection outcomes. Using transfer learning, the structure was trained for overhead person photographs and the additional feature layer was added. Further training enhances the detection architecture's performance by 0.96%. Face photographs from security cameras in a smart city's face database were processed utilizing image processing and sophisticated algorithms to overcome face identification restrictions. The approaches examined each pixel in a facial picture to determine its position and geometry. Finally, adaboost was applied to recognize faces (LAMSTAR). The newly built LAMSTAR face recognition technique effectively utilised memory to store face-related information [59]. A detailed study of facial characteristics, face shape model, and face pixel relationships facilitated face recognition. The LAMSTAR system's efficiency is examined utilizing MAT-LAB tool results and loss rate and efficiency measures. Using MATLAB, the system recognized images with 99.63% accuracy.

3.7.6 Data Management

3.7.6.1 Big Data Analytics

DBN-R-LSTM-NN classifies and predicts fire outbreaks using IoT sensor data. The Arduino MCU was utilized to analyze a large volume of IoT data, acting as a brain for gathering data and a preprocessor for classifying characteristics. Temperature, Flame, Smoke, FFMC, RH, and DMC were employed to identify '0' and '1' class fire breakouts [60]. The model spotted the fire with 98.4% accuracy and 0.14% error. 70% of the data is used for training and 30% for validation. This approach helped identify fires and allow quick response. In the framework of Smart Cities, a methodology based on visualization approaches for Bigdata has been presented, with the goal of improving the evidence-gathering process by supporting users in decision-making [61]. A case study [62] based on the call service of a fire department, in which data from IoT devices and incoming calls were examined. In this situation, the results were applied to data received through citizen calls [63]. As a result, the outcomes of this study aided resource optimization by providing decision-making evidence. When a call is received, firefighting battalions, for example, will be better positioned to respond.

Table 3.2 Comparative studies of different Models

Themes	Subthemes	Research gaps	Future research avenue
Environmental protection	Air quality	1. The utilization of real-world data sources raises uncertainty due to probable disturbances or malfunctioning measuring stations. 2. How can air pollution devices be explored for more accurate data?	Context aware AQ models can be used to measure the air quality.
	Environmental intelligence	Is the proposed architecture and model sufficient to assure the performance of each individual component of a smart city's 6G wireless network?	How can we build artificial general intelligence or artificial super intelligence (friendly AI).
	Water leakage	1. Why does the network provide such complicated results in the problem of location of leaks? 2. Is it possible for real data about the water net to be more effective if it is tested?	1. Implementation of improved algorithms to locate water supply network leaks where measurement points are few in monitoring systems. 2. What AI and ML approaches may be used to create an intelligent model?
Heath care	IoT health care monitoring	1. Is an IoT health care monitoring system capable of ensuring the immediate treatment of patients in a pandemic situation?	1. What percentage of the time can health monitoring technologies, such as temperature sensors, discover irregularities in the early stages of disease detection?
	Corona virus outbreak and smart city.	How to manage data access that may be sensitive to national security considerations.?	1. The standardization of protocols for improved communication in smart cities. 2.To assure the livability dimensions, smart city technology tools must be Established.
	Hospitals equipped with smart systems	1. How can the current automobile city of high-quality medical resources be adjusted for smart city environment	1. How to manage big data of smart cities for future business mode? 2. How can the original unsustainable healthcare infrastructure be modified, the conventional medical service model improved, and the existing automobile city of high-quality medical resources taken into account to raise the overall efficacy of the medical service system?

(continued)

Table 3.2 (continued)

Themes	Subthemes	Research gaps	Future research avenue
Transportation	Smart mobility	How do we solve the high computational issues and improve accuracy and decision making of autonomous cars?	To evaluate the CSK-enabled technique, deploy strong robots and better object detectors, with the assumption that CSK will improve object detection accuracy, decision-making in simulated automated driving and therefore improve autonomous cars. Solutions for difficulties relating to energy and mobility.
	Smart parking	1. Using forecasting algorithms and time series data to create meaningful predictive analytics framework is a difficult task. 2. One of the most exciting issues in smart city research is delivering novel services and obtaining new Knowledge from data generated by IoT devices.	Obtaining experimental data and conclusions from a wide range of real-world circumstances might be a useful resource for future research.
	License plate recognition	1. Combining diverse feature maps might be problematic. 2. The rare specific patterns that can use the majority of license plate detection systems to fail. These difficult patterns are seen on a sign or object that resembles a license plate. Correctly recognizing these patterns is a major challenge.	Reducing noise in feature maps to get better results and upgrading algorithm to detect misdetection or unidentified patterns more accurately can be future research avenue.
	Traffic management	1. Limited data is a major issue. 2. No research has been done in the context of monitoring drivers' behavior.	1. Improving the data set and improving the presented strategy by merging neuro-fuzzy methodologies. Further research into combining traffic sign systems with other aspects of driver behavior that can be combine utilizing AI technology could be Seen as a future development opportunity.

(continued)

Table 3.2 (continued)

Themes	Subthemes	Research gaps	Future research avenue
			2. Designing a solution, so that vehicles have worldwide knowledge of the traffic situation on the map. Furthermore, examine the usage of the MicroFogparadigm to carry out the decision-making process in route recommendation could be seen as a future development opportunity. 3. Incorporate vehicle-to-vehicle communication and the influence of speed breakers on traffic flow and congestion could also be a future avenue.
Safety	Privacy		Identify and test on real-world situations where data protection and privacy are needed and confirm the efficiency of disruptive implementations.
	Security	How to detect malicious attackers and penetrators to ensure the integrity of the virtual emotion information transmitted from a source user?	Issuing provider identity with anonymity should be prioritized. To support the system's reliability and confidence among users, an AI-based identification scheme and safe access control should be established.
Power and energy	Smart monitoring		Improve face shape generating model and facial point detection procedure with the use of optimized strategies.
Data management	Big data analytics		1. A potential path for future study may consist of concentrating on carrying out customized both local and international analytics throughout the course of time in order to determine the worth of the framework with its capacity to continually update depending on fresh data. 2. The architecture should be implemented in a cloud environment so that it can replicate the full local and global capabilities along with the multilayer connectivity.

The below table. 3.2 shows comprehensive analysis of different methods based on themes and sub-themes:

3.8 Conclusion

Cities are now facing a wide range of challenges, some of which include issues of privacy and security, healthcare, environmental concerns, and many more. Finding solutions to these problems, cities are starting to incorporate new technologies into their fundamental operations. The objective of this research was to demonstrate, by way of a review of the relevant existing literature, that artificial intelligence is one of the essential technologies of smart cities. This technology is utilized for a variety of purposes, including the improvement of infrastructure, the maximization of resources, and the guarantee of public safety. On the other hand, the implementation of AI in smart cities almost always leaves some room for improvement. In addition, we made an effort to bridge such gaps by proposing some future projects to strengthen the use of AI in smart cities. If successful, these initiatives would lead to an improvement in the quality of life for the general population.

References

1. Kagermann, H., Wahlster, W., & Helbig, J. (2013). *Acatech–national academy of science and engineering* (Vol. 4). Recommendations for Implementing the Strategic Initiative INDUSTRIE.
2. Johnson, P. A., Robinson, P. J., & Philpot, S. (2020). Type, tweet, tap, and pass: How smart city technology is creating a transactional citizen. *Government Information Quarterly, 37*(1), 101414.
3. Mohanty, S. P., Choppali, U., & Kougianos, E. (2016). Everything you wanted to know about smart cities: The internet of things is the backbone. *IEEE Consumer Electronics Magazine, 5*(3), 60–70.
4. Mehta, S., Bhushan, B., & Kumar, R. (2022). Machine learning approaches for smart city applications: Emergence, challenges and opportunities. In V. E. Balas, V. K. Solanki, & R. Kumar (Eds.), *Recent advances in internet of things and machine learning. Intelligent systems reference library* (Vol. 215). Springer. https://doi.org/10.1007/978-3-030-90119-6_12
5. Manchanda, C., Sharma, N., Rathi, R., Bhushan, B., & Grover, M. (2020). *Neoteric security and privacy sanctuary technologies in smart cities.* 2020 IEEE 9th International Conference on Communication Systems and Network Technologies (CSNT). https://doi.org/10.1109/csnt48778.2020.9115780
6. Vesco, A. (2015). *Handbook of research on social, economic, and environmental sustainability in the development of smart cities.* IGI Global.
7. Kaplan, A., & Haenlein, M. (2019). Siri, siri, in my hand: Who's the fairest in the land? On the interpretations, illustrations, and implications of artificial intelligence. *Business Horizons, 62*(1), 15–25.
8. Gurkaynak, G., Yilmaz, I., & Haksever, G. (2016). Stifling artificial intelligence: Human perils. *Computer Law & Security Review, 32*(5), 749–758.
9. Bhowmik, T., Bhadwaj, A., Kumar, A., & Bhushan, B. (2022). Machine learning and deep learning models for privacy management and data analysis in smart cites. In V. E. Balas, V. K. Solanki,

& R. Kumar (Eds.), *Recent advances in internet of things and machine learning. Intelligent systems reference library* (Vol. 215). Springer. https://doi.org/10.1007/978-3-030-90119-6_13

10. Li, L., Lin, Y.-L., Zheng, N.-N., Wang, F.-Y., Liu, Y., Cao, D., Wang, K., & Huang, W.-L. (2018). Artificial intelligence test: A case study of intelligent vehicles. *Artificial Intelligence Review, 50*(3), 441–465.

11. Shaan, A. A. M., Nausheen, T., & Haque, A. B. (2022). Blockchain for smart city: Opportunities and future research directions. In *International conference on digital technologies and applications* (pp. 267–275). Springer.

12. Haque, A., Bhushan, B., Hasan, M., Zihad, M., Mondol, O., et al. (2022). Revolutionizing the industrial internet of things using blockchain: An unified approach. In *Recent advances in internet of things and machine learning* (pp. 43–66). Springer.

13. Al-Hader, M., & Rodzi, A. (2009). *The smart city infrastructure development & monitoring* (Vol. 4, pp. 87–94). Theoretical and Empirical Researches in Urban Management.

14. Pranto, T. H., Noman, A. A., Rahaman, M., Haque, A. B., Islam, A. N., & Rahman, R. M. (2022). A blockchain, smart contract and data mining based approach toward the betterment of e-commerce. *Cybernetics and Systems, 53*(5), 443–467.

15. Haque, A. B., & Bhushan, B. (2021). *2 security attacks* (p. 17). Integration of WSNs into Internet of Things: A Security Perspective.

16. Toli, A. M., & Murtagh, N. (2020). The concept of sustainability in smart city definitions. *Frontiers in Built Environment, 6*, 77.

17. Haque, A., & Rahman, M. (2020). Blockchain technology: Methodology, application and security issues. *arXiv preprint arXiv:2012.13366.*

18. Haque, A. B., Bhushan, B., & Dhiman, G. (2021). *Conceptualizing smart city applications: Requirements, architecture, security issues, and emerging trends.* Expert Systems.

19. Haque, A. (2019). Need for critical cyber defence, security strategy and privacy policy in Bangladesh–hype or reality? *International Journal of Managing Information Technology (IJMIT), 11.*

20. Bansal, G., Zahedi, F. M., & Gefen, D. (2016). Do context and personality matter? Trust and privacy concerns in disclosing private information online. *Information & Management, 53*(1), 1–21.

21. Noy, N. F., McGuinness, D. L., et al. (2001). *Ontology development 101: A guide to creating your first ontology.* Stanford Knowledge Systems Laboratory.

22. Kaur, P., Dhir, A., Talwar, S., & Alrasheedy, M. (2021). *Systematic literature review of food waste in educational institutions: Setting the research agenda.* International Journal of Contemporary Hospitality Management.

23. Kraus, S., Mahto, R. V., & Walsh, S. T. (2021). The importance of literature reviews I in small business and entrepreneurship research. *J Small Bus Manage*, 1–12.

24. Chaudhary, S., Dhir, A., Ferraris, A., & Bertoldi, B. (2021). Trust and reputation in family businesses: A systematic literature review of past achievements and future promises. *Journal of Business Research, 137*, 143–161.

25. Jones, M. V., Coviello, N., & Tang, Y. K. (2011). International entrepreneurship research (1989–2009): A domain ontology and thematic analysis. *Journal of Business Venturing, 26*(6), 632–659.

26. Beccali, M., Strazzeri, V., Germana, M., Melluso, V., & Galatioto, A. (2018). Vernacular and bioclimatic architecture and indoor thermal comfort implications in hot-humid climates: An overview. *Renewable and Sustainable Energy Reviews, 82*, 1726–1736.

27. Schürholz, D., Kubler, S., & Zaslavsky, A. (2020). Artificial intelligence-enabled context-aware air quality prediction for smart cities. *Journal of Cleaner Production, 271*, 121941.

28. Rojek, I., & Studzinski, J. (2019). Detection and localization of water leaks in water nets supported by an ict system with artificial intelligence methods as a way forward for smart cities. *Sustainability, 11*(2), 518.

29. Bardoutsos, A., Filios, G., Katsidimas, I., Krousarlis, T., Nikoletseas, S., & Tzamalis, P. (2020). A multidimensional human-centric framework for environmental intelligence: Air pollution

and noise in smart cities. In *2020 16th International Conference on Distributed Computing in Sensor Systems (DCOSS)* (pp. 155–164). IEEE.

30. Gope, P., & Hwang, T. (2015). Bsn-care: A secure IoT-based modern healthcare system using body sensor network. *IEEE Sensors Journal, 16*(5), 1368–1376.

31. Hossain, M. S. (2015). Cloud-supported cyber–physical localization framework for patients monitoring. *IEEE Systems Journal, 11*(1), 118–127.

32. Islam, S. R., Kwak, D., Kabir, M. H., Hossain, M., & Kwak, K.-S. (2015). The internet of things for health care: A comprehensive survey. *IEEE access, 3*, 678–708.

33. Bahalul Haque, A., Bhushan, B., Nawar, A., Talha, K. R., & Ayesha, S. J. (2022). Attacks and countermeasures in iot based smart healthcare applications. In *Recent Advances in Internet of Things and Machine Learning* (pp. 67–90). Springer.

34. Haque, A., Naqvi, B., Islam, A., & Hyrynsalmi, S. (2021). Towards a gdpr-compliant blockchain-based covid vaccination passport. *Applied Sciences, 11*(13), 6132.

35. Allam, Z., & Jones, D. S. (2020). On the coronavirus (covid-19) outbreak and the smart city network: universal data sharing standards coupled with artificial intelligence (ai) to benefit urban health monitoring and management. In *Healthcare* (Vol. 8, p. 46). Multidisciplinary Digital Publishing Institute.

36. Haque, A. B., Muniat, A., Ullah, P. R., & Mushsharat, S. (2021). An automated approach towards smart healthcare with blockchain and smart contracts. In *2021 International Conference on Computing, Communication, and Intelligent Systems (ICCCIS)* (pp. 250–255). IEEE.

37. Kong, L. (2021). A study on the AI-based online triage model for hospitals in sustainable smart city. *Future Generation Computer Systems, 125*, 59–70.

38. Persaud, P., Varde, A. S., & Robila, S. (2017). Enhancing autonomous vehicles with commonsense: Smart mobility in smart cities. In *2017 IEEE 29th International Conference on Tools with Artificial Intelligence (ICTAI)* (pp. 1008–1012). IEEE.

39. Lützenberger, M., Masuch, N., Küster, T., Freund, D., Voß, M., Hrabia, C.-E., Pozo, D., Fahndrich, J., Trollmann, F., Keiser, J., et al. (2015). A common approach to intelligent energy and mobility services in a smart city environment. *Journal of Ambient Intelligence and Humanized Computing, 6*(3), 337–350.

40. Vazquez Salceda, J., Napagao, S. Á., Gomez, J. A. T., Felipe, L. J. O., Gasulla, D. G., Sebastia, I. G., & Busquet, V. C. (2014). Making smart cities smarter using artificial intelligence techniques for smarter mobility. In *SMARTGREENS 2014: proceedings of the 3rd International Conference on Smart Grids and Green IT Systems* (pp. IS7–IS11). SciTePress.

41. Piccialli, F., Giampaolo, F., Prezioso, E., Crisci, D., & Cuomo, S. (2021). Predictive analytics for smart parking: A deep learning approach in forecasting of IoT data. *ACM Transactions on Internet Technology (TOIT), 21*(3), 1–21.

42. Ke, R., Zhuang, Y., Pu, Z., & Wang, Y. (2020). A smart, efficient, and reliable parking surveillance system with edge artificial intelligence on iot devices. *IEEE Transactions on Intelligent Transportation Systems, 22*(8), 4962–4974.

43. Persaud, P., Varde, A. S., & Robila, S. (2017). Enhancing autonomous vehicles with commonsense: Smart mobility in smart cities. In *2017 IEEE 29th International Conference on Tools with Artificial Intelligence (ICTAI)* (p. 1008). IEEE.

44. Polishetty, R., Roopaei, M., & Rad, P. (2016). A next-generation secure cloud-based deep learning license plate recognition for smart cities. In *2016 15th IEEE International Conference on Machine Learning and Applications (ICMLA)* (pp. 286–293). IEEE.

45. Akter, R., Khandaker, M. J. H., Ahmed, S., Mugdho, M. M., & Haque, A. B. (2020). Rfid based smart transportation system with android application. In *2020 2nd International Conference on Innovative Mechanisms for Industry Applications (ICIMIA)* (pp. 614–619). IEEE.

46. Culita, J., Caramihai, S. I., Dumitrache, I., Moisescu, M. A., & Sacala, I. S. (2020). An hybrid approach for urban traffic prediction and control in smart cities. *Sensors, 20*(24), 7209.

47. Khan, S., Teng, Y., & Cui, J. (2021). Pedestrian traffic lights classification using transfer learning in smart city application. In *2021 13th International Conference on Communication Software and Networks (ICCSN)* (pp. 352–356). IEEE.
48. Vashisht, M., & Kumar, B. (2021). Effective implementation of machine learning algorithms using 3d colour texture feature for traffic sign detection for smart cities. *Expert Systems*, e12781.
49. Rocha Filho, G. P., Meneguette, R. I., Neto, J. R. T., Valejo, A., Weigang, L., Ueyama, J., Pessin, G., & Villas, L. A. (2020). Enhancing intelligence in traffic management systems to aid in vehicle traffic congestion problems in smart cities. *Ad Hoc Networks, 107*, 102265.
50. Haque, A. B., & Bhushan, B. (2021). Emergence of blockchain technology: A reliable and secure solution for iot systems. In *Blockchain technology for data privacy management* (pp. 159–183). CRC Press.
51. Huerta, J., & Salazar, P. (2018). Audit process framework for data protection and privacy compliance using artificial intelligence and cognitive services in smart cities. In *2018 IEEE International Smart Cities Conference (ISC2)* (pp. 1–7). IEEE.
52. Lv, Z., Qiao, L., Kumar Singh, A., & Wang, Q. (2021). Ai-empowered iot security for smart cities. *ACM Transactions on Internet Technology, 21*(4), 1–21.
53. Kim, H., & Ben-Othman, J. (2020). Toward integrated virtual emotion system with ai applicability for secure cps-enabled smart cities: Ai-based research challenges and security issues. *IEEE Network, 34*(3), 30–36.
54. Haque, A. B., Shurid, S., Juha, A. T., Sadique, M. S., & Asaduzzaman, A. S. M. (2020). A novel design of gesture and voice controlled solar-powered smart wheel chair with obstacle detection. In *2020 IEEE International Conference on Informatics, IoT, and Enabling Technologies (ICIoT)* (pp. 23–28). IEEE.
55. Kalra, D., & Pradhan, M. R. (2021). Enduring data analytics for reliable data management in handling smart city services. *Soft Computing, 25*(18), 12213–12225.
56. Haque, A., Hasan, M., Zihad, M., Mondol, O., et al. (2021). Smartoil: Blockchain and smart contract-based oil supply chain management. *arXiv preprint arXiv:2105.05338*.
57. Chui, K. T., Lytras, M. D., & Visvizi, A. (2018). Energy sustainability in smart cities: Artificial intelligence, smart monitoring, and optimization of energy consumption. *Energies, 11*(11), 2869.
58. Ahmad, M., Ahmed, I., & Jeon, G. (2021). An IoT-enabled real-time overhead view person detection system based on cascade-RCNN and transfer learning. *Journal of Real- Time Image Processing, 18*(4), 1129–1139.
59. Medapati, P. K., Tejo Murthy, P., & Sridhar, K. (2020). Lamstar: For iot-based face recognition system to manage the safety factor in smart cities. *Transactions on Emerging Telecommunications Technologies, 31*(12), e3843.
60. Zhang, Y., Geng, P., Sivaparthipan, C., & Muthu, B. A. (2021). Big data and artificial intelligence based early risk warning system of fire hazard for smart cities. *Sustainable Energy Technologies and Assessments, 45*, 100986.
61. Haque, A. B., & Bhushan, B. (2021). Blockchain in a nutshell: State-of-the-art applications and future research directions. In *Blockchain and AI technology in the industrial internet of things* (pp. 124–143). IGI Global.
62. Lavalle, A., Teruel, M. A., Mate, A., & Trujillo, J. (2020). Improving sustainability of smart cities through visualization techniques for big data from IoT devices. *Sustainability, 12*(14), 5595.
63. Haque, A. B., Islam, A. N., Hyrynsalmi, S., Naqvi, B., & Smolander, K. (2021). *Gdpr compliant blockchains – A systematic literature review* (Vol. 9, pp. 50593–50606). IEEE Access.

Chapter 4
Predictive Farmland Optimization and Crop Monitoring Using Artificial Intelligence Techniques

Antara Sahoo, Aniket Rathi, Shambhavi Bashishth, Sanghamitra Roy, and Chittaranjan Pradhan

Abstract India's economy is vastly affected by agriculture. Illiteracy has been a major concern among farmers which pulls them from identifying the crops that are perfect for their land and determining the type of diseases caused. Checking for diseases without any prior knowledge may result in overlooking some of the yields. The lack of awareness about certain crop diseases, land conditions and fertilizer has resulted in big losses in the past. Hence, the thought of automating the whole process using machine learning has been initiated. Crop selection, fertilizer selection and early disease prediction have been automated. In this research work, for crop yield and fertilizer prediction, various machine learning algorithms such as Support Vector Machine, Logistic Regression Random Forest, K-Nearest Neighbors and Artificial Neural Network (ANN) are used. The random forest algorithm for crop yield prediction gave an accuracy of 95.22% which is better compared to other algorithms, while in fertilizer prediction accuracy of 96% is achieved by ANN. The disease prediction model has been created using image datasets of wheat, maize and apple which were leveraged using convolution neural networks resulting in an average accuracy close to 98.5%.

Keywords Artificial intelligence · Crop monitoring · Deep learning · Fertilizer prediction · Image processing · Machine learning

---

A. Sahoo (✉) · A. Rathi · S. Bashishth · S. Roy · C. Pradhan
Kalinga Institute of Industrial Technology, Bhubaneswar, India

© The Author(s), under exclusive license to Springer Nature Switzerland AG 2023
M. A. Ahad et al. (eds.), *Enabling Technologies for Effective Planning and Management in Sustainable Smart Cities*, https://doi.org/10.1007/978-3-031-22922-0_4

4.1 Introduction

Machine learning has made a significant impact in all industries and agriculture sectors. Several sectors in each domain try to use past data and apply intelligent machine learning algorithms for prediction and analysis purposes. With a value of INR 56,564 billion in 2019, the agriculture industry plays a vital role in the nation's economy in terms of employment and contribution to GDP. Moreover, with 18% of the world's population, the demand for agro-products has increased year by year [1, 2].

Farmers encounter some obstacles in using conventional methods of farming:

- In the agriculture life cycle, climatic factors like temperature, rainfall, and humidity are crucial. The rise in deforestation and pollution are leading to climatic changes, so it's increasingly demanding for farmers to determine how to prepare the soil, sow seeds, and harvest. India is a land with varying temperature ranges and rainfall levels, which play an essential factor in farm management. This shows how a variety of crops can be grown in agricultural fields.
- Every crop demands a specific type of nutrition for the soil. The three major nutrients essential in soil include nitrogen (N2), phosphorus (P) and potassium (K). The inadequacy of nutrients, as well as their excessive use, can lead to harvest failure.
- For crop protection, weeds play a significant role most of the time. If unregulated, it can directly affect crop yield and cease its growth. It can also absorb nutrients from the soil, which can cause a shortage of nutrition. Then preserving damaged plants on large acres of land may require a substantial financial setup.

In our research work, these crucial problems are considered where artificial intelligence algorithms have been applied to enhance agronomic management in India since agriculture is one of the major occupations of many rural Indians. In India, there exist around 394.6 million acres of arable land. So growing more agricultural products helps not only humans but also the entire environment. However, as India is a significant producer of wheat, rice, maize, cereals, etc., growing these in every farming land is impossible due to different climatic conditions. However, this increases the scope of producing varieties of crops with an excellent yield depending upon suitable weather conditions.

The topic of our research is based on agriculture yield amplification. The main aim is to help farmers increase their production with the help of suitable fertilizers and make the farmers aware of what diseases the staple crops of India like rice, wheat, apple and tomato possess. The importance lies in the fact that the farmers are unaware of the various properties of their crops due to a lack of thorough knowledge and are misinformed. This misinformation leads to many faulty courses of action, leading to a lower yield of crops [3]. In this scenario, if the crop is infected, it becomes unwanted and no longer edible, which even hampers nutrients present in the soil. Therefore, they need to destroy the previous ones to develop fresh crops. For a long time in India, farmers have been practicing stubble burning, leading to a significant contribution to pollution and global warming. Here, an automated model envisages the crop yield above a specific soil type, and periodically checks the plant's health, whether it is infected, and its fertilizer content requirement [4].

With various machine learning techniques, one can feasibly predict the best type of crop that can be cultivated with a given set of parameters [5]. Further, the growth of the product can be moderated by fertilizer prediction and disease prediction models, which will help in the early detection of diseases and suggest a change in the type of fertilizers based on Nitrogen, Phosphorus Potassium (NPK) values and soil type. This will lead to proper crop management and yield amplification. Through AI techniques, the information will be unbiased and farmers will be able to make an informed decision regarding their net production [6]. This will help increase the profit margin of the farmers and hence, will increase the exports leading to an increase in the GDP of India. This research will have a more lasting impact than it currently appears to have.

The recent advancement of technology using the Internet of Things, machine learning and artificial technology is also applied in the agriculture domain for better productivity [7–9]. In our research, we have aimed at providing automation, where, using machine learning and neural network model, farmers can reduce their crop wastage rate. We divided our model into three subparts, i.e., crop prediction, early detection of plant diseases and fertilizer prediction. Our first model focuses on predicting an appropriate crop to be grown depending on climatic conditions and soil contents of the particular area. We have opted for the random forest classifier algorithm with hyper parameter tuning which helped improve the accuracy of the model and reduce the loss. Our next model is to identify any disease a crop can have before excessive damage using Convolutional Neural Network (CNN). CNNs are actively used for image detection purposes, and by feeding the picture of the diseased crop into the CNN model, through various layers of convolutional, dropout and pooling mechanisms, our model will identify the type of disease. Also, we have used the softmax activation function to reach maximum efficiency and reduced error. Consequently, after the disease is identified, our third model will suggest an appropriate kind of fertilizer that can be used to improvise the content of the rest of the crops depending on the nutrient content present in the soil. We have incorporated an Artificial Neural Network (ANN) model using Adam as an optimizer and regularization techniques to enhance the learning rate for predicting new inputs.

Using various algorithms, we did construct our model, whose detailed workflow is presented in the subsequent sections of the chapter. Section 4.2 contains the Literature Review on farmland optimization and crop monitoring techniques presented previously. Section 4.3 has an elaborated analysis of Related Works corresponding to our current research presented. Section 4.4 contains the Proposed Model which elicits a qualitative and quantitative analysis of our machine learning and ANN techniques proposed in this research. Section 4.5 has a Result Analysis that summarizes all our observations (subjective as well as pictorial) and computes various outputs based on tuning parameters of the algorithms. Section 4.6 contains the Conclusion that briefs on the three connected models that aid farmers to reduce crop wastage.

4.2 Literature Review

Agriculture, being a crucial sector of India, serves as the backbone of the economic system. The prediction of various crops under suitable conditions has been highlighted using data mining techniques [1]. The growth rate of three major crops in India is shown in Fig. 4.1 [2]. With exponential progress in agriculture, Singh et al. [3] reported a very sensitive issue of burning stubble and grasslands to control the growth of weeds, insects, plant infections, and excess crop residues that were vigorously practiced earlier. Even now in some parts of India, the stubble burning practice is still prevalent. Due to this quick, inexpensive and effective method, ease of seeding and other soil operations have been enhanced at a large scale. It is also the fact that it takes one-and-half months to decompose the wheat residue left by harvesters and when farmers don't have sufficient time to wait for sowing their fresh crops, stubble burning is practiced to prepare a new soil bed for their crops. But the dangers of burning wheat stubble can lead to major threats to the environment. This can directly harm the atmosphere, and indirectly the plants and humans as depicted in Fig. 4.2 [10].

The flaming can cause soil nutrient loss of organic carbon, nitrogen, phosphorous, and potassium and also deteriorate the ambient air quality [3]. Not only wheat but also burning of other agricultural residues discharge various trace gases like methane, oxides and ample quantities of suspended particulate matter causing adverse effects to humans. Till now there are many large-scale applications to tackle this deterioration. Many ways to conserve agriculture, mainly wheat-maize [5], can be effectively practiced if crop residue management plans are developed taking into consideration the demand, quality, feasibility, and economics of residue management which serves as an efficient way to preserve land. Figure 4.3 shows how important it is to take care of these leading crops like rice, wheat and maize due to their burning demands and exports. Still, there has been a minute sort of gaps in preserving soil as early as possible or early detection of any infection. Our work is to feature some improvement toward the conservation and preservation of natural soil.

Fig. 4.1 Growth rate of 3 major crops in India [2]

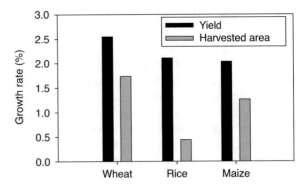

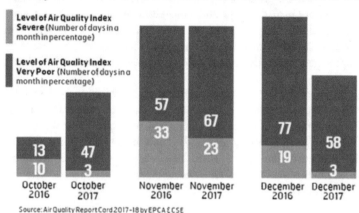

Fig. 4.2 Air quality in and after Harvest [10]

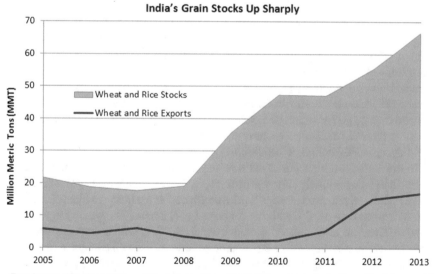

Fig. 4.3 A comparison of the wheat and rice stocks with their respective export

As soon as image processing is done to detect various infections, performing testing of soil samples can break the chain of spoil or destruction at a perfect time. There are many effective techniques to treat soil using suitable fertilizers as per requirements [11]. So this research is about performing tests of soil to know the present type of soil, weather conditions and contents of the fertilizer used. This way one can easily keep track and change fertilizers from time to time for a better outcome. Literature [11] reported the regulating of fertilizers used after inspecting the current soil content. There exist various efficient tests to find co-integration between consumption of fertilizer and food grain production. Kumar and Indira have reported [12] the effective methods and tests to support the cointegration relation. As far as classifying infection is concerned, there are various recent machine learning approaches and techniques to detect diseases and pests in agricultural products [13].

During the second phase, apple being the cure to everything – a well-accurate model has been set up for early detection and classification of its infection. Turkoglu et al. [14], highlighted proper measures using a multi-model Long short-term memory (LSTM) with good accuracy and bagful features. Our chapter will further add on techniques of early detection of infections in apples with better accuracy levels using various kinds of activation functions.

4.3   Related Work

Crop yield mapping, yield estimation, matching of supply with demand, and crop management to increase productivity [15, 16] are essential steps to boost the economy. Machine learning provides low-cost and efficient solutions for crop yield prediction. There are many efficient ways of predicting a crop yield under weather conditions over the field [17]. As mentioned earlier, crop production in India solely depends on temperature and moisture content in a specific area of growth. The review [18], has clearly shown the dependence of crop yield w.r.t change in diurnal temperature range by which one can know the impact of time and temperature to boost up their yield. Similarly, our research deals with amplifying any crop, and its yield under suitable climatic conditions.

In our work, we have portrayed how any spare land can grow its worthy crop rather than being a lonely site or growing up a factory. Growing ample amounts of crops make a path to greenery and a pristine atmosphere which can directly improve polluted air around us. So, with the context of [17] keeping an eye on crop-climate relationships, we have created a model which predicts which crop is suitable to grow under the area depending on climatic conditions and soil content. After a crop is produced, depending upon the soil conditions fertilizer levels are given initially. While applying any fertilizer to the soil, crucial care must be taken of the contents in the soil. Haynes and Naidu [19] explained the influence of fertilizers and manures on the soil's organic matter content and how it changes the physical conditions of the mineral-rich soil. Many times due to improper irrigation facilities available to the poor farmers, the soil gets extensively waterlogged and some of its nutrients may be diluted which in turn will affect crop yield. In [20], it is explained how the soil due to waterlogging loses some nutrients and causes infection itself. Hence, from there the need for fertilizers comes. A complete analysis of fertilizer used in India for the last 20 years is reported by Kumar and Indira [12]. This showed a long-run correlation between fertilizer use and food grains consumption over the last

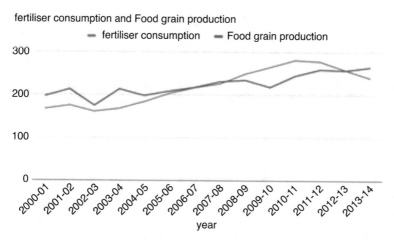

Fig. 4.4 Relation b/w fertilizer consumption and food grain production

20 years as in Fig. 4.4. They explained how farmers are increasing their production with increased fertilizer consumption without considering the environmental, health consequences, and sustainability of agriculture [12].

India is the leading producer of wheat and maize whose yield mostly depends on monsoon and temperature. Being the sole grain for all beings, producing an ample amount of the crop is necessary. A comparative analysis of their yield based on various machine learning techniques is elaborated in [15]. High-yielding varieties such as maize and wheat demanded more usage of fertilizers which is supported by the subsidy policy on fertilizers [12]. With vast acres of land and ample crop yield, the crop should be taken care of any blight. So our model is to timely inspect the condition of the crop with high accuracy to minimize any error.

Many plant leaf diseases were studied including maize (corn) with northern leaf blight, common rust and gray spot (shown in Fig. 4.5) with a well-detailed analysis [21–23]. The model proposed in this work has achieved a higher accuracy of 98.82% than that reported by Geetharamani and Pandian [22, 24].

Singh and Arora [23] have used a convolution neural network method to distinguish between healthy and unhealthy wheat. The unhealthy wheat crops affected by leaf rust and stem rust are shown in Fig. 4.6. In this work, we were successful in enhancing our prediction with an accuracy of 98.7% by learning effective algorithms and activation functions that one should use to pump up the accuracy than that reported in the literature [21, 23].

Fruit diseases can cause a literal economical loss if not controlled on time. An example has been taken to show how the apple scab, rust, and black rot diseases [22] affect the apple leaf and crop (shown in Fig. 4.7). Alharbi and Arif [25] have used CNN to detect and classify apple diseases. In our work, we have included some concepts and better algorithms to predict diseases with better accuracy of 98.93%.

If necessary action is not taken on time, this will result in wastage of crops, and fertilizers leading to financial loss and poor resource management. If the waste is

a. Northern Leaf Blight   b. Common Rust   c. Gray Spot

Fig. 4.5 Diseases found in maize

a. Leaf Rust in Wheat   b. Stem Rust in Wheat

Fig. 4.6 Diseases found in wheat

a. Apple scab   b. Cedar apple rust   c. Apple black rot

Fig. 4.7 Diseases found in apple

huge due to late inspection, this can lead to burning the residues to grow fresh crops which will directly affect the entire environment drastically. Our research will keep the four most important features – temperature, rainfall, moisture, and pH level of the soil to envisage a particular crop.

4.4 Proposed Model

India's prime source of economy is agricultural produce, because of the vast areas of cultivable land it is blessed with. As stated earlier, due to biochemical and environmental factors the crop yield may get affected. Hence, we have proposed three interconnected models, which when run in parallel can help the farmers produce more yield. Our first model is the crop prediction module, where based on parameters like temperature, humidity, pH and rainfall, we predict which crop should be ideally grown in a particular area. Then after the crop yield, a snapshot can be taken to check whether the particular crop has been affected or not. If the crop is healthy, then we continue with timely crop monitoring to prevent any crop loss. But, if the crop is affected, we can pass it through our model and predict which disease the crop is affected by. After the prediction is made, based on conditions of the soil one check which suitable fertilizer should be used to prevent the crops from being affected by any disease, based on parameters of the soil like the temperature of the surrounding, humidity levels of the region, the soil type, the crop type grown and the concentrations of nitrogen, potassium and phosphorus in that particular land. With the help of these parameters, an appropriate remedy can be provided to the farmer. Figure 4.8 gives a diagrammatic representation flow of our proposed model, where the relational connection between the various modules such as the crop prediction module, disease classification module and fertilizer prediction module is represented step by step.

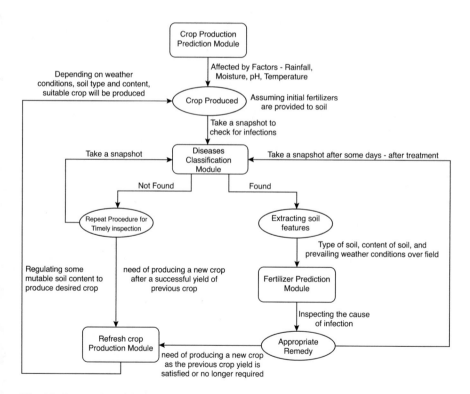

Fig. 4.8 Proposed model architecture

4.4.1 Machine Learning Approach for Crop Prediction

The use of statistics and mathematical models clubs together to build a machine learning model. Data and statistics help any model or network to learn relationships, dependencies, and equations among their participating factors. The development of this form of correlations between dependent and independent variables has been made. In [15], comprehensive research is presented on how machine learning is of importance in agriculture. To ensure the machine learning (ML) model is successful, we need to tune every step towards betterment. Figure 4.9 shows a layout of how a machine learns and analyzes patterns.

Here some trained data passes through which a model analyzes and learns all co-relations by a specific algorithm. Then the model infers some prediction or classification rules to predict new examples or future data. In Fig. 4.10, a detailed chart is presented on how the ML model works.

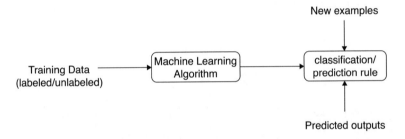

Fig. 4.9 Basic architecture of a machine learning model

Fig. 4.10 Working steps of a machine learning model

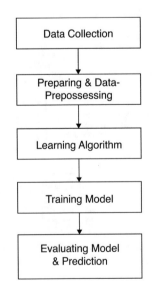

4.4.1.1   Data Collection

Gathering data is crucial for a model as the quality and quantity of data that we collect directly determines how good and accurate your predictive model can be. Mathematically, the amount of training data is directly proportional to model accuracy. Our source of data has been extracted from Kaggle datasets having 3100 entries with attributes temperature, rainfall, pH, and the humidity of the field to predict the desired crop that can be grown. Figures 4.11 and 4.12 depict the range of rainfall and temperature present in our data where the optimum range of temperature and rainfall for most of the crops produced is 14–38 °C and 20–250 cm, respectively.

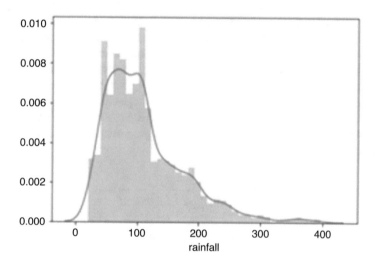

Fig. 4.11 Rainfall range for crop prediction in India

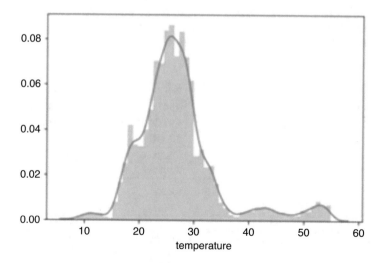

Fig. 4.12 Temperature range for crop prediction in India

4.4.1.2   Data Preparing and Pre-processing

Firstly in data preparation we read and load our data into a suitable set and prepare it for training. Pre-processing sometimes becomes very important because the data we collect can be irregular, absurd, and erroneous due to which data needs other forms of adjusting and manipulation like deduping, normalization, error correction, etc. Raw data should always be cleaned before feeding into the machine to enhance overall accuracy. Moreover, Bhaya and Wesam [26] have discussed various beneficial methods of preprocessing techniques in detail, which are used for data mining.

The next phase explains the need of splitting data into training and testing sets to get validated by the learning algorithm. To prepare this data, the test set is taken as 25% of the whole dataset with a random state tuned to 1. The random state is used in the data splitting module to ensure that the generated splits are reproducible. Feature scaling in entire data is needed in almost all models to give unbiased importance to every factor. In Table 4.1, a data frame is shown with varying data ranges in all columns.

Due to this irregularity, there can be a possibility of the machine giving utmost importance to a factor with a high data range and neglecting others due to low data range irrespective of their real contributing nature. So we need to standardize all variables in the same range. There are mainly 2 processes of normalizing as given in Eqs. 4.1 and 4.2.

$$X_{new} = \frac{X - X_{mean}}{Standard\ Deviation} \tag{4.1}$$

$$X_{new} = \frac{X - X_{min}}{X_{max} - X_{min}} \tag{4.2}$$

A broader perspective has been provided in [27] highlighting various methods of normalization and their influence. For our work, we have used a standard scalar to normalize all values under each attribute to develop equal importance as in Table 4.2. Using this scalar all values range from -3 to $+3$.

Table 4.1 Dataset sample for crop prediction

Temperature	Humidity	PH	Rainfall
51.395179	46.579188	6.332919	105.272329
51.750697	54.662403	6.511772	166.146187
53.017400	49.864205	5.299104	65.959049
53.211092	61.440867	5.322864	64.152838
50.875089	52.118891	7.377994	163.452682

Table 4.2 Normalized dataset sample

Temperature	Humidity	PH	Rainfall
−0.26197908	−0.16490876	−0.27393577	−0.48244424
−0.11746592	0.62523333	−0.05613165	−0.69880365
−0.28625737	−0.50470681	0.84887115	0.29740972

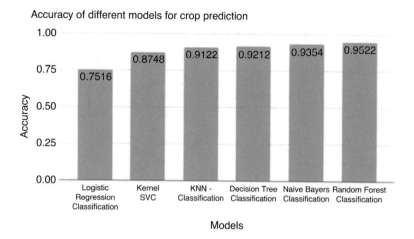

Fig. 4.13 Accuracy of different models

4.4.1.3 Learning Algorithm

Machine learning is backed by algorithms that predict output values within an acceptable range after analyzing input data. These algorithms are programmed to learn and optimize their calculations for better performance and efficiency when new data is allocated, developing intelligence over time. Machine learning marks the use of a wide range of algorithms to get a good correlation among the variables. We have used supervised algorithms like Logistic Regression, Naive Bayes classification, K-Nearest Neighbor Classification, and Support Vector Classification to make the machine learn correlations among variables [28–30]. Apart from Random Forest Classification which is derived from the Decision Tree was found to be at maximum accuracy (Fig. 4.13) with a great learning rate.

Since the best result is achieved using a decision tree with entropy, the criterion for the random forest is also chosen as entropy. This gave an accuracy of 95.22% and is the best among all other models.

4.4.1.4 Training the Model

As in the earlier section, it concluded that applying Random Forest Algorithm with the Decision Tree algorithm as its origin has increased the predictive nature of the model effectively with an accuracy of around 95%. In [17], a well-designed approach has been researched on crop prediction using Decision trees. So here in this work, we chose a random forest as our proposed algorithm. Figure 4.14 shows the working of the Random Forest Algorithm for any model.

We can understand the working of the Random Forest algorithm with the help of the following steps. These processes go over desired iterations to make the predictive model perfect and efficient.

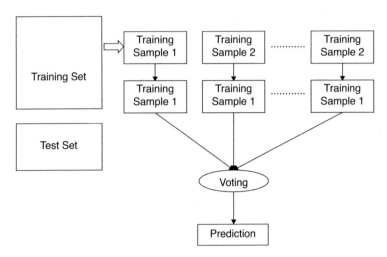

Fig. 4.14 Working of random forest classifier

```
from sklearn.ensemble import RandomForestClassifier
classifier = RandomForestClassifier(n_estimators = 1000,
                                     criterion = 'entropy',
                                     random_state = 1,
                                     max_depth=100)
classifier.fit(X_train, y_train)
```

Fig. 4.15 Parameters considered under random forest classification

– Step 1 – For a given data, a random number of samples are selected.
– Step 2 – For every sample, a decision tree is constructed which gives the prediction result.
– Step 3 – For every result, voting is performed.
– Step 4 – The most voted result is selected as the final result.

In Fig. 4.15, the code snippet shows the initiation of a random forest algorithm and fitting that classifier to learn co-relations among attributes for the prediction of future data.

This classifier object fits the training set to learn the relations, then validates with the testing test over iterations to figure out the best accuracy which is discussed in the section below. This final model is then used to predict future data in real-time scenarios.

4.4.1.5 Evaluating the Model and Prediction

To evaluate our model's performance [29], we use different types of evaluation metrics to improve the power of prediction before performing predictions on unseen data. To evaluate our models, we used metrics like f1-score, recall, and precision to validate at their best. In [23, 31], a proper dependency of evaluation/accuracy metrics is shown w.r.t. various predictive models.

Precision: When the model predicts a class, precision is used to determine how many times the model is predicting that class correctly as in Eq. 4.3

$$Precision = \frac{TP + TN}{TP + TN + FP + FN} \tag{4.3}$$

Where, TP = True Positive, TF = True Negative, FN=False Negative, FP=False Positive.

Recall: When the value is true, recall tells us how many times the model can predict it's true as in Eq. 4.4

$$True\ Positive\frac{Rate}{Recall} = \frac{TP}{TP + FN} \tag{4.4}$$

F1-score: The harmonic mean of precision and recall is F1-score, where its best value is 1 which means perfect precision and recall and the worst is 0 in Eq. 4.5

$$F1 = 2 \times \frac{Precision \times recall}{Precision + recall} \tag{4.5}$$

The study of data analysis [23] inferred that the higher the F1 score, the better is the predictive model, with 0 being the worst possible and 1 being the best. Taking into consideration all crops, the average of all evaluation metrics tends toward 1 which indicates our predictive model is well-developed and good.

The average of all evaluation components was found to be:

Precision = 0.9519354839
Recall = 0.9451612903
F1_score = 0.9464516129

These components generally should be near to 1 for any model to fit perfectly. The model accuracy for crop production amplification was found to be 95.22% with the proposed algorithm as Random Forest Classifier using entropy index.

4.4.2 Disease Detection Prediction

A Convolutional Neural Network (CNN) is a type of deep learning algorithm used for image classification. It can be termed a multi-layer neural network designed for analyzing visual inputs to perform tasks such as image classification, segmentation and object detection. So every CNN follows a flowchart where it can learn the pixels step by step and with that knowledge, it can predict and classify any image. The following steps are depicted in Fig. 4.16.

Fig. 4.16 The working
principle behind a CNN
model

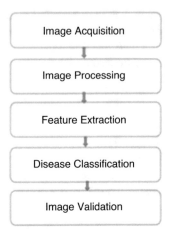

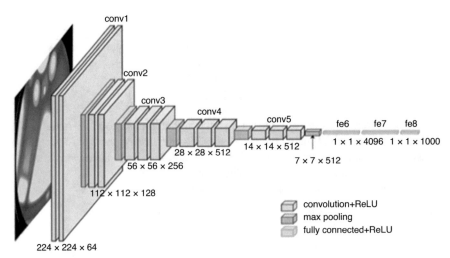

Fig. 4.17 Basic architecture of a CNN model [32]

In this research work, we would like to brief you on a basic CNN overview in Fig. 4.17. The initial pixels have been reduced for better machine interpretation. Abetting the pixels removes the complexity of any image and allows algorithms to learn images effectively. So now we will follow a step-by-step procedure where an applied algorithm can detect and classify diseases caused by maize, wheat and apple.

4.4.2.1 Image Acquisition

Image datasets for maize and apple diseases have been taken from the Kaggle data source and tested on real field image data. This data set is reformed using offline augmentation from the original data set. For wheat disease classification, images

Table 4.3 Number of training and testing sets of all types of each crop

Crop name	Type od disease	Number of training samples	Number of testing samples
Maize	Healthy	1859	465
	Northen blight	1908	477
	Cercospora gray spot	1642	410
	Common rust	1907	477
Wheat	Healthy	562	134
	Leaf-rust	562	134
	Stem-rust	562	134
Apple	Healthy	2008	502
	Cedar apple rust	1760	440
	Black rot	1987	497
	Apple scab	2016	504

come from a variety of sources. Some of the data is also from public images under Google.

Here for extracting images from source to machine, class_mode is assigned as 'sparse' due to multinomial variations of diseases for each crop. The following is some information and basics of how infections grow. We have highlighted all types of diseases focused on them in this research. As mentioned earlier, maize and wheat are important – utmost care should be taken to its cause and precautions adding to timely checkups.

The diseases specified in Table 4.3 are generally caused by wet springs and humid weather conditions. This disease may not kill the host but is involved in fruit deformation and premature fruit drop. The spread of these infections across the fields can also be determined by the windblown spores of the fungi which can carry disease long distances.

4.4.2.2   Image Pre-processing

Image pre-processing involves re-scaling or transforming every pixel value from the range (0, 255) to (0,1). Some images have a high pixel range and some have a low pixel range, due to which it can be quite perplexing for a machine to recognize its complete features. In this case, if we treat all the images in the same manner, the neural network module will also consider all images equally important. Also, scaling every image to the same range of (0,1) will make images contribute more evenly to the total loss existing. Moreover, a brief study about image processing is provided in [33].

From Keras, we import the Image Data Generator library to perform the enhancement of an image as shown in Fig. 4.18.

Here, in our proposed methodology, some mini processing steps have been taken for a better enhancement of images: such as every image being resized into 64*64 target size. The training data is processed in a way the machine can withstand any

Fig. 4.18 Step wise
procedure involved in
image processing

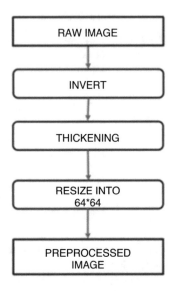

image flips i.e., rotations – left and right and also preserve the true classification of any crop disease. Also for better feature extraction in further steps, all images have been processed with a prior zoom limit of 0.2.

As mentioned above data augmentation has been used in all possible forms to make the learning better for the neural network which can help to increase the amount of relevant data in any dataset. Images of all crops for every disease after re-scaling are shown in Fig. 4.19.

In Fig. 4.20, it is shown how the whole image processing is well connected to image acquisition, and feature extraction processes extending data validation and classification. These procedural steps give clarity about which image has been in input, from noise removal to final classification via perfect validation accuracy.

4.4.2.3 Feature Extraction

To recognize any image, CNN must scan every image deeply. All the existing features in any image should be known for better extraction of key features to enrich the classification accuracy. Feature extraction has convolution layers followed by max-pooling and an activation function. The working principle of this step includes treating the pre-trained network as an arbitrary feature extractor, allowing the input image to propagate forward, stopping at the pre-specified layer, and features are the output of that layer. Also, Keiron and Ryan [34] have reported an overview of the working of CNN architecture.

The accuracy of learned models is increased using feature extraction by extracting features from input data. This phase not only helps in enhancing the final

Fig. 4.19 Re-scaled images of all crops diseases after pre-processing

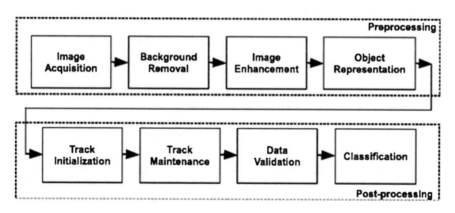

Fig. 4.20 Cycle of pre-processing and post-processing

accuracy but also removes redundant data and hence reduces the dimensionality of data. Hence, it increases training and inference speed.

In this research for the feature extraction process, we have created two deep convolutional layers, followed by two pooling layers and an activation function 'reLU' for each crop having the same parameters as shown in Table. 4.4. We found our

Table 4.4 Parameters used in the feature extraction of the CNN architecture

	Conv 2D				Max Pooling	
	Filters	Kernel size	Input shape	Activation	Pool size	Strides
Layer 1	32	(3, 3)	[64, 64, 3]	Relu	(2, 2)	2
Layer 2	32	(3, 3)	[64, 64, 3]	Relu	(2, 2)	2

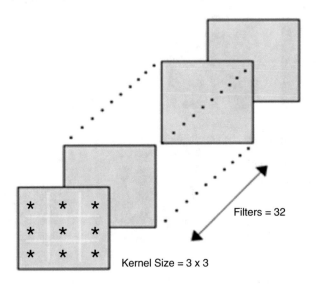

Fig. 4.21 Kernel size and filters used in conv2D model

model to be in a good perspective using 2-layers in feature extraction. A good amount of research has been done in [25] based on feature extraction. In agreement with their work, our model has been regenerated and optimized with greater accuracy.

4.4.2.3.1 Convolutional Layer

A conv2D layer has a filter or a kernel that consists of dimensions 3*3 kernel size and filters as 32 in our model as shown in Fig. 4.21. These are generally smaller than the input image so the whole image is covered. The area, called the receptive field, is where the filter is on the image area which is willing to consider or accept new suggestions and ideas.

There are three channels in an image mainly red, green, and blue through which the filter present in Conv2d extends with the possibility of each channel having different filters. Convolution is performed individually for each channel and then, they are integrated to get the final output called convoluted image. After the convolution operation, a feature map is received as an output of a filter.

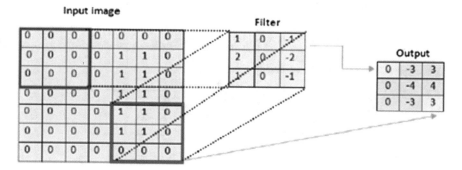

Fig. 4.22 Generic representation of a Conv2D network overlapping a filter dimension into input image to form the output shape [25]

Figure 4.22 represents a generic conv2D network used [25]. Convolution layer output is represented by Eq. 4.6.

$$M_j^p = f\left(\sum_{i \in M_j} M_i^{p-1} * k_{ij}^p + N_j^p\right) \tag{4.6}$$

Where p represents the pth layer, k_{ij} denotes convolutional kernel, N_j denotes bias and M_j denotes a set of input maps.

4.4.2.3.2 Pooling Layer

Extraction of sharp and smothered features is mainly done using the pooling layer. It is also done to reduce divergent features of data and computations for better estimation. Mathematically pooling is calculated as in Eq. 4.7.

$$\text{Output size} = \frac{\left(\text{Input size} - \text{Pool size} + 2 * \text{padding}\right)}{\text{stride}} + 1 \tag{4.7}$$

Gholamalinejad and Khosravi [35] have discussed various effective pooling methods in detail. In our work, we have used max-pooling represented as in Eq. 4.8. And a related diagram is shown to understand its working in Fig. 4.23.

$$V = \max_{i,j=1}^{h,w} S_{i,j} \tag{4.8}$$

4.4.2.4 Disease Classification

This is the last phase of the architecture where the disease is predicted. After the max-pooling feature, the process of flattening is done. The flattening method converts the output into a vector. The result of the classification can be obtained only

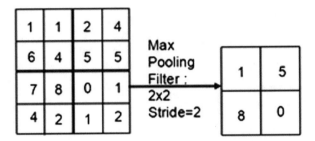

Fig. 4.23 Max pooling – Single Depth slice

Table 4.5 Number of units and activation function in a dense layer

| Number of Layers | Dense Layer | |
	Units	Activation
Layer 1	128	Relu
Layer 2	32	Relu
Layer 3	16	Relu
Layer 4	4	Softmax

through a vector. Hence, the conversion is necessary. Fully connected layers flatten the network's 2D spatial features into a 1D vector that represents image-level features for classification purposes [36].

Table 4.5 shows four multiple dense layers, a deeply connected neural network with the units and activation function used in each layer respectively. The hidden layers have used 'reLU' to increment the non-linearity in our images. The output layer has 4 units for each class of disease and softmax is used because it is suitable for mutually exclusive multi-class classification in the logistic regression model.

4.4.2.4.1 ReLU

The ReLU layer is used as an activation function here between the convolution layer and the feature maps (Fig. 4.24) [25] to convert all negative values to zero without affecting the size of the image and its dimensions.

So these 3 layers sum up to feature extraction giving a basic accuracy level. We added a dropout layer to achieve better accuracy. This regularization technique is used to prevent the model from overfitting as it randomly sets the input neural units to zero at each step during the training process [37]. It takes preventive measures to avoid complex co-adaptations on the training data which results in reduced overfitting.

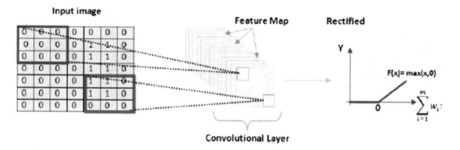

Fig. 4.24 Applying activation function Relu to feature maps of convolution layer [25]

Fig. 4.25 Graph of softmax activation function

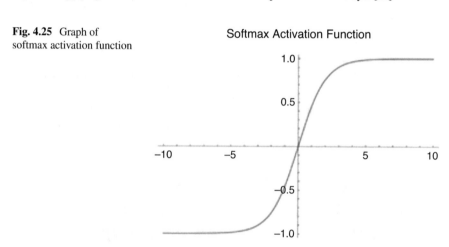

4.4.2.4.2   Softmax

Softmax is a combination of multiple sigmoid functions. A brief discussion about various activation functions used in the deep learning technique is provided in Fig. 4.25 [38].

In the compilation process for our CNN model, we have used the Adam optimizer because it gives the best accuracy among other optimizers available.

Figure 4.26 represents the overview of the internal mechanism of our model (including all the layers). The fully connected layers are finally formed by the last few flattened layers of our CNN model. These layers are instrumental in predicting the final output, i.e., predicting a particular disease.

4.4.2.5   Image Validation

Several sample images were selected from different sources for validation for which the model predicted diseases accurately. This was achieved due to the high accuracy of our models which was accomplished by tuning various parameters to enhance for

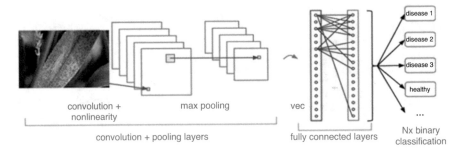

Fig. 4.26 Internal mechanism of how fully connected layers are formed using maize common rust image

```
Model: "sequential"

Layer (type)                    Output Shape
=====================================================
conv2d (Conv2D)                 (None, 62, 62, 32)

max_pooling2d (MaxPooling2D)    (None, 31, 31, 32)

conv2d_1 (Conv2D)               (None, 29, 29, 32)

max_pooling2d_1 (MaxPooling2    (None, 14, 14, 32)

flatten (Flatten)               (None, 6272)

dense (Dense)                   (None, 128)

dense_1 (Dense)                 (None, 32)

dense_2 (Dense)                 (None, 16)

dense_3 (Dense)                 (None, 4)
=====================================================
```

Fig. 4.27 Proposed model summary for disease detection using CNN

a more precise outcome. Later in Sect. 4.5.2, a detailed analysis will be presented on validation tests and overall accuracy. Further, it is discussed how regularization techniques can improve performance in a supportive manner reducing the margin of error.

The various parameters of the CNN such as the number of layers needed, the number of units per layer, the kernel size and the apt activation function for our model, were carefully tuned after several considerations. After making changes, we obtained a good accuracy for our CNN model. Figure 4.27 describes the summary of the model. It shows the output shape of the layers and the number of layers after each change.

4.4.3   Artificial Neural Networks for Fertilizer Prediction

Artificial neural networks are structures used for computing various tasks and their working is inspired by the human brain. These networks are similar to simulating tasks like clustering, pattern recognition, and classification on the computer. Presently, the usability of these networks has also forayed into the world of agriculture, helping our farmers to increase their profits.

The ANNs learn by adjusting the weights and biases for all the input parameters, it tries learning and gives a prediction. The process of learning is summed up in the steps in Fig. 4.28.

The description of the diagrammatic representation of the above steps is discussed below.

4.4.3.1   Data Collection

Our data source for the research work is Kaggle. The parameters (Fig. 4.29) used for predicting an apt fertilizer are the temperature conditions, the humidity level (an absolute value), and the moisture content of the soil. Sandy, loamy, red, etc. were

Fig. 4.28 Working of an ANN model

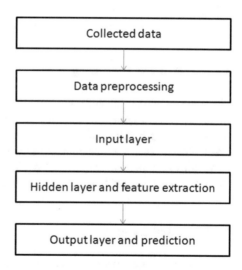

	Temparature	Humidity	Moisture	Soil Type	Crop Type	Nitrogen	Potassium	Phosphorous	Fertilizer Name
0	26	52	38	Sandy	Maize	37	0	0	Urea
1	29	52	45	Loamy	Sugarcane	12	0	36	DAP
2	34	65	62	Black	Cotton	7	9	30	14-35-14
3	32	62	34	Red	Tobacco	22	0	20	28-28
4	28	54	46	Clayey	Paddy	35	0	0	Urea

Fig. 4.29 First five readings of the fertilizer dataset

Fig. 4.30 Distribution of various fertilizers present in the dataset obtained

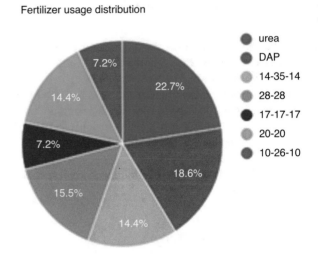

Fertilizer usage distribution

- urea
- DAP
- 14-35-14
- 28-28
- 17-17-17
- 20-20
- 10-26-10

some of the soil types which were the determinants of the correct fertilizer. The amount of nitrogen, potassium, and phosphorus, some of the essential nutrients required for the good growth of the crop, are also included as parameters. Some of the fertilizers which can be predicted by our model are- Urea, 14-14, DAP, 28-28, etc. (Fig. 4.30) among which urea is found to be of maximum use in India.

4.4.3.2 Data Pre-processing

The collected data is labeled encoded. There might be a substantial difference in the values of some columns of the data which may lead to prioritizing the columns which have larger values, hence normalization is done. Among various normalization methods [26], the mathematical representation for some of the normalization techniques like Standard Scalar and Min-Max Scalar is given in Eqs. 4.1 and 4.2. We have used Standard Scalar in our model.

4.4.3.3 Input Layer

Artificial neural networks need data to be fed into our systems as input. Then, the data is randomly assigned with weights and forwarded to the next hidden layer. Figure 4.31 shows the input layer parameters where the neuron is represented by a circle to which all the inputs are added. Then, an activation function is applied followed by bias.

A bias can be considered to be analogous to adding a constant value in a linear equation and finally combining it to form a network. After this internal computation, a predicted value is obtained. This is an abstract overview of how the computation is done.

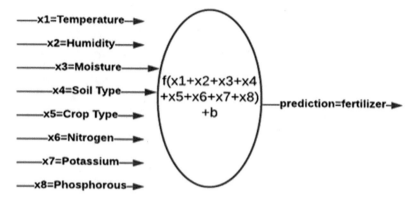

Fig. 4.31 Input layer showing various input parameters

Table 4.6 Hidden layers specification

	Units	Activation function
Layer 1	8	ReLU
Layer 2	8	ReLU

4.4.3.4   Hidden Layer and Feature Extraction

The hidden layers are used so that the machine gets enough to learn about the data and its co-relationship with other attributes which indeed helps in predicting the class for any future data. We have implemented our model using 2 hidden layers with 8 neurons each (Table 4.6).

When the input parameters are fed into the machine, due to the neurons in hidden layers some weights are multiplied by the input data to increase its learning rate. Finally, a bias is added to the result which serves as an additional parameter to adjust the output. Our developed neural network with hidden layers and its neuron is figured in Fig. 4.32.

Activation functions [38, 39] are generally used in deep learning models to introduce non-linearity. Arya and Ankit [40] have provided a brief analysis of the learning and recovery of 'reLU' function. The ReLU activation function (Eq. 4.9) is used after the features are extracted. ReLU activation function (Fig. 4.33) solves the problem of vanishing gradients which is computationally less expensive as compared to other activation functions like 'tanh'.

$$ReLU = f(x) = \{x, if \; x > 0 \; 0, if \; x < 0 \tag{4.9}$$

Later in Sect. 4.5.3, we have discussed how a regularization technique can render a better accuracy with increasing performance for our base model. In [39], a comparative analysis of various regularization techniques used in ANN is provided.

Fig. 4.32 Neural
connections in our ANN
model for fertilizer
prediction

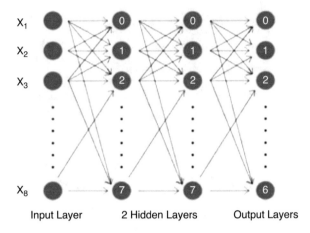

Fig. 4.33 ReLU activation
function

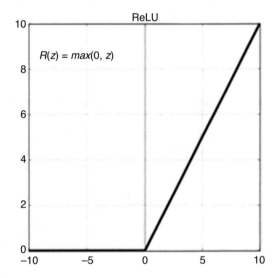

4.4.3.5 Output Layer and Prediction

The output layer is also referred to as the classification layer. The sigmoid function is being used for predicting the final output. The number of units used in the output layer is 7 (Fig. 4.34).

Then we call the compile module to combine all the layers to start its training phase and finally predict the favoring class. The optimizer used in the compilation is Adam as in Fig. 4.35. Among the various varieties of SGD such as RMSProp, Adagrad and Adam optimizer gives the best outcome. A more detailed analysis of Adam and a variation on it is in [41].

Many optimizers can be used such as SGD, and RMSProp [41]. But Adam optimizer is considered to be the best one due to its learning rate, reliability, efficiency

```
ann.add(tf.keras.layers.Dense(units=7, activation='sigmoid'))
```

```
ann.compile(optimizer = 'adam', loss = 'sparse_categorical_crossentropy',
            metrics = ['sparse_categorical_accuracy'])
```

Fig. 4.34 Output Layer configuration and compilation step

Fig. 4.35 Curve of Adam
optimizer

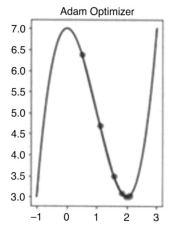

Table 4.7 Learning rate of various Optimizers

Optimizer	Learning rate
Adam	0.001
RMSProp	0.001
SGD	0.01

and cost-effectiveness as compared to others. Table 4.7 shows the learning rate of different algorithms.

Here, Adam and RMSProp show a good learning rate of 0.001. In Sect. 4.5.2, we will further discuss the results obtained from using these various optimizers.

After training the model with Adam optimizer, using metrics like precision, recall, and F1-score, the model was evaluated. The average values of these stated metrics were found close to 1 giving an insight that our model has nice accuracy and fitting.

The ANN model for fertilizer prediction was found to be 96% with our proposed network model with 2 hidden layers of 8 neurons each and the output layer of 7 neurons due to 7 classified fertilizers in our dataset.

4.5   Result Analysis

4.5.1   Crop Prediction

We have extended some scope of hyper-parameter tuning in our proposed random forest algorithm by scaling parameters like n-estimators and max-depth. N-estimators are the number of trees internally built by the algorithm before the averages of the predictions are made. Hence, the higher the number of trees, the algorithm will be able to choose from more options, which will help the classifier learn better. From Table 4.8, it is evident how an increase in the number of estimators yields better accuracy in the random forest classifier.

But n-estimators also depend on the shape of the original dataset or inputs. If n-estimators exceed the number of input rows, the model can lead to fainting situations. So, utmost care must be taken while tuning the parameters. However, reduced n-estimators can also raise problems in the designed model.

As the max_depth increases, the accuracy decreases due to over-fitting. Clearly, from Table 4.9, we can see how the accuracy decreases up to a certain level by increasing the max-depth and then reaches a threshold. The model learns patterns and various correlations to adopt predicting new data correctly. Hence, an optimal value for max-depth must be chosen based on the number of features present in the dataset.

For our final model, we have trained the Random forest classifier using 1000 n-estimators and max-depth as 10. Using these hyper-parameters, the evaluating metrics such as precision, recall, support and F1-score are close to 1.00.

To visualize the deviation of predicted output from the actual output, a graph was plotted for 100 observations. In the above graph (Fig. 4.36), the blue line indicates the predicted data and the red line indicates the test data. The coinciding lines depict that most of our predictions are in synchronization with the actual output which accounts for the accuracy of 95.22%.

Heatmap is a visualization technique to show the multicollinearity amongst the attributes present in the dataset. Values closer to 1 depict a positive correlation,

Table 4.8 Tabulation of accuracy achieved using different values of n-estimators

N-estimators used in the algorithm	Accuracy (in %)
1000	95.22
500	94.96
100	94.45

Table 4.9 Comparison of accuracy achieved using different max-depth values

Max-depth parameter value used	Accuracy (in %)
10	95.22
50	95.09
100	95.09

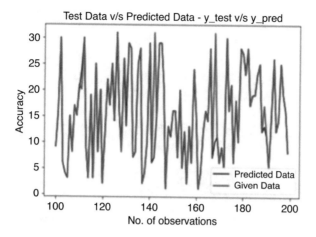

Fig. 4.36 Deviation of predictions from the actual result

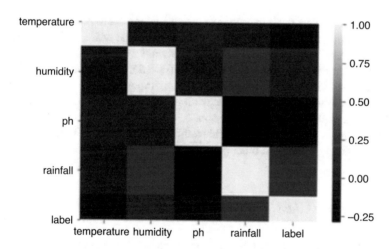

Fig. 4.37 Heatmap showing a correlation between different attributes in crop prediction

whereas being closer to 0 means there is no linear trend. The monochromatic scale parallel to the heatmap represents colour association to correlation. As shown in Fig. 4.37, highly correlated are defined using a lighter shade while the least ones are shown using a darker shade. And the correlation among the same variables is depicted by the white color, which is 1, as shown in the corresponding colour bar of the heatmap since the same attributes will always be completely correlated. The heatmap in Fig. 4.37 also shows how the characteristics like temperature, humidity, pH and rainfall are associated with our target variable. Some negative correlations are between pH and precipitation, temperature and the final label output. At the same time, some positive correlations are humidity and rain.

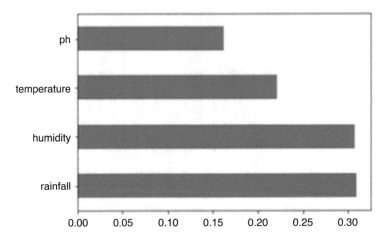

Fig. 4.38 Importance of different features in crop production

Figure 4.38 depicts the importance of the attributes used to predict the crop. India has a monsoon type of climate directly influenced by the water bodies surrounding the sub-continent. So as per the graph, the amount of rainfall is the most critical factor in determining the crops that can be cultivated in a particular region of India. Ensemble learning is used to determine the importance of features with the ExtraTreeClassifier. For better visualizations, the output of the feature_importances_ class is plotted as a "barh" graph.

Finally, the accuracy we have achieved using the Random Forest classifier is 95.22%, which is better than other proposed models [17].

4.5.2 Disease Classification

We will discuss the diseases that affect three crucial crops grown in India for our proposed CNN architecture. Better accuracy has been achieved through regularization techniques and varying the number of epochs. By training our model more times, the model will better understand patterns and produce more correct predictions. Hence, accuracy is a measure of how well our model will reduce mispredictions. Better the accuracy, the better the model we have developed. The relationship of accuracy with varying epochs for all the three crops is graphically depicted in Fig. 4.39.

Along with the increase in accuracy, another measure that provides insight into the model's robustness is the value of the loss function. Loss is a measure of the distance between the true values of the problem with the values which our model is predicting. Greater is the loss; more are the errors made on the dataset. In our model prediction, we have used the sparse categorical cross-entropy loss function as each dataset sample belongs to only one particular class. In the case of the loss function,

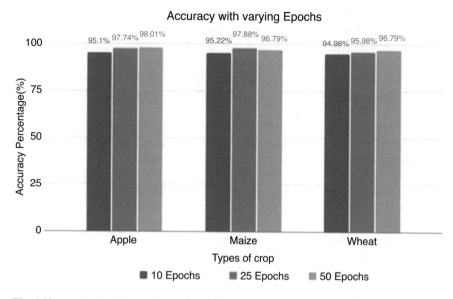

Fig. 4.39   Bar Graph depicting the varying values of accuracy with the number of epochs

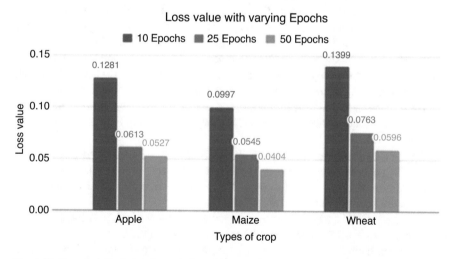

Fig. 4.40   Bar graph depicting the variation of loss values with the number of epochs

the lesser the value of the loss function, the better the model's training. The correlation between the loss values to the number of epochs is represented in Fig. 4.40.

It is evident from Figs. 4.39 and 4.40 that among various epochs, 50 epochs led to the best accuracy and least loss which allowed our model to be trained efficiently. Hence, we will be considering 50 epochs as a suitable benchmark for our further training process to improve model accuracy to a better pedestal.

While modeling any architecture, one must take utmost caution while selecting the optimal number of epochs for model training based on the size of the dataset and the quality of images. For instance, if the size of the dataset is small, then a large number of epochs will cause our model to overfit. Similarly, if a small number of epochs are employed for a large dataset, the model will be under-fitted. Both of these extreme conditions can lead to an increase in the loss function, degrading the model's efficiency.

Now the performance of our model has been amplified by using a regularization technique adding a dropout layer as mentioned earlier in Sect. 4.4.2. The dropout layer shuts off some neurons so our model does not overfit.

In Fig. 4.41, we can infer that with a decrease in dropout percentage, model accuracy increases to some extent which makes the learning better and even reduces the probability of overfitting. In Fig. 4.42, it is shown that with a decrease in dropout percentage, the loss function decreases, building the model less erroneous.

The percentage value of the dropout layer must be chosen carefully because if a very huge dropout percentage is taken, the maximum number of neurons will be switched off and our model will be unable to learn properly. If a low dropout percentage is used, it may lead to overfitting. While modeling our algorithm we observed that at 15% dropout we are obtaining somewhat good accuracy for some crops, but the graphs obtained showed that the learning process was not very efficient due to some inconsistency of validation curves. From Figs. 4.41 and 4.42, we got an optimum dropout percentage range. The best results with high accuracy and lower loss values were generated keeping the dropout percentage between 25% and 50%. Any value below that can lead to a scope of overfitting and any value above 50% may lead to a poor learning curve. Moreover, Alvin and Dae-Ki [42] have explained different dropout regularization techniques used in Neural Networks.

Here sparse categorical accuracy and sparse categorical cross-entropy are used to evaluate the model performance and efficiency in predicting new data (Figs. 4.43, 4.44 and 4.45).

The graphs compare the learning curves based on validation and training data where the gap area between them is significantly less and somewhat superimposing, which aligns with the general trend of CNN architecture. Table 4.10 contains the final accuracy of our described architecture.

Using our CNN architecture we obtained an accuracy of 98.70% for wheat prediction, which is 0.1% more than the best model used in [23].

The overall classifier accuracy for our model is 98.82% for the common diseases affecting the maize crop, which is higher than the one achieved by the model used in [21, 22]. In addition, we have also achieved a mean accuracy of 98.93% for classifications of apple infections, which is greater than the mean accuracy obtained using the model defined in [22].

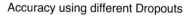

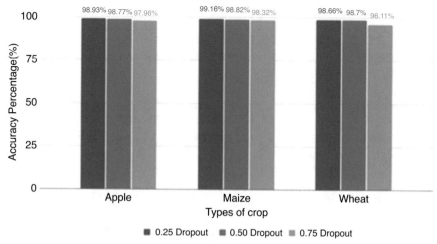

Fig. 4.41 Bar graph representing the varying accuracy values with different dropout values

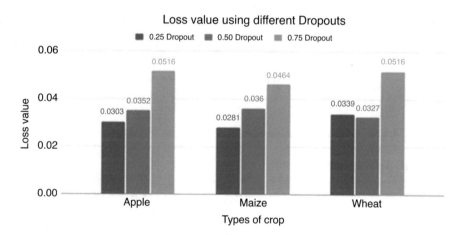

Fig. 4.42 Bar graph representing the varying loss values with different dropout values

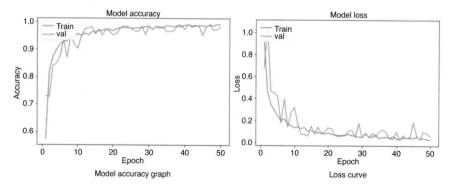

Fig. 4.43 Sparse validation performance curve for crop 'Apple' with dropout = 0.25

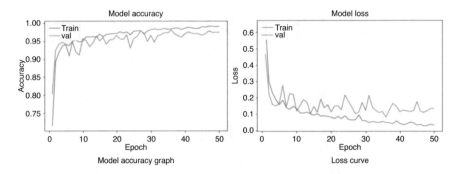

Fig. 4.44 Sparse validation performance curve for crop 'Maize' with dropout = 0.25

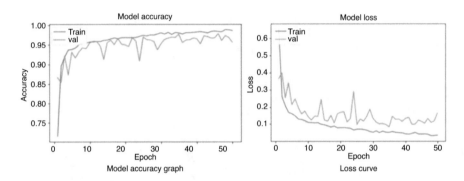

Fig. 4.45 Sparse validation performance curve for crop 'Wheat' with dropout = 0.5

Table 4.10 Accuracy of defined crops

Crop Type	Accuracy (in %)
Apple	98.93
Wheat	98.70
Maize	98.82

4.5.3 Fertilizer Prediction

As mentioned earlier in Sects. 4.4.2 and 4.4.3, Adam is the best-known optimizer used in CNN architecture. Adam is an acronym for the Adaptive Moment Estimation Algorithm, which estimates moments and utilizes them to optimize a function. It combines the gradient descent with the momentum algorithm and RMSProp algorithm.

Figures 4.46 and 4.47 show the validation accuracy score and validation loss parameter among various used optimizers like RMS Prop and SGD, which is why Adam is considered the best optimizer.

Fig. 4.46 Validation accuracy of various optimizers

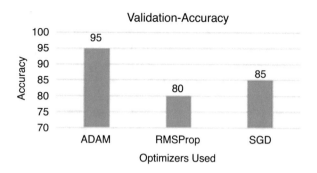

Fig. 4.47 Validation loss values of various optimizers

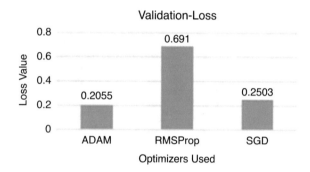

As is depicted in Fig. 4.46, the Adam optimizer's accuracy is the best optimizer. The accuracy used here is sparse categorical accuracy. Similarly in Fig. 4.47, Adam optimizer shows the lowest loss value among others. Less is the loss function, and more efficient is our model. So from Fig. 4.47, it is evident that RMSProp gives the maximum loss, hence the predictions made by using that optimizer are too far from the ground truths. The optimizer Adam gives the least amount of loss and greater accuracy. Hence, Adam optimizer is used.

Fewer epochs are used so that the neural network generalizes better on unseen data. On the other hand, multiple epochs help the neural network see the previous data and readjust the various parameters of the model so that our model is not biased towards the last few data points while being trained.

An optimal value must be chosen as epochs can affect the distance between predicted and actual values. As evident from the graphs in Fig. 4.48, the model with 500 epochs has reached the global minimum resulting in the lowest value of the loss. As the epochs are decreased to 250 and beyond, the loss increases. Similarly, when the epochs are increased to 1000, the loss increases significantly. Both the extreme cases are detrimental to the prediction model. Hence, for our model, the minimum loss is obtained at 500 epochs.

Our dataset has 99 rows of data for which the optimal range of epochs for our model was 350 to 700 beyond which the model can be erroneous. The best accuracy was obtained at around 500 epochs. If epochs are less than 350, there are chances of

Fig. 4.48 Validation loss
values with changing
Epochs

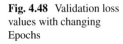

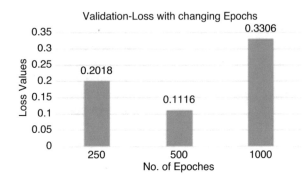

Validation-Loss with changing Epochs

0.35
0.3
0.25
0.2
0.15
0.1
0.05
0

Loss Values

0.2018

0.1116

0.3306

250   500   1000

No. of Epoches

Fig. 4.48 Validation loss values with changing Epochs

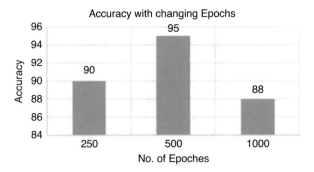

Accuracy with changing Epochs

96
94
92
90
88
86
84

Accuracy

90

95

88

250   500   1000

No. of Epoches

Fig. 4.49 Accuracy with changing Epochs

underfitting. Consequently, if epochs are taken more than 1000, there are chances of overfitting. So an optimal value of 500 epochs gave the best accuracy as depicted by the graphs in Fig. 4.49.

Concerning the detailed analysis of the heatmap in Sect. 4.5.1, we observe that in Fig. 4.50 the attributes are phosphorus, potassium, nitrogen, moisture, humidity and temperature. Among these, temperature and humidity are positively correlated while phosphorus and nitrogen are negatively correlated.

As discussed earlier we have set the optimal number of epochs used for training as 500. Along with only considering the number of epochs, we observed that although the accuracy was good still the validation curve showed a slight tendency of overfitting which was regularized using a dropout layer. After iterating our ANN model through different values of dropout percentages, we derived that with a dropout percentage of 25 we achieved a good accuracy and eliminated overfitting (Fig. 4.51).

Figure 4.52 shows the change in accuracy and loss function values obtained at various dropout percentages at an optimal value of 500 epochs. Maximum accuracy and minimum loss were obtained with the dropout parameter value of 0.25, hence we used this proposed technique.

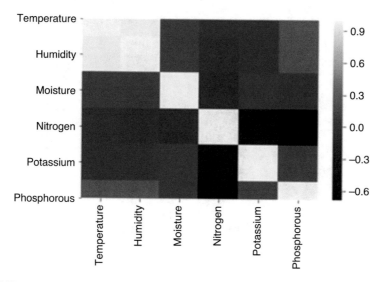

Fig. 4.50 Heatmap showing the correlation between attributes in fertilizer prediction

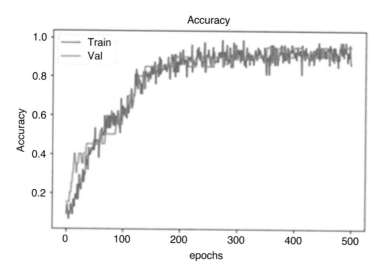

Fig. 4.51 Graph between epochs and accuracy for train and validation data

The optimal value of the loss is obtained within a range of 200–500 epochs. The values within this range returned a minimum loss. As in Fig. 4.53, the graphs show a decreasing trend which concludes our model to be well trained. Furthermore, the gap between training and validation loss curves is less or somewhat superimposing, proving that our proposed model is in good agreement with the general trend of perfect CNN architecture.

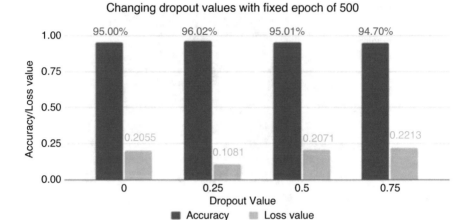

Fig. 4.52 Comparing accuracy and loss function for varying dropout values

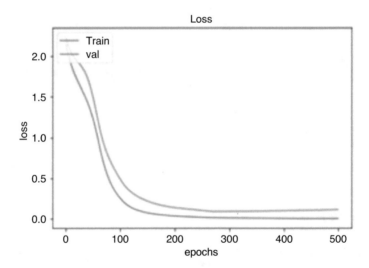

Fig. 4.53 Variation curve between epochs and loss function

4.6 Conclusions

Agriculture contributes to a substantial percentage of our Indian economy. But due to a lack of updated technology, the agricultural sector still suffers from various problems. This chapter aims to propose a machine learning kit that contains different data mining techniques for crop prediction and farm management. Automating such processes will increase the productivity of a farm to a large extent. Several techniques like CNN, ANN and random forest classifier will aid the farmers to understand what is best for their growth, owing to which their profits can increase. The various alterations made in the hyper-parameters of these techniques, helped us pick the most optimum parameters to build our model. Accuracy close to 95% was achieved in the first stage of our model of crop prediction using Random Forest Classifiers. Also, among the given input parameters, principal component analysis elicited criteria like rainfall and humidity to be most imperative. Secondly, for disease detection in crops, our designed CNN architectural model with 4 hidden layers and softmax activation function gave an accuracy of 98%. Lastly, our ANN model to predict fertilizers suitable for any infected soil gave us an accuracy of 95%, using adam optimizer and regularization dropout value set to 0.25. Also, using heatmaps, parameters like temperature and humidity were found to be positively correlated.

Machine learning and deep learning have been applied in various industries and if the agriculture sector adopts them quickly, we can see a boom in the agro-economic conditions. Precise and intelligent agriculture will be a research hotspot soon. With different advancements in AI and machine learning, the long wait for an intelligent farming solution will soon be over.

Further enhancement of this model is to use different IoT devices to directly gain on-field values of soil moisture, and NPK values and serve it on cloud technologies where the ML models can be hosted. This will help in understanding high dimensionality patterns between seasonal climatic changes, which can help predict the effects of drought and severe climatic repercussions.

References

1. Jambekar, S., Nema, S., & Saquib, Z. (2018). Prediction of Crop production in India Using data mining techniques. In *Fourth International Conference on Computing Communication Control and Automation (ICCUBEA).*
2. Madhukar, A., Kumar, V., & Dashora, K. (2020). Spatial and temporal trends in the yields of three major crops: Wheat, rice and maize in India. *International Journal of Plant Production, 14,* 187–207. Springer.
3. Singh, J., Singhal, N., Singhal, S., Sharma, M., Agarwal, S., & Arora S. (2018). Environmental implications of rice and wheat stubble burning in North-Western states of India. In *Advances in health and environment safety* (Transactions in civil and environmental engineering) (pp. 47–55). Springer.
4. Adebiyi, M. O., Ogundokun, R. O., & Abokhai, A. A. (2020). *Machine learning-based predictive farmland optimization and crop monitoring system* (pp. 1–12). Scientifica.
5. Pathak, S., Jain, N., & Bhatia, A. (2012). *Crop residues management with conservation agriculture: Potential, constraints and policy needs.* Published by Indian Agriculture Research Institute. https://www.researchgate.net/publication/256378461
6. Talaviya, T., Shah, D., Patel, N., Yagnik, H., & Shah, M. (2020). Implementation of artificial intelligence in agriculture for optimization of irrigation and application of pesticides and herbicides. *Artificial Intelligence in Agriculture, 4,* 58–73. Elsevier.
7. Kansal, N., Bhushan, B., & Sharma, S. (2021). Architecture, security vulnerabilities, and the proposed countermeasures in Agriculture-Internet-of-Things (AIoT) Systems. *Internet of Things and Analytics for Agriculture, 3,* 329–353. Springer.

8. Mehta, S., Bhushan, B., & Kumar, R. (2022). Machine learning approaches for smart city applications: Emergence, challenges and opportunities. *Recent Advances in Internet of Things and machine Learning*, 147–163. Springer.
9. Verma, B., Sharma, N., Kaushik, I., & Bhushan, B. (2021). Applicability of machine learning algorithms for intelligent farming. In *Advanced soft computing techniques in data science, IoT and cloud computing* (pp. 121–147). Springer.
10. Environment: No smoke without fire. http://www.businessworld.in/article/Environment-No-Smoke-Without-Fire/14-11-2018-164129/
11. Pathak, H., Aggarwal, P. K., Roetter, R., Kalra, N., Bandyopadhaya, S. K., Prasad, S., & Van Keulen, H. (2003). Modelling the quantitative evaluation of soil nutrient supply, nutrient use efficiency, and fertilizer requirements of wheat in India. *Nutrient Cycling in Agroecosystems, 65*(2), 105–113. Springer.
12. Kumar, L., & Indira, M. (2017). Trends in fertilizer consumption and Foodgrain production in India: A co-integration analysis. *SDMIMD Journal of Management, 8*(2), 45–50.
13. Tripathi, M. K., & Maktedar, D. D. (2016). Recent machine learning based approaches for disease detection and classification of agricultural products. In *International Conference on Computing Communication Control and Automation (ICCUBEA)*.
14. Turkoglu, M., Hanbay, D., & Sengur, A. (2022). Multi-model LSTM-based convolutional neural networks for detection of apple diseases and pests. *Journal of Ambient Intelligence and Humanized Computing, 13*, 3335–3345. Springer.
15. Liakos, K., Busato, P., Moshou, D., Pearson, S., & Bochtis, D. (2018). Machine learning in agriculture: A review. *Sensors, 18*(8), 2674. MDPI.
16. Tidake, A. H., Sharma, Y. K., & Deshpande, V. S. (2019). Design efficient model to increase crop yield using deep learning. In *International conference on innovative trends and advances in engineering and technology* (pp. 221–226). IEEE.
17. Veenadhari, V., Misra, B., & Singh, C. (2014). Machine learning approach for forecasting crop yield based on climatic parameters. In *International conference on computer communication and informatics* (pp. 1–5).
18. Lobell, D. B. (2007). Changes in diurnal temperature range and national cereal yields. *Agricultural and Forest Meteorology, 145*(3), 229–238.
19. Haynes, R. J., & Naidu, R. (1998). Influence of lime, fertilizer and manure applications on soil organic matter content and soil physical conditions: A review. *Nutrient Cycling in Agroecosystems, 51*, 123–137.
20. Ashraf, M. A. (2012). Waterlogging stress in plants: A review. *African Journal of Agriculture Research, 7*(13), 1976–1981.
21. Sibiya, M., & Sumbwanyambe, M. (2019). A computational procedure for the recognition and classification of maize leaf diseases out of healthy leaves using convolutional neural networks. *AgriEngineering, 1*(1), 119–131. MDPI.
22. Geetharamani, G., & Pandian, A. J. (2019). Identification of plant leaf diseases using a nine-layer deep convolutional neural network. *Computers & Electrical Engineering, 76*, 323–338. Elsevier.
23. Singh, A., & Arora, M. (2020). CNN based detection of healthy and unhealthy wheat crop. In *International Conference on Smart Electronics and Communication (ICOSEC)*. IEEE.
24. Subramanian, M., Narasimha, L.V.P., Janakiramaiah, B., Mohan, B.A., & Ve, S.K. (2022). Hyperparameter optimization for transfer learning of VGG16 for disease identification in corn leaves using Bayesian optimization. *Big Data*.
25. Alharbi, A.G., & Arif, M. (2021). Detection and classification of apple diseases using convolutional neural networks. In *International Conference on Computer and Information Sciences (ICCIS)* (pp. 1–6).
26. Bhaya, W. (2017). Review of data Preprocessing techniques in data mining. *Journal of Engineering and Applied Sciences, 12*, 4102–4107.

27. Raju, V. N. G., Lakshmi, K. P., Jain, V. M., Kalidindi, A., & Padma, V. (2020). Study the influence of normalization/transformation process on the accuracy of supervised classification. In *International Conference on Smart Systems and Inventive Technology (ICSSIT)* (pp. 729–735).
28. Gulati, P., Sharma, A., & Gupta, M. (2016). Theoretical study of decision tree algorithms to identify pivotal factors for performance improvement: A review. *International Journal of Computer Applications, 141*(14), 19–25.
29. Raileanu, L., & Stoffel, K. (2004). Theoretical comparison between the Gini Index and Information Gain Criteria. *Annals of Mathematics and Artificial Intelligence, 41*, 77–93.
30. Ali, J, Khan, R., Ahmad, N., & Maqsood, I. (2012). Random forests and decision trees. *International Journal of Computer Science Issues (IJCSI), 9*.
31. Davis, J., & Goadrich, M. (2006). The relationship between precision-recall and ROC curves. In *International conference on machine learning* (pp. 233–240). ACM.
32. https://i.pinimg.com/564x/fc/b8/35/fcb8358bbc2fd692e9ce9d85e0c2ebbf.jpg
33. Kawahara, M., Inoue, T., & Nishio, Y. (2010). Image processing application using CNN with dynamic template. In *International workshop on cellular nanoscale networks and their applications (CNNA 2010)*.
34. O'Shea, K., & Nash, R. (2015). An introduction to convolutional neural networks. *ArXiv*, abs/1511.08458.
35. Gholamalinejad, H., & Khosravi, H. (2020). Pooling methods in deep neural networks, a review. *arXiv*.
36. Jadhav, S. B., Udupi, V. R., & Patil, S. B. (2020). Identification of plant diseases using convolutional neural networks. *International Journal of Information Technology, 13*, 1–10.
37. Mumtaz, D., Jakhetiya, V., Nathwani, K., & Subudhi, B. N. (2021). Non-intrusive perceptual audio quality assessment for user-generated content using deep learning. *IEEE Transactions on Industrial Informatics*.
38. Sharma, S., Sharma, S., & Athaiya, A. (2020). Activation functions in neural networks. *International Journal of Engineering Applied Sciences and Technology, 4*(12), 310–316.
39. Gupta, S., Gupta, R., Ojha, M., & Singh, K. P. (2018). A comparative analysis of various regularization techniques to solve overfitting problem in artificial neural network. In *Communications in Computer and Information Science* (pp. 363–371).
40. Mazumdar, A., & Rawat, A. S. (2019). Learning and recovery in the ReLU model. In *Annual Allerton conference on communication, control, and computing (Allerton)* (pp. 108–115).
41. Zhang, Z. (2018). Improved Adam optimizer for deep neural networks. In *International Symposium on Quality of Service (IWQoS)* (pp. 1–2). IEEE.
42. Poernomo, A., & Kang, D.-K. (2018). Biased dropout and crossmap dropout: Learning towards effective dropout regularization in convolutional neural network. *Neural Networks, 104*, 60–67.

Chapter 5
Natural Language Processing (NLP) Based Innovations for Smart Healthcare Applications in Healthcare 4.0

Nemika Tyagi and Bharat Bhushan

Abstract Technology and computation have changed the backdrop of various aspects of our fast-paced lives. Healthcare is one such aspect that has been affected by this change and faces new challenges every day including the challenge of extracting relevant and valuable information from the enormous amount of data that is generated endlessly in this sector. Smart data analytics provides a solution to this problem through the use of Artificial Intelligence and Natural Language Processing (NLP). This paper elucidates the core concept of textual data analytics that is, NLP, its composition, and architecture. We also present the framework of Healthcare 4.0 and NLP's role in it. Subsequently, we give an elaborated and concise overview of state-of-art NLP technologies that have been employed in various aspects of healthcare and medicine. This paper aims to highlight the role of NLP in smart healthcare and its potential to solve the rising challenges of today's data-driven society.

Keywords Natural Language Processing · Healthcare · Smart city · Security · Privacy · Internet of Things · Cryptography

5.1 Introduction

The Information and Communication Technology (ICT) advances are being reflected in terms of our changing lifestyles through the concept of smart cities and sustainable development. The primary technologies leading the charge of the ongoing tech revolution also called Fourth Industrial Revolution or Industry 4.0 are the Internet of Things (IoT), Wireless Sensor Network (WSN), big data, cloud computing, machine learning, and data analytics [1]. When applied in the field of medicine, this phase of development is named Healthcare 4.0 and it aims to provide efficient

N. Tyagi (✉) · B. Bhushan
School of Engineering and Technology, Sharda University,
Greater Noida, Uttar Pradesh, India

© The Author(s), under exclusive license to Springer Nature
Switzerland AG 2023
M. A. Ahad et al. (eds.), *Enabling Technologies for Effective Planning and
Management in Sustainable Smart Cities*,
https://doi.org/10.1007/978-3-031-22922-0_5

and high-quality healthcare services [2]. The recent decade has especially seen higher investments and focus on the healthcare department from all over the world due to the globalization of this domain and increase in foreign direct investments towards the medical sector in terms of finance, infrastructure as well as technology [3].

Aceto et al. [4] has categorized the ICT aspect of Healthcare 4.0 into four subsets: Sensing – use of IoT devices, wearables, embedded systems; Actuation – robotics, IoT actuators; Communication – WSN, cloud computing, networks; and Processing – Machine Learning, Artificial Intelligence (AI), and Data analytics. Since Healthcare 4.0 is driven by data and the involvement of AI in processing medical data not only provides more efficient and precise results but also gives physicians more direct time with patients [5]. Healthcare analytics requires strategies for dealing with versatile, unstructured data from heterogeneous sources that vary based on semantics, ontologies, and conceptual understanding [6]. In this scenario, Natural Language Processing (NLP) comes into the picture as it presents an AI solution to language data-related problems in Healthcare 4.0.

NLP is an extensive domain of AI and is used in collaboration with machine learning and deep learning algorithms for clinical informatics and data processing. NLP helps in understanding human languages and can assist in automatically analyzing and making decisions by interpreting a large amount of textual data in a very short period. Most of the Clinical-NLP (CNLP) approaches are either rule-based corpus reliant or statistical methods using supervised or semi-supervised algorithms [7]. In healthcare, the data for processing is available in the form of pathology and radiology reports, clinical notes, Electronic Health Records (EHR), nursing documentation, and discharge summaries [8]. CNLP systems are modeled for the requirement of healthcare systems to fit the existing medical pipeline and provide smart solutions. The utilities of CNLP range from providing quick emergency department admissions [9], predicting mortality risk [10], disease prediction from clinical notes [11], identification of patients [12], prognosis of disease [13, 14], auto-prescriptions [15], probability of re-admission [16], predicting discharge disposition [17], providing healthcare assistants [18] and end-to-end decision support systems [19]. It is quite evident how CNLP has become an essential instrument in the intelligent medical domain and can take clinical analytics to new heights in the future as well.

In this paper, we shed light on the field of NLP and how it has integrated with smart healthcare over time to solve various medical problems that arise due to the increase in patient demands and simultaneous lack of resources. We found that the scope of NLP in medicine has been on a steady rise and detail-oriented studies have not been conducted that analyze the scope of NLP's applicability in Healthcare 4.0 and provide a review of research work conducted in those areas. The key features of this paper are given below:

• This work provides state-of-art NLP technologies that are setting a benchmark in the healthcare sector.

- This work also focuses on providing a deep understanding of CNLP and the various language tasks that contribute to the NLP pipeline
- The structure of Healthcare 4.0 has been discussed, including the essential aspect of identification of medical data origin sources.
- The applications of NLP in healthcare have been surveyed and analyzed by dividing into 3 separate categories: Healthcare Management and Administration, Assistive care and Clinical Decision Support Systems (DSS), and Disease Diagnosis, Prediction and Treatment.
- This work provides a review of Clinical-NLP systems used in the above domains and the types of methodologies adopted by them.

This paper has been organized as follows: Section 5.2 provides an overview of NLP, its language tasks, and the structure of the NLP pipeline. Section 5.3 explores the composition of Healthcare 4.0 and the role of smart data analytics in it. Section 5.4 throws light on the existing up-to-date NLP practices applied in the various healthcare domains such as management, assistance, and diagnosis. Finally, Sect. 5.5 condenses our thoughts about this study.

5.2 Natural Language Processing: An Overview

Processing human language-based data using computational methods or automated techniques is becoming a big challenge in today's data-driven society. NLP is a branch of computational science that helps in understanding as well as generating natural human language queries and responses. Therefore NLP is the right fit to bridge the gap between the rapid generation of language data and the need to rapidly process this data to produce relevant information. NLP uses a combination of Artificial Intelligence and linguistics to analyze the subject matter written or spoken in human languages [20]. NLP when used with machine learning and deep learning technologies produces highly accurate solutions to problems that require text analysis, classification, segmentation, summary generation, and machine translation among others [21].

5.2.1 What Is NLP?

NLP is a branch of Artificial Intelligence used for processing all kinds of language information such as shape, sound, tonality, semantics, and context [22]. It can be broadly classified into two major paradigms: Natural Language Understanding (NLU) and Natural Language Generation (NLG). NLU is the branch of NLP that is closely related to linguistics and it focuses on coarse to fine grain levels of language interpretation. NLU includes the study of Syntax – the structure of the sentence, Semantics – the meaningfulness of sentences or

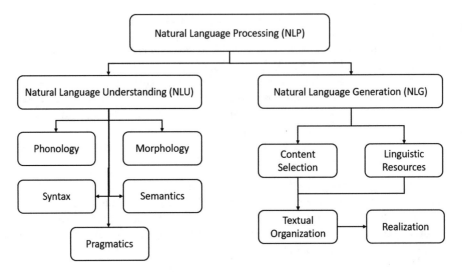

Fig. 5.1 Branches of NLP and their sub-sections

paragraphs, Phonology – the sound of the language, Morphology – the process of formation of words and Pragmatics – the understanding of contextual meaning of the language [20]. NLG is deployed in systems that require giving natural language responses. It consists of the following phases: Selection of Content – deciding the subject matter relevant to the query, Linguistic Resources – making use of the available resources for response generation, Textual organization – arranging the text to make syntactically and semantically correct sentences and Realization – the last phase where the final response is delivered in text or audio format. Figure 5.1 depicts these sub-sections of NLP.

NLP does not refer to a single algorithm or program but it is a consolidation of several processes and tasks that take place for understanding the actual meaning and context of the words including the temporal, spatial, and semantic insinuations. Consequently, NLP is regarded as a sub-domain of Artificial Intelligence since it requires intelligence on par with humans for the interpretation of language. As of now, we rely more on human-AI collaboration for executing NLP tasks than being solely dependent on computational acumen. The reason is, that several NLP processes still heavily depend on supervised learning approaches for high performance and need human intervention for understanding the NLP model's behavior, justify the predictions made by the model, and assess the uncertain or incorrect predictions [23].

5.2.2 Language Tasks in NLP

Depending on the purpose of the system or application, different NLP tasks can be used individually or in collaboration. Having an overview of the underlying NLP tasks can be useful while trying to solve a specific problem. This sub-section throws light on some of the most important natural language tasks and their role in the textual data processing.

5.2.2.1 Information Extraction

Information Extraction (IE) is one of the most important NLP processes and it is used for scraping the significant information from a large collection of related data. IE is a complex procedure and can be enhanced to extract information from structured as well as unstructured data sources [24]. This information is labeled and stored for further analysis under classes such as entity, object, temporal sequence, relations, types, and more. Fei et al. [25] made use of biomedical knowledge graphs on a big scale for biomedical IE to capture the contextualized concepts from available data. To identify, extract and timely arrange a mental health-related disorder, Zirikly et al. [26] used NLP to extract all the relevant information for diagnostic and treatment purposes.

5.2.2.2 Named Entity Recognition

Named Entity Recognition (NER) is a sub-task within IE and its main role is to extract proper nouns from a given structured or unstructured textual data [27]. It can be used to identify people, places, organizations, occupations, products, and other designators from the text. NER is a basic step that leads to several NLP tasks such as IE, question answering, machine translation, and even text summarization [28]. With a pre-trained BERT model, Li et al. [29] used clinical NER for the classification and identification of medical entities in Chinese medical records. Weber et al. [30] proposed a novel NER tagger called *HunFlair* for identifying biomedical entities.

5.2.2.3 Sentence Classification

Classification of text is another important NLP task that makes use of word embeddings and other representations of words to classify them separately. Bag of words models and word vector models are popular sentence classification approaches but nowadays deep learning and neural network especially Convolutional Neural networks (CNN) and Recurrent Neural networks (RNN) are producing more effective results [31]. Guo et al. [32] proposed a data augmentation method-based approach for the classification of sentences using word embeddings and sentence embeddings. To obtain a patient's past medical history from EHRs, Bagheri et al. [33] proposed enrichment by topic modeling for the task of sentence classification.

5.2.2.4 Document Classification

To maintain a large set of files and documents for archival, procedural, and management purposes document classification is necessary. Manual classification of documents can be a tedious process especially when big corporations and organizations are considered. To automate this process computer vision, deep learning classifiers, and NLP are used in combination to produce fast and accurate results [34]. Intending to evaluate the performance of Deep Neural Networks (DNN), Behera et al. [35] analyzed the different models used for biomedical document classification. Nadif et al. [36] made use of supervised and unsupervised text mining along with vector-based word embeddings for classifying documents.

5.2.2.5 Text Summarization

Going through an entire lengthy document to find significant information can be tiresome and wasteful. To accelerate this procedure automatic text summarization, both abstractive and extractive, can provide a gist of important subject matter from the document. Extractive summarization makes use of the frequency of word appearances to construct the summary, whereas abstractive summarization reconstructs the document information to focus on the central idea [37]. Belwal et al. [38] proposed a graph-based text summarization technique to rank sentences based on similarities with each other and the entire document. To improve the performance of the extractive summarization technique, Belwal et al. [39] further introduced another technique by integrating semantic measures and topic modeling with a vector space system.

5.2.2.6 Question Answering

Question answering systems have been gaining popularity due to the increase in the variety and usage of Artificial Intelligence empowered voice assistant services such as Apple's Siri, Amazon's Echo, and Google assistant. Besides the smartphone-based systems, many chatbot services and even IoT-based devices also make use of question answering either in text or speech mode. QA systems are used in combination with Information Retrieval (IR) to understand queries in human languages and deliver precise and appropriate responses [40]. Yin et al. [41] created a Spatio-temporal analysis and visualization tool using NLP-enabled-QA to give real-time instructions and queries. In another work, Meichanetzidis et al. [42] proposed a Quantum NLP model for constructing a grammar-aware QA model.

5.2.2.7   Machine Translation

Machine translation is a very practical NLP task that refers to the automatic translation of human languages using computers or machines. The most popular approaches for carrying out this task are rule-based, statistical, and neural machine translation [43]. The main focus during machine translation is retaining the actual meaning, grammar rules, and ideas behind the sentences where this translation is applied. Laskar et al. [44] demonstrated the use of neural machine translation with the help of two different models for translating English to the Hindi language. In another interesting scenario, Rahit et al. [45] proposed a machine learning system to convert natural language instructions to programming language codes. Table 5.1 gives a summary of the various language tasks in NLP and their recent advancements.

5.2.3   NLP Pipeline

Getting an overview of the language tasks in NLP gives an insight into how these tasks can not only be applied individually but also in combination with other tasks to solve a problem. Most NLP modules consist of four essential phases: *Data collection* – here the data that is to be processed is gathered from various sources be it text or speech, structured or unstructured. A lot of times if machine learning

Table 5.1 Comprehensive overview of NLP tasks and their recent applications

S. No.	NLP task	Purpose	Recent works	Unit of annotation
1.	Information extraction	Extracting task-relevant information from a large collection of data	Fei et al. [25] and Zirikly et al. [26]	Lexicon
2.	Named entity recognition	Identifying nouns from the data that can be tagged as an entity, event, person, and other classes	Li et al. [29] and Weber et al. [30]	Lexicon
3.	Sentence classification	Classifying sentences from data records to find a specific collection of information	Guo et al. [32] and Bagheri et al. [33]	Sentence
4.	Document classification	Classifying entire documents for better retrieval of information and reducing the amount of search	Behera et al. [35] and Nadif et al. [36]	Document
5.	Text summarization	Summarizing the content of large datasets into humanly comprehensible summaries	Belwal et al. [38] and Belwal et al. [39]	Document
6.	Question answering	Creating interactive dialogue to enable human-computer communication	Yin et al. [41] and Meichanetzidis et al. [42]	Document
7.	Machine translation	Translating one human language to another computationally	Laskar et al. [44] and Rahit et al. [45]	Sentence/ Document

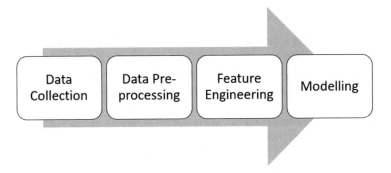

Fig. 5.2 NLP pipeline sequence

approaches are being used for carrying out a language task, the training corpus is also gathered or created in this phase. *Data preprocessing* – in this phase the collected data is processed to remove any noise, discrepancies, or inconsistencies to make it more uniform and accurate. Avoiding this phase may lead to complete failure of NLP application and heavily impact the performance of the system. *Feature engineering* – this is the process of obtaining required attributes from the preprocessed data and modifying them to fit the requisite NLP approach (rule-based, statistical, or neural network-based) of the given system. *Modeling* – this is the final step in which the kind of natural language task or combination of tasks required to tackle the problem is decided and modeled to fit the NLP pipeline. The final output is produced after the modeling phase and evaluated based on various performance metrics. The flow of the NLP pipeline is depicted in Fig. 5.2.

5.3   Healthcare 4.0

With the developments in ICT, we have witnessed the revolutionization of cities, industries, energy production, transportation, education, and healthcare services. Today we live in the era of Healthcare 4.0 where the healthcare industry is driven by numerous smart technologies such as IoT, Big Data Analytics (BDA), Artificial Intelligence, Machine Learning, Cloud computing, Virtual reality, Computer vision, and Augmented reality [46]. One common denominator in all these techniques is the presence and requirement of a large amount of data. Smart devices and embedded systems generate and collect an enormous quantity of medical data every single day. This data is stored via cloud architecture and processed using Machine Learning and Artificial Intelligence to conduct BDA to produce valuable insights. Manual data processing has taken a setback at present and given way to the large-scale automated processing of data for utilities such as NLP, computer vision, Virtual/ Augmented reality, and a lot more. The decision-making process is no longer solely human-reliant but is actively influenced by the knowledge provided via computational analytics.

5.3.1 Smart Data Analytics Using Machine Learning

Big data is defined by the 4 V's namely: Volume – the sheer amount of data being generated every day, Velocity – the high speed at which this data is being generated, Variety – the different formats in which this data is collected, and the Veracity – the inconsistencies and trustworthiness of the data that is collected. In the medical sector as well big data is generated around the clock through sensing and monitoring devices, patient logs, discharge summaries, clinical notes, prescriptions, reports, scans, and other paperwork. In this scenario, healthcare facilities have turned toward Smart Data Analytics techniques to increase the pace of decision-making systems. Most of the collected data consists of either redundant, inaccurate, irrelevant, or incomplete information which poses challenges for data analytics due to resource as well as time constraints [47]. Machine learning provides a respite from these impediments through various data mining, text mining, and data analytics methods. These machine learning-based smart data analytics techniques range from regression, classification, clustering, sequential pattern mining, NLP, temporal reasoning, anomaly detection, association rule mining, and a lot more [48]. These algorithms have contributed to the diagnostic and prognostic evaluation of patient reports [49] as well as the prediction of the mortality rate of patients based on their records [50]. The scope of machine learning algorithms in the healthcare industry has no bounds and new ways are discovered daily for optimizing the tedious processes and enhancing the decision-making processes in the medical field using this technology.

5.3.2 Medical Data Sources

The sources of data in the medical sector are diverse and it is imperative to pay attention to the quality of data as it leads to serious implications in healthcare analysis. Recognizing the source of data assists in devising more suitable strategies for dealing with the inconsistencies, inaccuracies, or redundancy of the data. The requirement of every data analytics model is different and even the pre-processing techniques of analysis also adapt accordingly. Being able to deal with data quality-related problems at the source itself reduces the amount of work that goes into processing low-quality data and prevents erroneous outcomes.

IoT devices and wearable gadgets produce a constant stream of timestamped data that is channeled via local networks and preferably stored using cloud systems. This data is generated at a very high speed and is also prone to latency issues [51] and inconsistent real-time streaming of sensor data. This kind of data requires high-speed processing with less computational overhead and minimum inaccuracies.

Monitoring devices with embedded systems [52] in healthcare facilities also produce constant data streams that are collected over time and are used in systems to alert patients and authorities instantaneously. The most prominent form of data in the medical sector to date is the manually generated or entered data, be it in electronic format or paper-based format. The admission forms and discharge summaries consist of valuable information about the state of a patient and the kind of diagnosis they have gone through. The clinical notes written by the doctors, nurses, or medical staff helps in understanding the treatment process of the administered patients. Reports in the form of descriptive, numeric, graphic, or visual data are used to gain insight into the present condition of a healthcare patient. Figure 5.3. shows the variants of medical data sources and the analytical processes applied on them.

A wide range of data sources are used for analytical procedures such as: checking the availability of resources, urgent patient care, diagnostic analysis, prognostic analysis, post-treatment risk analysis, and automatic prescriptions. Such kinds of analysis contribute to the formation of intelligent DSS. Zhan et al. [53] developed an assistive diagnosis and smart decision-making system that used sensor data for conducting an early diagnosis of NSCLC or Non-Small Cell Lung Cancer. To observe and effectively diagnose type-2 diabetes patients Abdel-Basset et al. [54] introduced an IoT and soft computing-based intelligent framework. In another work, Wadia et al. [66] implemented a NLP-based Clinical DSS for identifying post-colonoscopy patient cases that needed close follow-up and scheduling. Similarly, Shen et al. [68] proposed a CDSS to determine the order of sedation for outpatient endoscopy patients to rectify the sedation-type errors caused by human interventions. Table 5.2 gives a relative summary of the various CDSS used in medical healthcare system.

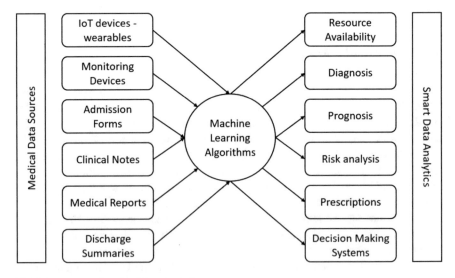

Fig. 5.3 Process of medical data analytics

Table 5.2 Overview of NLP based CDSS

S. No.	Work, year	Disease	Data source	Lexical unit
1.	Wadia et al. [66], 2017	Colon cancer care	Pathology reports	Lexicon
2.	Abdel-Basset et al. [54], 2019	Type-2 diabetes	IoT device observations	Lexicon
3.	Shen et al. [68], 2020	Outpatient endoscopy	EHR	Sentence
4.	Zhan et al. [53], 2021	Non-small cell lung cancer	Medical records	Document

5.4 Motivation

Clinical experts have always made use of medical data to conduct relevant studies but as healthcare becomes more accessible to the general public the amount of medical data is rapidly rising [8]. Manually conducting such analysis is becoming infeasible given the constraint of resources in healthcare facilities and time constrictions. This creates a need for automation of data processing and NLP provides the biggest solution to process language-based medical data. The popularity of Clinical-NLP has increased significantly in the last few years because of the introduction of several open-source NLP platforms such as Clinical Language Annotation, Modeling, and Processing Toolkit (CLAMP), clinical Text Analysis Knowledge Extraction System (cTAKES), SemEHR a tool for information extraction and general-purpose NLP tools like General Architecture For Text Engineering (GATE) [56]. An increase in the availability of electronic documents such as Electronic Health Records (EHRs) facilitates the easy structuring of data for obtaining diagnostic, semantic, and temporal information. Semantic analysis is an important aspect of CNLP for understanding the context behind words and making applications smarter and not just statistically driven.

Clinical text is different from regular language text since it consists of medical vocabulary and even telegraphic speech patterns [55]. The corpus used for training purposes is specialized to conduct domain-specific analysis and accurate tagging, annotation, and parsing of data. With further enrichment in the field of CNLP research and development, the prospects of improving smart healthcare systems are exceedingly bright. Healthcare 4.0 is a data-driven phase of the medical revolution and technology like NLP offers the chance to accelerate our vision of providing more efficient and accessible healthcare to people all around the world. Figure 5.4 depicts the current state of healthcare and its infrastructure in the top 5 most populated countries in the world as of 2022 [56, 57].

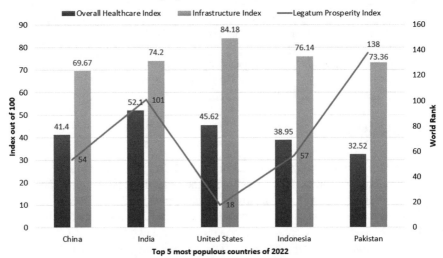

Fig. 5.4 Healthcare statistics of most populous countries of 2022

5.5 Smart Healthcare Applications of NLP

The possibilities of deploying NLP in Healthcare 4.0 are plenty especially since the commencement of the Precision Medicine Initiative (PMI) back in 2015. PMI helps in giving access to and connecting the large-scale medicinal and biological databases that consider individual variabilities in the form of genomics, proteomics, metabolomics, and mobile health technologies with powerful ways of analyzing these datasets using precision computing [58]. An initiative like this has encouraged researchers to find novel and creative ways for incorporating precision technologies using machine learning and NLP on textual data in every medical department. This section provides a deeper insight into the development of NLP models over time to suit the requirements of various clinical tasks. The applications of NLP in smart healthcare have been divided into 3 sub-sections: Healthcare Management and Administration, Assistive Care and Clinical DSS, and Disease Diagnosis, Prediction, and Treatment.

5.5.1 Healthcare Management and Administration

Overcrowding in emergency departments (ED) leads to crucial waste of time and to resolve this issue Zhang et al. [59] proposed a prediction model for ED admission using initial presentation data. In a similar work, Sterling et al. [60] used nursing triage documentation to predict final ED disposition. Risk analysis of a patient is a fundamental research field to estimate the severity, time of stay, chances of mortality, and cost of procedures. For predicting the severity of an Intensive Care Unit (ICU) admitted patient's ailment and the in-hospital mortality risk Jin et al. [61] proposed a neural network-based NLP model.

Nawab et al. [62] developed a system to extract insight from patient feedback forms for reimbursement-related studies. Discharge planning involves predicting the length of stay of a patent and Bacchi et al. [63] proposed a model to predict the general medical admission length of stay with NLP and deep learning. In 2021 Arnaud et al. [64] proposed a prediction model using triage notes to project medical specialties at hospitals in advance. To compare the performance of the Confusion Assessment Method for intensive care unit (CAM-ICU) and Natural Language Processing (NLP) diagnosed behavioral disturbance (NLP-Dx-BD) for delirium, Young et al. [65] developed an analytical system. Table 5.3 provides an overview of the NLP systems described in this section.

5.5.2 Assistive Care and Clinical DSS

Decision support systems are great assistance to healthcare professionals when making a dynamic prediction based on knowledge, cognition, and analytical skills. Wadia et al. [66] described a Clinical-DSS based on NLP designed for colon cancer care coordinators which can be used to monitor post-colonoscopy patients. In another work, Zikos et al. [67] introduced a CDSS reference model for designing contextually relevant DSS. Shen et al. [68] developed a CDSS for adopting a suitable endoscopy sedation strategy for patients dealing with outpatient endoscopy using NLP and consensus-derived logic. A Portuguese CDSS system was proposed by Leite-Moreira et al. [69] to promote the use of NLP in clinical decision-making.

Social or nursing robots in healthcare and assistive chatbots have a lot of use in the care, monitoring, and treatment procedures of patients. NLP provides a means of communication and understanding between these assistive care units and the end-users. Dino et al. [70] developed a Socially Assistive Robot, Ryan, for providing internet-delivered cognitive-behavioral therapy (CBT) to elderly depression patients. For assisting patients that don't know the workings of the outpatient department, Chen et al. [71] proposed an attention-based bidirectional long short-term memory (Att-BiLSTM) system for service robots. Christopherjames et al. [72] introduced a healthcare chatbot for assisting people with their medical concerns and corresponding treatments. In a similar work, Hassan et al. [73] presented a chatbot system for e-mental health care. Table 5.4 provides an overview of the NLP systems described in this section.

Table 5.3 A comprehensive review of NLP applications in Healthcare Management and Administration

S.No.	Author, year	Purpose	Data source	Methodology	Performance	Limitation
1.	Jin et al. [61], 2018	Mortality risk analysis of ICU patients	MIMIC-III data set	Word embeddings, LSTM, and multi-modal Neural Network	AU-ROC (%) – LSTM: 0.8531; Multi-modal: 0.8734	Extracted entities could not be normalized
2.	Zhang et al. [59], 2019	Prediction of admission to ED	NHMACS US ED dataset	LR and MLNN with NLP	AUC – LR: 0.824; MLNN: 0.823	Contextual information was ignored
3.	Sterling et al. [60], 2019	Predict ED disposition at admission	Data from 3 academically-affiliated EDs	Neural network regression-based NLP model	AOC – Bag-of-words: 0.737; para-vectors: 0.785	Prone to mis-classification and biases
4.	Nawab et al. [62], 2020	Analysis of patient experience	Press Ganey Database of patient feedback	POS tagging and sentiment analysis	Positive and negative feedback classification	Lacks entity linking and contextual understanding
5.	Bacchi et al. [63], 2020	Length of stay prediction	AMU of the Royal Adelaide Hospital	NLP and LR, CNN, ANN, Random Forrest	ANN had highest AUC: 0.75	Limited sample size
6.	Arnaud et al. [64], 2021	Medical specialties at hospital prediction	Amiens-Picardy University Hospital dataset	NLP, word embeddings, CNN and MLP	Accuracy: 0.68	Model sensitivity was low
7.	Young et al. [65], 2022	NLP-Dx-BD vs CAM-ICU to assess delirium in ICU patients	Nursing Progress notes	NLP-based behavioral diagnosis and CAM analysis	NLP-Dx-BD identifies more patients likely to receive antipsychotic medications	No evaluation was done by independent, psychiatrically trained clinician

Abbreviations: *MIMIC* Medical Information Mart for Intensive Care, *AU-ROC* Area Under the Receiver Operating Characteristic Curve, *NHAMCS* National Hospital Ambulatory Medical Care Survey, *LR* Logistic Regression, *MLNN* Multilayer Neural Network Models, *POS* Part of Speech, *AMU* Acute Medical Unit, *MLP* Multi-Layer Perceptron

5.5.3 *Disease Diagnosis, Prediction, and Treatment*

EHRs, clinical notes, reports, and discharge summaries contain a lot of information about a patient's medical history, present condition, statistics, clinical procedures or surgeries, prescriptions, and final comments. These data sources have been used in

Table 5.4 A comprehensive review of NLP applications in assistive care and clinical DSS

S.No.	Author, year	Purpose	Data source	Methodology	Result/Performance	Limitation
1.	Wadia et al. [66], 2017	CDSS for post-colonoscopy patients	VA Connecticut Health Care System pathology reports	Structured Query Language (SQL) function and text categorization using NLP	Accuracy: 0.985	Does not have a web-based user interface
2.	Zikos et al. [67], 2018	CDSS reference model	External data providers	Conceptual development of CDSS using NLP	Generalized CDSS-RM framework	Infrastructural aspects of health facilities not considered
3.	Dino et al. [70], 2019	CBT for older adults with depression	Dialogue training on human language data	AIML–based dialogue manager system using NLP	Positive survey responses	Small-sample size and short research period
4.	Shen et al. [68], 2020	CDSS for outpatient endoscopy	EHR from Brigham and Women's hospital	SQL, NLP using heuristic check and validation	Sedation-type order error rate decreased to 0.037%	Relied heavily on historical endoscopy data
5.	Chen et al. [71], 2020	Service robot for outpatient department	Dialogue data from Taiwan E Hospital	NLP, TF–IDF for text processing and Att-BiLSTM	Accuracy: 0.96; Precision: 0.96	The dialogue system is not operative for other departments
6.	Christopherjames et al. [72], 2021	Healthcare chatbot	Chatbot trained with Google assistant	NLP and ML algorithms by Dialogflow	Real-time application	Does not provide health parameters to the user
7.	Hassan et al. [73], 2021	e-Mental health chatbot	MBTI dataset	NLTK, LSTM and computer vision	A web-based application	Dataset requires further expansion
8.	Leite-Moreira et al. [69], 2022	Portuguese CDSS	EHR: Clinical notes, discharge summaries, test results	Transition-based parser, MATPD, and SAACE	Favorable and rapid predictions	Semantic contextualization is lacking

Abbreviations: *TF–IDF* Term Frequency-Inverse Document Frequency, *NLTK* Natural Language Toolkit

CNLP to make predictions about diseases and risks related to them, the prospective diagnosis after analyzing the present condition, suggesting treatments and medication, forecasting post-operative complications, and finding patterns in clinical data. More importantly, chronic diseases benefit the most from smart analysis of data since they have a longitudinal nature and consist of plenty of temporal information and trends that might be overlooked when conducting clinical analysis [74]. This section reviews various CNLP models that were used for the diagnosis, prediction, and treatment of the following medical conditions: Mental healthcare, Cancer research, Circulatory system diseases, and miscellaneous diseases.

5.5.3.1 Mental Healthcare

Early prediction of mental health-related illnesses at the time of their onset can help doctors and physicians devise better treatments at an early stage itself. Jackson et al. [75] used NLP to construct a language model that can detect the symptoms of severe mental illness (SMI) from clinical text. Detecting patients at risk of self-harm can be done using NLP of case notes in EHR, as demonstrated in a work by Van Le et al. [76]. In another work, Mulyana et al. [77] proposed case-based reasoning (CBR) computer system to diagnose medical illnesses from health records using NLP to compensate for the lack of professional psychologists. An Internet-Delivered Psychological Treatment (IDPT) system was developed with the help of patient-authored clinical data and NLP [78]. Ridgway et al. [79] introduced an NLP model to detect mental disorders or indicators of substance abuse among HV patients.

5.5.3.2 Cancer Research

Research in the field of cancer has been a very demanding and progressive field for decades including studies related to pathology, radiology reports, narrative reports, histopathology, information extraction from clinical notes, and more. Karunakaran et al. [80] applied NLP to find lung cancer patients from CT-scan notes created by radiologists using Geisinger's Close-the-Loop clinical program. In another approach, Si et al. [81] proposed an NLP model for extracting information about cancer diagnosis, cancer therapeutic procedure, and tumor description from EHR. To determine the onset of familial breast cancer and colorectal cancer from Family health history (FHH), Mowery et al. [82] made use of NLP classifiers. Alawad et al. [83] introduced a deep learning NLP-based privacy-preserving transfer learning model for cancer-related information from pathology documents. Deshmukh et al. [84] used NLP for extracting vital cancer information at the prognostic stage itself from breast cancer medical records. To quantify the privacy of deep learning models for IE from cancer pathology reports Yoon et al. [85] developed a vocabulary selection NLP method.

5.5.3.3 Circulatory System Disease

Circulatory system disorders are related to heart failure, cardiology, arterial diseases, cardiovascular disorders, and risk prediction for the onset of such diseases. To investigate how cardiovascular disease operates in HIV patients, Patterson et al. [86] developed an NLP system to analyze echocardiogram reports. Afzal et al. [87] introduced an algorithm for identifying Critical limb ischemia (CLI) cases in narrative clinical notes of peripheral artery disease (PAD) patients. For classifying patients with heart disease and predicting various cardiovascular disorders, Thaiparnit et al. [88] proposed a technique for clinical data extraction. Bagheri et al. [89] designed a system for cardiovascular risk prediction using multimodal BiLSTM on structured EHR documents. In another work, Sammani et al. [90] aimed to create a model for automated classification of reliable ICD-10 codes using free medical text available in the cardiology department. Zaman et al. [91] created a framework using semi-supervised NLP for automated diagnosis categorization of Cardiovascular MRI from clinical text reports.

5.5.3.4 Miscellaneous

The prospects of applying NLP in smart healthcare prediction, diagnosis, and prognosis are immense and go beyond the categorizations provided in the above sections. Weng et al. [92] made use of NLP for the classification of medical notes into sub-domains using a machine-learning-based model. For bridging the gap between clinical experts and NLP, Trivedi et al. [92] proposed an interactive NLP tool called NLPReViz. Chen et al. [93] used EHR clinical notes to automatically procure patients' geriatric syndromes from the medical text. Septic shocks are a major health concern, yet often overlooked by smart healthcare experts. Using a gradient boosting algorithm on clinical notes, Liu et al. [94] computed the time-impending risk of developing septic shocks. Oliwa et al. [95] developed a predictive model to identify symptoms of lost to follow-up (LTFU) HIV patients from unstructured notes. For detecting adverse drug events (ADEs), Chen et al. [96] introduced a knowledge-based NLP system and relation identifier using an attention-based BiLSTM network. An NLP tool called COVID-19 SignSym for extracting Covid-19 symptoms from free text EHRs was created by Wang et al. [97] using CLAMP. In a different work Song et al. [98] used NLP for the automatic extraction of medical data from unstructured esophagogastroduodenoscopy (EGD) reports. Table 5.5 provides an overview of the various NLP models discussed in the above section in a detailed yet precise manner.

Table 5.5 A comprehensive review of NLP applications in healthcare diagnosis, prediction, treatment

Cate-gory	Author, year	Purpose	Data source	Methodology	Result/Performance	Limitation
Mental health	Jackson et al. [75], 2017	Detecting SMI from clinical text	CRIS data resources and EHR from hospitals	Information extraction, annotation, and classification	Median F1 score: 0.88 for 46 SMI symptoms	Underestimation of symptoms occurred
	Van Le et al. [76], 2018	Risk analysis of self-harm-prone patients	EHR of de-identified forensic inpatient notes	Bagging, J48, Jrip, Logistic Model Trees (LMT), LR, and SVM	LMT and SVM algorithm were best	Synonyms and language variants were not incorporated
	Mulyana et al. [77], 2019	CBR system for mental disorders	Medical records	NLP and CBR processing	Pattern matching was successful	Limited dataset and scope
	Mukhiya et al. [78], 2020	IDPT system to diagnose depression	PHQ-9 questionnaire	Depression2Vec for word embedding and cosine similarity	Performance is comparable to WordNet	Evaluation is done on a human-annotated dataset
	Ridgway et al. [79], 2021	Mental illness or substance abuse in HIV patients	Structured and unstructured EMR data	CoreNLP and NegEx for NLP	PPV of 98% and NPV of 98%	Cases of false detection are present

Cate-gory	Author, year	Purpose	Data source	Methodology	Result/Performance	Limitation
Cancer research	Karunakaran et al. [80], 2017	Identifying lung cancer patients from radiology reports	Scanned radiology reports	Hadoop for data storage, cTAKES PoS tagging, NER	F1-score: 0.908; precision: 0.873	Study on a specific use case and has not been generalized
	Si et al. [81], 2018	Cancer-related information extraction	Clinical notes from UT physicians data warehouse	Bi-LSTM CRF networks and word embeddings	F1: Cancer diagnosis – 93.70; therapy procedure: 96.33	Multi-step evaluation not conducted
	Mowery et al. [82], 2019	Extract breast and colorectal cancer from FHH	EHR from the university of Utah health enterprise	Frequency pattern and NLP classifiers	NLP classifier outperformed; precision: 96%	Study based on a single academic healthcare network
	Alawad et al. [83], 2020	Cancer IE from pathology documents	Text corpora of cancer pathology reports	Multitask learning CNN NLP algorithm	F1-score: Micro – 0.823; Macro - 0.580	Performance is not as good in low prevalence class labels
	Deshmukh et al. [84], 2021	Prognostic stage of breast cancer prediction	Pathological and clinical reports	NLP, Decision tree, K-fold cross-validation	Prediction accuracy: Urban – 0.92; rural – 0.82	Small-sample size to quantify the privacy data
	Yoon et al. [85], 2022	Securing patients' information while IE	Cancer pathology reports	Multitask CNN and membership inference attacks	Lower privacy vulnerability and good IE performance	The study requires multiple data providers

(continued)

Table 5.5 (continued)

Cate-gory	Author, year	Purpose	Data source	Methodology	Result/Performance	Limitation
Circulatory system disease	Patterson et al. [86], 2017	Cardiovascular disease identification in HIV patients	General clinic notes, echo-cardiogram, and radiology reports	Apache UIMA AS) framework for NLP	F1-scores: 0.872, 0.844, and 0.877 for each report type	Poor performance for rare measures
	Afzal et al. [87], 2018	Identifying CLI cases among PAD patients	Clinical notes from Mayo clinical data warehouse	CLI-NLP algorithm for patient classification	CLI-NLP PPV: 0.96; F1-score: 0.90	Data from only a single medical center was used
	Thaiparnit et al. [88], 2019	Extraction of data for cardio-disease	University of California Irvine dataset	Vertical Hoeffding decision tree algorithm	Accuracy: 0.8543;	The system can be made more accurate
	Bagheri et al. [89], 2020	Cardiovascular risk prediction	EHR from SMART study	Multimodal BiLSTM for NLP	AUC: 0.847; misclassification rate: 0.143	Not integrated with clinical DSS
	Sammani et al. [90], 2021	Automated classification of reliable ICD-10 codes	Discharge letters from cardiology patients	Bidirectional Gated Recurrent Unit Neural Network	F1 scores: 0.76–0.99 for 3-char codes; 0.87–0.98 for 4-char codes	Required manual assessment for discrepancies in performance
	Zaman et al. [91], 2022	Automatic Diagnosis Labeling of MRI reports	Cardiac MRI reports	BERT, rule-based model, and SVM model	BERT model performed best; F1-score: 0.86	The model was not fully accurate across all categories

Cate-gory	Author, year	Purpose	Data source	Methodology	Result/Performance	Limitation
Miscellaneous	Weng et al. [92], 2017	Sub-domain classification	MGH, and iDASH data repository	CRNN with neural word embedding and TF-IDF, cTAKES	CRNN AUC: iDASH – 0.975; MGH – 0.991	cTAKES may not be the most suitable NLP tool here
	Trivedi et al. [92], 2018	Interactive NLP tool for binary concept	Colonoscopy reports	NLPReViz using bag-of-words and SVM	F1 scores: Between 0.78 and 0.91	Integration with other NLP tools not explored
	Chen et al. [93], 2019	Determining patients with geriatric syndromes	Anonymized EHR data multispecialty organization	cTAKES and CRF	Macro F1-score: 0.834; Micro F1-score: 0.851	Annotations were slightly inconsistent
	Liu et al. [94], 2019	Predicting septic-shock onset patients	MIMIC-III clinical database	text2vec, GloVe, and XGBoost	AUC: 0.92; PPV: 0.49; early warning: 7 hrs	Better labels for annotations are available
	Oliwa et al. [95], 2020	Classify LTFU and retained HIV patients	Outpatient HIV care clinical notes	Bag-of-words, TF-IDF, ten-fold cross-validation	Weighted F1-score mean of 0.912	An automatic ontology match was not used
	Chen et al. [96], 2020	ADEs detection from clinical text	MIMIC-III Clinical care database	Knowledge-based NLP system and BiLSTM	F-measure of 0.9442	Sense ambiguity, relation classifier matching error
	Wang et al. [97], 2021	Extracting covid-19 symptoms	Notes from MIMIC-III, UTP, KUMC, Johns Hopkins	COVID-19 SignSym, deep learning, pattern-based rules	F1-measure: 0.972; recall: 0.992	Not generalized, more extraction of information is possible
	Song et al. [98], 2022	Gastric disease detection	EGD reports	IE and concept summarization	F1 score: 0.967; PPV: 0.972	Not adaptable with document formats

Abbreviation: *CRIS* Clinical Record Interactive Search, *PPV* Positive Predictive Value, *NPV* Negative Predictive Value, *UIMA-AS* Unstructured Information Management Architecture Asynchronous Scaleout, *SMART* Second Manifestations of Arterial Disease Study, *BERT* Bidirectional Encoder Representations from Transformers, *MRI* Magnetic Resonance Imaging, *iDASH* Integrating Data for Analysis, Anonymization, and Sharing, *CRF* Conditional Random Fields, *GloVe* Global Vectors for Word Representation, *CLAMP* Clinical Language Annotation, Modeling, and Processing

5.6 Conclusion

The healthcare domain is a challenging technical field, especially since the flooding of the enormous amount of data started due to ICT advancements. The twenty-first century is regarded as the century of data which is quite evident from how much information is being generated every single day. In the field of medicine and healthcare, language-based data is present from the admission into a hospital to the discharge of a patient while also including the monitoring data, reports, diagnosis, and clinical notes. There is a lot of valuable information in this data that can be extracted for progressive healthcare research. Manually doing data analytics is not a feasible option due to time and resource restraints and hence AI technologies like NLP have taken the forefront. This paper begins by throwing light on the concept of NLP and the tasks used to make an NLP pipeline. Next, the features of Healthcare 4.0 were explored along with the concept of smart data analytics. Then the paper devolves into the details of specific NLP models and systems that have been created to assist smart healthcare. This is a study that provides an impression of present NLP technologies in Healthcare 4.0 and it intends to serve as a basis for understanding the landscape of smart healthcare systems and their applications in the future as well.

References

1. Quasim, M. T., Khan, M. A., Algarni, F., & Alshahrani, M. M. (2021). Fundamentals of smart cities. In *Smart cities: A data analytics perspective* (pp. 3–16). Springer.
2. Bajaj, D., Bhushan, B., & Yadav, D. (2021). Healthcare 4.0: An insight of architecture, security requirements, pillars and applications. *Biomedical Data Mining for Information Retrieval*, 103–129. https://doi.org/10.1002/9781119711278.ch4
3. Shenkar, O., Liang, G., & Shenkar, R. (2022). The last frontier of globalization: Trade and foreign direct investment in healthcare. *Journal of International Business Studies, 53*(2), 362–374.
4. Aceto, G., Persico, V., & Pescapé, A. (2018). The role of information and communication technologies in healthcare: Taxonomies, perspectives, and challenges. *Journal of Network and Computer Applications, 107*, 125–154.
5. Bahalul Haque, A. K. M., Bhushan, B., Nawar, A., Talha, K. R., & Ayesha, S. J. (2022). Attacks and countermeasures in IoT based smart healthcare applications. In V. E. Balas, V. K. Solanki, & R. Kumar (Eds.), *Recent advances in Internet of Things and machine learning. Intelligent systems reference library* (Vol. 215). Springer. https://doi.org/10.1007/978-3-030-90119-6_6
6. Sharma, N., Kaushik, I., Bhushan, B., Gautam, S., & Khamparia, A. (2020). Applicability of WSN and biometric models in the field of healthcare. In *Deep learning strategies for security enhancement in wireless sensor networks advances in information security, privacy, and ethics* (pp. 304–329). https://doi.org/10.4018/978-1-7998-5068-7.ch016
7. Wen, A., Fu, S., Moon, S., El Wazir, M., Rosenbaum, A., Kaggal, V. C., et al. (2019). Desiderata for delivering NLP to accelerate healthcare AI advancement and a Mayo Clinic NLP-as-a-service implementation. *NPJ Digital Medicine, 2*(1), 1–7.
8. Sheikhalishahi, S., Miotto, R., Dudley, J. T., Lavelli, A., Rinaldi, F., & Osmani, V. (2019). Natural language processing of clinical notes on chronic diseases: A systematic review. *JMIR Medical Informatics, 7*(2), e12239.

9. Klang, E., Kummer, B. R., Dangayach, N. S., Zhong, A., Kia, M. A., Timsina, P., et al. (2021). Predicting adult neuroscience intensive care unit admission from emergency department triage using a retrospective, tabular-free text machine learning approach. *Scientific Reports, 11*(1), 1–9.

10. Mahbub, M., Srinivasan, S., Danciu, I., Peluso, A., Begoli, E., Tamang, S., & Peterson, G. D. (2022). Unstructured clinical notes within the 24 hours since admission predict short, mid & long-term mortality in adult ICU patients. *PLoS One, 17*(1), e0262182.

11. Abokhzam, A. A., Gupta, N. K., & Bose, D. K. (2021). Efficient diabetes mellitus prediction with grid based random forest classifier in association with natural language processing. *International Journal of Speech Technology, 24*(3), 601–614.

12. Weissler, E. H., Zhang, J., Lippmann, S., Rusincovitch, S., Henao, R., & Jones, W. S. (2020). Use of natural language processing to improve identification of patients with peripheral artery disease. *Circulation: Cardiovascular Interventions, 13*(10), e009447.

13. Sohn, S., Wi, C. I., Wu, S. T., Liu, H., Ryu, E., Krusemark, E., et al. (2018). Ascertainment of asthma prognosis using natural language processing from electronic medical records. *Journal of Allergy and Clinical Immunology, 141*(6), 2292–2294.

14. Hossain, M. T., Talukder, M. A. R., & Jahan, N. (2022). Depression prognosis using natural language processing and machine learning from social media status. *International Journal of Electrical and Computer Engineering, 12*(3), 2847.

15. Mahatpure, J., Motwani, M., & Shukla, P. K. (2019). An electronic prescription system powered by speech recognition, natural language processing and blockchain technology. *International Journal of Science & Technology Research (IJSTR), 8*(08), 1454–1462.

16. Dhanalakshmi, T. S., & Meleet, M. (2020, June). Predicting Clinical Re-admission using Discharge Summaries (PCRUDS). In *2020 5th International Conference on Communication and Electronics Systems (ICCES)* (pp. 772–777). IEEE.

17. Muhlestein, W. E., Monsour, M. A., Friedman, G. N., Zinzuwadia, A., Zachariah, M. A., Coumans, J. V., et al. (2021). Predicting discharge disposition following meningioma resection using a multi-institutional natural language processing model. *Neurosurgery, 88*(4), 838–845.

18. Bharti, U., Bajaj, D., Batra, H., Lalit, S., Lalit, S., & Gangwani, A. (2020, June). Medbot: Conversational artificial intelligence powered chatbot for delivering tele-health after covid-19. In *2020 5th International Conference on Communication and Electronics Systems (ICCES)* (pp. 870–875). IEEE.

19. Laxmi, P., Gupta, D., Gopalapillai, R., Amudha, J., & Sharma, K. (2021). A Scalable multi-disease modeled CDSS based on Bayesian network approach for commonly occurring diseases with a NLP-based GUI. In *Intelligent systems, technologies and applications* (pp. 161–171). Springer.

20. Khurana, D., Koli, A., Khatter, K., & Singh, S. (2017). Natural language processing: State of the art, current trends and challenges. *arXiv preprint arXiv:1708.05148.*

21. Lavanya, P. M., & Sasikala, E. (2021, May). Deep learning techniques on text classification using Natural language processing (NLP) in social healthcare network: A comprehensive survey. In *2021 3rd International Conference on Signal Processing and Communication (ICPSC)* (pp. 603–609). IEEE.

22. Liu, D., Li, Y., & Thomas, M. A. (2017, January). A roadmap for natural language processing research in information systems. In *proceedings of the 50th Hawaii international conference on system sciences*.

23. Lertvittayakumjorn, P. (2021). *Explainable NLP for human-AI collaboration*.

24. Adnan, K., & Akbar, R. (2019). An analytical study of information extraction from unstructured and multidimensional big data. *Journal of Big Data, 6*(1), 1–38.

25. Fei, H., Ren, Y., Zhang, Y., Ji, D., & Liang, X. (2021). Enriching contextualized language model from knowledge graph for biomedical information extraction. *Briefings in Bioinformatics, 22*(3), bbaa110.

26. Zirikly, A., Desmet, B., Newman-Griffis, D., Marfeo, E. E., McDonough, C., Goldman, H., & Chan, L. (2022). Information extraction framework for disability determination using a mental functioning use-case. *JMIR Medical Informatics, 10*(3), e32245.
27. Liu, X., Chen, H., & Xia, W. (2022). Overview of named entity recognition. *Journal of Contemporary Educational Research, 6*(5), 65–68.
28. Li, J., Sun, A., Han, J., & Li, C. (2020). A survey on deep learning for named entity recognition. *IEEE Transactions on Knowledge and Data Engineering, 34*(1), 50–70.
29. Li, X., Zhang, H., & Zhou, X. H. (2020). Chinese clinical named entity recognition with variant neural structures based on BERT methods. *Journal of Biomedical Informatics, 107*, 103422.
30. Weber, L., Sänger, M., Münchmeyer, J., Habibi, M., Leser, U., & Akbik, A. (2021). HunFlair: An easy-to-use tool for state-of-the-art biomedical named entity recognition. *Bioinformatics, 37*(17), 2792–2794.
31. Hassan, A., & Mahmood, A. (2018). Convolutional recurrent deep learning model for sentence classification. *Ieee Access, 6*, 13949–13957.
32. Guo, H., Mao, Y., & Zhang, R. (2019). Augmenting data with mixup for sentence classification: An empirical study. *arXiv preprint arXiv:1905.08941*.
33. Bagheri, A., Sammani, A., van der Heijden, P. G., Asselbergs, F. W., & Oberski, D. L. (2020). ETM: Enrichment by topic modeling for automated clinical sentence classification to detect patients' disease history. *Journal of Intelligent Information Systems, 55*(2), 329–349.
34. Audebert, N., Herold, C., Slimani, K., & Vidal, C. (2019, September). Multimodal deep networks for text and image-based document classification. In *Joint European conference on machine learning and knowledge discovery in databases* (pp. 427–443). Springer.
35. Behera, B., Kumaravelan, G., & Kumar, P. (2019, December). Performance evaluation of deep learning algorithms in biomedical document classification. In *2019 11th International Conference on Advanced Computing (ICoAC)* (pp. 220–224). IEEE.
36. Nadif, M., & Role, F. (2021). Unsupervised and self-supervised deep learning approaches for biomedical text mining. *Briefings in Bioinformatics, 22*(2), 1592–1603.
37. Yadav, D., Lalit, N., Kaushik, R., Singh, Y., Yadav, A. K., Bhadane, K. V., ... & Khan, B. (2022). Qualitative analysis of text summarization techniques and its applications in health domain. *Computational Intelligence and Neuroscience, Article ID 3411881* (pp. 1-14).
38. Belwal, R. C., Rai, S., & Gupta, A. (2021). A new graph-based extractive text summarization using keywords or topic modeling. *Journal of Ambient Intelligence and Humanized Computing, 12*(10), 8975–8990.
39. Belwal, R. C., Rai, S., & Gupta, A. (2021). Text summarization using topic-based vector space model and semantic measure. *Information Processing & Management, 58*(3), 102536.
40. Soares, M. A. C., & Parreiras, F. S. (2020). A literature review on question answering techniques, paradigms and systems. *Journal of King Saud University-Computer and Information Sciences, 32*(6), 635–646.
41. Yin, Z., Zhang, C., Goldberg, D. W., & Prasad, S. (2019, March). An NLP-based question answering framework for spatio-temporal analysis and visualization. In *Proceedings of the 2019 2nd international conference on geoinformatics and data analysis* (pp. 61–65).
42. Meichanetzidis, K., Toumi, A., de Felice, G., & Coecke, B. (2020). Grammar-aware question-answering on quantum computers. *arXiv preprint arXiv:2012.03756*.
43. Yang, S., Wang, Y., & Chu, X. (2020). A survey of deep learning techniques for neural machine translation. *arXiv preprint arXiv:2002.07526*.
44. Laskar, S. R., Dutta, A., Pakray, P., & Bandyopadhyay, S. (2019, December). Neural machine translation: English to Hindi. In *2019 IEEE conference on information and communication technology* (pp. 1–6). IEEE.
45. Rahit, K. M., Nabil, R. H., & Huq, M. H. (2019, October). Machine translation from natural language to code using long-short term memory. In *Proceedings of the future technologies conference* (pp. 56–63). Springer.

46. Kumar, A., Krishnamurthi, R., Nayyar, A., Sharma, K., Grover, V., & Hossain, E. (2020). A novel smart healthcare design, simulation, and implementation using healthcare 4.0 processes. *IEEE Access, 8,* 118433–118471.
47. Li, W., Chai, Y., Khan, F., Jan, S. R. U., Verma, S., Menon, V. G., & Li, X. (2021). A comprehensive survey on machine learning-based big data analytics for IoT-enabled smart healthcare system. *Mobile Networks and Applications, 26*(1), 234–252.
48. Islam, M. S., Hasan, M. M., Wang, X., Germack, H. D., & Noor-E-Alam, M. (2018, May). A systematic review on healthcare analytics: Application and theoretical perspective of data mining. In *Healthcare* (Vol. 6, No. 2, p. 54). MDPI.
49. Fleuren, L. M., Klausch, T. L., Zwager, C. L., Schoonmade, L. J., Guo, T., Roggeveen, L. F., et al. (2020). Machine learning for the prediction of sepsis: A systematic review and meta-analysis of diagnostic test accuracy. *Intensive Care Medicine, 46*(3), 383–400.
50. Thorsen-Meyer, H. C., Nielsen, A. B., Nielsen, A. P., Kaas-Hansen, B. S., Toft, P., Schierbeck, J., et al. (2020). Dynamic and explainable machine learning prediction of mortality in patients in the intensive care unit: A retrospective study of high-frequency data in electronic patient records. *The Lancet Digital Health, 2*(4), e179–e191.
51. Azari, A., Stefanović, Č., Popovski, P., & Cavdar, C. (2019). On the latency-energy performance of NB-IoT systems in providing wide-area IoT connectivity. *IEEE Transactions on Green Communications and Networking, 4*(1), 57–68.
52. Khan, S. F. (2017, March). Health care monitoring system in Internet of Things (IoT) by using RFID. In *2017 6th International conference on industrial technology and management (ICITM)* (pp. 198–204). IEEE.
53. Zhan, X., Long, H., Gou, F., Duan, X., Kong, G., & Wu, J. (2021). A convolutional neural network-based intelligent medical system with sensors for assistive diagnosis and decision-making in non-small cell lung cancer. *Sensors, 21*(23), 7996.
54. Abdel-Basset, M., Manogaran, G., Gamal, A., & Chang, V. (2019). A novel intelligent medical decision support model based on soft computing and IoT. *IEEE Internet of Things Journal, 7*(5), 4160–4170.
55. Velupillai, S., Mowery, D., South, B. R., Kvist, M., & Dalianis, H. (2015). Recent advances in clinical natural language processing in support of semantic analysis. *Yearbook of Medical Informatics, 24*(01), 183–193.
56. Mittal, Y. K., Paul, V. K., Rostami, A., Riley, M., & Sawhney, A. (2020). Delay factors in construction of healthcare infrastructure projects: A comparison amongst developing countries. *Asian Journal of Civil Engineering, 21*(4), 649–661.
57. CEOWORLD Magazine. (2021, April 27). *Revealed: Countries with the best health care systems, 2021.* https://ceoworld.biz/2021/04/27/revealed-countries-with-the-best-health-care-systems-2021/
58. Collins, F. S., & Varmus, H. (2015). A new initiative on precision medicine. *New England Journal of Medicine, 372*(9), 793–795.
59. Zhang, X., Kim, J., Patzer, R. E., Pitts, S. R., Patzer, A., & Schrager, J. D. (2017). Prediction of emergency department hospital admission based on natural language processing and neural networks. *Methods of Information in Medicine, 56*(05), 377–389.
60. Sterling, N. W., Patzer, R. E., Di, M., & Schrager, J. D. (2019). Prediction of emergency department patient disposition based on natural language processing of triage notes. *International Journal of Medical Informatics, 129,* 184–188.
61. Jin, M., Bahadori, M. T., Colak, A., Bhatia, P., Celikkaya, B., Bhakta, R., ... & Kass-hout, T. (2018). Improving hospital mortality prediction with medical named entities and multimodal learning. *arXiv preprint arXiv:1811.12276.*
62. Nawab, K., Ramsey, G., & Schreiber, R. (2020). Natural language processing to extract meaningful information from patient experience feedback. *Applied Clinical Informatics, 11*(02), 242–252.

63. Bacchi, S., Gluck, S., Tan, Y., Chim, I., Cheng, J., Gilbert, T., et al. (2020). Prediction of general medical admission length of stay with natural language processing and deep learning: A pilot study. *Internal and Emergency Medicine, 15*(6), 989–995.

64. Arnaud, É., Elbattah, M., Gignon, M., & Dequen, G. (2021, August). NLP-based prediction of medical specialties at hospital admission using triage notes. In *2021 IEEE 9th International Conference on Healthcare Informatics (ICHI)* (pp. 548–553). IEEE.

65. Young, M., Holmes, N., Kishore, K., Marhoon, N., Amjad, S., Serpa-Neto, A., & Bellomo, R. (2022). Natural language processing diagnosed behavioral disturbance vs confusion assessment method for the intensive care unit: Prevalence, patient characteristics, overlap, and association with treatment and outcome. *Intensive Care Medicine, 48*(5), 559–569.

66. Wadia, R., Shifman, M., Levin, F. L., Marenco, L., Brandt, C. A., Cheung, K. H., et al. (2017). A clinical decision support system for monitoring post-colonoscopy patient follow-up and scheduling. *AMIA Summits on Translational Science Proceedings, 2017*, 295.

67. Zikos, D., & DeLellis, N. (2018). CDSS-RM: A clinical decision support system reference model. *BMC Medical Research Methodology, 18*(1), 1–14.

68. Shen, L., Wright, A., Lee, L. S., Jajoo, K., Nayor, J., & Landman, A. (2021). Clinical decision support system, using expert consensus-derived logic and natural language processing, decreased sedation-type order errors for patients undergoing endoscopy. *Journal of the American Medical Informatics Association, 28*(1), 95–103.

69. Leite-Moreira, A., Mendes, A., Pedrosa, A., Rocha-Sousa, A., Azevedo, A., Amaral-Gomes, A., ... & Pimenta, T. (2022). An NLP solution to foster the use of information in electronic health records for efficiency in decision-making in hospital care. *arXiv preprint arXiv:2202.12159*.

70. Dino, F., Zandie, R., Abdollahi, H., Schoeder, S., & Mahoor, M. H. (2019, November). Delivering cognitive behavioral therapy using a conversational social robot. In *2019 IEEE/RSJ International Conference on Intelligent Robots and Systems (IROS)* (pp. 2089–2095). IEEE.

71. Chen, C. W., Tseng, S. P., Kuan, T. W., & Wang, J. F. (2020). Outpatient text classification using attention-based bidirectional LSTM for robot-assisted servicing in hospital. *Information, 11*(2), 106.

72. Christopherjames, J. E., Saravanan, M., Thiyam, D. B., Sahib, M. Y. B., Ganapathi, M. V., & Milton, A. (2021, August). Natural language processing based human assistive health conversational agent for multi-users. In *2021 Second International Conference on Electronics and Sustainable Communication Systems (ICESC)* (pp. 1414–1420). IEEE.

73. Hassan, A., Ali, M. D., Ahammed, R., Bourouis, S., & Khan, M. M. (2021). Development of NLP-integrated intelligent web system for E-mental health. In *Computational and mathematical methods in medicine*.

74. Sheikhalishahi, S., Miotto, R., Dudley, J. T., Lavelli, A., Rinaldi, F., & Osmani, V. (2019). Natural language processing of clinical notes on chronic diseases: Systematic review. *JMIR Medical Informatics, 7*(2), e12239.

75. Jackson, R. G., Patel, R., Jayatilleke, N., Kolliakou, A., Ball, M., Gorrell, G., et al. (2017). Natural language processing to extract symptoms of severe mental illness from clinical text: The clinical record interactive search comprehensive data extraction (CRIS-CODE) project. *BMJ Open, 7*(1), e012012.

76. Van Le, D., Montgomery, J., Kirkby, K. C., & Scanlan, J. (2018). Risk prediction using natural language processing of electronic mental health records in an inpatient forensic psychiatry setting. *Journal of Biomedical Informatics, 86*, 49–58.

77. Mulyana, S., Hartati, S., & Wardoyo, R. (2019, October). A processing model using natural language processing (nlp) for narrative text of medical record for producing symptoms of mental disorders. In *2019 Fourth International Conference on Informatics and Computing (ICIC)* (pp. 1–6). IEEE.

78. Mukhiya, S. K., Ahmed, U., Rabbi, F., Pun, K. I., & Lamo, Y. (2020, July). Adaptation of IDPT system based on patient-authored text data using NLP. In *2020 IEEE 33rd international symposium on Computer-Based Medical Systems (CBMS)* (pp. 226–232). IEEE.

79. Ridgway, J. P., Uvin, A., Schmitt, J., Oliwa, T., Almirol, E., Devlin, S., & Schneider, J. (2021). Natural language processing of clinical notes to identify mental illness and substance use among people living with HIV: Retrospective cohort study. *JMIR Medical Informatics, 9*(3), e23456.
80. Karunakaran, B., Misra, D., Marshall, K., Mathrawala, D., & Kethireddy, S. (2017, December). Closing the loop—Finding lung cancer patients using NLP. In *2017 IEEE international conference on big data (big data)* (pp. 2452–2461). IEEE.
81. Si, Y., & Roberts, K. (2018). A frame-based NLP system for cancer-related information extraction. In *AMIA annual symposium proceedings* (Vol. 2018, p. 1524). American Medical Informatics Association.
82. Mowery, D. L., Kawamoto, K., Bradshaw, R., Kohlmann, W., Schiffman, J. D., Weir, C., et al. (2019). Determining onset for familial breast and colorectal cancer from family history comments in the electronic health record. *AMIA Summits on Translational Science Proceedings, 2019*, 173.
83. Alawad, M., Yoon, H. J., Gao, S., Mumphrey, B., Wu, X. C., Durbin, E. B., et al. (2020). Privacy-preserving deep learning NLP models for cancer registries. *IEEE Transactions on Emerging Topics in Computing, 9*(3), 1219–1230.
84. Deshmukh, P. R., & Phalnikar, R. (2021). Information extraction for prognostic stage prediction from breast cancer medical records using NLP and ML. *Medical & Biological Engineering & Computing, 59*(9), 1751–1772.
85. Yoon, H. J., Stanley, C., Christian, J. B., Klasky, H. B., Blanchard, A. E., Durbin, E. B., et al. (2022). Optimal vocabulary selection approaches for privacy-preserving deep NLP model training for information extraction and cancer epidemiology. *Cancer Biomarkers, 33*(2), 185–198.
86. Patterson, O. V., Freiberg, M. S., Skanderson, M. J., Fodeh, S., Brandt, C. A., & DuVall, S. L. (2017). Unlocking echocardiogram measurements for heart disease research through natural language processing. *BMC Cardiovascular Disorders, 17*(1), 1–11.
87. Afzal, N., Mallipeddi, V. P., Sohn, S., Liu, H., Chaudhry, R., Scott, C. G., et al. (2018). Natural language processing of clinical notes for identification of critical limb ischemia. *International Journal of Medical Informatics, 111*, 83–89.
88. Thaiparnit, S., Kritsanasung, S., & Chumuang, N. (2019, July). A classification for patients with heart disease based on hoeffding tree. In *2019 16th International Joint Conference on Computer Science and Software Engineering (JCSSE)* (pp. 352–357). IEEE.
89. Bagheri, A., Groenhof, T. K. J., Veldhuis, W. B., de Jong, P. A., Asselbergs, F. W., & Oberski, D. L. (2020). Multimodal learning for cardiovascular risk prediction using EHR data. *arXiv preprint arXiv:2008.11979.*
90. Sammani, A., Bagheri, A., van der Heijden, P. G., Te Riele, A. S., Baas, A. F., Oosters, C. A. J., et al. (2021). Automatic multilabel detection of ICD10 codes in Dutch cardiology discharge letters using neural networks. *NPJ Digital Medicine, 4*(1), 1–10.
91. Zaman, S., Petri, C., Vimalesvaran, K., Howard, J., Bharath, A., Francis, D., et al. (2022). Automatic diagnosis labeling of cardiovascular MRI by using semisupervised natural language processing of text reports. *Radiology. Artificial Intelligence, 4*(1), e210085.
92. Weng, W. H., Wagholikar, K. B., McCray, A. T., Szolovits, P., & Chueh, H. C. (2017). Medical subdomain classification of clinical notes using a machine learning-based natural language processing approach. *BMC Medical Informatics and Decision Making, 17*(1), 1–13.
93. Chen, T., Dredze, M., Weiner, J. P., Hernandez, L., Kimura, J., & Kharrazi, H. (2019). Extraction of geriatric syndromes from electronic health record clinical notes: Assessment of statistical natural language processing methods. *JMIR Medical Informatics, 7*(1), e13039.
94. Liu, R., Greenstein, J. L., Sarma, S. V., & Winslow, R. L. (2019, July). Natural language processing of clinical notes for improved early prediction of septic shock in the ICU. In *2019 41st Annual International Conference of the IEEE Engineering in Medicine and Biology Society (EMBC)* (pp. 6103–6108). IEEE.

95. Oliwa, T., Furner, B., Schmitt, J., Schneider, J., & Ridgway, J. P. (2021). Development of a predictive model for retention in HIV care using natural language processing of clinical notes. *Journal of the American Medical Informatics Association, 28*(1), 104–112.

96. Chen, L., Gu, Y., Ji, X., Sun, Z., Li, H., Gao, Y., & Huang, Y. (2020). Extracting medications and associated adverse drug events using a natural language processing system combining knowledge base and deep learning. *Journal of the American Medical Informatics Association, 27*(1), 56–64.

97. Wang, J., Abu-el-Rub, N., Gray, J., Pham, H. A., Zhou, Y., Manion, F. J., et al. (2021). COVID-19 SignSym: A fast adaptation of a general clinical NLP tool to identify and normalize COVID-19 signs and symptoms to OMOP common data model. *Journal of the American Medical Informatics Association, 28*(6), 1275–1283.

98. Song, G., Chung, S. J., Seo, J. Y., Yang, S. Y., Jin, E. H., Chung, G. E., et al. (2022). Natural language processing for information extraction of gastric diseases and its application in large-scale clinical research. *Journal of Clinical Medicine, 11*(11), 2967.

Chapter 6
Evolving of Smart Banking with NLP and Deep Learning

Bibhu Dash, Swati Swayamsiddha, and Azad I. Ali

Abstract The banking world is moving faster with digital reality, where financial transactions, customer care, fraud prevention, and trading analysis are no longer handled by humans but by computers. Digitalization is marching ahead, and financial industries are not in the back seat to realize the same. Banks are producing a lot of information as part of their daily processes. This information stored either in legacy platforms or in the cloud is amorphous, and a lot of confidential information is kept inside it. Our objective is to read those unstructured data elements and extract meaning from them, which can be used for enterprises for managerial insights and business process innovation. With the evolution of deep neural networks, a sub-domain of artificial intelligence (AI), extracting and classifying unstructured data is much easier nowadays. This chapter is forwarding our research to use deep learning algorithms with natural language processing (NLP) to solve the challenges banks face in reading these unstructured data and extracting meanings. Our approach uses cognitive neural networks (CNN) and recurrent neural networks (RNN) in NLP to obtain performance results that substantially improve Spearman correlation scores above other traditional models. We will also perform a qualitative study of the importance of these unstructured data on why and when it is critical to utilize this framework to improve enterprises in insights extraction and classification. This chapter illustrates the role of deep learning in NLP for sentiment analysis and emotion detection using the extracted features from unstructured data for smart banking.

B. Dash (✉) · A. I. Ali
School of Computer and Information Sciences, University of the Cumberlands, Williamsburg, KY, USA
e-mail: bdash6007@ucumberlands.edu; azad.ali@ucumberlands.edu

S. Swayamsiddha
School of Electronics Engineering, KIIT University, Bhubaneswar, India
e-mail: swayamsiddhafet@kiit.ac.in

© The Author(s), under exclusive license to Springer Nature Switzerland AG 2023
M. A. Ahad et al. (eds.), *Enabling Technologies for Effective Planning and Management in Sustainable Smart Cities*, https://doi.org/10.1007/978-3-031-22922-0_6

Keywords Smart banking · Structured and unstructured data · Deep learning · AI · Deep-NLP · Chatbot · Cyberthreats

6.1 Introduction

In the last decade, the number of banks focusing on developing cutting-edge technologies to create a realistic 24 × 7 banking experience for their customers has risen exponentially. With the rise of social media and technological evolution, banks are getting a lot of pressure to match other industry types. Smart banking focuses on mobility banking, next-generation self-service, advanced security, remote advisory with the chatbot, social computing, and digital signage. As the world is getting digitalized faster, Fintech has been rapidly penetrating the financial core markets by filling in the gaps left by the legacy financial institutions and significantly improving the user experience [1]. E-banking has transferred to innovative banking with better product lines, better service capabilities, and competency. These smart features are integrated with AI technology to streamline processes and strengthen security.

6.1.1 Motivation

Several disruptive concepts, such as peer-to-peer banking, are gaining traction. The world produces 2.5 quintillion bytes of data daily, and the banking and financial industry has one quintillion bytes of data, so the transaction volume has become vast to thrust data-driven banking [2]. If we study these data further, the modern financial or banking industry produces more unstructured data than structured data as part of their daily operation. These unstructured data are the key to understanding customer expectations for business process innovation and quick adaptation. The banking experience is being put under the microscope like never before to attract more and more customers. With the evolution of machine learning (ML) and Deep-NLP learning, extracting and classifying these unstructured data is much easier nowadays than before. Deep-NLP plays a pivotal role in developing knowledgeable virtual assistants and chatbots in Fintech. In the recent past, deep learning models have successfully solved a variety of natural language processing (NLP) problems in the banking domain [3]. It's worth pointing out that financial sectors that will respond slowly to the adaptation of deep learning suffer lower Returns on Investment (ROI) and profits and could face extinction. In recent years, practitioners and scientists in NLP have been leveraging the power of modern Artificial Neural Networks (ANNs) with many prolific results in Financial Technology (FinTech) [4]. Many technologies are being employed to overcome the drawbacks of traditional financial services in the financial revolution period.

6.1.2 Objective

The objective of the present work is to show where the banking system is now and to lay the groundwork for future studies. With the current technological advancement, the financial industry is evolving daily. Our research uses the technology as an indexing tool (natural language processing (NLP) and deep learning) to showcase how these technologies modernize FinTech.

6.1.3 Contribution

In this chapter, we are forwarding our research to use ML and deep learning algorithms with natural language processing (NLP) to show the usability of modern-day Deep-NLP technologies in Fintech for an intelligent banking experience. The paper focuses on the complicated issues in smart banking and solutions to these issues using deep learning and natural language processing techniques. This study focuses on the works produced between 2018 and 2022. The work's most important contribution is demonstrating the importance of deep NLP techniques in redesigning intelligent banking experiences. The technical aspects and the applicability of these technological tools are discussed thoroughly for smart banking.

The rest of the chapter is organized as follows: Section 6.2 presents the traditional banking approach. The rise of FinTech and the new era of banking is described in Sect. 6.3. Section 6.4 offers the technologies used for smart banking. Transitions from Now to the Future are given in Sect. 6.5. Section 6.6 describes various applications of Deep-NLP in smart banking. Finally, the conclusion is given in Sect. 6.7.

6.2 Traditional Banking

The brick-and-mortar model of traditional banking was the heart of economic transactions. These traditional banks, referred to as "borrowing short and lending long," depended on short-term deposits and long-term lending to generate money through interest payments [5]. There were no customer-first policy and no customer lifetime value notions to give more focus to customer expectations. Banks were dictating their rules, and the paper-based transactions were very puzzling and hard to manage. Low risk and high return policy were the fundamental economic factors to drive the profits for traditional banks. It was believed that launching more products and seeking new sources of revenue in derivatives banks may be taking a high risk that could ultimately put them in danger and possibly a threat to the stability of the banking system [5]. But with time, the fundamental economic forces have undercut the role of traditional banks by forcing diminished deposits. In the United States and other developing countries, specialized banking institutions declined their market share from 20% in 1970 to 10% in the early 1990's [6]. The rise of many private and social banking machinery also created pressure on traditional banks for self-existence. The declining role of conventional banking in the world has forced countries around the globe to have banking regulatory policies and develop customer-centric products. The decline of traditional banking forced executives to think beyond innovation, technology adaptation, and risk mitigation to be customer-centric. The banking revolution 2.0 came into the picture with internet banking through innovation and communication technologies. The development of 3G and 4G communication pushed financial institutions to break the barriers and reach every household through mobiles. Automatic Teller machines (ATMs) and online banking helped bring the lost glory back for many institutions. The same tradition and popularity continued till 2005. After 2005, a new era of banking called revolution 3.0 emerged with innovative banking, which helped customers meet their needs 24×7 with the help of Artificial intelligence 5G and blockchain-like technologies. With greater freedom, innovative banking is now changing the world of finance. It is available at our fingertips anytime, anywhere, with a robot greeter, smart front desk, biosignature, interactive kiosk, video teller machine (VTM), and self-help chatbots [7].

6.3   Rise of FinTech and the New Era of Banking

Financial Technology (FinTech) is one of the expanding domains worldwide, and it is continuously getting new shapes and colors with the advancement of technology. According to the statistics from Google Trends, financial topics and trends are rapidly rising debated topics globally [8]. The financial industry runs with three basic application scenarios: Know Your Customer (KYC), Know Your Product (KYP) and Satisfy Your Customer (SYC). As the FinTech industry, directly and indirectly, influences everyone's daily life, it is highly regulated by the government. But with modern technologies, the traditional financial sector is going through a revolution while keeping itself compliant with government rules. Every year, many financial and banking-related workshops are organized worldwide to prioritize and transform this sphere.

As a highly regulated industry, the banking industry always emphasizes knowing its customers well (KYC). This industry uses structured and unstructured textual data for customer identification and credit evaluation. As the banking industry deals with corporate and personal customers, AI-enabled technology is crucial in updating customer information and status from news articles and financial statements. Zheng et al. (2019) constructed an end-to-end model using a transformer encoder [9]. Early detection and evaluation of situations for any personal customer is essential for banks when dealing with private customers [10]. With the popularity of social media sites, using daily posts to track the lifelong of a person has become possible [11]. These logs and events are helpful for banks and financial watchdogs rapidly capture the situation and better strategy for the future course of action.

To capture the price movement and understand the financial instruments, it's always crucial for banks to know their products well (KYP). Banks often have a common problem; they need to learn from their peers to learn from their mistakes to innovate themselves. Some models are in place to predict products and related pricing well to capture the risks [12]. Hu developed a hybrid attention network (HAN) to predict the trends in stocks with the swing in the news. Devlin and his team (2019) developed a model to read the textual data to find the fear index of customers using bidirectional encoder representations from Transformers (BERT) [13]. The crowd's information has proved to be very useful in reading changing financial trends. Satisfying customers and providing them with the best product they need is the primary goal of the FinTech industry. Many startups in the money exchange market and online lending services are leveraging the best technologies available to better customer satisfaction in customer-to-customer (C2C) or business-to-customer (B2C) segments. So, to remain competitive, banks implement technology for their shake and need to be flexible enough to keep it up to meet customer trends, as highlighted in Fig. 6.1 [14].

6.3.1 Smart Banking

A banking service that permits users to perform various banking activities using smartphones anytime and anywhere is considered smart banking [15]. Smart banking allows banks to present their new product offerings and services, allowing them

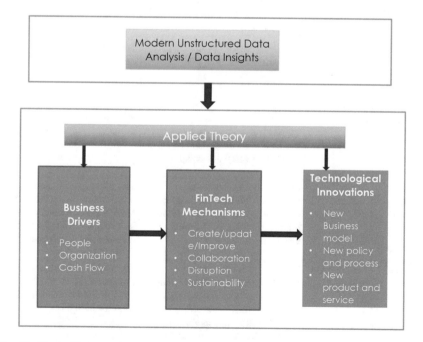

Fig. 6.1 The architecture of unstructured data processing in a banking framework

to enhance their business and sustain in this completive era [16]. Currently, it is the physical image of banking systems and services that customers will access to measure the quality through it. The systems and services can include debit and credit cards, e-banking, convenience, security, real-time chatbots, virtual assists, speed, the accuracy of their transactions, etc. [17]. Smart banking is prevalent but brings more operative risks, such as security and privacy concerns, including personal information and financial status [18]. Also, the 24 × 7 nonstop accessibility to bank products and transactions leads to significant threats, like malware, computer viruses, and hackers [19]. Per a survey conducted by Arcand et al. [20], banks' responsiveness in handling queries has increased up to 45% through different innovative banking channels. But in one sentence, we can iterate that it's the core empathy to ensure the customer feels that he is unique and special to his bank.

6.3.2 Data-Driven Fintech Industry and Literature Review

Digitalization in the finance industry came very late, but it is currently going in full fledge to affect the banking world. Many researchers have done significant studies to track the developments in this industry and how it impacts customers' daily lives across the industry. Table 6.1 below highlights the type of research design and its findings, along with the gaps in the study. All those gaps will be critical indicators when analyzing the technical aspects of this banking industry.

Table 6.1 Systematic literature reviews and gaps in Fintech

Study details	Study design	Research findings	Research gaps
Tian et al. (2021) [21]	Cross-sectional	Research provides comprehensive comparisons, including the advantages and disadvantages of data-driven algorithms in Fintech.	The study didn't include non-Fintech firms for reliability
Seng et al. (2018) [22]	Longitudinal cohort	The research examines the non-traditional data analytics approach and sentiment analysis on Big Data for a financial multi-case study and supply-demand framework.	It is a single-dimensional study restricted only to 'Big Data on finance.'
Suryono et al. (2020) [23]	Cross-sectional	Research focuses on – (a) state-of-art Fintech advancement, (b) identity challenges and future trends, and (c) gaps in Fintech research.	This study is very detailed but only focuses on the theoretical basis of Fintech research. It lacks the applied technological concepts and task-technology fit mock-ups.
Gai et al. (2018) [24]	Longitudinal cohort	The study proposes an active Fintech framework using technical aspects – security and privacy, data techniques, hardware and infrastructure, application management, and service models.	The study is limited to one framework, DF2, which is not practically implemented for overall validity.

6.4   Technology: A Catalyst for Smart Banking

Technologies in the banking industry are evolving at breath-keeping speed, forcing customers to be more engaging and dynamic. The virtual banking workplace in mobiles and smart devices is becoming more collaborative when processes become more flexible. Customers are trying hard to understand bank products, and banks are trying to understand their diverse customer base better. This creates an ever-connected and collaborative workforce for high-quality service experiences. These experiences are captured and analyzed to predict customer lifetime value and product decision-making. All these are possible due to AI-powered technological advancement, and these technologies are discussed in detail below.

6.4.1   Natural Language Processing

In this section, we review the recent technological advancements in natural language processing, and also, we will also understand the classical and rational models of language analysis.

6.4.1.1   The First Wave and Classicalism

Natural language processing (NLP) is broadly defined as the computerized approach to analyzing text based on statistical theories and a set of technologies. NLP investigates the use of computers and statistical analysis to understand human languages to perform various tasks. With digitalization at its peak, it is hard to believe a modern intelligent system like a chatbot, voice translator, or recommendation engine without NLP [25]. A range of computational techniques is required to accomplish a particular language analysis, and modern NLP processes bind those in a package for better accuracy and swiftness. It all starts with data, then reading it to find pattern meanings, and then the machines reply to all user questions to get the work done. In the first wave of language classification, NLP was mainly designed to understand human-like responses. In 1954, NLP was used to demonstrate the first machine learning translation system capable of translating more than 60 Russian sentences into English. This period coincided with the early development of artificial intelligence and was characterized by different domain experts who devised computer programs and symbolic logical rules like 'if-then-else' to get the most from the NLP process. The use of machine learning during the initial phases is shallow, with many data quality issues. But such systems have minimal scope and, unfortunately, worked for only a few use cases [26].

6.4.1.2   The Second Wave and Rationalism

The second wave of NLP started in the mid-nineties and was characterized by exploring data quantities and deep machine learning to use such data. The second phase is data-intensive machine learning and focuses more on data-driven decision-making [27]. More significantly, the analysis-by-synthesis deep generative process gave rise to the first commercial success of deep learning, which is the driving force behind the third generation of Deep-NLP models. The second wave promoted the knowledge-based speech recognition NLP and attempted to generalize from one condition to another and one domain to another [28]. When talking about NLP, we talk about areas such as speech recognition, machine translation, pattern matching, automatic text summarization, part-of-speech tagging, sentiment analysis, etc. [29]. Generally, NLP is a modern-day necessity to manage smart homes and smart offices like Alexa, Cortana, Siri, Google assistance, etc. NLP has experienced significant breakthroughs with the emergence of AI [30, 31]. Language is an essential means of delivering communication, thoughts, and ideas. But when this communication channel is mixed with mathematical rules and fed to machines, it significantly evolves human-machine interaction. Making engines understand the core of communication by understanding the language and returning the response efficiently is the basis of NLP adaptation.

6.4.2   Deep Learning

Deep Learning (DL), a subfield of machine learning, is a solid and robust advanced computational field that has reached significant success recently in many research areas. DL can be viewed as cascading models of cell types inspired by biological neural systems. With the advancement of backpropagation techniques, training deep neural networks from scratch attracted many researchers at the beginning of the twentieth century [32]. In the early days of DL research, without a large volume of training data and proper model design, the learning signals vanish significantly with the number of layers propagated from layer to layer, making it difficult to tune the models for better outcomes [26]. Hinton et al. [26] overcame this challenge by using an unsupervised pre-training method to detect valuable features. Then the process is further polished to train with supervised learning to classify the level data. This significant discovery considerably impacted the deep neural network's evolution and started to be used in many high-level representations where low-level data representations exist. The present DL can discover intricate structures in high-dimensional data, and deep stacking and deep neural networks have been successfully applied to real-world artificial intelligence tasks, including NLP and speech recognition [33].

The model presented by Hinton et al. [26] above is considered the beginning of deep learning. Unlike classical machine learning models, DL uses Neural Networks (NNs), including several hidden layers of variables to perform automatically, preprocessing, feature extraction, feature selection, and feature learning [34–37].

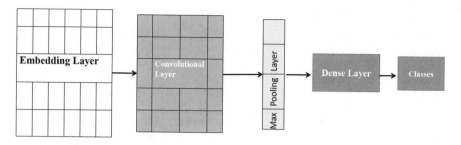

Fig. 6.2 The architecture of a CNN-based model for text classification

Convolutional Neural Networks (CNN) is one of the deep learning theorems with two convolution layers: pooling and fully connected dense layers. Figure 6.2 shows the CNN model for a text classification framework [35]. CNN's are extensively used in image and video processing and speech and NLP [38]. It is often not essential to know where certain features occur; instead, whether they appear in certain localities or not. Therefore, pooling operations can minimize the size of feature maps [39]. The CNN model has been applied in the existing literature on NLP and has shown to be very productive in handling sentiment analysis problems.

DL profoundly impacts people's lives or societies since its applications are consistently the need of the day. It drives advances in many standard technologies, such as self-driving vehicles, image and speech recognition, and natural language processing. DL algorithms depend highly on artificial neural networks for predictive modeling and recognition of complex patterns [38]. The fundamental framework of Deep Neural Networks (DNNs) comprises an input layer, hidden layers, and an output layer, as in Artificial Neural Networks (ANNs). The variation between DNNs and ANNs is the number of hidden layers, which is more than one in DNNs, and this directly affects the depth of the algorithm in DNNs [39]. Also, in DL, the repeated analysis of massive datasets eradicates errors and discrepancies in findings, leading to a reliable conclusion. Therefore, DL is suitable for handling large and complex data. The most famous types of DL networks are Convolutional Neural Networks (CNN), Recurrent Neural networks (RNN), and Recursive Neural Networks (RvNNs). DL gains enormous significance because of a new emerging field called big data analytics. This field offers various business benefits: more viable marketing strategies, better client service, improved operational efficiency, etc. [40].

The modern DL algorithms excel at unsupervised learning as the data is not labeled in this category. DL algorithms require Graphics Processing Units (GPUs), so the complex computation can be optimized efficiently. Neural networks consist of interconnected nodes or neurons, each having several inputs and supplying one output [41]. Each of these output nodes conducts weighted sum computation on the values they receive from the input nodes. These outputs are the sum result of these nonlinear transformation functions. Corrections to these weights are made in response to the network's individual errors or losses at the output nodes [41]. Such corrections are usually made in modern networks using stochastic gradient descent, considering the derivatives of errors at the nodes, an approach called

Table 6.2 Deep Learning popular algorithms and their features

Algorithm	Type	Input data type	Main features
Auto encoders (AE)	Unsupervised	Various	Dimensionality reduction, feature extraction
Convolutional neural network (CNN)	Supervised	2D data (image, audio, etc.)	Dimensionality reduction, computations, and visual task
Recurrent neural networks (RNN)	Supervised	Serial, time-series	Useful for IoT applications with time-dependent data
Restricted Boltzmann machine (RBM)	Both supervised and unsupervised	Various	Dimensionality reduction, feature extraction, and classification
Deep belief network (DBN)	Both supervised and unsupervised	Various	Best for hierarchical feature discovery. Greedy training of the network layer by layer
Long short-term memory (LSTM)	Supervised	Serial, time-series, long time-dependent data	Good performance with data of long-time lag
Variational auto encoder (VAE)	Semi-supervised	Various	Suitable for the scarcity of labeled data
Generative adversarial networks (GAN)	Semi-supervised	Various	It consists of a generator and a discriminator. This model can handle noisy data.
Ladder net	Semi-supervised	Various	It consists of two encoders and one decoder. This model can handle noisy data.

backpropagation [33]. The main factors influencing the output are the number of layers and the nodes' connection. While deep neural networks (DNN), there is no clear consensus on precisely what defines a DNN. Generally, networks with multiple hidden layers are considered deep, and those with many layers are considered very deep [42].

Big data is an essential component of building an intelligent banking framework. It can be processed through batch mode or real-time mode. With the advancement of real-time technologies like Apache Spark, Apache Storm, Hive, and Map Reduce to handle streaming data [42, 43], the intelligent banking concept is becoming modernized daily. The problem is how to extract data from different banking components, third-party systems, and subsystems for batch or real-time processing. DL algorithms are evolving with data types, volume, and velocity changes. Table 6.2 details the most popular algorithms of Deep Learning in practical use [34].

6.4.3 Deep-NLP: A Revolution

Machine learning is everywhere in today's NLP models. But with the advancement of deep learning, the process of NLP has reached its highs in developing features and handling complex interpretation tasks. If we analyze different approaches holistically at a deeper level, we can identify the aspects of a conceptual revolution in human-machine interaction. The cost of analyzing these human-centric 'rationalistic' linguistic rules was very high. Still, with the development of Deep-NLP, the cost has been significantly decreased, and accuracy has been increased with the help of bidirectional Long Short-term memory (LSTM) networks. LSTMs are designed to avoid long-term dependency problems faced during RNN architectures. Advances in techniques and hardware for training deep neural networks have recently enabled impressive accuracy improvements across many fundamental NLP tasks [39].

Deep learning in NLP is on the rage and exponentially growing over the past few years due to its supremacy in terms of accuracy and applicability to a broad scope of applications. Deep learning for NLP truly shines to mitigate the problem of combinatorial counting sparseness [40]. Recent advances in deep learning with NLP design have diversely contributed significantly to AI. Even more significantly, DL has outperformed notable Machine Learning (ML) methods in domains like NLP, robotics, optimization, cybersecurity, bioinformatics, and healthcare, among others [41]. Whether it is fraud or anomaly detection, healthcare digital record analysis, FinTech predictions, or automation, NLP methods using DL algorithms are reshaping the world of digitalization. With the evolution of Meta-learning, a learning-to-learn paradigm to learn new tasks faster by reusing previous experience than teaching everything in isolation, the NLP has become a more intelligent system than before. Meta and federated learning contribute more value to NLP research by assisting organizations in managing real-time data analytics for improved decision management, cost reduction, and process optimization.

6.5   Transitions from Now to Future

The banking industry is in the race for insightful digitalization. Banks globally plan to invest US$ 9.7 billion in the last couple of years to enhance digital banking capabilities in the front office alone [42]. Online and mobile banking channels have become as crucial as branches and ATMs. Banks worldwide are already invested in digital technologies and now realizing to get benefits from customer satisfaction and acquisition. If we study the benefits of digitalization in the banking industry, Bank of America confirmed that it received more deposits from mobile channels than directly from its branches [43]. But satisfaction is relative, and different business entities are trying to become leading digital brands like Apple, Amazon, or Google, as these are considered the gold standard of digital engagement. If banks want to keep it up, they must offer a better digital experience to keep the customers emotionally attached to their products and values.

A survey conducted by Deloitte in 2018 took 17,100 banking consumers in more than 17 counties, resulting in restructuring organizations around different stages of customer interaction, which will be the next frontier for digital banking [44]. Banks now focus on integrated digital services with five steps to drive holistic engagement: adoption, consideration, application, onboarding, and servicing. The above study by Deloitte also highlights that transforming banks is the need of the hour than increasing and enhancing digital offerings. Banks need to be aware that if the banking system is unmoved and only focuses on consumer behaviors, it will raise a trust liability between the banks and their consumers.

The rate of digital adaptation is directly proportional to more transactions. Modern consumers are ready for a higher level of digital engagement, which creates more opportunities for banks to increase engagement through improved digital offerings. Currently, 43% of consumers embrace online banking in the global banking system, and 29% embrace digital adventurers. Still, the satisfaction rate of digital adventurers is higher than that of online customers [44]. So, there is a massive opportunity for banks to attract younger tech-savvy customers to digital banking as they are familiar with mobile apps and modern technologies. Putting real in digital and digital in real is route banks need to take seriously to make their digital transformation successful.

In the future, consumers are more likely to increase the use of digital channels and will prefer smart banking outside of brick-and-mortar locations. That will pressure banks to add more self-service screens and preparedness to mitigate cyber threats. AI and NLP will play a key role in self-service analytics to understand customer behaviors and prevent online threats. NLP-enabled Older Adult Technology Assistance (OATA) programs will take center stage for banking on-the-go models [45]. The self-training videos with speech recognition technologies will educate seniors and new bankers about the convenience of digital banking. Digital adventurers are avid mobile users and always expect more from banks, creating a gap in emotional connection. Banks need to work with intelligent chatbots as the go-to help tool for real-time problem-solving to fill that gap. Some banks may consider digital-only banking with limited product features to attract millennials and new-age customers. Also, future banking needs to have a seamless flow of data, and it should break the channel silos. All the branches, ATMs, online and mobile banking, and third-party services need to be connected with popular products like Google Home, Alexa, or Siri to facilitate omnichannel experiences [45]. This experience will boost customer expertise in a Smart Banking Management System (SBMS).

6.6   Application of Deep-NLP in Smart Banking

The banking industry is highly regulated, and executives are very possessive about frequent changes. There are established global regulations to follow standards and guidance around modern technologies as the bank handles sensitive and personally identifiable information (PII). However, deep learning and NLP are vital in the modern banking system as enablers of risk management, better user experience, and self-service analytics. With the evolution of cloud infrastructure, financial institutes now live in a hybrid environment where they manage traditional and smart banking for users. Digital transformation is underway in all kinds of financial sectors in front, back, and shadow office operations [46]. The section below highlights some of the very market-leading use cases of deep learning and NLP in the below section.

6.6.1 *Application of NLP in Smart Banking*

With the aid of contemporary NLP technology, several viable applications have shown to be highly valuable for the modern banking revolution. Some of the most popular NLP-based technology characteristics are listed and discussed below.

6.6.1.1 Chatbots

Self-service chatbots are in high demand for providing 24 × 7 support to banking customers. To avoid duplicate questioning and prompt response, a chatbot works as a conversational agent for particular domains and specific topics with the help of NLP. These agents are built on understanding users' input and providing meaningful sentences using a preloaded knowledge base [46–49]. Figure 6.3 below highlights a sample chatbot application and how this is shaping the world of real-time customer interaction. From testing and developing the model to query handling, all are done by NLP models with the help of machine learning logic.

The architecture model is a stepping stone in building banks' and financial institutions' intelligent query handling programs for self-learn support. Chatbots are in high demand in Chat-Apps like WhatsApp, Messenger, and Telegram and on many online platforms for quality customer service. There are many successful use cases of chatbots across the banking world. For instance, according to [50], Erica (the virtual assistant of Bank of America), COIN (contract intelligence platform of JPMorgan), Eno (chatbot assistant of Captial One), Clinc (by USAA), Amy (by HKBC), Haro and Dori (by Hang Seng Bank), Emma (by OCBC Bank), Ceba (by Commonwealth Bank in Australia), POSB by (DBS bank), etc. All these bots can interact with customers via text and voice commands.

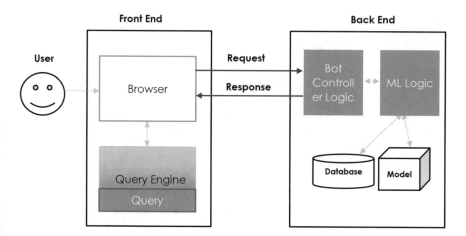

Fig. 6.3 Chatbot architecture with NLP and ML logic

6.6.1.2 Auto Feedback and Offline Messaging System

There are situations where bots are not enough to answer all the queries. So, in that situation, sending questions offline and getting a response from an actual customer support representative later is a prevalent option [50]. In these options, the users are not required to call or visit any physical location to get an answer to their queries. The model keeps similar questions in the database if there is no PII information attached to them, and if similar queries are asked in the future, the feedback system will respond to them quickly. In another way, the self-feedback system captures the user feedback on any survey or product experience. If users have 'disliked' any of these feedbacks, the system sends the responses to proper authorities to address the concerns. In that way, the enterprise can maintain customer feedback logs to study the Customer Lifetime Value (CLV). The same feedback system can be evaluated using machine learning models later for better decision-making and product development. Figure 6.4 shows the architecture of the feedback and auto messaging system.

6.6.1.3 Developing Self-Learning and Training Models

The knowledge gap in banking due to the lack of proper educational resources is a very costly affair and is undesirable. It is crucial to address the real meaning of all terms and regulations and review the most up-to-date progress. That prompts many organizations to leverage text and speech analytics to build learning and training models for their employees. These self-learning programs benefit online kiosks, ATMs, and self-service portals for off-hour operations. These machines are integrated with Interactive Voice Response (IVR) machines to build a collaborative tech center. These speech-to-meaning and text-to-meaning setups are more efficient, easy to use, and help resolve cases faster [50]. Many banks and enterprises sound like these technologies create a positive and lasting impression on users. Many third-party tech companies offer these services for optimizing and classifying large datasets, resource management, and saving a lot on money-human efforts.

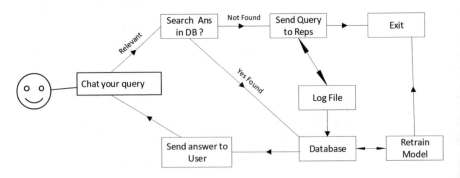

Fig. 6.4 The architecture of auto feedback and offline messaging system

6.6.1.4 Detecting Phishing Attacks Using NLP

Phishing attacks are the most common security threats in the banking system. But the new NLP-enabled semantic analysis can help analyze the texts to detect malicious intent in any email. Security of private information is a significant concern for all organizations irrespective of their domains, and phishing, like social engineering attacks, is there to steal sensitive customer information. Machine learning and NLP are used to blacklist the topics and email subjects whose presence in an email or command suggests malicious intent. The phishing algorithms report five values: true positive (TP), false positive (FP), false negatives (FN), precision, and recall. The precision and recall are calculated as below. The decrease in false negatives shows that semantic information helps detect phishing attacks [51].

$$precision = \frac{TP}{TP+FP} \text{ and } recall = \frac{TP}{TP+FN}$$

Many researchers focus on combing NLP with ML models to address information retrieval (IR) problems to detect if any check payment or loan documents are fabricated to cheat the system. All those systems also detect fraudulent transactions by studying archives of content-based formal documents. Many banks and financial institutes use automated NLP models to examine customers through e-KYC (AI-based Know Your Customer). Also, antifraud chatbots detect scams used in social-banking network services. This field is evolving, and recently the development of efficient NLP models by DistilBERT with traditional ML methods has lower resource computing costs and faster execution in real-time to detect malicious behaviors [52].

6.6.2 Application of Deep Learning in Smart Banking

The latest trend shows that most enterprises are embracing data-driven decision-making and catching up with all new-age technologies that are rapidly evolving to manage data. As unstructured Big Data currently overshadows the total data cloud platforms, organizations encourage relevant skills and technologies to extract information from Big Data using the latest Artificial Intelligence (AI) technologies. The banking industry is one of the most influential domains that directly or indirectly impact people's daily lives. Hence, this industry actively develops and implements advanced data-driven technologies to prosper globally [53]. AI, ML, and deep learning have rapidly grown over the last few years. Among all these latest trends, deep learning shows the steepest exponential growth curve due to its rapid advancements with closely connected technologies. In many banking enterprises, deep learning is closely implemented with other domains like marketing, customer relationship management (CRM), and risk management (RM) [54].

6.6.2.1 Deep Learning in Marketing

Deep learning has been an effective tool for strategic marketing activities in all industry segments, including banking [55]. In general, under intense competition, deep learning is used for online assessments to acquire the right customers for the right banking products to enhance the effectiveness of marketing campaigns. Many researchers have attempted to implement deep learning techniques for personal and retail banking needs. Deep learning is primarily used to study customer behaviors to prioritize more accurate offers and referrals. Yan [56] demonstrated the application of a convolutional neural network via Kaggle completion on Santander's data to study customer response behavior for predicting the usage of bank products. For a large retail bank in Poland, Ładyżyński et al. [57] used deep belief networks and stacked Boltzman machines to analyze direct marketing scenarios, showing significant improvements in the performance of a marketing campaign.

6.6.2.2 Deep Learning in CRM

Banking is a data-rich sector that produces and stores much customer-related information. As customer personal and transactional data are vital for personalized services and product design, deep learning is integrated with CRM to improve the productivity of customer interaction [58]. Customer profiling and segmentation are vital for KYC implementation and a customer hierarchy system. Zhou et al. [59] compared the performance of neural networks with other data mining techniques by taking the customer data from the Saman Bank in Iran, and they achieved over 97% in customer behavior segmentation.

Customer satisfaction study is another primary usage of deep learning in banking [60]. Deep learning with NLP is broadly used in many banking systems for improving customer satisfaction with chatbots and feedback systems. Customer churn is a method to evaluate business success and retain existing customers. A recent study by Caigny et al. [61] using CNN models on customer churn prediction proved the improved performance of CNN in text analysis. It is widely noticed that deep learning plays a vital role in the broad scale of CRM in image processing and audio/video processing for information extraction from these unstructured data. Seeing the importance of CRM in any industry, researchers are still working to utilize deep learning capabilities in all segments of the CRM module.

6.6.2.3 Deep Learning in RM

Risk Management is an essential pillar of the banking sector. RM aims to protect assets and prevent potential losses to the banking assets. As this is a crucial task, deep learning is vital in alerting and protecting bank assets to prevent banks from going into solvency. Some of the most critical elements of risk management in banking, like investment, asset risk assessment to loan approval, are done using deep learning techniques [62].

Investment and portfolio management is one of the future-focused areas in any banking operation. Deep learning accurately evaluates repricing, option, and third-party investment risks. Culkin et al. [63] used deep learning in option pricing, and robust performance was confirmed compared to traditional methods. A recent study by Vo et al. [64] used the environmental, social, and governance metrics and the long short-term memory (LSTM) deep learning technique for portfolio optimization with sustainable consideration of social impact. It was considered a highly productive experiment in measuring and calculating portfolio impacts.

Loan approval and fraud detection are a significant portion of day-to-day bank operations. Deep learning successfully evaluates customers' risks and predicts their credit risks to assess customer risk proportions. Many researchers have investigated these areas to determine the customer risk portfolios before loan approvals. A study by Kvamme et al. [65] investigated the real-world Norwegian mortgage portfolio data set using applied convolutional neural networks for credit risk prediction. Similarly, another research was conducted by Sirignano et al., using USA mortgage data using deep learning to evaluate mortgage risks [66]. Fu et al. applied CNN to a Chinese commercial bank's real-world transactional data set to study credit and fraud behavior [67]. All USA credit bureaus like TransUnion, Equifax, and Experian use modern AI techniques to research and predict customer credit risks from their daily transactions.

6.6.2.4 Deep Learning on Detecting Cyber Threats

With the advance in technology, Cyberthreats are increasing daily. Financial institutions are the most susceptible to cyber threats. Banks are adopting a cyber resilience strategy to mitigate cyber-attacks. The manage detection and response technique powered by deep learning is useful for investigating potential compromises and providing real-time remediation to those threats. Deep learning techniques are widely used in the context of data-driven cyber security research like malware detection and vulnerability detection [68–71]. A study by Fang et al. [72] using the BRNN-LSTM framework for predicting cyberattack rates showed that this framework significantly outperforms other ML models in terms of prediction accuracy and decreasing cyber-attack rates. With the advancement of the Internet of Things (IoT) and internet-enabled devices around the banking domains, a high volume of data is generated from these smart environments. By integrating deep learning with these IoT data, institutions can prevent inference attacks using the Deep Variational Autoencoder (DVAE) [73]. These fields still need more attention from researchers to manage the patterns in Commercial Internet of Things (CIoT) environments.

6.6.2.5 Deep Learning on Real-Time Detection in Banks

Financial institutions like banks and Automated Teller Machines (ATMs) are high-security premises heavily guarded by Closed-Circuit Televisions (CCTVs) and video cameras. It is critical to extract data from CCTV footage and process it in

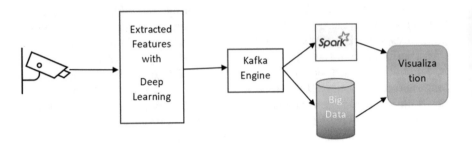

Fig. 6.5 Data flow architecture

real-time or batch processing for better physical security. Video footage is collected from CCTV installed inside and outside the banking premises, and objects are extracted with deep learning algorithms (Fig. 6.5). Object attributes like class, name, type, relative coordinates, and timestamp are processed using DL. Class or class-Id is the key used for object classification identity e.g., human = 1, animals = 2, vehicles = 3 etc. Generated features are then sent from the CCTV servers to the model using the Spark engine. These features are stored in big data systems as logs about the bank premise's activity history generated by deep learning algorithms. Apache flame duplicates the data from Spark to HDFS in big data systems [72]. The data flow ends with real-time analytics dashboards using visualization tools like Tableau, Qlik Sense, or PowerBI [74].

6.7   Conclusion

The service quality dimensions of the banks are essential to promote offerings and gain customer confidence. Implementing the smart banking environment will give banks the edge to better serve customers. As the growth in the number of banks across the globe is increasing every year, in the future, the performance of the banks will be measured according to their sustainability and technological adaptability. The latest deep learning trends and NLP indicate rapidly rising global interest in these technologies to reshape financial bottlenecks. These technologies hugely contribute to overcoming the knowledge gap between technical experts and the public by promoting their broad applicability in modern data-rich enterprises. There are still many potential deep learning implementations that banks will adapt in the near future, for instance, face recognition, biometric authorization, audio/video processing, etc. This chapter is expected to provide insights into future research by connecting academics, researchers, and practitioners in deep learning, NLP, and banking.

References

1. Truong, T. (2016). *How the FinTech industry is changing the world*. Thesis.
2. Marr, B. (2018). *How much data do we create every day? The mind-blowing stats everyone should read*. Retrieved October 2, 2019, from https://www.forbes.com/sites/bernard-marr/2018/05/21/how-much-data-do-we-create-every-daythe-mind-blowing-stats-everyone-should-read/#2aa86a2b60ba
3. Alshemali, B., & Kalita, J. (2020). Improving the reliability of deep neural networks in NLP: A review. *Knowledge-Based Systems, 191*, 105210.
4. Collobert, R., Weston, J., Bottou, L., Karlen, M., Kavukcuoglu, K., & Kuksa, P. (2011). Natural language processing (almost) from scratch. *Journal of Machine Learning Research, 12*, 2493–2537.
5. Edwards, F. R., & Mishkin, F. S. (1995). *The decline of traditional banking: Implications for financial stability and regulatory policy.*
6. Benston, G. J., & Kaufman, G. G. (1988). *Risk and solvency regulation of depository institutions: past policies and current options* (Vol. 88–1). Federal Reserve Bank of Chicago.
7. Sahu, P., Elezue, C. J., & Kushawaha, R. (2022). An analysis of consumer expectations, nature and economic implications of smart banking system in India. In *Internet of things and its applications* (pp. 271–279). Springer.
8. Chen, C. C., Huang, H. H., & Chen, H. H. (2020). NLP in FinTech applications: past, present and future. *arXiv*. Preprint arXiv:2005.01320.
9. Vaswani, A., Shazeer, N., Parmar, N., Uszkoreit, J., Jones, L., Gomez, A. N., ... & Polosukhin, I. (2017). Attention is all you need. In *Advances in neural information processing systems* (pp. 5998–6008).
10. Losada, D. E., Crestani, F., & Parapar, J. (2019). Overview of early risk prediction on the internet. In *International conference of the cross-language evaluation forum for European languages* (pp. 340–357). Springer.
11. Yen, A. Z., Huang, H. H., & Chen, H. H. (2020). Multimodal joint learning for personal knowledge base construction from Twitter-based lifelogs. *Information Processing & Management, 57*(6), 102148.
12. Hu, Z., Liu, W., Bian, J., Liu, X., & Liu, T. Y. (2018, February). Listening to chaotic whispers: A deep learning framework for news-oriented stock trend prediction. In *Proceedings of the eleventh ACM international conference on web search and data mining* (pp. 261–269).
13. Devlin, J., Chang, M. W., Lee, K., & Toutanova, K. (2018). Bert: Pre-training of deep bidirectional transformers for language understanding. *arXiv*. Preprint arXiv:1810.04805.
14. Legowo, M. B., Subanija, S., & Sorongan, F. A. (2020). Role of FinTech mechanism to technological innovation: A conceptual framework. *International Journal of Innovative Science and Research Technology, 5*(5), 1–6.
15. Alhosani, F. A., & Tariq, M. U. (2020). Improving service quality of smart banking using quality management methods in UAE. *International Journal of Mechanical Production Engineering Research and Development (IJMPERD), 10*(3), 2249–8001.
16. Manikandan, D., Madhusudhanan, J., Venkatesan, V. P., Amrith, V., & Britto, M. A. (2011). Smart banking environment based on context history. *International Conference on Recent Trends in Information Technology (ICRTIT), 2011*, 450–455. https://doi.org/10.1109/ICRTIT.2011.5972335
17. Drigă, I., & Isac, C. (2014). E-banking services–features, challenges and benefits. *Annals of the University of Petroşani Economics, 14*, 49–58.
18. Mani, Z., & Chouk, I. (2018). *Smart banking: Why it's important to take into account consumers' concerns?* halshs-01678806f
19. Jain, H. C., & Godara, A. (2021). Smart banking services resistance across the income levels. *Hem Chand Jain, Anubha Godara, Smart Banking Services Resistance across the Income Levels International Journal of Management, 11*(11), 2020.

20. Arcand, M., PromTep, S., Brun, I., & Rajaobelina, L. (2017). Mobile banking service quality and customer relationships. *International Journal of Bank Marketing.*
21. Tian, X., He, J. S., & Han, M. (2021). Data-driven approaches in FinTech: A survey. *Information Discovery and Delivery, 49*(2), 123–135. https://doi.org/10.1108/IDD-06-2020-0062
22. Seng, J. L., Chiang, Y. M., Chang, P. R., Wu, F. S., Yen, Y. S., & Tsai, T. C. (2018). Big data and FinTech. In *Big data in computational social science and humanities* (pp. 139–163). Springer.
23. Suryono, R. R., Budi, I., & Purwandari, B. (2020). Challenges and trends of financial technology (Fintech): A systematic literature review. *Information, 11*(12), 590.
24. Gai, K., Qiu, M., & Sun, X. (2018). A survey on FinTech. *Journal of Network and Computer Applications, 103*, 262–273.
25. Johri, P., Khatri, S. K., Al-Taani, A. T., Sabharwal, M., Suvanov, S., & Kumar, A. (2021). Natural language processing: History, evolution, application, and future work. In *Proceedings of 3rd international conference on computing informatics and networks* (pp. 365–375). Springer
26. Hinton, G. E., & Salakhutdinov, R. R. (2012). A better way to pretrain deep Boltzmann machines. In *Advances in neural information processing systems* (p. 25)
27. Xiong, W., Droppo, J., Huang, X., Seide, F., Seltzer, M., Stolcke, A., ... & Zweig, G. (2016). Achieving human parity in conversational speech recognition. *arXiv.* Preprint arXiv:1610.05256.
28. Murphy, K. P. (2012). *Machine learning: a probabilistic perspective.* MIT press.
29. Liu, B. (2012). Sentiment analysis and opinion mining. *Synthesis lectures on human language technologies, 5*(1), 1–167.
30. Hirschberg, J., & Manning, C. D. (2015). Advances in natural language processing. *Science, 349*(6245), 261–266.
31. Lu, Y. (2019). Artificial intelligence: A survey on evolution, models, applications and future trends. *Journal of Management Analytics, 6*(1), 1–29.
32. Rumelhart, D. E., Hinton, G. E., & Williams, R. J. (1986). Learning representations by back-propagating errors. *Nature, 323*(6088), 533–536.
33. Yu, Z., Black, A. W., & Rudnicky, A. I. (2017). Learning conversational systems that interleave task and non-task content. *arXiv.* Preprint arXiv:1703.00099.
34. Lima, S. & Terán, L. (2019). Cognitive smart cities and deep learning: A classification framework. In *2019 Sixth International Conference on eDemocracy & eGovernment (ICEDEG)* (pp. 180–187). https://doi.org/10.1109/ICEDEG.2019.8734346
35. Jain, P. K., Saravanan, V., & Pamula, R. (2021). A hybrid CNN-LSTM: A deep learning approach for consumer sentiment analysis using qualitative user-generated contents. *Transactions on Asian and Low-Resource Language Information Processing, 20*(5), 1–15.
36. Bhowmik, T., Bhadwaj, A., Kumar, A., & Bhushan, B. (2022). Machine learning and deep learning models for privacy management and data analysis in smart cites. In *Recent advances in internet of things and machine learning* (pp. 165–188). Springer.
37. Chandana Mani, R. K., Bhushan, B., Rajyalakshmi, V., Nagaraj, J., & Ramathulasi, T. (2022). A Pilot study on detection and classification of COVID images: A deep Learning approach. In *Innovations in electronics and communication engineering* (pp. 187–193)
38. Zhang, Y., & Wallace, B. (2015). A sensitivity analysis of (and practitioners' guide to) convolutional neural networks for sentence classification. *arXiv.* Preprint arXiv:1510.03820.
39. Otter, D. W., Medina, J. R., & Kalita, J. K. (2020). A survey of the usages of deep learning for natural language processing. *IEEE Transactions on Neural Networks and Learning Systems, 32*(2), 604–624.
40. Schmidhuber, J. (2015). Deep learning in neural networks: An overview. *Neural networks, 61*, 85–117.
41. Dozat, T. & Manning, C. D. (2017). Deep biaffine attention for neural dependency parsing. In *ICLR.*
42. Deng, L., & Liu, Y. (Eds.). (2018). *Deep learning in natural language processing.* Springer.

43. Alzubaidi, L., Zhang, J., Humaidi, A. J., Al-Dujaili, A., Duan, Y., Al-Shamma, O., et al. (2021). Review of deep learning: Concepts, CNN architectures, challenges, applications, future directions. *Journal of Big Data, 8*(1), 1–74.
44. Mayo, D., Cheparthi, A., Gattu, N. S., Pabba, P. G. (2021, December 20). *It banking spending predictor: Corporate & amp; Retail – 2021*. Omdia. Retrieved March 27, 2022, from https://omdia.tech.informa.com/OM018213/IT-Banking-Spending-Predictor-Corporate%2D%2DRetail%2D%2D2021
45. Rogers, T. N. (2018, July 16). *Mobile deposits surpass in person transactions at Bank of America*. TheStreet. Retrieved March 27, 2022, from https://www.thestreet.com/technology/mobile-deposits-surpass-in-person-transactions-at-bank-of-america-14652141
46. Srinivas, V., & Ross, A. (2018, December). *Accelerating digital transformation in banking*. Deloitte Insights. Retrieved March 27, 2022, from https://www2.deloitte.com/global/en/insights/industry/financial-services/digital-transformation-in-banking-global-customer-survey.html
47. Röcker, C., & Kaulen, D. (2014). Smart banking: User characteristics and their effects on the usage of emerging banking applications. *Journal ISSN, 2368*, 6103.
48. Kulkarni, C. S., Bhavsar, A. U., Pingale, S. R., & Kumbhar, S. S. (2017). BANK CHAT BOT–an intelligent assistant system using NLP and machine learning. *International Research Journal of Engineering and Technology, 4*(5), 2374–2377.
49. Dash, B. (2021). *A hybrid solution for extracting information from unstructured data using optical character recognition (OCR) with natural language processing (NLP)*. Research Gate.
50. Marous, J. (2018). *Meet 11 of the most interesting chatbots in banking*. The Financial Brand. Available online: https://thefnancialbrand.com/71251/chatbots-banking-trends-ai-cx/. Accessed on 26 Mar 2020.
51. Bhagat, P., Prajapati, S. K., & Seth, A. (2020). Initial lessons from building an IVR-based automated question-answering system. In *Proceedings of the 2020 international conference on information and communication technologies and development* (pp. 1–5).
52. Peng, T., Harris, I., & Sawa, Y. (2018). Detecting phishing attacks using natural language processing and machine learning. In *2018 IEEE 12th international conference on semantic computing (icsc)* (pp. 300–301). IEEE.
53. Chang, JW., Yen, N. & Hung, J.C. (2022). Design of a NLP-empowered finance fraud awareness model: the anti-fraud chatbot for fraud detection and fraud classification as an instance. *J Ambient Intell Human Comput, 13*, 4663–4679.
54. Hassani, H., Huang, X., Silva, E., & Ghodsi, M. (2020). Deep learning and implementations in banking. *Annals of Data Science, 7*(3), 433–446.
55. Bose, I., & Chen, X. (2009). Quantitative models for direct marketing: A review from systems perspective. *European Journal of Operational Research, 195*(1), 1–16.
56. Yan C. (2018). *Convolutional Neural Network on a structured bank customer data*. Towards data science. Available online: https://towardsdatascience.com/convolutional-neural-network-on-astructured-bank-customer-data-358e6b8aa759. Accessed on 25 Mar 2020.
57. Ładyżyński, P., Żbikowski, K., & Gawrysiak, P. (2019). Direct marketing campaigns in retail banking with the use of deep learning and random forests. *Expert Systems with Applications, 134*, 28–35.
58. Ogwueleka, F. N., Misra, S., Colomo-Palacios, R., & Fernandez, L. (2015). Neural network and classifcation approach in identifying customer behavior in the banking sector: A case study of an international bank. *Human Factors and Ergonomics in Manufacturing & Service Industries, 25*(1), 28–42.
59. Zhou, X., Bargshady, G., Abdar, M., Tao, X., Gururajan, R. & Chan, K. C. (2019). A case study of predicting banking customers behaviour by using data mining. In *2019 6th international conference on behavioral, economic and socio-cultural computing (BESC)* (pp. 1–6). IEEE.
60. Vieira, A. & Sehgal, A. (2018). How banks can better serve their customers through artificial techniques. In *Digital marketplaces unleashed* (pp. 311–326). Springer.

61. De Caigny, A., Coussement, K., De Bock, K. W., Lessmann, S. (2019). Incorporating textual information in customer churn prediction models based on a convolutional neural network. *International Journal of Forecasting* (In Press).
62. Lin, W. Y., Hu, Y. H., & Tsai, C. F. (2011). Machine learning in financial crisis prediction: A survey. *IEEE Transactions on Systems, Man, and Cybernetics, Part C (Applications and Reviews), 42*(4), 421–436.
63. Culkin, R., & Das, S. R. (2017). Machine learning in finance: The case of deep learning for option pricing. *Journal of Investment Management, 15*(4), 92–100.
64. Vo, N. N., He, X., Liu, S., & Xu, G. (2019). Deep learning for decision making and the optimization of socially responsible investments and portfolio. *Decision Support System, 124*, 113097.
65. Kvamme, H., Sellereite, N., Aas, K., & Sjursen, S. (2018). Predicting mortgage default using convolutional neural networks. *Expert Systems with Applications, 102*, 207–217.
66. Sirignano, J., Sadhwani, A. & Giesecke, K. (2018). *Deep learning for mortgage risk.* Available at: https://doi.org/10.2139/ssrn.2799443
67. Fu, K., Cheng, D., Tu, Y., & Zhang, L. (2016, October). Credit card fraud detection using convolutional neural networks. In *International conference on neural information processing* (pp. 483–490). Springer.
68. Li, D., Baral, R., Li, T., Wang, H., Li, Q., & Xu, S. (2018). *Hashtran-dnn: a framework for enhancing robustness of deep neural networks against adversarial malware samples.* CoRR. abs/1809.06498: http://arxiv.org/abs/1809.06498
69. Z. Li, D. Zou, S. Xu, X. Ou, H. Jin, S. Wang, Z. Deng & Y. Zhong (2018). *In 25th annual network and distributed system security symposium, NDSS 2018, San Diego, California, USA, February 18–21, 2018.* Vuldeepecker: A deep learning-based system for vulnerability detection (Internet Society San Diego).
70. Singh, R. V., Bhushan, B., & Tyagi, A. (2021). Deep learning framework for cybersecurity: Framework, applications, and future research trends. In *Emerging Technologies in Data Mining and Information Security* (pp. 837–847). Springer.
71. Malhotra, L., Bhushan, B., & Singh, R. V. (2021). *Artificial intelligence and deep learning-based solutions to enhance cyber security.* Available at SSRN 3833311.
72. Fang, X., Xu, M., Xu, S., & Zhao, P. (2019). A deep learning framework for predicting cyber-attacks rates. *EURASIP Journal on Information security, 2019*(1), 1–11.
73. Kumar, P., Kumar, R., Gupta, G. P., Tripathi, R., & Srivastava, G. (2022). P2TIF: A blockchain and deep learning framework for privacy-preserved threat intelligence in industrial IoT. In *IEEE transactions on industrial informatics.*
74. Supangkat, S. H., Hidayat, F., Dahlan, I. A. & Hamami, F. (2019). The Implementation of traffic analytics using deep learning and big data technology with Garuda Smart City framework. In *2019 IEEE 8th GLOBAL Conference on Consumer Electronics (GCCE)* (pp. 883–887). https://doi.org/10.1109/GCCE46687.2019.9015300

Chapter 7
Blockchain Based Smart Card for Smart City

Kazi Tamzid Akhter Md Hasib, Rakibul Hasan, Mubasshir Ahmed, and A. K. M. Bahalul Haque

Abstract We are living in the age of various modern technologies and Blockchain is one of the newest among them. Smart contract are used with Blockchain as an add on which brings automation in application. Smart card are also used nowadays widely to access smart services in various domains. Since the vast majority of people nowadays do not want to carry a lot of cards with them at all times. As a result, we came up with a solution to this conundrum. A single Card, which will function as the key card for all municipal services, will serve as the core hub for all of this decentralization. Also planned is the development of a Cryptocurrency wallet, which will allow smart cities to access anything inside the Blockchain Network directly from peer to peer. There will be no intermediates who will be able to access any citizen's information or data; yet, if an event happens, such as criminal activity, there will be no one to blame. Using blockchain technology, law enforcement will be able to follow down the perpetrators of these crimes since all timestamps will be saved on our platform. Because of this, smart cities will be less prone to criminal activity in general. We can ensure a more efficient smart city by using blockchain technology. Therefore, people will have a greater sense of security at every level of service where Card will play a vital part. Finally, we can say that a Blockchain-based Smart Card will serve as a one-stop solution for all of humanity. Consequently, we don't have to be worried with all of the services that are offered in any certain place. Life will be far better than it has ever been in the past. Blockchain technology, which was initially introduced in 2008 and is based on cryptography, is the fundamental technology that underpins the bitcoin cryptocurrency. Initially, it was exclusively utilized by the cryptocurrency bitcoin.

K. T. A. Md Hasib (✉) · R. Hasan · M. Ahmed
Department of Electrical and Computer Engineering, North South University,
Dhaka, Bangladesh
e-mail: kazi.hasib@northsouth.edu; rakibul.hasan25@northsouth.edu;
mubasshir.ahmed@northsouth.edu

A. K. M. Bahalul Haque
LUT School of Engineering Science, LUT University, Lappeenranta, Finland
e-mail: bahalul.haque@lut.fi

Keywords Blockchain · Smart City · Smart card · Smart contract · Industry 4.0 · Privacy · Security

7.1 Introduction

During this time of industrialization, an increasingly large number of people are moving into urban cities. Cities with growing populations have significant challenges in terms of urban infrastructure, greater demand for resources and public services, and increased environmental impact, among other things. At this moment, the normal approach to city management is not adequate to meet the needs of the metropolitan region and its residents. The idea of a smart city is crucial in solving these kinds of issues. Smart cities may be made more efficient and environmentally friendly by connecting the notion of Blockchain technology with them. The economic breakthrough brought about by the COVID-19 epidemic revealed the need for more effective and sustainable urban management practices progressive technology, such as Blockchain. Blockchain, has the potential to address these socioeconomic concerns while simultaneously improving the efficiency of urban planning.

Smart cities are the ultimate solution in resolving these issues while maintaining optimal comfort for the citizens. Modern smart cities need some essential facilities, services, and supporting technologies to process and function its infrastructures [1]. For all of these activities, blockchain provides a complete framework that controls these operations and ensures that they are managed as effectively as possible. Blockchain is among the most growing and highly effective technologies, and it is constantly evolving with more features to improve our way of life [2]. Besides having an impact on our daily lives, it also facilitates many areas of city management.

Blockchain is a decentralized ledger that securely and permanently records transactions between two parties without requiring any central authentication [3]. This technology for conducting Internet-based verifications and safe transactions has the potential to transform smart city management. In a P2P network, blockchain leverages cryptographic security, which is one of the most critical elements for the protection of data and processes security [4]. Blockchain keeps all the logged transactions. Once the transaction is accepted and saved in blockchain, nobody has the power to alter these transactions and agreements [5]. Regardless of its features like transparency, security, and distribution, blockchain has the potential to become one of the most essential technological answers to the new difficulties that smart cities will face in the future. Moreover, with the advancement of technology, the need for connected devices and technologies is growing in smart cities [6]. The cost of developing and maintaining a separate database (with high reliability and performance, safe & secure with disaster recovery abilities) for these services is very high. Moreover, blockchain technology can solve all of the issues associated with centralization databases and lack of flexibility and transparency [7]. Without relying on centralized control, Blockchain allows network users to share their data with very high levels of reliability and transparency.

Urban city where we are facing high level of accumulation and concentration of economic activities. The number of people using public transport in urban cities is constantly growing. In fact, transportation facilities such as bus stations, airports, and railyards are located within metropolitan regions, which assists cities in their incorporation into regional and global mobility systems [8]. Furthermore, every transportation system has its own payment or ticketing system. And if a person needs to travel from one part of a city to another, and on the way there, he needs to take the metro, then the bus, and then the train, there will be a different ticketing system for bus, train and metro. And people generally want to get from point A to point B as quickly as possible, combining numerous modes of transportation in a flexible manner without having to worry about fare categories, different providers, or the boundaries between various ticketing system. As a result, all of these transportation systems require payment. And there is a chance that customers will have to carry multiple cards (such a bus card, metro card, or subway card) when travelling because each of these forms of transportation may have its own payment system.

As a result, we have developed a solution for public transportation in which every transportation system payment in a city will be integrated, allowing us to pay for all types of transportation cost with only one card. It connects numerous modes of public transportation, including ridesharing services, to a single payment link. Using blockchain technology, a person who takes both a cab and a bus may make their payments using a single way. It aids in the maintenance of an accurate record of the residents' payment papers and information about their identities [9]. This technology will make it possible for the government to provide services that are more targeted and individualized. When it comes to the processing of payment cards, the use of private blockchains limits the number of participants to just those who are actively involved in the current transaction. Participating parties are the only ones who can see the transaction information. Participants need only consist of the customer (or cardholder), the merchant (or POS), and the bank that the merchant uses. Because anybody may participate in the public blockchain, and the list of transactions is seen by anyone, the public blockchain cannot function as a sustainable business model.

This initiative will solve the disorganized transportation system and the widespread public suffering caused by it [10]. The transportation owners and drivers form a syndicate, influencing consumers to pay extra for the service in an indirect way. But they pay less tax to the government. In the existing monitoring system, it is difficult for the government to keep track of these things, and one important aspect is that the truth does not always come out. It will take a lot of human resources to keep track of all of those transactions, and there's a chance that the individuals watching the system may be the root of the problem. The existing system makes it challenging to tackle these challenges. Our recommended approach shines in this regard. In our system, there will be no human involvement. Blockchain based smart card are taking the place of human resources. All transactions will be appropriately supervised and monitored with no human involvement and no danger of failure [11]. Each transaction will preserve total transparency for all parties engaged in the transaction. Owners and drivers of public transit will not be permitted to charge extra for the service. In addition, the government will automatically get the total tax. As a result, both the government and the people will benefit from our system.

This paper starts with a brief introduction to Blockchain and smart city architecture. First, it introduces the important role of the blockchain in smart cities, its basic concepts, and its key technologies. Then it shows an overview of the Blockchain's characteristics and benefits, demonstrating that the technological aspects of the blockchain based smart card and how it is suitable for managing smart cities by reducing high costs for centralized database maintenance, and user privacy leaks. Then it introduced the smart card-based solution for smart cities composed of smart transaction for Transportation System. The report then goes through the smart card analysis in detail, showcasing all of the services such as crypto wallet associated with smart card infrastructure as well as the advantages of combining blockchain technology with smart cards. Finally, it discusses the threats and countermeasures that all services linked to smart cards in smart city infrastructure face and how to avoid them. A working solution is offered to assist in the future use of blockchains in future of smart cities.

7.2 Blockchain Overview

Blockchain is made up of concepts that are essential for its own incorporation into any context. Those concepts would include distinct characteristics of cryptocurrency, transaction scenarios, consensus algorithms [12] and so on. A concise and accurate description of blockchain basics can aid in a thorough knowledge of the technology. As a result, the essentials are listed below. A simple and precise representation of the blockchain fundamentals may help people understand the underlying technology. As a result, the fundamental concepts are listed below.

7.2.1 Characteristics of Blockchain System

There are certain fundamental properties of blockchain. These characteristics are very important for industry and commerce [13]. The following is a brief description of their work:

- **Decentralization**: A peer-to-peer network is formed when each node in a decentralized system is connected to the other nodes in the system. There seems to be no central body or intermediaries, as in a centralized system, which reduces infrastructure, maintenance, and expenditures [14].
- **Immutability**: It is extremely challenging to undo any of the data that has already been placed into the public ledger. Users will never be able to change the information in the ledger [15]. It's an excellent method for assessing one's data as well as their financial activity [16].

- **Persistency**: Other nodes in the network check the validity of each block on a blockchain. As a direct consequence of this, nodes will never include fraudulent transactions [17]. If a block engages in any illegal conduct, other blockchains will be notified, and the algorithms will track it down and settle the transaction [18].
- **Anonymity**: An unidentified transaction that occurred between the sender and the receiver is required to establish long-term privacy. Only a ledger address could be used to accomplish a solid impact. As a result, it does not expose the user's true identify [19, 20].
- **Traceability**: Users can track down records by using transaction details such as timestamps [21]. As a result, blockchain improves the trust and transparency of network data [22].
- **Transparency**: A public ledger makes the information available to users when each transaction is completed [23]. For example, blockchain can identity the environment every 10 min and recombine data exchange in bitcoin. Visibility is created by this degree of transparency, which improves the misunderstanding [24].
- **Autonomy**: A distributed network's nodes may safely update and transfer information without interfering with one another. As a direct consequence of this, there is no one authority that is responsible for keeping track of the transactions [25].

7.2.2   Properties of a Block

There are two distinct components that make up a block structure (Fig. 7.1) [26]. The data, transactions, and transaction counter are stored in the block body, while metadata like a nonce, timestamp, Merkle tree root hash, parent block hash, and many more are placed in the block header. The transaction counter is also included in the block body. While the block header is fixed at 80 bytes, the block content is flexible in size. The block's size decides how many transactions may be processed within it. The very first block, which has no additional blocks as parents, is known as the genesis block [27].

- **Hashing**: Function of a hash, analogous to a biometric template, which creates a unique value code of a predetermined length. Relying on the supplied data, a hash number of 64 characters is created to use a unique technique called SHA-256 [28].
- **Timestamp**: The timestamp maintains track of when a block was generated and when another block data was updated [29]. By designating a precise date and time to the transaction, it is made much simpler to track and validate the transaction.
- **Merkle Tree Root Hash**: The Merkle tree improves the effectiveness of storing vast quantities of data quickly. Every node is tagged as a leaf by a block, and

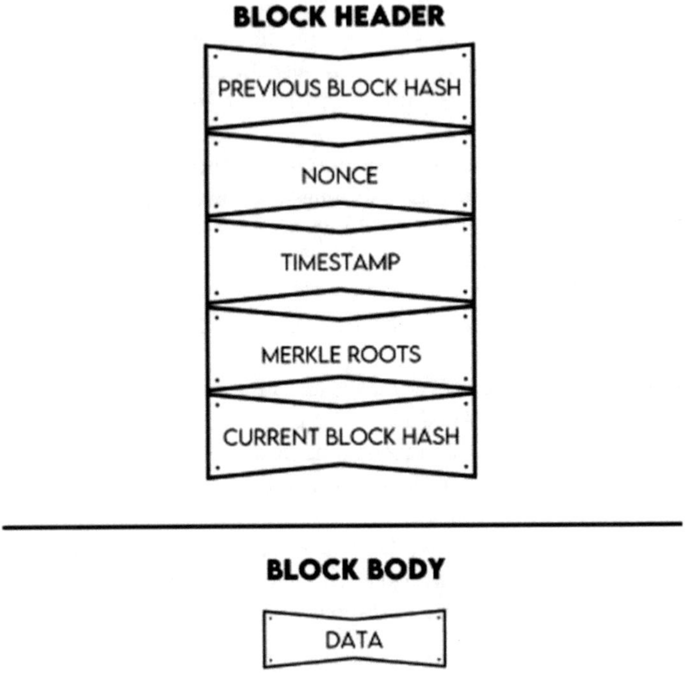

BLOCK HEADER

PREVIOUS BLOCK HASH
NONCE
TIMESTAMP
MERKLE ROOTS
CURRENT BLOCK HASH

BLOCK BODY

DATA

Fig. 7.1 Properties of block header and block body

each transaction is linked via a Merkle tree [30]. Every time a unique Merkle root is created to process all the transactions via the hashing process.

- **Nonce**: The nonce is a four-byte value associated with a hashing algorithm. Miners use it to validate blocks while utilizing PoW. The hash will change entirely if the nonce is modified due to the cascade effect [31].

7.2.3 Blockchain Classification

Blockchainisdividedintothreecategories.Foreachofthem,abriefsummaryisprovidedbelow-

- **Public Blockchain**: This form of the blockchain network is open to the public and accessible to everyone. It is built on the decentralized principle, which makes it possible for anybody to examine the transparent of all the transactions and determine how the mining process works [32]. Nonetheless, the users' true identities are always kept confidential. In this scenario, the transaction is peer-to-peer, which grants all members in the network the ability to direct the OS [33]. It is protected from dangers like as network congestion and Sybil attacks according to the procedure that is the public blockchain. The PoW and PoS protocols restrict the ability of any node or malicious player to generate a block [34]. As a result, public blockchains have a very high level of security. One of the unique advantages of the blockchain is that it functions as a distributed ledger while still preserving user privacy [35]. However, it has certain downsides in terms of cost and speed. As more nodes are added, the cost of electricity rises and the system becomes slower. However, compared to earlier methods, it is faster and less expensive. Examples of public blockchains accessible to the general public include Bitcoin, Ethereum, Litecoin, and many more [15].

- **Private Blockchain**: This type of blockchain network is not open to the public. It is controlled by a centralized body that operates according to network regulations [36]. It restores the historical centralized mechanism for granting access authorization. It is based on rigorous management and deterministic decentralized consensus, and is known as "Practical Byzantine Fault Tolerance (PBFT) " [37]. This consensus is followed in the mining process by a professional team, an industry or numerous organizations to provide transparency and restrict unfamiliar users. The absence of decentralized characteristics on a private blockchain is the major drawback. However, compared to other blockchain variations, it is faster and consumes less power. Therefore, private businesses and organizations, as well as governments, are ideal candidates for this version of blockchain that is operated privately [38].

- **Federated Blockchain**: it is kinds of a hybrid of the two previously stated blockchain types. It is somewhat decentralized, enabling some form of control for authentication to the nodes. Instead of an individual, nodes have the ability to validate the transaction [39]. Transactions, like public blockchain, may be made available as open source. It has many problems with immutability. Nodes have the ability to be malicious and alter transactions. However, it is particularly useful to enterprises comprised of several partners [40].

7.2.4   Consensus Algorithm

In a decentralized system that works on a peer-to-peer (P2P) model, like blockchain, when no one authority has control over the whole network, it may not be easy to get all of the ledgers on the network to agree on anything. As a result, there are a number of protocol or algorithm known as Consensus Protocols or Algorithms that can be used to achieve consensus in a distributed context. Consensus algorithms are used to achieve consensus in a distributed setting. Consensus algorithms, which are used in blockchain technology, also act as a defense against attackers [41, 42]. The following is a description of some of the consensus algorithms:

7.2.4.1 Details of PoW

It is a well-known and widely used consensus protocol. The key principle is that miners must provide proof in order for a block to be validated [43]. The program examines a block to determine its integrity before adding it to the chain. Nonetheless, the miner, also known as a node, is responsible for solving the cryptographic issue first. It operates by establishing a threshold. Miners must estimate a suitable hash by adjusting the nonce in order to verify a block. To validate the information, the previous hash of the block and its timestamp are also utilized. The threshold shifts over time, making authentication challenging. The block will be validated if and only if the new hash value that results from changing the nonce is lower than the threshold value [44, 45]. Nonetheless, finding the secret nonce is difficult owing to the SHA-256 algorithm, which makes it more secure. After completing this problem, the node will be able to introduce the new block into the system. The miner is compensated for his 'labor,' and the block is regarded mined successfully. This method effectively protects double-spending attacks and the forking problem. However, there are certain disadvantages to mining in terms of energy costs [46, 47].

7.2.4.2 Algorithmic Approach of PoS

The strategy gets rid of all of the problems that the PoW had, such as its high energy consumption and computing power requirements. PoW is subjected to a 51 percent attack scenario in which a pool with greater computing power can accomplish the majority of the work. As a result, PoS is implemented differently from PoW. It utilizes cash as a stake. Coinage is calculated by multiplying the currency quantity by the holding time. After 10 days of holding ten coins, one will have one hundred coins in their possession. It, together with the cash, is termed a stake, and it eventually serves to lower the complexity of mining. Additionally, the node with the most stake represents legitimate miners who are unlikely to damage the system. PoS can be purely stack-based, or it can be a combination of stack and grid-based [48, 49].

7.2.4.3 DPoS: Proof of Stake

Daniel Larimer first created DPoS in April 2014 as an enhanced version of PoS with the goal of speeding up transactions and compensating for PoS's shortcomings. DPoS is a type of representative or delegated democracy, whereas PoS is a type of direct democracy. The DPoS method is composed of two components: witnesses as well as interested parties. The block may be generated by witnesses, and witnesses can also profit from the block. The delegates modify the process of creating these blocks and also determine how much money is charged for transactions. The members of these two roles are chosen by the votes of the stakeholders. To ensure the system's integrity, the delegates vote in turn. The person who validates the block is the most significant differential between PoS and DPoS [50]. In a Proof of Stake

(PoS) system, the stakeholder validates the block. In DPoS, on the other hand, the function is carried out by delegates who have been nominated by the stakeholders. It has some benefits over the point of sale. Among them would be the quantity of people participating in the DPoS causes it to move at a slower pace. Aside from that, it is a highly successful, efficient, and adaptive consensus process. Consequently, the confirmation time is lowered to seconds, bringing the bitcoin system up to date [51].

7.2.4.4 Development of the PBFT Protocol

The permissioned consensus method is used in the development of the PBFT protocol. The complexity of the network is reduced to a polynomial rather than an exponential as it is in BFT because it is possible for individual nodes to make decisions on major rules. PBFT is comprised of three separate phases [52]. There are three of them, and they are as follows: from before, the, trained, and dedicated. There are two different kinds of nodes, including the leader and the backup nodes are responsible for the operation of the mining process. Any requests that are received by the leader node are sent to the backup nodes for processing. All nodes can share their contact information in order to demonstrate the integrity of the majority votes [53]. It is resilient to fault nodes because it can sustain up to f fault nodes, and if at least 3f + 1 node remains in the system. It is capable of handling one-third of malicious nodes. Only after receiving two-thirds of the votes cast by the participating nodes is the request forwarded through the stages. PBFT satisfies the time requirement for commercial implementation but has a poor synchronous protocol. As a result, PBFT is best suited to environments dependable, such as private or consortium blockchains [54, 55].

Other consensus techniques exist for specialized jobs and situations. There are around thirty algorithms in all. PoB [56], PoC [57], Ripple [58], PoET [59, 60], and more cryptocurrencies exist for the Network. Those are utilized in the creation of the primary algorithm for the blockchain system, which was previously discussed. Some of them are intended for particular use in certain scenarios. However, no consensus method is ideal for all systems, and there is no such algorithm. As a result, further research is being conducted to address the challenges in diverse applications.

7.2.5 Blockchain Architecture

Blockchain technology may be built using a mix of technologies such as digital signatures, cryptographic hashes, consensus algorithms, transactions, apps, and so on. These technologies may be thought of as network layers. The type of layer may change based on the environment and application [61, 62].

7.2.5.1   Data Level of Blockchain

The location where the processes and procedures pertaining to the data are kept. Block structures make up the majority of the layer's composition like timestamps, Merkle trees, data blocks, hash functions, asymmetric encryption, and chain structures. The primary purpose of the data layer is to generate data and attach for validation The block has both a hash function for itself and a hash function for its parent [63]. It is validated when it is added to the chain, the location from which the original hash is retrieved. The chain continues to grow as miners add new blocks to the system. The Merkle root tree is the name given to this structure, and the root node is known as the genesis block. An additional method through which the Merkle tree may validate the reliability and consistency of the system by verifying the timestamp [64].

7.2.5.2   Components of the Blockchain Network

Network Layer for Blockchain, there are a variety of data verification methods that may be utilized. Some examples of these processes include Data transmission, network design, decentralized networking, and packet forwarding, amongst others [65]. In a peer-to-peer network structure, blockchain employs digital signatures. Asymmetric cryptography ensures the legitimacy of this form of public network.

7.2.5.3   Consensus Layer

A huge challenge lies ahead in order to successfully deploy the system without encountering any security issues. Whenever threats or viruses alter any data, there is no way to use blockchain technology, and the network becomes vulnerable to harmful activity. As a result, it is critical to have a great appearance in order to defend the architecture and avoid all types of attacks. Different consensus algorithms, are suggested to prevent attacks and handle security challenges [66]. The consensus layer's primary goal is to offer a framework for verifying blocks, transactions, and security [67].

7.2.5.4   Process Inside Incentive Layer

Nodes are encouraged to participate in the blockchain process through the incentive layer. In exchange for incentives, in the block construction and data validation procedures, each node must contend with self-interest. As a result, this layer is made up of a system for distribution and issuance. Additionally, it creates a secure setting for business transactions [68].

7.2.5.5 Mechanism of Contract Layer

The layer offers a set of rules that govern how transactions involving currencies, assets, rights, and so on may be communicated throughout the network. In this example, the layer conducts the transaction using smart contracts, algorithms, and numerous scripts. Furthermore, smart contracts serve as a ledger between nodes. If the nodes agreed to the rules, the contract is signed cryptographically [69].

7.2.5.6 Network Insider: Application Layer

The application layer represents a variety of situations such as smart cities, market security, commercial applications, IoT, digital identification, intellectual property, and so on [70]. It does, in fact, deliver the result of a blockchain-based system that can be put into operation. It is composed of application programming interfaces (APIs). Not only that it also composed of a variety of frameworks. You will find out that a user interfaces as well as scripts that enable users to take part inside the whole network [71].

7.2.6 Transaction Phase

In most circumstances, there are five stages involved in the transaction process. These procedures may differ from one model to another, but the underlying concept is nearly identical. Suppose, Alice wishes to offer Bob 10 bitcoin (BTC) [72].

Figure 7.2 is describing our whole architecture model. Distributed Network Mode (DNM) is interacting with Wallet. Inside the DNM it's validating data in the block where public key, private key will be maintained from wallet data.

- **Generate Transaction**: Alice must first construct the transaction data by using the Unspent Transaction Outputs (UTXOs). It refers to the fact that the transferable bitcoin must remain unspent. Following SHA-256, Alice creates a hash of the source data and the receiver's public key. It contains the bitcoin amount as well as data encrypted using Alice's private key. The input transaction may be uniquely recognized using this hash value. It may also cancel the transaction if it differs or changes. As a result, the hash will operate as a digital signature, protecting the transaction from manipulation [73].
- **Verifying the Transaction**: Bob, the recipient, must confirm the deal after it has been generated. Bob must now look for a number of items. He must be certain that the transaction is not an instance of double-spending. It can be resolved by confirming both parties' signatures. Only after this verification can the output transaction be redeemed. Once again, only genuine blocks may be added to the network. As a result, if the transaction becomes a part of the blockchain, it is also regarded genuine. A transaction is lawful if the total input UTXOs equals or

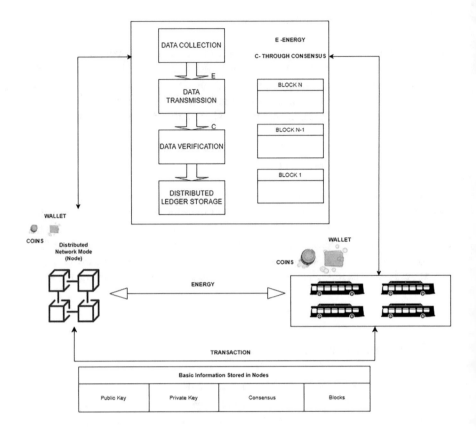

Fig. 7.2 Blockchain transactions in network with smart card

exceeds the total output UTXOs. This is called the law of conservation of values [74].

- **Making a Claim to Ownership**: In order to claim ownership of the transaction, Bob will now need both a private key and a public key. Using the private key, the receiver may produce a valid signature. The hash from the transaction creation stage that contains the receiver's public key decrypts precisely when the sender transmits the transaction. This digital signature must match; otherwise, the transaction will be invalidated since it is deemed fraudulent [75].

- **Mining process and Mechanism of Consensus**: Distributed ledger blocks must be produced after encryption with particular authentication requirements. Different algorithms define these requirements, allowing the parties, Alice and Bob, to agree that the block is genuine. Algorithms such as PoW can function well since they must solve the cryptographic problem with tremendous labor to validate the validity of the block. With block information such as previous hash, timestamp, block version, nonce, and Merkle root hash, a hash value less than the goal value is constructed. This target value is likewise updated on a regular basis to ensure the block's legitimacy [76].

- **Blocking Validation**: During the validation step, Bob must confirm that the occurrence of the transaction follows the reference. Again, the prior hash must be included in the current block, and the timestamp must be correct. Finally, Bob must confirm that the block is verified using PoW [77].

After all of these phases are completed, Bob will get the transaction, and Alice will receive confirmation of the completed transaction.

7.3 Industrial Adoption

Blockchain is a relatively recent development of technology that has expanded rapidly over the last several years. Its qualities and benefits open up a world of possibilities for many applications. Blockchain includes properties like as immutability and transparency, which are uncommon. The protection of user data is an additional crucial aspect of blockchain, which is essential in business. Blockchain may be used to solve problems in transactions, supply chain management, workforce management, and legal difficulties. Blockchain technology provides innovative features [78]. The Characteristics serve as the foundation for numerous company concepts. The current corporate landscape is being transformed by these new models, which are having a significant impact on industries including healthcare, banking, supply chain management, apparel, IoT, vehicles, and more.

There have been four industrial revolutions up to this point. A high level of automation, optimization, efficiency, production rates, and sustainability are all desirable, are made feasible as a result of recent revolutions [79]. There are several components (technological enablers) that contribute to the modernization of the industry. Industry 4.0 is no longer concerned with individual computerized equipment; rather, [80, 81] it is concerned with the entire network [82]. It includes resource control, among other things, in order to finish the manufacturing process which replace traditional manufacturing environments with optimized, cutting-edge distributed systems. Some Industry 4.0 design concepts enable firms to study a potential transition from their present systems to Industry 4.0 technology. In general, there are six design tenets [83] based on the commercial situation. It may be more or lesser. The six design tenets are characterized as being blow.

- **Interoperability**: It establishes a common communication platform for gadgets, people, and other entities. It used networks for IoT and IoS to interact.
- **Service-Oriented**: The IoS must be considered while developing an Industry 4.0 framework.
- **Decentralization**: Cyber-physical systems (CPS) should be self-contained.
- **Real-time monitoring Capability**: CPS must operate in real-time to give real-time insights into company processes and identify production concerns [84].

- **Modularity of System**: It is expected that every component is "plug and play" with very minimal initial setup required. Because of the system setup, businesses will be able to successfully adjust in response to the requirement of the market.
- **Virtualization**: Here's how to recreate tangible goods and services digitally. The CPS should be capable of simulating conditions similar to those seen in the normal world while operating inside a digital setting. Furthermore, it will aid in the execution of scenario simulations [85].

Blockchain is the most recent addition for offering automation, security, privacy, product racing, and other benefits [86].

7.3.1 Automation of Supply Chain Management

Depending on the product, supply chain management might be quite complicated. A supply chain network is made up of several pieces that are spread out over different areas and stages. These numerous parts provide the network that needed to meet user requests. Due to the complexity and lack of transparency in our supply chain, it might be divided into different entities. These organizations can use blockchain. The unique characteristics of blockchain technology have the potential to revolutionize the sector [87].

7.3.2 Security and It's Privacy

Furthermore, the technology is required to ensure the confidentiality, integrity, and availability of the information. The technology known as blockchain may be implemented in decentralized environments. Its primary characteristics are immutability, transparency, and non-repudiation. Given these characteristics, blockchain has the potential to deliver an extremely efficient, secure, and reliable industrial solution for the sector. Identity management, authentication, and the defense against cyberattacks are some potential applications for blockchain technology, such as resistance against DDoS assaults in the IoT context [88].

7.3.3 Tracking of Product Manufacturing Phases

There is a lifespan for every process. The same may be said of the production process. The lifespan of every product manufacturing process necessitates a number of stages. It is critical to keep track of what is going on in each of these stages. The product life cycle management method encompasses everything from gathering raw materials to logging the products in a server to commencing the production process and ending with trash management [89]. With all of these processes incorporated in any production process, blockchain can be advantageous. This provides an opportunity for stakeholders to keep a track of the production process in real time, without the need to analyze or contact customers. On the other hand, suppliers using the outdated system are unable to do manual monitoring of the product life cycle. As a result, the whole system suffers from a lack of openness and transparency. Throughout an individual's working life, blockchain technology may find applications in a number of settings. Some examples are shown below [90].

- System for controlling and managing versions of files.
- Maintain a record of past, current, and future ideas and developments.
- Creating an index of the basic ingredients
- Managing the expectations of the clients and the goals of the product.
- Tracking of the production line.
- Keeping track of and organizing a number of different chemical and physical characteristics.
- Bringing corporate systems together.
- Maintain an up-to-date product knowledge base for the company.

7.3.4 Payment Systems

The accounts linked is now fully automated thanks to the Internet of Things. Moreover, now, it is possible for all IoT devices to decide for themselves when required. For instance, the amount of power that devices consume is immediately compensated. We no longer have the means to do, and the existing method of making payments is insufficient because of the transaction cost and limited capacity it has. When it comes to making payments, using the credit card system and exchanging card information with our various gadgets comes with its own set of unique obstacles. The use of blockchain technology in this situation could be beneficial. The following list includes some of these reasons –.

- **Low pace of Transaction**: We often use Third party payment processors, which are relatively costly. We can prevent it and begin using blockchain to lower transaction rates. Also, we may employ crypto transactions. Also, we may employ crypto transactions, which have a minimal transaction cost that will be decreased further in the future.
- **Instant payment**: In the case of cryptocurrencies, funds are credited immediately rather than 2 or 3 days. The transactions can easily be done 24 h a day, 7 days a week.
- **Fair distribution**: The whole system might be automated using smart contracts. Therefore, no human intervention will be needed [91].

7.4 Smart Card Usage in Smart Transportation

Smart transportation has achieved broad appeal in recent years, owing mainly to the advancement of Information and communication technology. It enhances the quality of transportation, increases pedestrian safety for vehicles, and makes both passengers and drivers more comfortable. Blockchain technology could make it easier to share information, track vehicles, and network lifespan reliability [92]. Also, blockchain helps the transportation industry by making security checks, inspections, and data management faster. The following document outlines research on blockchain-based smart cards in the smart transportation system in urban cities.

Smart mobility or transport is a notion that aims to enhance the mobility of people in cities by developing modern transportation systems. Today, Urban cities need to manage their transportation networks to meet the needs of their citizens. Blockchain technology can improve vehicle and passenger tracking, as well as the payment of transportation fees effectively. One of the biggest hurdles a city faces is effective transportation network management. It can also be utilized to plan for the different needs of different commuters. It can also help transport authorities improve their efficiency and effectiveness. Blockchain technology can be used with IoT devices and systems to keep track of vehicles and their passengers in real time [93]. And also, all vehicle users can use their smart cards to pay directly to the car or bicycle owner even after the trip.

Various applications of blockchain technology allow transportation decision-makers to optimize routing strategies and timetables to meet the diverse needs of commuters and achieve greater impact in relation to environmental and sustainability goals [94]. An efficient transportation network powered by blockchain technology allows users to safely pay for transportation services throughout the transportation ecosystem by using a smart card. Blockchain has the tech of storing enormous amounts of sensitive data, as well as maintaining a complete and unchangeable history of traveling, distance, maintenance, and other activities while providing businesses a greater knowledge of user profiles without breaching any privacy. Blockchain will also be an enabler of mobility as a Service solution that can provide citizens with a variety of additional services such as car sharing, payments, insurance, and maintenance [95].

Additionally, we can ensure secure and real time data flow in smart cities by using blockchain technology. However, in a smart city context, it also facilitates smooth interactions between users of autonomous technologies. The peer-to-peer network can benefit the integration of numerous devices used in different smart city applications for authentication and resistance against cyberattacks [96]. As a result, the two most significant problems are preserving user privacy and guaranteeing transactional data security. Unauthorized access, data theft, and data tampering are just a few of the challenges facing smart transportation. Attackers can cause social and economic harm by disrupting the transportation system. People use public transport for their daily commute. If they cannot get to work, this can negatively influence the economy. The attacker can cause the electrical flow and power supply might be disrupted by an attacker, forcing transport units to halt. In addition, attackers can alter traffic signs on the streets or at transportation terminals to create instability, interrupt ticket vending machines, and harm others.

Smart healthcare must be properly safeguarded since it deals with sensitive personal data. In the healthcare sector, a data breach might be disastrous. Patients' private data will be made public, which may be exploited for identity theft, blackmail, and other purposes [97].

By using smart cards in this sector, we can encounter the regular daily life problem. They function by being pre-loaded with cash and credit subtracted each time the user scans it at a ticket date. It reduces the need for customers to stand in line for tickets and allow them to move quickly through a congested train station. That's great if you're running late for your morning commute! The automated fare collecting gates make passing through a station much faster and easier.

7.4.1 Benefits of Smart Transportation?

It is not easy to execute smart transportation solutions or to build "smart cities" by merging information and communication technology and other essential technologies into a city's transportation network. A collaboration of national and local governments works closely with smart mobility solution providers to develop solutions that will make citizens' lives and workplaces better, safer, and more enjoyable places to live and work [98]. Sometimes choosing which solutions will benefit the largest number of people is sometimes the most challenging challenge that decision-makers face. On the other hand, governments and city authorities can make cities more livable, workable, and sustainable – both economically and environmentally, with the correct planning and investment.

Smart transportation systems throughout the world are aiming to increase the safety of life for everyone in urban places. The key advantages of smart mobility are improved transportation system safety, accessibility, and sustainability.

7.4.1.1 Sustainability

All enterprises, including local and national governments, must be concerned with sustainability. A smart city's interconnected bike and pedestrian routes tempt people to leave their automobiles at home more often, promoting environmental sustainability. Organizations must work to provide enough charging stations to accommodate the growing number of electric vehicles so that owners may conveniently charge their vehicles and add to the overall sustainability of a community [99]. The infrastructure also becomes more environmentally friendly by making public transportation as efficient as private automobiles for traveling from one place to another.

7.4.1.2   Livability

An effective, practical, and reliable transportation network is one of the most prized components of every modern city. Smart mobility solutions allow individuals to travel more effectively for both professional and leisure purposes, resulting in less time spent stuck in traffic. Smart transportation options also help reduce traffic, leading to cleaner air in and around "smart cities," improving the livability of city life and the standard of living in general [100].

7.4.1.3   Workability

A lot of us spend a notable portion of time commuting to work or coming back to work to home by public transport. An intelligent transportation network provides convenient, affordable, and reliable ways to get to our work.

Furthermore, smart mobility systems also can attract business. Companies assess the transportation network when determining where to locate or move employees since they realize how dependent they are on it [101]. It creates new job possibilities for individuals while also making a city more appealing to people wishing to relocate.

7.4.1.4   Increased Safety

Nowadays, many road accidents are caused by human mistakes or a lack of information about one's surroundings. Smart transportation can assist in mitigating the impact of these variables. Driverless automobiles, semi-autonomous assistance systems, and networked cars will extend communication channels between commuters and give technical assistance when human senses fail [102].

7.4.1.5   Better Accessibility

Every city's smart mobility plan must consider the demands of all persons who want to use the public transportation system. For persons with disabilities, seamless transit and route planning and payment for transportation via a single smart card can considerably improve their quality of life. Hearing and speaking aids, as well as accessibility for wheelchairs, service animals, and other special needs, are all essential components of a smart transportation system.

We will use a crypto wallet to create our blockchain-based smart cards in smart cities, and consumers will be able to pay or transfer money throughout the transportation network using this card. It will give citizens privacy safeguards for the large volumes of data created in smart cities, such as healthcare, transportation, and service data [103]. Collection of location-based data, its transmission across the area networks, new technologies may offer considerable privacy risks if appropriate privacy safeguards are not applied. With blockchain, however, overcoming the complexity and the system's privacy constraints associated with distributed servers. We can ensure allowed access to many data types, including health and financial records, by employing a blockchain-based smart card.

7.5 Crypto Wallet with Smart Card

Cash exchange is facilitated using a cryptocurrency wallet. Transactions are secure because they are cryptographically signed. Mobile and web devices may access the wallet, and the user's identity and privacy are both safeguarded. As a consequence, a blockchain-based crypto wallet has every feature needed for risk-free financial transactions and capital transfers between various parties [104]. Most of the time, it works much like sending or receiving money using PayPal or any other popular payment option.

7.5.1 Security

It is possible to transfer and receive cryptocurrencies like Bitcoin and Ethereum using a crypto wallet, which protects the private keys (the passwords that enable anyone access to your cryptocurrency). From crypto wallets like Ledger (which looks like a USB stick) to mobile wallets like Coinbase, utilizing crypto is as simple as using your credit card to buy goods and services on the internet [105].

A Bitcoin wallet functions similarly to a traditional currency wallet. In the same way that you wouldn't carry a thousand dollars in your pocket, you may want to take the same precautions with your Bitcoin wallet. General rule of thumb: keep only modest quantities of bitcoins on your computer, mobile device, or server for daily usage and store the remainder of your assets in a more secure location [106].

Below you will find how to secure your wallet:

7.5.2 Backup Wallet

Some wallets have a large number of concealed private keys that are used internally. If you only have a backup of the private keys for the Bitcoin addresses that are available to the public, it is possible that you may not be able to retrieve a significant portion of your assets [107].

7.5.3 Encrypt Online Backups

Any backup that is kept on the internet is very susceptible to being stolen. Even a computer that is linked to the Internet might become a victim of malicious software if not protected. A recommended security practice is thus encrypting any backups that are made available to the public over a network [108].

7.5.4 Use Many Secure Locations

Single points of failure are harmful to the security of a system. If your backup is not reliant on a single place, it is less probable that a catastrophic incident would prohibit you from recovering your wallet information. You may also want to think about employing multiple types of media, such as USB keys, papers, and CDs [109].

7.5.5 Make Regular Backups

To ensure that any recent Bitcoin change identities as well as any new Bitcoin addresses you establish are included in your backup, you must backup your wallet on a regular basis. All programs, on the other hand, will soon be utilizing wallets that will only need to be backed up once.

Traditional banking systems provide a number of challenges while conducting any transaction. Transaction's speed is slow because each transaction must go via an intermediary, such as a bank, which validates the transaction. And there is a high point of failure. There are other difficulties in keeping track of all accounts and balances; data may be compromised, manipulated, or corrupted across the multiple systems where the accounts and balances are stored [110]. Blockchain wallets mitigate or eliminate these issues.

7.6 Crypto Wallet Features

- It's simple to use. It works simply like any other piece of software or wallet we use on a daily basis.
- Extremely safe. It uses peer-to-peer transactions, and there are no third parties involved. That means it's very secure.
- Enables cross-border transactions in real-time. These are also barrier-free, as there are no intermediaries.
- Transaction costs are low. Compared to regular banks, the cost of moving cash is significantly lower.

- Enables transfers between different cryptocurrencies. This makes currency conversions simple.

7.6.1 Blockchain Wallet Types

There are two kinds of blockchain wallets based on private keys: hot and cold wallets [111]. Hot wallets resemble the everyday wallets we carry with us for daily transactions. Hot wallets are online wallets that allow for the fast transfer of cryptocurrency. They are available on the internet. Coinbase and Blockchain are two examples. Cold wallets are similar to vaults in that they securely store cryptocurrency.

Furthermore, there are other types of Digital offline wallets known as "cold wallets," which sign transactions offline before publishing them online [112]. They are not kept in the cloud on the internet; instead, they are kept offline, which is called cold storage for maximum protection. Trezor and Ledger are two examples of cold wallets.

7.7 Research Directions and Security

Blockchain has enormous business potential. But we do not yet fully understand its opportunities. As a result, it is obvious that some challenges would arise in the system's implementation, which will necessitate more research. Blockchain is seen to be beneficial for the industrial sector due to its concrete security. It does, however, have certain security risks. There are hazards such as message hijacking, smart contract program flaws, and so on [113]. Another issue to be concerned about is data leaking. Blockchain is a completely internet-based program that creates a massive network. As a result, it is vulnerable to assaults such as hacking, theft, spying efforts, and DoS attacks. Another issue is double-spending, which results in an invalid transaction. It offers a solution to prevent this, but its implementation across several platforms and participants still takes a lot of work [114, 115].

7.7.1 Integration

Blockchain is a collection of technologies that act in tandem. It must retain coherence with diverse sorts of components in order to be implemented in industrial sectors. As a result, integrating all of it at once requires a highly complicated system. Any integration procedure with a large number of functions should be understandable and speedy. If one of the pieces fails to function properly, the other should serve backup or it will be vulnerable to attacks, privacy problems, and lack of availability. Future research should focus to increase the effectiveness and speed of its integration [116].

7.7.2 Resource Limitations

The system must have the significant processing power, not only that but also the scalability. Stability in order to reap the advantages of blockchain. Numerous blockchain operations, including mining, block generation, and validation, need to be carried out continuously. However, this is a difficult process. For the time being, IoT devices used in blockchain may support it. It is critical to do research in this field in order to fulfill the future demands for blockchain resources and to deploy them in large enterprises [117].

7.7.3 System Scalability

A certain blockchain size has been defined for the distributed ledger, where transactions & data protection are fully assured. On a broader scale, The slower the procedure becomes as the blockchain grows in size. The mining process requires a specific time for the consensus mechanism. It is more challenging to synchronize with the system in the more critical case [118].

7.7.4 System Regulations

It lacks a third party who can serve as an authority figure and oversee activities. Yet, in order to accomplish anything on a significant scale, certain guidelines need to be acknowledged and adhered to, in conjunction with the standards that are now prevalent in the business [119]. The long-term viability of blockchain industrial applications would be endangered otherwise.

7.8 Conclusion

We developed a smart city transportation and other service solution. Everything will be centered on a single smart card, which will be the city's sole mode of mobility. We also intend to create a Cryptocurrency wallet so that smart cities can directly peer to peer within the Blockchain Network. There will be no intermediaries who can get access to any citizen's information or data. If any incident occurs, such as criminal conduct. Because all timestamps will be stored on our system, law enforcement will be able to track these perpetrators using blockchain technology. As a smart city role model, Dubai has successfully implemented 24 use cases of blockchain technology, including eight primary sectors: business, real estate, transportation, security, health, financial services, education, and tourism. Both the government and private organizations are working on these problems. The usage of blockchain technology has increased by 24% in Dubai, which is far more than the average rise of 19% found around the world. Currently, Dubai has more than 100 blockchain startups. Adopting blockchain technology in Dubai would help the government save around 5.5 billion dirhams annually. If all goes according to plan, Dubai will become the world's first government to be run by blockchain technology. This thriving ecosystem will help organizations to grow and expand their operations, which will attract additional investors and collaborations in the region. We are working on putting up a strategy to limit the risk to privacy and security. Using blockchain technology, we can ensure a better smart city. As a consequence, individuals will feel safer at every level of service where smart card will play a significant role. Finally, we can state that a Blockchain-based smart card will be a one-stop solution for everyone. As a result, we do not need to be concerned about all of the services available within any city. Life will be considerably better than it has ever been.

References

1. Nakamoto, S. & Bitcoin, A. (2008). A peer-to-peer electronic cash system. In *Bitcoin*. https://doi.org/10.1007/978-3-030-17740-9_3.
2. Collomb, A. & Sok, K. (2016). Blockchain/distributed ledger technology (DLT): what impact on the financial sector? *Digiworld Economic Journal*.
3. Joshi, A. P., Han, M., & Wang, Y. (2018). A survey on security and privacy issues of blockchain technology. *Mathematical Foundations of Computing, 1*(2), 121–147. https://doi.org/10.3934/mfc.2018007
4. Andoni, M., Robu, V., Flynn, D., Abram, S., Geach, D., Jenkins, D., McCallum, P., & Peacock, A. (2019). Blockchain technology in the energy sector: A systematic review of challenges and opportunities. *Renewable and Sustainable Energy Reviews, 100*, 143–174. https://doi.org/10.1016/j.rser.201810.014
5. Saxena, S., Bhushan, B., & Ahad, M. A. (2021). Blockchain based solutions to Secure Iot: Background, integration trends and a way forward. *Journal of Network and Computer Applications, 181, 103050*. https://doi.org/10.1016/j.jnca.2021.103050
6. Kumar, A., Abhishek, K., Bhushan, B., & Chakraborty, C. (2021). Secure access control for manufacturing sector with application of ethereum blockchain. *Peer-to-Peer Networking and Applications, 14*, 3058–3074. https://doi.org/10.1007/s12083-021-01108-3
7. Chase, M., Kohlweiss, M., Lysyanskaya, A., & Meiklejohn, S. (2014) Malleable signatures: new definitions and delegatable anonymous credentials. In *2014 IEEE 27th computer security foundations symposium* (pp. 199–213). IEEE.
8. Biswas, K. & Muthukkumarasamy, V. (2016). Securing smart cities using blockchain Technology. In *IEEE Conference publications* (pp. 1392–1393).
9. Christidis, K., & Devetsikiotis, M. (2016). Blockchains and smart contracts for the internet of things. *IEEE Journals & Magazines, 4*, 2292–2303.

10. Chen W. (2017). Urban parking problem analysis and solving countermeasures: taking Xian as the example. In *3rd international conference on social science and technology education* (pp. 1–6). https://doi.org/10.12783/dtssehs/icsste2017/9301.

11. Plosz, S. & Varga, P. (2018). Security and safety risk analysis of vision guided autonomous vehicles. In *2018 IEEE Industrial Cyber-Physical Systems (ICPS)* (pp. 193–8). https://doi.org/10.1109/ICPHYS.2018.8387658.

12. Gupta, R., Tanwar, S., Kumar, N., & Tyagi, S. (2020). Blockchain-based security attack resilience schemes for autonomous vehicles in industry 4.0: A systematic review. *Computers and Electrical Engineering, 86*, 106717. https://doi.org/10.1016/j.compeleceng.2020.106717

13. Lin, I.-C., & Liao, T.-C. (2017). A survey of blockchain security issues and challenges. *International Journal of Network Security, 19*, 653–659. https://doi.org/10.6633/IJNS.201709.19(5).01

14. Wang, L., Kwok, S. K., & Ip, W. H. (2010). A radio frequency identification and sensor-based system for the transportation of food. *Journal of Food Engineering, 101*(1), 120–129.

15. Atzori, L., Iera, A., & Morabito, G. (2010). The internet of things: A survey. *Computer Networks, 54*(15), 2787–2805.

16. Buterin, V. (2014). *A Next-Generation Smart Contract and Decentralized Application Platform*. White Paper.

17. Wu, J., Guo, S., Huang, H., Liu, W., & Xiang, Y. (2018). Information and communications technologies for sustainable development goals: State-of-the-art, needs and perspectives. *IEEE Communications Surveys and Tutorials, 20*(3), 2389–2406.

18. Goyal, S., Sharma, N., Kaushik, I., & Bhushan, B. (2021). Blockchain as a solution for security attacks in named data networking of things. *Security and Privacy Issues in IoT Devices and Sensor Networks*, 211–243. https://doi.org/10.1016/b978-0-12-821255-4.00010-9

19. Peters, G. W., Panayi, E., & Chapelle, A. (2015). Trends in crypto-currencies and blockchain technologies: A monetary theory and regulation perspective. *Journal of Financial Perspectives, 3*, 46.

20. Sasson, E.B., Chiesa, A., Garman, C., Green, M., Miers, I., Tromer, E. & Virza, M. (2014) Zerocash: Decentralized anonymous payments from Bitcoin. In *Proceedings of 2014 IEEE symposium on Security and Privacy (SP)* (pp.459–474).

21. Tayal, A., Solanki, A., Kondal, R., Nayyar, A., Tanwar, S., & Kumar, N. (2021). Blockchain-based efficient communication for food supply chain industry: Transparency and traceability analysis for sustainable business. *International Journal of Communication Systems, 34*, e4696. https://doi.org/10.1002/dac.4696

22. Zyskind, G. & Nathan, O. (2015). Decentralizing privacy: Using blockchain to protect personal data. In *Proceedings of the 2015 IEEE security and privacy workshops* (pp. 21–22).

23. Peters, G.W. & Panayi, E. (2016). Understanding modern banking ledgers through blockchain technologies: Future of transaction processing and smart contracts on the internet of money. In *Banking beyond banks and money* (pp. 239–278). Springer.

24. Zheng, Z., Xie, S., Dai, H., Chen, X., & Wang, H. (2018). Blockchain challenges and opportunities: A survey. *International Journal of Web and Grid Services, 14*(4), 352–375. https://doi.org/10.1504/IJWGS.2018.095647

25. Al-Riyami, S. S., & Paterson, K. G. (2003). Certificateless public key cryptography. In C. S. Laih (Ed.), *Advances in cryptology – ASIACRYPT 2003* (pp. 452–473). Springer.

26. Ao, W., Fu, S., Zhang, C., & Xu, M. (2020). A secure certificateless identity authentication scheme based on Blockchain. In W. Han, L. Zhu, & F. Yan (Eds.), *Trusted computing and information security* (pp. 251–266). Springer.

27. Yinxia, S., & Futai, Z. (2010). Secure certificate less encryption with short ciphertext. *Chinese Journal of Electronics, 19*(2), 313–318.

28. Purohit, S., Calyam, P., Alarcon, M. L., et al. (2021). HonestChain: Consortium blockchain for protected data sharing in health information systems. *Peer-to-Peer Networking and Applications*. https://doi.org/10.1007/s12083-021-01153-y

29. Alsunaidi, S. J. & Alhaidari, F. A. (2019). A survey of consensus algorithms for blockchain technology. In *2019 international conference on computer and information sciences* (pp. 1–6). IEEE, https://doi.org/10.1109/iccisci.2019.8716424.
30. Christidis, K., & Devetsikiotis, M. (2016). Blockchains and smart contracts for the internet of things. *IEEE Access, 4,* 2292–2303. https://doi.org/10.1109/ACCESS.2016.2566339
31. Fan, K., Ren, Y., Yan, Z., Wang, S., Li, H., & Yang, Y. (2018). Secure time synchronization scheme in IoT based on Blockchain. In *2018 IEEE international conference on internet of things (IThings) and IEEE green computing and communications (GreenCom) and IEEE cyber, physical and social computing (CPSCom) and IEEE smart data (SmartData)* (p. 1068). IEEE, https://doi.org/10.1109/cybermatics_2018.2018.00196.
32. Vigil, M. A. G., Weinert, C., Demirel, D., & Buchmann, J. A. (2014). An efficient timestamping solution for long-term digital archiving. In *IEEE 33rd international performance computing and communications conference* (pp. 1–8). IEEE Computer Society. https://doi.org/10.1109/PCCC.2014.7017099
33. Li, X.H. (2021). Blockchain-based Cross-border E-business Payment Model. In *2021 2nd International Conference on E-Commerce and Internet Technology (ECIT)*. https://doi.org/10.1109/ECIT52743.2021.00022.
34. Hepp, T., Schoenhals, A., Gondek, C., & Gipp, B. (2018). OriginStamp: A Blockchain-backed system for decentralized trusted timestamping. *Information Technology, 60*(5–6), 273–281. https://doi.org/10.1515/itit-2018-0020
35. Jie, X., Xue, K., Tian, H., & Hong, J. (2020). Peilin Hong, an identity management and authentication scheme based on redactable blockchain for mobile networks. *IEEE Transactions on Vehicular Technology, 69*(6), 6688–6698.
36. Gertner, Y., Goldwasser, S., & Malkin, T. (1998). Random server model for private information Retrievalî, In *International workshop on randomization and approximation techniques in computer science* (pp. 200–217). Springer.
37. Yassein, M.B., Shatnawi, F., Rawashdeh, S., Mardin, W. (2019). Blockchain technology: Characteristics, security and privacy; issues and solutions. In *2019 IEEE/ACS 16th international conference on computer systems and applications* (pp. 1–8). AICCSA. https://doi.org/10.1109/AICCSA47632.2019.9035216.
38. Ray, S., Puthal, D., Sharma, S., Mohanty, S. P., & Zomaya, A. Y. (2018). Building a sustainable Internet of Things. *IEEE Consumer Electronics Magazine, 7*(2), 42–49.
39. Eyal, I., Gencer, A., Sirer, E. & Renesse, R. (2016). Bitcoin-NG: A scalable blockchain protocol. In *Proceeding 13th USENIX symposium networked systems design and implementation* (pp. 45–59).
40. Mukhopadhyay, U., Skjellum, A., Hambolu, O., Oakley, J., Yu, L., & Brooks, R. (2016). A brief survey of cryptocurrency systems. In *2016 14th annual conference on privacy, security and trust* (pp. 745–752). IEEE. https://doi.org/10.1109/PST.2016.7906988.
41. Lai, J., Ding, X. & Wu, Y. (2013). Accountable trapdoor sanitizable signatures. In *International conference on information security practice and experience* (pp. 117–131). Springer.
42. Zhu, P., Hu, J. & Li, X., Zhu, Q. (2021). Using blockchain technology to enhance the traceability of original achievements. *IEEE Transactions on Engineering Management*. https://doi.org/10.1109/TEM.2021.3066090.
43. Hughes, L., Dwivedi, Y. K., Misra, S. K., Rana, N. P., Raghavan, V., & Akella, V. (2019). Blockchain research, practice and policy: Applications, benefits, limitations, emerging research themes and research agenda. *International Journal of Information Management, 49,* 114–129.
44. Xu, G., Dong, J. & Ma, C. (2021). A certificate less encryption scheme based on blockchain. *Peer-to-Peer Networking and Applications*. https://doi.org/10.1007/s12083-021-01147-w.
45. Wan, S., Li, M. & Liu, G., et al. (2019). Recent advances in consensus protocols for blockchain: A survey. *Wireless Network*. https://doi.org/10.1007/s11276-019-02195-0.
46. Sayeed, S., & Marco-Gisbert, H. (2019). Assessing blockchain consensus and security mechanisms against the 51% attack. *Applied Science, 9*(9), 1788.

47. Hardjono, T., Lipton, A., & Pentland, A. (2020). Toward an interoperability architecture for blockchain autonomous systems. *IEEE Transactions on Engineering Management, 67*(4), 1298–1309.
48. Mood, B., Gupta, D., Butler, K. & Feigenbaum, J. (2014). Reuse it or lose it: more efficient secure computation through reuse of encrypted values. In *Proceedings of the ACM SIGSAC conference on computer and communications security.*
49. Yuan, Y. & Wang, F. (2016). Towards Blockchain-based intelligent transportation systems. In *2016 IEEE 19th international conference on intelligent transportation systems* (pp. 2663–2668). ITSC. https://doi.org/10.1109/ITSC.2016.7795984
50. Wu, Y., Song, P., & Wang, F. (2020). Hybrid consensus algorithm optimization: A mathematical method based on POS and PBFT and its application in blockchain. *Mathematical Problems in Engineering.*
51. Manimuthu, A., Sreedharan, V. R., Rejikumar, G., & Marwaha, D. (2019). A literature review on bitcoin: Transformation of crypto currency into a global phenomenon. *IEEE Engineering Management Review, 47*(1), 28–35. https://doi.org/10.1109/emr.2019.2901431
52. Mondal, S., Wijewardena, K., Karuppuswami, S., Kriti, N., Kumar, D., & Chahal, P. (2019). Blockchain inspired RFID-based information architecture for food supply chain. *IEEE Internet of Things Journal, 6*(3), 5803–5813.
53. Gueta, G. G., Abraham, I., Grossman, S., Malkhi, D., Pinkas, B., Reiter, M., Seredinschi, D., Tamir, O. & Tomescu, A. (2019). SBFT: A scalable and decentralized trust infrastructure. In *Proceedings of the 49th annual IEEE/IFIP international conference on dependable systems and networks (DSN'19).* (pp. 568–580). https://doi.org/10.1109/DSN.2019.00063
54. Harry, H. (2017). Introduction to security and privacy on the Blockchain. In *2nd IEEE European symposium on security and privacy workshops.* EuroS and PW.
55. Castro, M., & Liskov, B. (1999). Practical byzantine fault tolerance[J]. *Symposium on Operating Systems Design & Implement, 20*(4), 173–186.
56. Sharma, S., Jain, S., & Chandavarkar, B. R. (2021). Nonce: Life cycle, issues and challenges in cryptography. In A. Kumar & S. Mozar (Eds.), *ICCCE 2020* (Lecture notes in electrical engineering) (Vol. 698). Springer. https://doi.org/10.1007/978-981-15-7961-5_18
57. Ølnes, S. (2016). Beyond Bitcoin enabling smart government using blockchain technology. In H. J. Scholl et al. (Eds.), *EGOVIS 2016. LNCS* (Vol. 9820, pp. 253–264). Springer. https://doi.org/10.1007/978-3-319-44421-520
58. Fotiou, N. & Polyzos, G. C. (2016). Decentralized name-based security for content distribution using Blockchains. In *2016 IEEE conference on computer communications workshops* (pp. 415–420). INFOCOM WKSHPS.
59. Bhushan, B., Khamparia, A., Sagayam, K. M., Sharma, S. K., Ahad, M. A., & Debnath, N. C. (2020). Blockchain for smart cities: A review of architectures, integration trends and future research directions. *Sustainable Cities and Society, 61*, 102360. https://doi.org/10.1016/j.scs.2020.102360,ISSN2210-6707
60. Intel Software GuardExtensions (IntelSGX). https://software.intel.com/en-us/sgx
61. Xie, J., Tang, H., Huang, T., Yu, F. R., Xie, R., Liu, J., & Liu, Y. (2019). A survey of blockchain technology applied to smart cities: Research issues and challenges. *IEEE Communication Surveys and Tutorials, 21*(3), 2794–2830. https://doi.org/10.1109/comst.2019.2899617
62. Gupta, S., Sinha, S. & Bhushan, B. (2020). Emergence of blockchain technology: fundamentals, working and its various implementations. *SSRN Electronic Journal.* https://doi.org/10.2139/ssrn.3569577.
63. Wang, X., Zheng, X., Zhang, X., Zeng, K., & Wang, F. (2017). Analysis of cyber interactive behaviors using artificial community and computational experiments. *IEEE Transactions on Systems, Man, and Cybernetics: Systems, 47*(6), 995–1006. https://doi.org/10.1109/tsmc.2016.2615130
64. Lv, Z., Qiao, L., Hossain, M. S., & Choi, B. J. (2021). Analysis of using blockchain to protect the privacy of drone big data. *IEEE Network, 35*(1). https://doi.org/10.1109/MNET.011.2000154

65. Neudecker, T., & Hartenstein, H. (2019). Network layer aspects of permissionless Blockchains. *IEEE Communication Surveys and Tutorials, 21*(1), 838–857. https://doi.org/10.1109/comst.2018.2852480
66. Song, H., Zhu, N., Xue, R., He, J., Zhang, K., & Wang, J. (2021). Proof-of-contribution consensus mechanism for blockchain and its application in intellectual property protection. *Information Processing & Management, 58*(3), 102507. https://doi.org/10.1016/j.ipm.2021.102507
67. Hyla, T., & Pejas´, J. (2020). Long-term verification of signatures based on a Blockchain. *Computers and Electrical Engineering, 81*, 106523. https://doi.org/10.1016/j.compeleceng.2019.106523
68. Li, J., Ni, X., & Yuan, Y. (2018). The reserve price of ad impressions in multi-channel real time bidding markets. *IEEE Transactions on Computational Social Systems, 5*(2), 583–592. https://doi.org/10.1109/tcss.2018.2831234
69. Kosba, A., Miller, A., Shi, E., Wen, Z. & Papamanthou, C. (2016). Hawk: The blockchain model of cryptography and privacy-preserving smart contracts. In *2016 IEEE symposium on Security and Privacy (SP)*. https://doi.org/10.1109/sp.2016.55.
70. Haque, A.K., Bhushan, B. & Dhiman, G. (2021). Conceptualizing smart city applications: require- ments, architecture, security issues, and emerging trends. Expert System. https://doi.org/10.1111/exsy.12753.
71. Bamakan, S. M. H., Faregh, N., & ZareRavasan, A. (2021). Di-ANFIS: An integrated Blockchain–IoT–big data-enabled framework for evaluating service supply chain performance. *Journal of Computational Design and Engineering, 8*(2), 676–690. https://doi.org/10.1093/jcde/qwab007
72. Bhushan, B., Sahoo, C., Sinha, P., et al. (2020). Unification of blockchain and internet of things (BIoT): Requirements, working model, challenges and future directions. *Wireless Networks, 27*, 55–90. https://doi.org/10.1007/s11276-020-02445-6
73. Liu, X. F., Jiang, X., Liu, S., & Tse, C. K. Knowledge discovery in cryptocurrency transactions: A survey. *IEEE Access, 9*, 37229–37254. https://doi.org/10.1109/ACCESS.2021.3062652
74. Zhang, R., Xue, R., & Liu, L. (2019). Security and privacy on Blockchain. *ACM Computing Surveys, 52*, 1–34. https://doi.org/10.1145/3316481
75. Tabassum, A., Jeba, H.A., Mahi, T.K., Salim Reza, S.M. & Hossain, D.A. (2021). Securely transfer information with RSA and digital signature by using the concept of fog computing and Blockchain. In *2021 International Conference on Information and Communication Technology for Sustainable Development*. ICICT4SD. https://doi.org/10.1109/ICICT4SD50815.2021.9396987.
76. Yadav, A. S., Agrawal, S., & Kushwaha, D. S. (2021). Distributed ledger technology-based land transaction system with trusted nodes consensus mechanism. *Journal of King Saud University – Computer and Information Sciences, 34*(8), 6414–6424. https://doi.org/10.1016/j.jksuci.2021.02.002
77. Kim, H. J. (2021). Technical aspects of Blockchain. In H. K. Baker, E. Nikbakht, & S. S. Smith (Eds.), *The emerald handbook of blockchain for business* (pp. 49–64). Emerald Publishing Limited. https://doi.org/10.1108/978-1-83982-198-120211006
78. Swan, M. (2015). *Blockchain: Blueprint for a new economy*. O'Reilly Media.
79. Zhou, K., Liu, T. & Zhou, L. (2015). Industry 4.0: towards future industrial opportunities and challenges. In *Proceedings of 12th international conference on fuzzy system and knowledge discovery*. (pp. 2147–2152). FSKD. https://doi.org/10.1109/FSKD.2015.7382284.
80. Alladi, T., Chamola, V., Parizi, R. M., & Raymond Choo, K. K. (2019). Blockchain applications for industry 4.0 and industrial IoT: A review. *Journals & Magazines, 7*, 176936. https://doi.org/10.1109/ACCESS.2019.2956748
81. Digital and Emerging Technology Strategy. intueriglobal.com/digital-and-emerging-technology-strategy/

82. Weyer, S., Schmitt, M., Ohmer, M., & Gorecky, D. (2015). *Towards industry 4.0-standardization as the crucial challenge for highly modular, multi-vendor production systems* (Vol. 48, pp. 579–584). IFAC-Papersonline. https://doi.org/10.1016/j.ifacol.2015.06.143

83. Mohamed, N., & Al-Jaroodi, J. (2019). *Applying blockchain in industry 4.0 applications* (pp. 0853–0854). IEEE. https://doi.org/10.1109/CCWC.2019.8666558

84. Tonelli, F., Demartini, M., Pacella, M., & Lala, R. (2021). Cyber-physical systems (CPS) in supply chain management: From foundations to practical implementation. *Procedia CIRP, 99*, 598–603. https://doi.org/10.1016/j.procir.2021.03.080

85. Semenkov, K., Promyslov, V., Poletykin, A., & Mengazetdinov, N. (2021). Validation of complex control systems with heterogeneous digital models in industry 4.0 framework. *Machines, 9*(3), 62.

86. Al-Jaroodi, J., & Mohamed, N. (2019). Blockchain in industries: A survey. *IEEE Access, 7*, 36500–36515. https://doi.org/10.1109/ACCESS.2019.2903554

87. Sethi, R., Bhushan, B., Sharma, N., Kumar, R. & Kaushik, I. (2020). Applicability of industrial IoT in diversified sectors: evolution, applications and challenges. In *Studies in big data multimedia technologies in the internet of things environment* (pp. 45–67). https://doi.org/10.1007/978-981-15-7965-3_4.

88. Pilkington, M. (2016). 11 Blockchain technology: principles and applications. In *Research handbook on digital transformations* (p. 225). https://doi.org/10.4337/9781784717766.00019
.

89. Luu, L., Chu, D.H., Olickel, H., Saxena, P. & Hobor, A. (2016). Making smart contracts smarter. In *Proceedings of the 2016 ACM SIGSAC Conference on Computer and Communications Security* (pp. 254–269). https://doi.org/10.1145/2976749.2978309.

90. Hofmann, E. & Rüsch, M. (2017). Industry 4.0 and the current status as well as future prospects on logistics. *Computers in Industry*, 23–34. https://doi.org/10.1016/j.compind.2017.04.002.

91. Saxena, S., Bhushan, B. & Yadav, D. (2020). Blockchain-powered social media analytics in supply chain management. *SSRN Journal of Electronic*. https://doi.org/10.2139/ssrn.3598906.

92. Sicari, S., Rizzardi, A., Grieco, L. A., & Coen-Porisini, A. (2015). Security, privacy and trust in Internet of Things: The road ahead. *Computer Networks, 76*, 146–164. https://doi.org/10.1016/j.comnet.2014.11.008

93. Weber, R. H. (2010). Internet of things–new security and privacy challenges. *Computer Law and Security Review, 26*(1), 23–30. https://doi.org/10.1016/j.clsr.2009.11.008

94. Chelladurai, U. & Pandian, S. (2021). A novel blockchain based electronic health record automation system for healthcare. *Journal of Ambient Intelligence and Humanized Computing*. https://doi.org/10.1007/s12652-021-03163-3.

95. Roman, R., Zhou, J., & Lopez, J. (2013). On the features and challenges of security and privacy in distributed internet of things. *Computer Networks, 57*(10), 2266–2279. https://doi.org/10.1016/j.comnet.2012.12.018

96. Kurkin, O. & Janu˘ska, M. (2010). Product life cycle in digital factory Knowledge management and innovation: a business competitive edge perspective. In *Cairo: International Business Infor-mation Management Association* (pp. 1881–1886). IBIMA. ISBN 978–0–9821489–4–5.

97. BradleyShawSwathiSambhani,"Data,data,everywhere!productlifecyclemanagementin the world of iot.".

98. Nam, T., & Pardo, T. A. (2011). Conceptualizing smart city with dimensions of technology, people, and institutions. In *Proceedings of the 12th annual international digital government research conference: Digital government innovation in challenging times* (pp. 282–291).

99. Emanate: Emanate intro series 2. *Blockchain, micro-payments and streaming*. https://medium.com/emanate-live/emanate-intro-series-2-blockchain-micro-payments-and-streaming-102698859420.

100. Kshetri, N. (2017). Can blockchain strengthen the internet of things. *IT professional, 19*, 68–72. https://doi.org/10.1109/MITP.2017.3051335

101. Li, J., Liu, Z., Chen, L., Chen, P. & Wu, J. (2017). Blockchain-based security architecture for distributed cloud storage. *In Proceedings of IEEE international symposium on parallel and distributed processing with applications and IEEE international conference on ubiquitous computing and communications.* ISPA/IUCC. (pp. 408–411). https://doi.org/10.1109/ISPA/IUCC.2017.00065.
102. Fernández-Caramés, T. M., Fraga-Lamas, P., Suárez-Albela, M., & Vilar-Montesinos, M. (2018). A fog computing and cloudlet based augmented reality system for the industry 4.0 shipyard. *Sensors, 18*, 1798–1961. https://doi.org/10.3390/s18061798
103. Suárez-Albela, M., Fraga-Lamas, P., & Fernández-Caramés, T. M. (2018). A practical evaluation on RSA and ECC-based cipher suites for IoT high-security energy-efficient fog and mist computing devices. *Sensors, 18*, 3868. https://doi.org/10.3390/s18113868
104. Guo, Y., & Liang, C. (2016). Blockchain application and outlook in the banking industry. *Financial Innovation, 2*, 24. https://doi.org/10.1186/s40854-016-0034-9
105. Tripoli, M. & Schmidhuber, J. (2018) *Emerging opportunities for the application of blockchain in the agri-food industry.* FAO and ICTSD. Licence: CC BY-NC-SA, 3.
106. Czachorowski, K., Solesvik, M., & Kondratenko, Y. (2019). The application of blockchain technology in the maritime industry. In V. Kharchenko, Y. Kondratenko, & J. Kacprzyk (Eds.), *Green IT engineering: Social, business and industrial applications. Studies in systems, decision and control* (Vol. 171). Springer. https://doi.org/10.1007/978-3-030-00253-4_24
107. Fraga-Lamas, P., & Fernández-Caramés, T. M. (2019). A review on blockchain technologies for an advanced and cyber-resilient automotive industry. *IEEE Access, 7*, 17578–17598. https://doi.org/10.1109/ACCESS.2019.2895302
108. Jovović, I., Husnjak, S., Forenbacher, I., & Maček, S. (2019). Innovative application of 5G and blockchain technology in industry 4.0. *EAI Endorsed Transactions on Industrial Networks and Intelligent Systems, 6*(18). https://doi.org/10.4108/eai.28-3-2019.157122
109. Fernández-Caramés, T. M., & Fraga-Lamas, P. (2019). A review on the application of blockchain to the next generation of cybersecure industry 4.0 smart factories. *IEEE Access, 7*, 45201–45218. https://doi.org/10.1109/ACCESS.2019.2908780
110. Ozdemir, A.I., Ar, I.M. & Erol, I. (2019). Assessment of blockchain applications in travel and tourism industry. *Quality & Quantity*, 1–15. https://doi.org/10.1007/s11135-019-00901-w.
111. Lu, H., Huang, K., Azimi, M., & Guo, L. (2019). Blockchain technology in the oil and gas industry: A review of applications, opportunities, challenges, and risks. *IEEE Access, 7*, 41426–41444. https://doi.org/10.1109/ACCESS.2019.2907695
112. Papathanasiou, A., Cole, R., Murray, P. (2020). The (non-) application of blockchain technology in the Greek shipping industry. *The European Management Journal.* https://doi.org/10.1016/j.emj.2020.04.007.
113. Chen, J., Cai, T., He, W., Chen, L., Zhao, G., Zou, W., & Guo, L. (2020). A Blockchain-driven supply chain finance application for auto retail industry. *Entropy, 22*(1), 95. https://doi.org/10.3390/e22010095
114. Alladi, T., Chamola, V., Parizi, R. M., & Choo, K. R. (2019). Blockchain applications for industry 4.0 and industrial IoT: A review. *IEEE Access, 7*, 176935–176951. https://doi.org/10.1109/ACCESS.2019.2956748
115. Madaan, G., Bhushan, B. & Kumar, R. (2021). Blockchain-based cyberthreat mitigation systems for smart vehicles and industrial automation. In *Studies in Big Data Multimedia Technologies in the Internet of Things Environment* (pp. 13–32). https://doi.org/10.1007/978-981-15-7965-3_2.
116. Soni, S. & Bhushan, B. (2019). A comprehensive survey on Blockchain: working, security analysis, privacy threats and potential applications. In *2019 2nd International Conference on Intelligent Computing, Instrumentation and Control Technologies (ICICICT).* https://doi.org/10.1109/icicict46008.2019.8993210.
117. Yadav, A. K., & Singh, K. (2021). Comparative analysis of consensus algorithms and issues in integration of blockchain with IoT. In S. Tiwari, M. Trivedi, K. Mishra, A. Misra, K. Kumar, & E. Suryani (Eds.), *Smart innovations in communication and computational*

sciences. Advances in intelligent systems and computing (Vol. 1168). Springer. https://doi.org/10.1007/978-981-15-5345-5_3

118. Sajid, S., Haleem, A., Bahl, S., Javaid, M., Goyal, T. & Mittal, M. (2021). Data science applications for predictive maintenance and materials science in context to Industry 4.0. In *2021 Elsevier Ltd. All rights reserved. Second International Conference on Aspects of Materials Science and Engineering (ICAMSE 2021)*. https://doi.org/10.1016/j.matpr.2021.01.357.

119. Karame, G. (2016). On the security and scalability of bitcoin's block chain. In *Proceedings of ACM SIGSAC Conference on Computer and Communications Security (CCS)* (pp. 1861–1862). https://doi.org/10.1145/2976749.2976756.

Chapter 8
Blockchain-Powered Smart E-Healthcare System: Benefits, Use Cases, and Future Research Directions

Ayasha Malik, Bharat Bhushan ⓘ, Veena Parihar, Lamia Karim, and Korhan Cengiz

Abstract Blockchain technologies are deeply distributed and used in several dominions, including for E-healthcare. Internet of Things (IoT) strategies can arrange real-time sensual information from patients for their treatment. Composed information is aimed to combine for computation, dealing, and storing. Such centralism can be challenging, as it can be the only reason for lack of success, uncertainty, document management, interfering, and confidentiality elusion. Blockchain is able to resolve these kinds of consequent complications by giving distributed computation and proper storage for IoT data records. Consequently, the mixture of blockchain technologies in healthcare can convert into a realistic selection for the scheme of distributed Blockchain-powered smart E-healthcare systems. This paper discusses the background of blockchain technology with its features and categories. The paper explores the collaboration of blockchain with IoT for E-healthcare. Further, this paper highlights some popular consensus algorithms used in blockchain in the circumstance of E-health. Finally, this paper examines some use cases of E-healthcare that illustrate how key characteristics of the IoT and blockchain can be leveraged to maintain healthcare facilities and environments.

A. Malik
Delhi Technical Campus (DTC), GGSIPU, Greater Noida, India

B. Bhushan (✉)
School of Engineering and Technology (SET), Sharda University, Greater Noida, India

V. Parihar
KIET Group of Institutions, Ghaziabad, India

L. Karim
National School of Applied Sciences of Berrechid (ENSA), Hassan 1st University, Settat, Morocco

K. Cengiz
Department of Computer Engineering, Istinye University, Istanbul, Turkey
e-mail: korhan.cengiz@istinye.edu.tr

© The Author(s), under exclusive license to Springer Nature
Switzerland AG 2023
M. A. Ahad et al. (eds.), *Enabling Technologies for Effective Planning and Management in Sustainable Smart Cities*,
https://doi.org/10.1007/978-3-031-22922-0_8

203

Keywords Blockchain · E-healthcare · Data management · Internet of Things (IoT) · Security · Data analysis

8.1 Introduction

E-healthcare programs or E-healthcare systems are planned to fulfil our healthcare desires, and the necessity for efficacy is growing because of aged people and their movement [1]. For illustration, the current eruption of the 2019 fresh coronavirus (2019-nCoV, also acknowledged as SARS-CoV-2 and COVID-19) determines the significance of sharing data records in real-time. Healthcare styles i.e. Mobile Healthcare (MHealth) and Worldwide Healthcare (WHealth). Whereas mobile and Internet-enabled devices that are mobile and available everywhere (such as Internet-based Medical Devices (IoMD)) have contributed to faster, more effective, more economical, and have also carried new tasks [2] like the most important task in electronic healthcare is the safety of IoT devices, blockchain devices and health statistics substructure. With the advent of IoT and the proliferation of healthcare occupied devices and requests (applications), a large sum of medicinal data is noted down and transmitted hourly, daily, weekly, and so on. Present E-healthcare systems face problems such as collaboration, lengthy procedures, process and diagnostic delays, information sharing delays, high operating costs and procedures, time-consuming and cost-effective insurance procedures, secrecy, safety, data possession, and data mechanism [3].

Blockchain medical devices can support the collection of important patient's information, programmed workflow, deliver the best information about disease indications and mechanisms, contribution to enlarged long-lasting care, and provide better control on patients' treatment to improve their health [4]. With IoT-blockchain-based devices, patients are observed in real-time without any movement of patients as well as doctors. The visits of hospitals and hospital stays or the cost of admittance can be reduced by the E-healthcare system. Blockchain-enabled medical devices can help diagnose using warnings and trigger alerts before they become critical [5]. Sensors implanted in several portions of a patient's medical equipment, may collect and refer information to a hospital, where the physician may diagnose the irregularities. Unquestionably, the growth of blockchain with IoT has managed to the sustained invention in the healthcare sector. Conversely, safe management of *Electronic Medical Records/Electronic Health Records* (EHR/EMR) has turn out to be a major challenge as data is still being distributed to various medical institutions [6]. Most surviving healthcare systems are at risk of single failure and information leaks due to increased cyber security attacks [7]. Leaks of patients' personal and sensitive information can lead to serious follow-up. Likewise, present medical systems fail to provide transparency, reliable tracking, consistency, auditing, secrecy and safety, while handling EHR/EMR [8]. Bearing in mind these challenges in current healthcare systems are very problematic, but blockchain technology can solve them [9]. It is projected that blockchain acquisition could lead to savings of money up to

$110–$160 billion per year by 2026, saving in data breach and reduction of fraud and fake products [10].

In terms of licensing management, the blockchain is distributed into four main classifications; Public blockchain, Private blockchain, Consortium blockchain and Hybrid blockchain [11] are explained in a further section. Depending on the unambiguous needs or circumstances of the use case, health administrations may use any category of blockchain to create a network as they all have their own advantages as well as disadvantage. Blockchain is an auspicious technology that can help simplify health information management tasks by giving unparalleled data efficacy and forcing trust. It proposes a variety of outstanding and built-in characteristics, like shared stowage, transparency, consistency, authenticity, the flexibility of data access, centralized communication, and security, enabling greater use of blockchain technology for healthcare data management. Blockchain uses the idea of smart agreements that introduce terms and circumstances where all healthcare associates elaborate in the network are granted upon, so no mediator is needed. It decreases excessive managerial costs [12]. Furthermore, a summary of the involvement of this effort is enumerated as below:

- The work discusses the background of E-healthcare system and its application.
- The work highlights the development, simple functioning, features and categories of blockchain in detail.
- The work redefines the inspiration for blockchain incorporation with IoT to form an E-healthcare system that eases medical facilities.
- The work explores some recently proposed consensus algorithms and use cases of E-healthcare system based on blockchain technology.

The remainder of the paper is organised as follows. Section 8.2 elaborates the background, features, application and categorisation of blockchain for E-healthcare. Moreover, various blockchain consensus algorithms in E-healthcare are described. Section 8.3 described the benefits of blockchain in healthcare data management. Section 8.4 defined some related use cases of E-healthcare system based on IoT-blockchain technology. Section 8.5 deliberates some recent case studies and ongoing projects towards the blockchain technology that collaborates in E-healthcare. Section 8.6 discusses some future research directions. Finally, the paper concludes with Sect. 8.7.

8.2 Background and Application of Blockchain for E-Healthcare

In this section, the background of blockchain is explained in corelation with its numerous applications that help to build an E-healthcare system to reduce overall cost and offer safety by providing untouchable treatment to the patient by doctors.

8.2.1 Background of Blockchain

Blockchain is a rising list of data, termed as blocks, interconnected through cryptographic techniques. All blocks carry the cryptographic hash function of the preceding block. In easy terms, by blockchain technology consumers can easily convey the data as of A to B in a completely computerized and harmless. One transaction event promises the procedure by building a safe block. This block is validating by lacks of successful transactions, can be millions in count, of a computer that is distributed over the net. A fresh certified block generates a series, which is deposited above the internet, not only creating a distinctive record but a distinctive record with a distinctive history [13].

- Blockchain technology: A blockchain is a public record of everything that has been done (like Bitcoin and Ether) that has been already implemented and sucessful. These ledgers of previous trades call it as a block chain, like a series of blocks. It is constantly evolving, as miners add new blocks to it to keep track of all the latest developments. Blocks are always added sequentially and in chronological order to the blockchain [14].
- Blockchain Mining: Blockchain Mining is the process of addition in record transactions to a public/private blockchain ledger. A blockchain mining worker is connected to a node, for instance, a participant of the same set-up with the ability to authorize a transaction in a particular type of contract.
- 51% Attack: 51% attack on blockchain technology talk about a miner or a crowd of miners trying to take access of more than 50% of the grid's retrieving authority along with computer energy and hash function. The individuals in control of such retrieving authority can prevent new transactions from mishappening [15].
- Intelligent Contract: A program developed to obey certain computer principles to facilitate digital work, to verify, or to prosecute partnerships or implementation of contracts. Intelligent contracts allow for unresolved, reliable, complex and tracked transactions without any involvement of third parties [16].

8.2.2 Blockchain Features for E-Healthcare

Some features of blockchain are discussed below that make blockchain so famous and successful in providing security in such an easy way.

- Decentralization: Transferring technology contributes to the ability to store all services (like agreements and official papers), which says that they can be retrieved via the internet. At this time, the owner takes complete access to his/her account; means that the owner having a power to transmission his/her services wherever he/she wishes [17].

- Transparency: Blockchain transparency is based on the statement that the capture and execution of each societies address are exposed to the public. All information used to recognize the consumer is kept protected.
- Blockchain is virtually impossible to break: In the out-dated networks all data files are in one unit so it is easy to modify or discard by attackers. But in blockchain all data files are not in one unit, due to this feature of blockchain, it is difficult to hack as each official call testifies to countless locations of the system.
- Secured: All the internal and confidential data records are remained protected by using encryption or decryption techniques.
- Immutability: If the data record is stowed in a block, then that data record cannot be altered by anyone. Even consumer has not the power to change it during transmission. If any blunder happens during the transaction, a new transaction must be performed to undo that blunder. At that point, both transactions are visible so that blunder and correction can be seen properly [18].
- Blockchain provides encoding, authentication and confirmation: In blockchain technology information is encoded, unchanged and it is already proven that all single data of the blockchain is completely encoded and signed digitally.
- No Third-Party: Distributed feature of the blockchain technology creates it an organisation that doesn't depend on third-party companies; no third-party, no added risk. Blockchain technology is an independent system i.e. not any need for a third person. All the transaction and communication is done between two required persons without any additional interference of any person, no third party, and no additional danger.
- Fewer Scams: Since the blockchain structure works on algorithms, there remains very little chance that people will cheat on you with anything. No one can use the blockchain to their advantage.

8.2.3 Categories of Blockchain

At present-day, there are four natures of blockchain systems, i.e., public, private, consortium, and hybrid. Furthermore, this section discusses all the natures of blockchain in detail.

- Public blockchain: This category of blockchain does not have any kind of restriction applied to it. Every single person can easily connect to the public blockchain through the internet and can do any kind of transaction. Also, it can serve as a main validator (contributing to the competence of the compatibility algorithms of blockchain). Public blockchain tend to depend on commercial motivations to protect the structure over the actual and best use of an exceptional type of consensus algorithm for compliance [19].
- Private blockchain: This nature of blockchain is repeatedly referred to as permitted, i.e., an individual essential to be requested by system superintendent of blockchain, where the job of all involvement and validator stays much constrained.

The association and applications that need treating delicate data records, record-keeping is chosen in particular that prefer a privately approved approach to blockchain infrastructure [20].

- Consortium blockchain: Defined as a semi-dispersed blockchain, in which numerous administrations collectively decide to simplify blockchain service delivery to consumers. Therefore, the permissible approach is modified over consumers while placing rights limitations above the blockchain structure [21].
- Hybrid blockchain: Illuminated as a collection of public and private blockchain system services. Hybrid blockchain is used for legitimacy where public and private data can able to access in the collection is infinitely installed over the consumer. Therefore, the consumer on this blockchain might be granted or able for free access depending on the precise suggestions as required by the application [22]. The differences between previously mentioned categories of the blockchain-based on some properties are shown in Table 8.1.

8.2.4 IoT and Blockchain for E-Healthcare

IoT is an Internet connection grant for mobile devices and daily use objects. Internet connection and other kinds of hardware are bound electronically, and this device can be monitored as well as remotely controlled for further communication and interaction. Specified the strong needs of IoT webs, the blockchain appears to be the most suitable for both; may protect the whole network from fraudulent data attacks and can provide a protected environment for all devices on the web. The boundaries of existing models and the capabilities of the blockchain-based E-healthcare IoT model are discussed [23].

- Most recent used IoT systems are built into a client-server model, where everything is recognized, validated, and associated to cloud hubs that require a large

Table 8.1 Difference between categories of blockchain

Properties	Private blockchain	Public blockchain	Consortium blockchain	Hybrid blockchain
Speed	Fastest	Slow	Faster	Slow/faster
Effectiveness	High	Low	High	High/low
Immutability	Yes	Yes	Yes	Yes
Centralised	Yes	No	Partial	Depend on nature
Read agreement	Public/limited	Public	Public/limited	Public/limited
Consensus process	Permissioned	Permission less	Permissioned	Depend on nature
Consensus determination	One organisation	All miner	A selected set of nodes	Miner/one organisation
Network	Partially decentralised	Decentralised	Partially decentralised	Depend on nature
Asset	Any asset	Native asset	Any asset	Native/any

volume of processing and stowage dimensions. In accumulation, if the IoT devices are nearby to another IoT device then communication among these devices must pass through a channel over the internet. Conversely, this model is used for small IoT set-ups, it is not able to measure well [24]. Likewise, the cost of setting up a lot of network connections, central cloud storage and connecting all the tools is important for large IoT systems. In contrast to cost, relying on cloud hubs creates the infrastructure vulnerable to a distinct point of failure. Besides, IoT devices can survive the attack on data and physical modification in data. While selected some recent methods make IoT devices safer, those methods are composite and inappropriate for resource-inhibited IoT devices along with restricted controlling power [25].

- Blockchain launches a peer-to-peer set-up, which reduces the rate of installing and maintaining intermediate clouds, hub systems, record centres, and communication apparatus by sharing computer and storage needs all across the network's devices. One point of failure problem that arrived earlier is now resolved by the communiqué model. Using encryption and decryption algorithms, blockchain addresses all the confidentiality concerns and provides full security to IoT networks. Similarly, it solves the issues of reliance in IoT networks by using interfere-resilient records [26].

Figure 8.1 introduces the standard construction of the IoT-based blockchain structure for E-healthcare. The properties are divided into four functional categories named: IoT E-healthcare, the blockchain environment, communication and IoT devices. The blockchain environment plays a main role in the blockchain data distribution inside the IoT system also in numerous facilities such as law enforcement, buildings and authentication. Investigators believe, using two-aspect and multi-aspect schemes to prove the authenticity of the object, as described consistently. Both certification schemes will allow blockchain site users to interact well with blocks while marking actual certification. Therefore, surviving cyber-physical communication will be brighter and more understandable. The proposed structures have been proven to be better suited to the IoT-based blockchain-centric surroundings [27]. Table 8.2 provides a comparison of blockchain platforms in the state of IoT-based healthcare.

8.2.5 Blockchain Consensus Algorithms in E-Healthcare

In blockchain, consensus is used to deliver a contract between all blockchain nodules. For different cryptocurrency consensus procedures are many types. A list of selected consensus algorithms is declared as follows. These consensus algorithms could be used in various use cases of E-healthcare specifically in E-health facility provisioning [28].

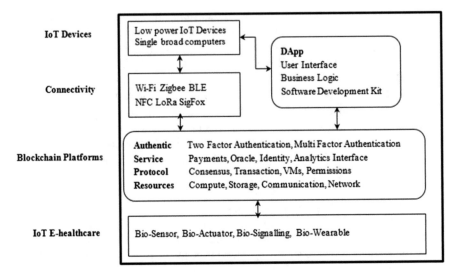

Fig. 8.1 Architecture of IoT for blockchain e-healthcare

8.2.5.1   Proof of Work

This impression was designed and accessible in 1993s magazine article. Originally named and legalized in the 1999, Proof of Work (PoW) is too recognized as the following: *Central Processing Unit (*CPU) charge utility, customer riddle, computer riddle, and CPU estimating function. Not suitable for IoT due to the need for extraordinary grid bandwidth. As PoW is widely used on various platforms, there remains an intermediate chance of finding PoW that is hidden in healthcare services [29].

8.2.5.2   Proof of Stake

Proof of Stake (PoS), Node is selected by random to resolve the succeeding block to mine. There are no mining coin production rewards available but are pleased lone by contract fees. The nothing at stake issue might reason behind the re-awarded of a node in the same contract fees. We accept that it can be used as an effective communication tool for E-health requests [30].

8.2.5.3   Delegated Proof of Stake

Delegated Proof of Stake (DPoS), it is a popular PoS perception, in which network operators do polling and select representatives to verify the succeeding block. It makes for quick transactions but is more expensive to refer to in the middle. A

Table 8.2 Comparison of blockchain environments for IoT-based E-healthcare

Platforms/Features	Qtum	EthereumM	Neo	Wanchain	Lisk	Ark	Eos	Straits	Waves
Symbol	QTUM	ETH	NEO	WAN	LSK	ARK	EOS	STRAT	WAVES
Consensus	PoS	PoW/PoS	dBFT	PoS	DPoS	DPoS	DPoS	PoS	LPoS
Block time in second	120	15	15	Not found	10	8	0.5	60	3
Transaction per second	70	15	1000	Not found	5	25	100K	20k	100
Smart agreement	Yes	Yes	Yes	Yes	In evolution	In evolution	Yes	Yes	In evolution
Atomic switches	Yes	Yes	No	No	No	In evolution	No	No	In evolution
DApps	Yes	Yes	Yes	Yes	Yes	Yes	Yes	Yes	Yes
Side cables	Yes	Yes	Yes	Yes	In evolution	Yes	No	Yes	In evolution
Software Development Kit (SDK)	Yes	Yes	Yes	In evolution	In evolution	In evolution	Yes	Yes	Yes
Smart agreement language	Solidity	Solidity	C#, Java, Python	Solidity	JavaScript	JavaScript	C, C++	C#, .NET	Scale
Smart agreement	Yes	Yes	Yes	Yes	In evolution	In evolution	Yes	Yes	In evolution

protocol for identifying and selecting a dangerous mediator exists. Therefore, it can be used in healthcare situations with the great openings [31].

8.2.5.4 Leased Proof of Stake

Leased Proof of Stake (LPoS), PoS permits for the resolution of state difficulties in areas with low stabilities and contractual agreements, and divides recompenses per prosperity management. Agree to token owners to "rent" their tokens to complete nodes and receive a pay-out percentage as compensation. In a standard pole authentication platform, each nodule is capable to combine a fresh block to the blockchain. By using such algorithm, the best E-health facility can be maintained [32].

8.2.5.5 Proof of Importance

It is an enhancement of PoS. Checks the equilibrium of network's nodes and the status of nodes. It remains a highly productive set-up. By way of Proof of Importance (PoI), the nodes prerequisite to enter the amount of money to be eligible for the creation of blocks and are nominated to create a block equal to the school that limits their contribution to the network. We agree to use E-healthcare services as physicians' statuses can be demoralized to assist in choice-creating of patients [33].

8.2.5.6 Practical Byzantine Fault Tolerance

Practical Byzantine Fault Tolerance (PBFT) every node of the network could take part in the elective procedure to enhance the subsequent block. Additional 2/3 nodes' agreement is essential. This knowledge is virtuous for remote blockchain and efficient as well as healthier as compare to PoW and PoS. Likewise, it has little broad-mindedness in contradiction of malevolent nodes. We would help it for pretentious usage for E-health facilities [34].

8.2.5.7 Delegated Byzantine Fault Tolerance

It is a development of PBFT. There are additional methods to enable blockchain. Delegated Byzantine Fault Tolerance (dBFT) is a process used to implement an arrangement that makes it difficult to accept blockchain and cryptocurrency. It is a complex idea that not appreciated like PoW or PoS. Nodules are selected as messengers of another place. Therefore, it appears that E-healthcare facilities can-not be fully functional when using dBFT in IoT-blockchain infrastructure [35].

8.2.5.8   Proof of Capacity

It is an enhancement above PoW. Proof of Capacity (PoC) is a valid algorithm used in blockchain that allows mining devices on the system to use their accessible hard drive area to determine mining rules and secure transactions. It desires to accumulate big data to mine blocks following other nodes. Not worthy of the IoT. It is not suggested to be used for blockchain based health-care services [36].

8.2.5.9   Proof of Activity

Proof of Activity (PoA), it is a combination of PoW and PoS. PoW is completed before. After that, a team of verifiers' symbols is composed to enter a transaction in the minor's heads keep an eye on by the PoS. Not appropriate for IoT due to prolonged interruptions; therefore, it is not a worthy selection for E- healthcare [37].

8.2.5.10   Proof of Burn

Proof of Burn (PoB), it talks about distributing coins to an invalid statement. Many hot coins organise for the miner to go to the mine. It is ready for the formation of cryptocurrency and not for IoT because of its pecuniary and financial structure. Because of its improper combustion method, it is not appropriate for health-related applications [38]. A comparison of all the interviewed algorithms discussed is presented in Table 8.3.

8.3   Benefit of Blockchain Technology in E-Healthcare Record Administration

Various benefits of using blockchain technology in E-healthcare record administration are discussed in the subsections below.

8.3.1   Health Records Exactness

Patient medicinal data is often distributed across multiple locations, medicinal care facilities, and assurance suppliers. To obtain all relevant patient medicinal olden times, all sections of patient information prerequisite to be compiled in a computerised fashion. This can be accomplished by keeping whole patient medical information (such as, his or her documentation, symptom details, curing process, developed properties, payment details, and some additional statistics) in a continually

Table 8.3 Comparison among various blockchain consensus algorithms

Characteristics	PoW [29]	PoS [30]	DPoS [31]	LPoS [32]	PoL [33]	PBFT [34]	dBFT [35]	PoC [36]	PoA [37]	PoB [38]
Self-conscious	No	No	Partial	Partial	No	No	No	No	No	No
Flexibility	High	High	Med	Med	Med	Low	Low	Low	Med	Very low
Acceptance	Very high	Very high	Med	Med	Med	Low	Low	Low	Low	Low
Ease of access	Exposed	Exposed	Exposed	Exposed	Exposed	Prop	Prop	Exposed	Prop	Prop
E-health sustenance	Med	High	High	High	High	High	Low	Low	Low	Low
IoT acquiescent	No	Partial	Partial	Partial	No	No	No	No	No	No
Simple idea	CPU	Stake	PoS	PoS	PoS	67% node	PBFT	PoW	PoW-PoS	Burn coin
Liveliness	Very high	Med	Med	Med	Med	Low	Low	Low	Med	High
Illustration	Bitcoin	Etherium	Bitshare	Waves	NEM	Hyperledger	NEO	Burstcoin	Bitcoin	Slimcoin

up-to-date blockchain, tracked, and records disruptive. This supports healthcare professionals to provide patients with effective, timely, and appropriate care. Healthcare suppliers can have a comprehensive representation of the medicinal history of patients using blockchain technology. All information stored in the blockchain is undeniable, recognizable, noticeable, and protected [39].

8.3.2 Health Records Interoperability

Collaboration speaks to the capability to exchange statistics amid programs, developed by unlike constructors. Maximum EHR/EMR goods are constructed on a variety of scientific technologies, mechanical stipulations, and operational competencies. Such variations postpone the creation and sharing of facts in a single set-up. In the best instance, single-built EHR structures are unusable because they are designed to meet the specific needs and preferences of a health organization. For the two EHR systems to work together, the transmission of messages must be based on standard coded data. However, the lack of standard data is a serious problem that binds the ability to share information electronically inpatient care. This limit can be overcome by using a blockchain-based healthcare data management system. All HER/EMR stored in a blockchain system follows a standard data code, so it can be easily accessed and used in any area related to healthcare [40].

8.3.3 Health Records Safety

In the past, numerous healthcare administrations have condemned victims to preventable cyber security attacks. A huge amount of healthcare activities used hands-based infrastructure systems to manage digital medicinal accounts. These organizations are out-dated, so they can be effortlessly replaced for fake purposes. Likewise, health records may disappear in the event of usual disasters since the focus is on one area of failure. Blockchain can support eliminate the risk of data theft or abuse of the static aspect of cryptographic terms. The health data stored in the blockchain is also protected from injury from natural disasters or medical facility failure because the same data is stored in multiple locations, so there is no significant point of disappointment [41].

8.3.4 Health Data Managing Costs

Extraordinary managing cost connected through patient documents records recovery and data transmission is one more main anxiety upraised by existing healthcare systems. Patient medical prescription is divided towards numerous health services.

Gathering comprehensive medical prescription and data logs of the patients from verbal or unsystematic hospital data administration schemes can lead to extra time and charges. Blockchain technology can aid to decrease the managerial price modelled by third person associations in existing healthcare systems. Similarly, it empowers elastic access of data files to the patient medical prescription, which is collected and stowed from several foundations, likewise patient records, private carry able and hand handling expedients. Towards this mode, blockchain can contribute to decreasing the expenses of medicinal corporations since they can straightforwardly operate far-reaching patients' data files deprived of moving to various positions wherever these data files used to be deposited [42].

8.3.5   Worldwide Health Records Distribution

In some medicinal emergencies, a systematic awareness of past medical history is required before any appropriate medical treatment. For instance, a patient with a serious illness has travelled abroad, and he may need to consult a physician in a situation of a crisis. In this case, the medicinal specialised will regularly need a patient's previous data to provide healthier and qualitative health facilities. A patient's past medicinal records can assist physicians to evaluate a variety of factors, such as past medical history, details of drug and drug allergies, and previous treatment records, which can lead to the development of more effective treatment strategies. On the other hand, most of the present health managing networks are based on personal and preventive measures, and therefore do not suggest worldwide accessibility and tracking structures [43]. These structures can be accessed via blockchain machinery.

8.3.6   Enhanced Healthcare Records Audit

Audits are performed in the healthcare industry to determine whether or not compliance with policies, processes, guidelines, protocols, and rules set by health facilities. The audit procedure helps to assess the efficiency of the healthcare acquiescence system through systematic and targeted valuation [44]. Many modern health data organization systems are hands-on and absent of brainy integration and assimilation purposes. Besides, they are at risk of document openings and illegal modifications. As a result, such restrictions interfere with the audit procedure and its excellence. Blockchain technology enables healthcare professionals to achieve their data in a secure, confusing, and sustainable technique, thus demonstrating the reliability of the health information. This allows examiners to effortlessly validate communications made on blockchain structure. Blockchain-based healthcare testing can help advance the excellence of patient services, as well as preserving health facilities in line with important lawful necessities. Likewise, it may aid to escape needless data breaks [45].

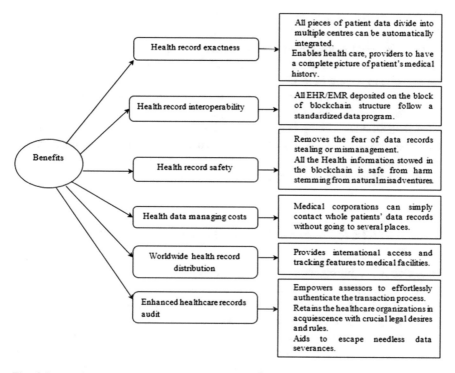

Fig. 8.2 Benefits of leveraging blockchain technology for E-healthcare record administration systems

Figure 8.2 summarizes the key reimbursements of leveraging blockchain technology for E-healthcare record administration.

8.4 Use Cases of E-Healthcare System

These are some use cases of E-healthcare system based on blockchain listed in subsection that is very important and mandatory to fulfil all the use cases required to generate a successful E-healthcare system that based on blockchain as well as IoT.

8.4.1 Medical Record Access

A mixture in a healthcare incrusted environment is projected relating to a smart meeting organization, patient-driven interactions and blockchain incorporation in a composite IoT-based methodology. The art of architecture can serve the patient through interferences from the Local Health Organization (LHO) or healthcare administrations, in established professional contracts [46]. Business integration is done within n number of healthcare organizations, where patient-determined and blockchain-based is integrated seamlessly with IoT-grounded sensor, actuator, and facilities. A Patient-Based novel Applications Programming Interface (APIs) can be used to obtain patient EHR data from such administrations. The patient is enabled by smart indentures to approve the distribution of EHR amongst 1 and n organizations, where past business associations may not exist. The blockchain layer lastingly adheres to all rules relating to permission, the patient's public key, and EHR access data logs. Many organizations can accomplish the intelligent communication of a patient's public key to their private patient company individually while exercising whole liberty for patients to access their EHR data [47].

8.4.2 EHR Claim and Billing Valuation

Fake claims and billing are the utmost important sufferers in E-healthcare that requisite to be escaped and rejected. Such deceitful payment-linked actions occur in the general health sector. Claims relating to the charging of unused E-healthcare facilities, overpricing of real E-health facilities, misuse of non-medical E-health amenities of a patient, improper representation of unattended healthcare services often lead to such actions. While the surviving situation permits mediators to verify and adjudicate information related to a claim, it does not have active communication amid the person elaborate in the payment of the bill. The IoT-enabled blockchain E-healthcare ecology can support alleviate much of these challenges by making the required workflow and allowing teams to distribute a solitary replica of business deal and agreement statistics while claiming litigation and payment procedures are not fraudulent [48].

8.4.3 Medical Research

Medical trials necessitate highly targeted patient records. The procedure of integrating patient data identification takes a lot of time and determination, therefore, a great increase in costs. The main experiment in determining the accuracy of the results of basic clinical examinations depends on the findings of analysis and availability of a huge patient database, which essential to be recognized [49]. Meta-investigation is similarly required in the next stage of practice, which requires ensuring that the mainstream of E-health customers are prepared to give their EHR with medical examination and studies, as long as confidentiality and confidentiality are preserved. That kind of power-saving effort can be seen in building a blockchain, with excessive transparency. A full-fledged E-health patient could use IoT formats to publicly convert and confidentially store EHR data with the help of a combined hybrid blockchain. One can use a hybrid key encryption technique to give

Distributed Ledger Technology (DLT) to simplify safe clinical information between community-based research and community-based study. IoT blockchain-based patients can quickly access and manage their EHR and open up the rights to allowance or rescind EHR-data access to the medicinal maintenance public, thereby providing greater sustenance to medical organizations to access DLT with more accurate EHR data with complete clinical data [50].

8.4.4 Drug Supply Chain Administration

Each and all year, huge numbers of patient's pain or expire from the use of counterfeit drugs. Next to similar, pharmacists are experiencing huge financial and psychological losses as a result of that drug. From drug production to the patient, the procurement procedure may include the succeeding categories: transference, management, storage, redistribution and marketing. The situation may be tense because of human error or the target's behavior. In its place of using the out-dated procurement management system, the creation of an IoT-based blockchain can take part in this procedure to make every step visible. Drug purchase records can be easily incorporated into a blockchain DLT that is perpetual, stable, and enabled to debug. Therefore, the risk of fraudulent activities can be completely reduced [51].

8.4.5 IoBHealth

Researchers introduced the formation of an E-healthcare structure based on IoT united with blockchain (IoBHealth) data stream to simplify all-in-one incorporation between IoT and blockchain for the provision of health-related facilities. This agenda contains three key sub-methods: IoT-constructed health administrative nodule, IoT-blockchain structure and IoT-built healthcare patient's nodule. Nodule of healthcare suppliers and patient nodule these two nodules of blockchain used. Both of these nodes are intended with the support of an EHR appliance, a back collection, a gate caretaker and a cryptocurrency user. Nodes are permissible to accumulate certain service information and transaction data [52].

8.5 Recent Case Studies

This segment deliberates the recent case studies and on-going real-time projects in the direction of the disposition of blockchain technology worldwide. The main purpose is to demonstrate how blockchain technology has been leveraged to convey inventions and evolutions in relation to healthcare data administration.

8.5.1 Estonian E-Healthcare System

The speedy invention in calculating techniques besides employment of E-explanations has transfigured Estonia's health organisation. In Estonia, 95.98–98.99% of patients have electrical health documents (like medicaments, their inquiries, and payment information) that can be chased and retrieved authoritatively through the E-patient online portal. An E-portal empowers a surgeon to access patients' records (medical reports and X-rays) from one file [53]. In 2016, the Estonian administration originated a blockchain-based assignment to protect the health data records and network access of its 1.5 million occupants. The purpose of the project is to stock record files that support maintaining a track status of all data handling happenings achieved on the health records. Key welfare of blockchain technology may be to reduce the danger of data breaks due to a mischievous hacker or a fake insider in the healthcare region. A personal digital block ledger was used to keep an eye and timestamp every minute to retrieve the patient's medicinal data records. Cryptographic hash functions generate an immutable review track of patient personal data. The assignment has the capability to attain the objective of having real-time attentiveness of the truthfulness of stowed patient personal data, which allows superintendents to recognize violations and act on time to restrict harm. Additionally, it improves the cost-efficiency, strength, and efficacy of Estonian healthcare systems in a way to be distributed, safe, translucent, interfere-proof, irreversible, and perceptible [54].

8.5.2 Healthcare and Pharma Data in UAE Using Blockchain

The UAE Ministry of Health and Prevention (MoHAP) has declared to introduce a platform based on blockchain for stowing healthcare data (such as healthcare services, medicinal physicians and medicines). The main concern of the platform is to increase stowage and toughen data safety in nationwide health organisations. The structure constructed on a blockchain is projected through examinations aimed at healthiness doctors, their medicinal warrant data, pharmacological documents, and MoHAP's application to government and private facilities. This application is similarly predictable to offer the utmost trustworthy and irreplaceable pharmaceutical facts in relation to industrial, permitted mediator, vigorous material, and charge. MoHAP's solutions could be leveraged to keep noticed data logs of health employees and administrations, bring about relaxed authentication of government institutions. In addition, it supports increasing records authentication plus stability, additional implements a higher level of transparency also faiths in the healthcare area. Grounded on unchallengeable records, all healthcare suppliers may have admittance to dependable data that helps in making suitable conclusions. Besides, MoHAP's resolution can help systematise working procedures and expand stability and functioning competence [55].

8.5.3   Medical Device Tracking in Swiss Hospitals by Permission Blockchain

Swiss hospitals have seen several embed and fake scams in current decades. On the way to overwhelm such matters, Swiss hospitals have designed a healthcare system constructed on blockchain that permits well-organized and reliable chasing of medicinal strategies. On an agreement basis among hospitals, all connections are stowed in the blockchain in an unchallengeable and noticeable method. This stage is grounded on hyper-laser technology allowing a blockchain. All communication formats of the transaction are associated with the Global Standard 1 (GS1) (Switzerland: GS1FG EDI 3.1 XML). Not like out-dated structures, this substructure removes the requirement of a third person when gathering medicinal strategies. Every dealing phase in a stockchain is stowed in the blockchain network atmosphere. The specific recogniser of every medicinal expedient permits the blockchain to create it noticeable, thereby enlightening patient security. The platform based on a blockchain allows incorporation amongst all performers (from producer to clever logistics, and data records) into the stock chain, creating it conceivable to create a safe and detectable stage for medicinal strategies in Swiss hospitals [56]. A summarised view of the above discussed cases is presented in Table 8.4.

8.6   Future Research Directions

The pragmatic study in the collected works is regularly around the plan and training of blockchain environment or structure. On the other hand, understudied regions continue, which need further study to resolve the present challenging problems already put on the blockchain-based healthcare system to real-life systems [57]. For this objective, fresh investigation in *Artificial Intelligence* (AI), Machine Learning (ML), fog computing, big data, data analytics and cloud computing can be co-operative through the distributed perception of blockchain. Likewise, some worries in systems constructed on the blockchain, the stress-free guideline in addition to normalization of these organizations.

8.6.1   AI and Data Analytics in Combination with Blockchain

Uniting blockchain technology with AI technology as well as data analytics can support in transformation of medicinal cure choices, health research, and clinical trials. Healthcare seeks to combine blockchain and AI to expand records administration and medicinal cure decision constructing. The accurateness and legitimacy of expectation are discussed, and extra deep investigation is required. One key challenge in implementing blockchain with AI in the healthcare environment is the

Table 8.4 Recent case studies of E-Healthcare

Case studies	Year	Description
Estonian E-health system	2016	Estonia stayed the first country in the universe to execute the EHR structure, recording almost every history of the population since birth to death Estonia used its surviving digital software identified as X-road to build the EHR system The Estonian program was supervised by the Department of Public Affairs till Estonia was established at the Health Foundation. Meanwhile, its inception, 95% of health information has been used The cost of this program was € 7.50 for a single individual at the period of formation
Healthcare and pharma data in the UAE using blockchain	2020 (accessed)	The key apprehension is to improve data security in health systems across the country This system will support and protect a consistent, fragmented and encoded record with great safety to ensure data accuracy and dependability Medical information based on drug inhale by community and reserved hospitals and healthcare workers can be noted on the MoHAP blockchain such as this one is there so that the public can be used
Medical device tracking in Swiss hospitals by permission blockchain	2020 (accessed)	Swiss hospitals have developed a healthcare system that is grounded on blockchain that allows for systematic and trustworthy monitoring of medical equipment The structure is centered on hyperactive record machinery All types of transactional messages comply with the GS1 standard Distinct out-dated structures, this organisation removes the necessity for the third person during the collection of medicinal equipment
Patientory Decentralized Application (DApp) solution	2020 (accessed)	Patientory has industrialised an application-sharing solution named DApp, which uses a reserved blockchain to offer elastic access to EMR in a collaborative and safe method Confirms that whole business deal or sharing of records have proof of interference and are consistent DApp is an essential healthcare resolution, also an exceptional instrument for handling appropriateness and nutrition

phonological to social changes of EHR structures worldwide. The conversion of medicinal information as of one phonologic to alternative is remaining a challenging task in medicinal exploration and medical trials. Conversely, if universal structure files and infers reports for alike analysis and cure, AI methods like ordinary philological handling and other data analytics resolutions make more real transformation or explanation of medicinal policy approaching from surgeons in diverse nations may facilitate.

8.6.2 Parallel Blockchain-Based Healthcare Organizations

Additional future investigation way for healthcare systems constructed on the blockchain is to design then implement corresponding healthcare systems in conjunction with blockchain's distributed independent bodies to integrate parallel healthcare systems and dissimilar healthcare dominions. Altogether healthcare groups, together with patients, medicine stores, hospitals, billing, health administrations, medicinal scholars, healthcare associations, and health assurance corporations, participate in the "Co-proprietorship, Co-creation and Co-distributing" of the Decentralized Parallel Healthcare Organizations (DPHO) ecology. The grouping of equivalent blockchain, healthcare structures, big data and data mining allows for an authoritative medical cure decision sustenance device.

8.6.3 Cloud Computing in Combination with Blockchain

Another most significant task of blockchain is to properly manage the enormous quantity of data records that are produced and protected hooked on every node of a network. A growth in the total amount of network nodes and communications will strengthen this experiment; added, IoT strategies had not sufficient computing ability and storing capability. Hence, one important future indicator is to reduce the volume of data manufactured or increase accessible stowage volume and further research on improving the mining process with power, time, resources and the use of new technologies in IoMT devices to expand computer energy and speed. Numerous scholars have deliberated the effectiveness of cloud and fog computing in healthcare system dominions. Other investigations have similarly established healthcare organisations that manage data extra efficiently as well as securely in healthcare using cloud computing.

8.6.4 Healthcare Regulations and Standardization Based on Blockchain

Presently, designers and scientists are going in the direction of designing. On the other hand, some blockades derivative from the absence of standards and authorized control creates through designed structures even more interesting and problematic. There is a silent controlling challenge for illuminating the relations of usage and instruct all related peoples of real-world systems. Due to, cross-edge distribution of EHR, wherever repeatedly varied and self-contradictory authorities may reduce the profits of blockchain data records distribution. Thus, developing a compliance code becomes a most significant future direction, containing united rules, normalizations, and cross-edge guidelines for smearing a blockchain to all definite healthcare dominion. Also, controlling barricades alike Health Insurance Portability and Accountability Act (HIPAA) are compulsory to guarantee the suitable usage of records though attacker can interrupt developing determinations.

8.6.5 Development of E-Healthcare System Considering Blockchain

With the growth of research on merging AI, edge computing, cloud computing, deep learning and blockchain, several additional entrances will be exposed to numerous dominions, containing healthcare study. Besides the continuing investigation, many essential stages to be followed however, emerging healthcare applications that built on blockchain, counting the succeeding.

- Examining the key features of the exact system of healthcare dominion centred on a blockchain.
- Threat examination of the use of blockchain locally and universally.
- Trade-off examination of blockchain uses.
- Smart agreement expansion

8.7 Conclusion

The paper explored how blockchain and IoT technology could be used to expand E-healthcare programs and facilities. Blockchain is a novel branch allocation that can renovate out-dated trades into a safe and reliable organization. Existing safety, confidentiality, and collaboration concerns in out-dated healthcare systems have enlarged the ability to use blockchain in this dominion. EHR is a key area where blockchain can be used to resolve data administration and uniqueness administration. In other healthcare facilities, the blockchain can be used to recover the efficacy and excellence of procedures at a low cost. Thus, this paper discusses a brief background, features, categories and application of blockchain. Furthermore, the paper enlightens the need for collaboration of blockchain with IoT to provide an improved E-healthcare system. Additionally, the paper elaborates some famous consensus algorithms used in blockchain in circumstance of E-healthcare system. Moreover, the paper deliberates the benefit of blockchain technology in healthcare data management. Besides, some use cases are systematically specified to demonstrate how some important structures of IoT with blockchain can be leveraged to sustenance E-healthcare facilities and ecologies. Finally, the paper presents some recent case studies along with some future research directions. In addition, we want to study more in this domain and will provide enhanced version of security with proper collaboration and adoption of new technologies along with ease.

References

1. Adler-Milstein, J., Holmgren, A. J., Kralovec, P., Worzala, C., Searcy, T., & Patel, V. (2017). Electronic health record adoption in US hospitals: The emergence of a digital "advanced use" divide. *Journal of the American Medical Informatics Association, 24*(6), 1142–1148. https://doi.org/10.1093/jamia/ocx080

2. Bhushan, B., Sinha, P., Sagayam, K. M., & Andrew, J. (2020). Untangling blockchain technology: A survey on state of the art, security threats, privacy services, applications and future research directions. *Computers & Electrical Engineering, 106897.* https://doi.org/10.1016/j.compeleceng.2020.106897

3. Madaan, G., Bhushan, B., & Kumar, R. (2020). Blockchain-based cyberthreat mitigation systems for smart vehicles and industrial automation. *Studies in Big Data Multimedia Technologies in the Internet of Things Environment, 13*–32. https://doi.org/10.1007/978-981-15-7965-3_2

4. Griggs, K. N., Ossipova, O., Kohlios, C. P., Baccarini, A. N., Howson, E. A., & Hayajneh, T. (2018). Healthcare blockchain system using smart contracts for secure automated remote patient monitoring. *Journal of Medical Systems, 42*(7), 130. https://doi.org/10.1007/s10916-018-0982-x

5. Folorunso, S. O., Chakraborty, C., & Awotunde, J. B. (2021). A secured transaction based on blockchain architecture in mobile banking platform. *International Journal of Internet Technology and Secured Transactions, 1*(1), 1. https://doi.org/10.1504/ijitst.2021.10039177

6. Tripathi, G., Abdul Ahad, M., & Paiva, S. (2020). Sms: A secure healthcare model for smart cities. *Electronics, 9*(7), 1135. https://doi.org/10.3390/electronics9071135

7. Ali, F., El-Sappagh, S., Islam, S. M. R., Kwak, D., Ali, A., Imran, M., & Kwak, K.-S. (2020). A smart healthcare monitoring system for heart disease prediction based on ensemble deep learning and feature fusion. *Information Fusion, 63*, 208–222. https://doi.org/10.1016/j.inffus.2020.06.008

8. Awais, M., Raza, M., Ali, K., Ali, Z., Irfan, M., Chughtai, O., & Ur Rehman, M. (2019). An Internet of Things based bed-egress alerting paradigm using wearable sensors in elderly care environment. *Sensors, 19*(11), 2498. https://doi.org/10.3390/s19112498

9. Ahad, M. A., Tripathi, G., Zafar, S., & Doja, F. (2019). IoT data management—Security aspects of information linkage in IoT systems. *Intelligent Systems Reference Library, 439*–464. https://doi.org/10.1007/978-3-030-33596-0_18

10. Jiang, L., Chen, L., Giannetsos, T., Luo, B., Liang, K., & Han, J. (2019). Toward practical privacy-preserving processing over encrypted data in IoT: An assistive healthcare use case. *IEEE Internet of Things Journal, 6*(6), 10177–10190. https://doi.org/10.1109/jiot.2019.2936532

11. Farouk, A., Alahmadi, A., Ghose, S., & Mashatan, A. (2020). Blockchain platform for industrial healthcare: Vision and future opportunities. *Computer Communications, 154*, 223–235. https://doi.org/10.1016/j.comcom.2020.02.058

12. Kumar, A., Abhishek, K., Bhushan, B., & Chakraborty, C. (2021). Secure access control for manufacturing sector with application of ethereum blockchain. *Peer-to-Peer Networking and Applications.* https://doi.org/10.1007/s12083-021-01108-3

13. Akhtar, M. M., Khan, M. Z., Ahad, M. A., Noorwali, A., Rizvi, D. R., & Chakraborty, C. (2021). Distributed ledger technology based robust access control and real-time synchronization for consumer electronics. *PeerJ Computer Science, 7.* https://doi.org/10.7717/peerj-cs.566

14. Malik, A., Gautam, S., Abidin, S., & Bhushan, B. (2019). Blockchain technology-future of IoT: Including structure, limitations and various possible attacks. In *2nd International Conference on Intelligent Computing, Instrumentation and Control Technologies (ICICICT), Kannur, India*, pp. 1100–1104. https://doi.org/10.1109/ICICICT46008.2019.8993144

15. Ray, P. P., Dash, D., Salah, K., & Kumar, N. (2021, March). Blockchain for IoT-based healthcare: Background, consensus, platforms, and use cases. *IEEE Systems Journal, 15*(1), 85–94. https://doi.org/10.1109/JSYST.2020.2963840

16. Yang, X., Chen, Y., & Chen, X. (2019). Effective scheme against 51% attack on proof-of-work blockchain with history weighted information. In *IEEE international conference on Blockchain (Blockchain), Atlanta, GA, USA*, pp. 261–265. https://doi.org/10.1109/Blockchain.2019.00041

17. Bhushan, B., Khamparia, A., Sagayam, K. M., Sharma, S. K., Ahad, M. A., & Debnath, N. C. (2020). Blockchain for smart cities: A review of architectures, integration trends and future research directions. *Sustainable Cities and Society, 61*, 102360. https://doi.org/10.1016/j.scs.2020.102360

18. Saxena, S., Bhushan, B., & Ahad, M. A. (2021). Blockchain based solutions to secure Iot: Background, integration trends and a way forward. *Journal of Network and Computer Applications, 103050.* https://doi.org/10.1016/j.jnca.2021.103050

19. Aich, S., Chakraborty, S., Sain, M., Lee, H., & Kim, H. (2019). A review on benefits of IoT integrated blockchain based supply chain management implementations across different sectors with case study. In *21st International Conference on Advanced Communication Technology (ICACT), PyeongChang, Korea (South)*, pp. 138–141. https://doi.org/10.23919/ICACT.2019.8701910

20. Kumar, A., Krishnamurthi, R., Nayyar, A., Sharma, K., Grover, V., & Hossain, E. (2020). A novel smart healthcare design, simulation, and implementation using healthcare 4.0 processes. *IEEE Access, 8*, 118433–118471. https://doi.org/10.1109/ACCESS.2020.3004790

21. Srivastava, G., Crichigno, J., & Dhar, S. (2019). A light and secure healthcare blockchain for IoT medical devices. In *IEEE Canadian Conference of Electrical and Computer Engineering (CCECE), Edmonton, AB, Canada*, pp. 1–5. https://doi.org/10.1109/CCECE.2019.8861593

22. Salimitari, M., & Chatterjee, M. (2019). *A survey on consensus protocols in blockchain for IoT networks.* https://arxiv.org/pdf/1809.05613.pdf

23. Kim, J., Jin, J., & Kim, K. (2018). A study on an energy-effective and secure consensus algorithm for private blockchain systems (PoM: Proof of Majority). In *International Conference on Information and Communication Technology Convergence (ICTC), Jeju, Korea (South)*, pp. 932–935. https://doi.org/10.1109/ICTC.2018.8539561

24. Altarawneh, A., & Skjellum, A. (2020). The security ingredients for correct and Byzantine Fault-tolerant blockchain consensus algorithms. In *International Symposium on Networks, Computers and Communications (ISNCC), Montreal, QC, Canada*, pp. 1–9. https://doi.org/10.1109/ISNCC49221.2020.9297326

25. Goyal, S., Sharma, N., Bhushan, B., Shankar, A., & Sagayam, M. (2020). Iot enabled technology in secured healthcare: Applications, challenges and future directions. In *Cognitive internet of medical things for smart healthcare* (pp. 25–48). https://doi.org/10.1007/978-3-030-55833-8_2

26. Bhushan, B., Sahoo, C., Sinha, P., & Khamparia, A. (2020). Unification of Blockchain and Internet of Things (BIoT): Requirements, working model, challenges and future directions. *Wireless Networks.* https://doi.org/10.1007/s11276-020-02445-6

27. Goyal, S., Sharma, N., Kaushik, I., & Bhushan, B. (2021). Blockchain as a solution for security attacks in named data networking of things. In *Security and privacy issues in IoT devices and sensor networks* (pp. 211–243). https://doi.org/10.1016/b978-0-12-821255-4.00010-9

28. Sethi, R., Bhushan, B., Sharma, N., Kumar, R., & Kaushik, I. (2020). Applicability of industrial IoT in diversified sectors: Evolution, applications and challenges. In *Studies in big data multimedia technologies in the Internet of Things environment* (pp. 45–67). https://doi.org/10.1007/978-981-15-7965-3_4

29. Blockchain and healthcare: Use cases today and opportunities for the future. https://mlsdev.com/blog/blockchain-and-healthcare-use-cases-today-and-in-the-future. Accessed 2020.

30. Dagher, G. G., Mohler, J., Milojkovic, M., & Marella, P. B. (2018). Ancile: Privacy-preserving framework for access control and interoperability of electronic health records using blockchain technology. *Sustainable Cities and Society, 39*, 283–297. https://doi.org/10.1016/j.scs.2018.02.014

31. Alam Khan, F., Asif, M., Ahmad, A., Alharbi, M., & Aljuaid, H. (2020). Blockchain technology, improvement suggestions, security challenges on smart grid and its application in

healthcare for sustainable development. *Sustainable Cities and Society, 55*, 102018. https:// doi.org/10.1016/j.scs.2020.102018

32. Vazirani, A. A., O'Donoghue, O., Brindley, D., & Meinert, E. (2020). Blockchain vehicles for efficient Medical Record management. *Npj Digital Medicine, 3*(1). https://doi.org/10.1038/ s41746-019-0211-0

33. Kumar, T., Ramani, V., Ahmad, I., Braeken, A., Harjula, E., & Ylianttila, M. (2018). Blockchain utilization in healthcare: Key requirements and challenges. In *2018 IEEE 20th international conference on e-health networking, applications and services (Healthcom)*. https://doi. org/10.1109/healthcom.2018.8531136

34. Xia, Q., Sifah, E. B., Asamoah, K. O., Gao, J., Du, X., & Guizani, M. (2017). MeDShare: Trust-less medical data sharing among cloud service providers via blockchain. *IEEE Access, 5*, 14757–14767. https://doi.org/10.1109/access.2017.2730843

35. Gordon, W. J., & Catalini, C. (2018). Blockchain technology for healthcare: Facilitating the transition to patient-driven interoperability. *Computational and Structural Biotechnology Journal, 16*, 224–230. https://doi.org/10.1016/j.csbj.2018.06.003

36. Yang, X., Li, T., Liu, R., & Wang, M. (2019). Blockchain-based secure and searchable EHR sharing scheme. In *2019 4th International Conference on Mechanical, Control and Computer Engineering (ICMCCE), Hohhot, China*, pp. 822–8223. https://doi.org/10.1109/ ICMCCE48743.2019.00188

37. Singh, P., & Wilkie, D. J. (2019). Development of advanced clinical research application: PAINRelieveIt using patient feedback. In *2019 IEEE International Conference on Electrical, Computer and Communication Technologies (ICECCT), Coimbatore, India*, pp. 1–5. https:// doi.org/10.1109/ICECCT.2019.8869466

38. Nakhai, I., & Jafari, S. (2010). Developing smart and active packaging of inventory model in drug supply chain for special diseases. In *IEEE international conference on management of inno- vation & technology, Singapore*, pp. 550–555. https://doi.org/10.1109/ICMIT.2010.5492762

39. Qiu, J., Liang, X., Shetty, S., & Bowden, D. (2018). Towards secure and smart healthcare in smart cities using blockchain. In *2018 IEEE International Smart Cities Conference (ISC2), Kansas City, MO, USA*, pp. 1–4. https://doi.org/10.1109/ISC2.2018.8656914

40. Healthcare. https://e-estonia.com/solutions/healthcare/e-health-record/. Accessed 2020.

41. Blockchain and healthcare: The estonian experience. https://nor tal.com/blog/blockchain- healthcare-estonia/. Accessed 2020.

42. UAE launches blockchain for healthcare and pharma data. https://www.ledgerinsights.com/ blockchain-healthcare-pharma-uae/. Accessed 2020.

43. Swiss hospitals track medical products by blockchain. https://fintechnews.ch/blockchainbit- coin/swiss-hospitals-track-medical-products-by-blockchain/32699/. Accessed 2020.

44. Salah, K., Rehman, M. H., Nizamuddin, N., & Al-Fuqaha, A. (2019). Blockchain for AI: Review and open research challenges. *IEEE Access, 7*, 10127–10149. https://doi.org/10.1109/ access.2018.2890507

45. Mamoshina, P., Ojomoko, L., Yanovich, Y., Ostrovski, A., Botezatu, A., Prikhodko, P., Izumchenko, E., Aliper, A., Romantsov, K., Zhebrak, A., Ogu, I. O., & Zhavoronkov, A. (2018). Converging blockchain and next-generation artificial intelligence technologies to decentralize and accelerate biomedical research and healthcare. *Oncotarget, 9*(5), 5665–5690. https://doi. org/10.18632/oncotarget.22345

46. Wang, F.-Y., Yuan, Y., Rong, C., & Zhang, J. J. (2018). Parallel blockchain: An architecture for CPSS-based smart societies. *IEEE Transactions on Computational Social Systems, 5*(2), 303–310. https://doi.org/10.1109/tcss.2018.2832379

47. Li, X., Huang, X., Li, C., Yu, R., & Shu, L. (2019). EdgeCare: Leveraging edge computing for collaborative data management in mobile healthcare systems. *IEEE Access, 7*, 22011–22025. https://doi.org/10.1109/access.2019.2898265

48. Mamoshina, P., Ojomoko, L., Yanovich, Y., Ostrovski, A., Botezatu, A., Prikhodko, P., Izumchenko, E., Aliper, A., Romantsov, K., Zhebrak, A., Ogu, I. O., & Zhavoronkov, A. (2017). Converging blockchain and next-generation artificial intelligence technologies to decentralize

and accelerate biomedical research and healthcare. *Oncotarget, 9*(5), 5665–5690. https://doi.
org/10.18632/oncotarget.22345

49. Charles, W., Marler, N., Long, L., & Manion, S. (2019). Blockchain compliance by design:
Regulatory considerations for blockchain in clinical research. *Frontiers in Blockchain, 2.*
https://doi.org/10.3389/fbloc.2019.00018

50. Gautam, S., Malik, A., Singh, N., & Kumar, S. (2019). Recent advances and countermeasures
against various attacks in IoT environment. In *2019 2nd International Conference on Signal
Processing and Communication (ICSPC).* https://doi.org/10.1109/icspc46172.2019.8976527

51. Haque, A. B., Najmul Islam, A., Hyrynsalmi, S., Naqvi, B., & Smolander, K. (2021). GDPR
compliant blockchains – A systematic literature review. *IEEE Access,* 1–1. https://doi.
org/10.1109/access.2021.3069877

52. Haque, A. B., Shurid, S., Juha, A. T., Sadique, M. S., & Asaduzzaman, A. S. (2020). A novel
design of gesture and voice controlled solar-powered smart wheel chair with obstacle detection. In *2020 IEEE International Conference on Informatics, IoT, and Enabling Technologies
(ICIoT).* https://doi.org/10.1109/iciot48696.2020.9089652

53. Pranto, T. H., Noman, A. A., Mahmud, A., & Haque, A. B. (2021). Blockchain and smart contract for IoT enabled smart agriculture. *PeerJ Computer Science, 7.* https://doi.org/10.7717/
peerj-cs.407

54. Indumathi, J., Shankar, A., Ghalib, M. R., Gitanjali, J., Hua, Q., Wen, Z., & Qi, X. (2020).
Block chain based internet of medical things for UNINTERRUPTED, ubiquitous, USER-
FRIENDLY, UNFLAPPABLE, UNBLEMISHED, unlimited health care services (BC Iomt
U6 HCS). *IEEE Access, 8,* 216856–216872. https://doi.org/10.1109/access.2020.3040240

55. Bhardwaj, A., Shah, S. B., Shankar, A., Alazab, M., Kumar, M., & Gadekallu, T. R. (2020).
Penetration testing framework for smart contract blockchain. *Peer-to-Peer Networking and
Applications.* https://doi.org/10.1007/s12083-020-00991-6

56. Kumar, A., Abhishek, K., Nerurkar, P., Ghalib, M. R., Shankar, A., & Cheng, X. (2020). Secure
smart contracts for cloud-based manufacturing using Ethereum blockchain. *Transactions on
Emerging Telecommunications Technologies.* https://doi.org/10.1002/ett.4129

57. Azad, C., Bhushan, B., Sharma, R., Shankar, A., Singh, K. K., & Khamparia, A. (2021).
Prediction model using SMOTE, genetic algorithm and decision tree (PMSGD) for classification of diabetes mellitus. *Multimedia Systems.* https://doi.org/10.1007/s00530-021-00817-2

Chapter 9
A Comprehensive Review of Wireless Medical Biosensor Networks in Connected Healthcare Applications

Duaa Alhusein and Ali Kadhum Idrees (iD)

Abstract The development of the hardware platform, as well as the underlying software, led to the emerging Internet of Healthcare Things (IoHT). The demand for remote healthcare continuous monitoring systems using limited resources and biosensors has increased. This paper provides a comprehensive review of the wireless medical biosensor networks in Connected Healthcare Applications. The main aim is to provide a basic overview of WMBNs and to discuss current achievements, particularly applications concentrating on remote patient monitoring for the elderly and chronically ill. A detailed examination of WBSN architecture, challenges, healthcare applications, and their needs is necessary to fulfil the scientific notion of WMBN. Following that, the main critical features of the WBSN are discussed, including data gathering, fusion, telemedicine and remote patient monitoring, rehabilitation and therapy, biofeedback, assisted living technologies, risk assessment, and decision making. It also offers insight into machine learning techniques and their applications in medical environments.

Keywords IoT · WBSN · Data reduction · Patient risk assessment · Decision making energy efficiency

9.1 Introduction

Over the last years, an increasing amount of interest was focused upon the wireless body sensor networks (WBSNs) due to their vast, innovative, accurate and simultaneous applications of monitoring in various areas, which include healthcare, sport training and fitness, social interactions, and monitoring industrial workers. People are getting increasingly aware of the importance of health-care in their daily lives as

D. Alhusein · A. K. Idrees (✉)
Department of Computer Science, University of Babylon, Babylon, Iraq
e-mail: ali.idrees@uobabylon.edu.iq

© The Author(s), under exclusive license to Springer Nature Switzerland AG 2023
M. A. Ahad et al. (eds.), *Enabling Technologies for Effective Planning and Management in Sustainable Smart Cities*, https://doi.org/10.1007/978-3-031-22922-0_9

the standard of living rises and the population ages. Wearable health monitoring (WHM) can be defined as a new technology which allows for continuous ambulatory monitoring of potions for recording the vital sign about their body and health without causing undue discomfort or interfering with their daily activities when they're at home, work, or other exercise-focused locations, or in a clinical setting. The technical WHM device designs have been focused on four major areas: reliability and safety, low power consumption, ergonomics, and comfort.

The smart WHM systems can be provided in different forms skin- touch devices, implantable devices as well as another wearable tiny devices and were used to monitor the vital signals regarding body and health body activity and location On the other hand, the agreement level of (WHM) devices by end employer is low, in order to the data treatment technologies applied in the WHM devices or systems can't manage data gathering by the set of the sensors composite in a system through the phase of data preprocessing, origin of discriminative and salient characteristics, and data identification in the status of the body activity. In the present day, the clinicians usually perform the diagnoses and classification of the diseases, according to the information that has been obtained from many physiological sensor signals. None-the-less, the sensor signal could be vulnerable easily to specific interference or noise cases and as a result of the large individual variation sensitivity to various physiological sensors might vary as well. Which is why, multiple sensor signal fusion is necessary for providing more reliable and robust decisions.

The principal contribution of this paper is to introduce a comprehensive show of Wireless Medical Biosensor Networks in connected healthcare applications. This review covers the background of the Wireless Body Sensor Networks, their applications, and the principal challenges of network. The data collection, data fusion, local emergency detection, and decision making about of the patients situation investigated. The machine learning applications in smart cities are explored.

This paper is set up as follows: The Wireless Body Sensor Networks (WBSNs) are presented in the next section. Section 9.3 introduces the architecture of WBSN. The biosensor is given in Sect. 9.4. The WBSN applications are illustrated in Sect. 9.5. The main challenges of WBSNs are shown in Sect. 9.6. Section 9.7 presents the Early Warning Score (EWS). The data gathering is given in Sect. 9.8. Section 9.9 introduces data fusion in WBSNs. Telemedicine and remote patient monitoring are investigated in Sect. 9.10. Section 9.11 demonstrates the decision making. Section 9.12 shows energy consumption. Section 9.13 explores machine learning techniques and their applications in smart cities. Finally, the conclusions are indicated in Sect. 9.14.

9.2 Wireless Body Sensor Networks (WBSNs)

The WBSNs had set up as follows an inexpensive resolution allowing the continuous control of the physiological and physical parameters of the patient body. A lot of research has been made and is still being made in the design of medical accurate invasive and noninvasive sensors and the design of comfortable wearable health monitoring systems. Firstly the most commonly employed sensors in WBSNs. capture physiological parameters including vital signs and physiological signals as well as physical parameters related to body movement. In additionally to the discussion of the differences of several commercially available wearable sensor nodes on the market [1]. Having health related data being continuously collected leads to a palette of body sensor network (BSN) applications. A particular focus is given to healthcare applications given that it is the main focus of this thesis. All types of population can benefit from BSN healthcare applications, starting from toddlers to elderly, depending on the monitoring phenomenon of interest. Furthermore, diverse monitoring tasks can be achieved such as event detection, prediction, diagnosis etc.

Thus a discussion about these tasks and depict them is provide as a function of three different dimensions: the type of user, the type of processing and the monitoring location However, BSN healthcare applications should meet a set of requirements in order to achieve user satisfaction, perform as desired, have an impact on people's life and ensure continuity, especially that WBSNs have limited resources, are subjected to interference as well as faulty measurements and that are dealing with sensitive medical data [2].

In the previous years, the entire world has been facing an growing number of patients and illnesses. Moreover, The relationships between humans and animal led to the introduction and prevalence of new types of viruses and unknown ailments such as covid-19. Consequently, this will increase health observation and evaluation a complex task for hospitals and medical staff. In addition, the connected healthcare applications are overcoming some significant obstacles such us keep the power of the biosensor devices to guarantee as much a time period of monitoring as possible for the patients, and speeding up the discovery of the patient's state sending it to a medical expert so they can make an appropriate conclusion.

9.3 The Architecture of WBSN

A WBSN include the biosensor nodes and a coordinator, The former is deployed on a person's body. They may be either implanted inside the human body or placed on it. They continuously sense physiological signals, vital signs, an example of physiological signals include ECG, EEG and PPG etc. Whereas an example of vital signs includes the RR, HR, temperature, BP and oxygen saturation etc. The acquired data is periodically and wirelessly transmitted to the coordinator of the network [3]. The latter can be any portable device close to a person's body such as his/her smartphone or PDA. Its role is to manage the network and perform the fusion of the collected data. Thus, emergencies, abnormal events as well as the continuous follow-up of the person's health condition can be ensured by the coordinator. Moreover, it can provide the person advice, reminders and take action in emergency situations such as call the doctor. The collected data as well as results of the process of fusion are sent

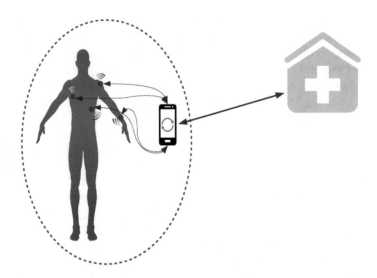

Fig. 9.1 WBSN architecture [3]

by the coordinator to the medical center (healthcare experts, doctors) where further processing can be made [3].

The main motivations for using the WBSN are (1) reducing the energy consumed by the biosensor devices make ensure the patient receives the longest possible monitoring and (2) fast detection of the patient's urgency and sending it to the medical professionals to provide the best decision to save their lives. (3) monitoring and tracking the patient's situation Whenever he wants, from anywhere, the patient can give professionals remote access to patient data (Fig. 9.1).

9.4　Biosensor

Biosensors are miniature, lightweight, low power, limited-resources and intelligent sensor nodes that sense, process and transmit human physiological parameters such as the ECG, the heart rate, the body temperature, the body movement etc. Figure 9.2 illustrates the components of a wireless biosensor node. It is composed of three units powered by a battery: the sensing, the processing and the transmission units.

All three units require power for performing tasks. However, the transmission has been viewed as the most power-hungry of tasks. The unit of sensing includes a sensor and an ADC, converting the analog signal that is sensed with a certain frequency (Nyquist-Shannon), to a digital signal.

The latter is given to processing unit (i.e. memory and processor) where the algorithms of processing are run. In addition to that, the processor regulates the transmission and sensing units and it changes and/or activates their status based on applications and utilized protocols [4].

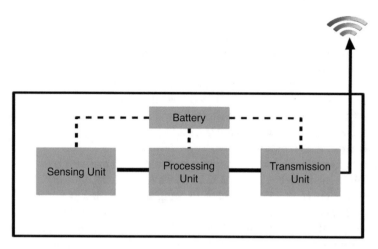

Fig. 9.2   The components of a biosensor node [4]

9.5   WBSN Applications

These applications are comprehensive for multiple areas such as health care, assistance to the elderly and provision response to emergency case [5] an overview of potential medical applications will be presented in this section.

- **Telemedicine and Remote Patient Monitoring**
  Increasing cost of medical care and old age in the world's population leads to a major development in the telemedicine network for the purpose of providing many medical services. Telemedicine uses an integrated medical system and modern communication techniques to enable the delivery of a remote patient care service and also provides the possibility for health professional in the world such as physicians, scientists and others to take care of more patients. In this case, the patient can remain under the continuous monitoring of the doctor under normal physiological conditions without affecting the daily activities and at the lowest cost. WBSNs are able to supply constant monitoring for the biomedical parameters and failure detection in the devices when it occurs, as well as early detection of emergencies. Such patient monitoring systems will be more secure, more compatible and inexpensive [5].
- **Rehabilitation and Therapy**
  Aim of rehabilitation application is permitting for sick people after leaving the hospital to recover their functional abilities and return to normal condition by convenient treatment Rehabilitation is a dynamic operation designed for correction any wrong behavior by using the available facilities to arrive the optimal state. In order to reach a person with a brain stroke to the highest level of stability, the movement of the patient during rehabilitation period should be constantly monitored and corrected. Thus, patients' movement tracking becomes necessary in the scheme of rehabilitation [5].

- **Biofeedback**
  Biofeedback indicates to the possibility of measuring biomedical activity and potential medical parameters and returning them to the user in order to allow him to modify his biological activity and control it for the purpose of enhancing his health. It is beneficial for controlling certain conditions and for non- voluntary human body functions such as blood pressure plus migraines. The devices of biofeedback can involve those designed for monitoring the human heart functions, breathing apparatus, brainwaves and others [6].
- **Assisted Living Technologies**
  Aging in the world population and the high cost of formal healthcare institutions as well as the tendency of some individuals to live independently all this led to an expansion of innovative living techniques for an independent and secure aging. These applications use house automation to enhance living and preserve an independent style for life. Actually, supported living techniques have been used as an alternative for older people, people with special needs and disabilities persons who cannot be independent and the same time do not need health care all the time.

  The ambient health sensor network can obtain the bio parameters of the environment of living and then send them to a centralized station due to medical constant monitoring system. The health of these people can be guessed by knowing the blood pressure, heart rate, etc. These systems could be linked to a medical center for the purpose of emergency response or sudden changes (if the parameters deviate from the physical range) [7].

9.6 Main Challenges of WBSNs

- Reliably – the major problem is to ensure that information reaches is intended destination in reliable manner. Many factors contribute to the reliability of wireless body sensor network, including stable software programing, dependable wireless communications between nodes sensor and efficient processing in every sensor node.
- Biocompatibility – for sensors node that directly interact with patient body, the shape, size and materials are limited. Packaging the sensor in biocompatible materials is the solution.
- Portably – the size and Wight of the sensors node employed in wireless physiology measuring device must be tiny and light Wight, whether they are placed on or swallowed.
- Privacy and security – the major security concerns include eavesdropping, identity spoofing and disclosure of personal information to the unauthorized persons. It is possible to be secure improved by incepting data, privet data must be

safeguarded against unauthorized access "Consented data acquisition, proper data storage, secure transmissions, and integrity of the data and authorized data access are vital areas for developing software or hardware solutions" [8].

- Light-weight wireless communication protocols have to be able to handle self-organization networks (include security features) as well as data gathering and routing.
- Enrage aware communication nodes should transmit at allow power level to permit. The nodes bargain to reduce their transmission power, an emerge-were protocol is required.

9.7 Early Warning Score

The healthcare doctors at the hospital use the National Early Warning Score (NEWS), a physiological scoring system, to assess each patient's condition and determine how best to treat instances with high risks. This system of scoring uses six physiological measures that presented in Fig. 9.3 [9]. The key benefit of NEWS is how easily it can calculate the patient's overall risk using the appropriate scores for each type of sensor. The NEWS can assess the patient's condition by evaluating the sensed values from various biosensors [10, 11].

9.8 Data Gathering

Data collection is a method of gathering and measuring data, that are collect from several source of information so as to supply answers to pertinent questions [7].

The process of gathering, measuring, and evaluation of the correct information for the study, utilizing approved established processes has been known as the data collection. According to the obtained facts, a study could evaluate the hypothesis. Despite the subject of study, the collection of data is typically the first and most important stage in the process of the research. For the dialysis, the different methods to the data acquisition are utilized in various disciplines of study, relying on the information needed [7].

The most significant aim of data gathering is collecting the information-rich and accurate data for the statistical analyses so that the data-driven study decisions could be made. There are two type of data collection: primary data and secondary data, the primary data are un processed data that have been obtained for the first time. The secondary data represents the information that was gathered and tested already [12].

PHYSIOLOGICAL PARAMETERS	3	2	1	0	1	2	3
Respiration Rate	≤8		9 - 11	12 - 20		21 - 24	≥25
Oxygen Saturations	≤91	92 - 93	94 - 95	≥96			
Any Supplemental Oxygen		Yes		No			
Temperature	≤35.0		35.1 - 36.0	36.1 - 38.0	38.1 - 39.0	≥39.1	
Systolic BP	≤90	91 - 100	101 - 110	111 - 219			≥220
Heart Rate	≤40		41 - 50	51 - 90	91 - 110	111 - 130	≥131
Level of Consciousness				A			V, P, or U

Fig. 9.3 NEWS

9.9 Data Fusion

Currently, developing intelligent algorithms for a variety of tasks in healthcare applications has been attracting the research community. Hence, the treatment and processing of the collected data is an important aspect in WBSNs. For instance, data fusion in WBSNs allows to combine, to correlate and to associate physiological data and medical information coming from one or multiple biosensor nodes in order to achieve accurate situation assessments about the monitored person. Particularly, multi-sensor fusion has been gaining an ever-increasing interest driven by its potential in ensuring a unified picture about the health condition of the patient. However, several challenges exist in WBSNs, especially that the collected data is subject to noise, interference and faulty measurements, thus leading to the fusion of imperfect and inconsistent data.

Furthermore, real-time fusion and good accuracy, which are two important aspects in healthcare applications, should be satisfied by multi-sensor fusion approaches.

The Data fusion is multilevel operation that deals with associations, correlations, combination of the data and information from multiple as well as single sources for achieving the identity estimations, refined position, and complete timely evaluations of the situations, threats in addition to their relevance [13].

The following definition for Multisensor fusion enables to obtain a unified image and a globalized view of the system by combining information from several sources [2, 14].

There are three different data fusion approaches based on the processing architecture are identified: distributed, centralized and hybrid. The centralized method depends on a fusion center where all processing is carried out. A distributed method is adopted when the sensor nodes perform independent processing on the data they have captured and transmit the results to a fusion node. In this case, the fusion node executes a global analysis based on the results sent by all the sensor nodes [15, 16].

Finally, hybrid fusion concerns approaches where the sensor nodes only perform pre-processing and/or perform partial lightweight computation on the collected data in a distributed approach fashion while a central node fuses the gathered data and performs high-level fusion [17].

9.10 Telemedicine and Remote Patient Monitoring

In clinical uses, multiple devices placed on the bodies of the patients are being used to sense their vital signs. These devices continuously transmit each signal they have detected to the Gateway. Every period, the gateway collects massive observed data. Therefore, before sending the data to the gateway, each device must reduce the data. Data cleaning at the sensor devices can reduce cost and maximize system longevity. Additionally, it can lower the amount of data that is received at the Edge gateway to make it easier to analyze and provide an accurate assessment of the patient's situation.

NEWS claims that the devices only transmit measures with results greater than 0 to the healthcare experts. The data of the patients' normal state won't have been sent to gateway. It is obvious that less time will be spent periodically checking on the patient's condition and sending data to the gateway. This issue can be resolved by determining the relationships between the detected data per period and then send them to the gateway.

9.11 Decision Making

After receiving the readings of the biosensor nodes that executing the emergency detection algorithm, the Edge gateway achieves the fusion for the readings of biosensor nodes to provide meaningful information about the situation of the patient health.

This health condition of the patient is utilized to assess the health risk of the patient and then take the appropriate decision. The Edge gateway transmits the taken decision and the collected data to the experts in the medical center. The Edge gateway collects the first readings of biosensor nodes at the beginning of each period, then each time t receives reading from appropriate biosensor k, it computes its updated score US. Finally, the Edge gateway calculates the aggregated score AS for the whole biosensor nodes using their updates scores. For example, if the Edge gateway only receives the scores of the biosensor nodes HR, RESP, and ABPsys at the time t, it calculates the updated score for them. Then, it uses the last saved updated score of the remaining two biosensor nodes BLOODT and SpO$_2$. Finally, it computes the aggregated score.

9.12   Energy Consumption

This model can be characterized as the design and analysis of mathematical representation of the WBSN for studying the effects of the alteration of the parameters of the system. The behavior of this model represents a function of its parameters [18]. The reduction of power that is consumed in the communication by the wireless sensor nodes may be highly effective, due to the fact that radio transceiver is a component with maximum power consumption. The wireless sensor node is comprised of three components that are powered by battery: the sensing, the processing and the transmission units. All those three units need power for performing their tasks. The energy consumption of this thesis was evaluated based on typical power consumption concerning wearable node, where 1 energy unit equals 152 J: the task of the sensing consumes 6 J, the task of processing consumes 24 J, transmission task (TX) consumes 60 J and receiving task (RX) consumes 62 J [19] (Fig. 9.4).

9.13   Machine Learning Applications in Smart Cities

The goal of a smart city is to maximise the efficient use of limited resources while also improving residents' quality of life. To develop a sustainable urban existence, smart cities used the Internet of Things (IoT). In smart cities, IoT devices such as sensors, actuators, and smartphones create data. The data created by smart cities is submitted to analytics in order to obtain insight and uncover new information for increasing the smart cities' efficiency and effectiveness. Several works are focused on the machine learning in the internet of health and things [20–24]. In this section, some machine learning methods are presented [25].

9.13.1   Convolutional Neural Network (CNN)

The mathematical technique 'convolution' is used in the convolutional neural network (ConvNet) displayed in Fig. 9.5. The processing of numerous convolution applications that run simultaneously is referred to as "convolution" in this context.

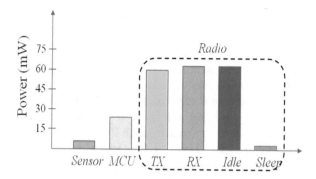

Fig. 9.4 Typical Power Consumption in Wearable Nodes [19]

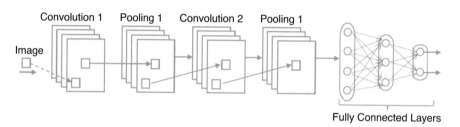

Fig. 9.5 The CNN

It is a particular linear transformation action in its levels that substitutes convolution for conventional matrix multiplication. The 1st parameter is called the input, the 2nd parameter is called the kernel, and the output is called the feature map, according to TheConvNet.

Whereas the input is a matrix of data, the kernel is an array of variables. These two matrices are known as tensors because the input and kernel parts should be kept independently. ConvNet's main inspiration is based on three factors: sparse interactions, parameter sharing, and equivariant representation. The kernel is smaller than the input because to the sparse interaction, and parameter sharing is used in a model. Equivariant representations imply that when the input modified, the output would likewise change [26].

The ConvNet components are divided into two layers: left and right. The left layer is made up of a limited number of complicated layers, each of which has many stages. These stages are also known as the input stage, output stage, and numerous hidden stages, with convolutional, pooling, fully connected, and normalising hidden layers being the most common. There are three steps in a pooling layer: The first stage involves running a series of convolutions one after another to produce a collection of linear activations. Each linear activation is carried out in the second step using function of activation. The pooling function is used in the third stage to affect the output of the following layer. Because it may utilise lower pooling units than detector units, pooling enhances the network's computational and statistical efficiency while also reducing the amount of storage needed to hold the parameters [26].

9.13.2   The RNN (Recurrent Neural Network)

It is efficient network that provides a succession of learning [27]. RNNs are temporal state-structured dynamical systems. They're rather powerful, and they're used in a variety of temporal processing situations and digital applications. Both the Hopfield and Cohen Grossberg models use a kinetic basic feature to hold data, and serves as an associate memory respectively for storing knowledge and finding solutions to optimization problems, are two common RNN models. The RNN is divided into two types: global and local. Local RNN tight feed forward connection organised using dynamic neuron models, whereas global RNN applies the connection between the neurons as feed forward. The time-delayed and simultaneous RNNs are two static time models for RNNs. First of which is taught to minimise error of prediction and the 2nd is learned to create broad approximation function skills [28]. In contrast to the shallow RNN, the deep RNN has numerous hidden layers (see Fig. 9.6).

9.13.3   The DRL (Deep Reinforcement Learning)

The DRL algorithm works in the environment to take action with the purpose of maximising rewards and improving the learning algorithm's efficiency [29]. The reinforcement learning block diagram is shown in Fig. 9.7.

9.13.4   Support Vector Machine

SVM one of the common tools of supervised machine learning, it is commonly utilized for the efficient classification. The SVMs demonstrate high accuracy of the classification with many applications, like the object detection, speech recognition, bio-informatics, image classification, medical diagnosis, and so on [30]. The supervised machine learning is typically composed of 2 fundamental stages, learning/training phase and classification phase. The training phase of the SVMs constructs a model to be utilized to classify any testing data which has been based upon the Support Vectors (SVs).

Support Vectors have been identified from training data-set throughout the process of the training, to be utilized then in the phase of the classification for the prediction of proper class of input testing data. The SVMs showed high rates of the classification accuracy, as they outperform other common algorithms of classification in a wide range of the applications and cases [31, 32]. There is a growing interest for the exploitation of the SVMs in several of the embedded systems of detection and different applications of image processing.

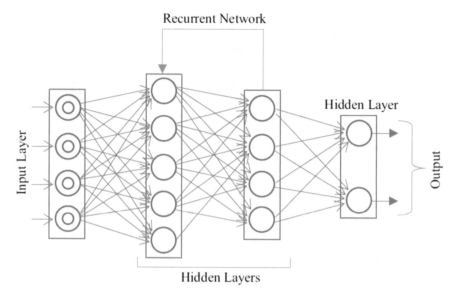

Fig. 9.6 Deep RNN

Fig. 9.7 Reinforcement
learning

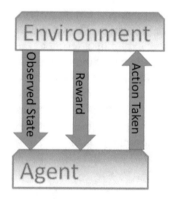

SVM represents a powerful algorithm for machine learning, showing high precision in various problems of classification [33]. The SVMs are based upon the theory of decision boundary, efficiently differentiating between 2 different data sample classes. There are two main phases in this model of supervised learning, training/learning and classification phases. In phase of training, a trained model is advanced with the use of input training data-set, where a decision boundary has been formed from optimal separating hyper-plane which optimally separates the data samples of those 2 classes. SVs represent data samples which lie on decision boundary, and they have been defined in the phase of the training and are utilized after that for the tasks of the classification in classification stage.

The reason for using the SVMs in machine learning The SVMs are utilized in some applications such as the hand-writing recognition, face detection, intrusion detection, gene classification, e-mail classification, and in web pages. It is a reason for using the SVM in machine learning. It has the ability of handling the classification as well as the regression on the linear and the nonlinear data. An additional reason for using the SVMs is due to the fact that they have the ability of finding complex relationships between one's data without needing to perform many transformations on their own. It is one of the best options in the case of working with smaller data-sets having tens-hundreds of thousands of the features. Usually, they find more precise results in comparison with other algorithms due to their capability in handling small, complex data-sets [34]. Below is a set of advantages and disadvantages for utilizing the SVMs.

9.14 Conclusions

The rapid development of the Internet of Things (IoT) has led to increasing advancements in the healthcare industry. The development of the hardware platform, as well as the underlying software, led to the emerging Internet of Healthcare Things (IoHT). The demand for remote healthcare continuous monitoring systems using limited resources and biosensors has increased. In Connected Healthcare Applications, this study presents a detailed assessment of wireless medical biosensor networks. The main goal is to present a fundamental introduction of WMBNs and to highlight recent advances, with a focus on remote patient monitoring for the elderly and chronically ill. To fulfil the scientific idea of WMBN, a detailed investigation of WBSN architecture, problems, healthcare applications, and their demands is required. The WBSN's primary important elements are then covered, including data collection, fusion, telemedicine and remote patient monitoring, rehabilitation and therapy, biofeed-back, assisted living technologies, risk assessment, and decision making. It also gives an overview of machine learning techniques and how they're used in medical settings.

References

1. Idrees, A. K., & Witwit, A. J. H. (2021). Energy-efficient load-balanced RPL routing protocol for internet of things networks. *International Journal of Internet Technology and Secured Transactions, 11*(3), 286–306.
2. Idrees, S. K., & Idrees, A. K. (2021). New fog computing enabled lossless EEG data compression scheme in IoT networks. *Journal of Ambient Intelligence and Humanized Computing, 13*, 3257–3270.
3. Idrees, A. K., Deschinkel, K., Salomon, M., & Couturier, R. (2018). Multiround distributed lifetime coverage optimization protocol in wireless sensor networks. *The Journal of Supercomputing, 74*(5), 1949–1972.
4. Poon, C. C. Y., Lo, B. P. L., Yuce, M. R., Alomainy, A., & Hao, Y. (2015). Body sensor networks: In the era of big data and beyond. *IEEE Reviews in Biomedical Engineering, 8*, 4–16.

5. Idrees, A. K., Deschinkel, K., Salomon, M., & Couturier, R. (2016). Perimeter-based coverage optimization to improve lifetime in wireless sensor networks. *Engineering Optimization, 48*(11), 1951–1972.
6. Idrees, A. K., & Al-Yaseen, W. L. (2021). Distributed genetic algorithm for lifetime coverage optimisation in wireless sensor networks. *International Journal of Advanced Intelligence Paradigms, 18*(1), 3–24.
7. Habib, C. (2018). *Energy-efficient data collection and fusion in wireless body sensor networks for continuous health monitoring. Data Structures and Algorithms [cs.DS].* Université Bourgogne Franche-Comté. English. NNT: 2018UBFCD046. tel-02744180.2018.
8. Al-Qurabat, A. K. M., & Idrees, A. K. (2020). Data gathering and aggregation with selective transmission technique to optimize the lifetime of Internet of Things networks. *International Journal of Communication Systems, 33*(11), e4408.
9. Alomari, A., Comeau, F., Phillips, W., & Aslam, N. (2017). New path planning model for mobile anchor-assisted localization in wireless sensor networks. *Wireless Networks, 24,* 2589–2607.
10. Cui, L., Wang, F., Luo, H., Ju, H., & Li, T. (2004). A pervasive sensor node architecture. In *IFIP international conference on network and parallel computing*, pp. 565–567.
11. Rassam, M. A., Zainal, A., & Maarof, M. A. (2013, August 7). Advancements of data anomaly detection research in wireless sensor networks: A survey and open issues. *Sensors (Basel), 13,* 10087–10122.
12. Negra, R., Jemili, I., & Belghith, A. (2016). Wireless body area networks: Applications and technologies. *Procedia Computer Science, 83,* 1274–1281.
13. https://www.rcplondon.ac.uk/file/8504/download
14. Miyazaki, M. (2003). *The future of E-health – Wired or not wired.* Business Briefing: Hospital Engineering & Facilities Management.
15. Laiymani, D., & Makhoul, A. (2013, July). Adaptive data collection approach for periodic sensor networks. In *9th international wireless communications and mobile computing conference*, pp. 1448–1453.
16. https://searchcio.techtarget.com/definition/data-collection
17. Hall, D. L., & Llinas, J. (1997). An introduction to multisensor data fusion. *Proceedings of the IEEE, 85*(1), 6–23.
18. Khaleghi, B., Khamis, A., Karray, F. O., & Razavi, S. N. (2013). Multisensor data fusion: A review of the state-of-the-art. *Information Fusion, 14*(1), 28–44.
19. Castanedo, F. A. (2013). Review of data fusion techniques. *The Scientific World Journal, 2013,* 1–19.
20. Swain, S., Bhushan, B., Dhiman, G., & Viriyasitavat, W. (2022). Appositeness of optimized and reliable machine learning for healthcare: A survey. *Archives of Computational Methods in Engineering, 1,* 3981–4003.
21. Bajaj, D., Bhushan, B., & Yadav, D. (2021). Healthcare 4.0: An insight of architecture, security requirements, pillars and applications. In *Biomedical data mining for information retrieval: Methodologies, techniques and applications* (pp. 103–129). Wiley/Scrivener Publishing.
22. Mehta, S., Bhushan, B., & Kumar, R. (2022). Machine learning approaches for smart city applications: Emergence, challenges and opportunities. In *Recent advances in Internet of Things and machine learning* (pp. 147–163). Springer.
23. Goyal, S., Sharma, N., Bhushan, B., Shankar, A., & Sagayam, M. (2021). Iot enabled technology in secured healthcare: Applications, challenges and future directions. In *Cognitive internet of medical things for smart healthcare* (pp. 25–48). Springer.
24. Khamparia, A., Singh, P. K., Rani, P., Samanta, D., Khanna, A., & Bhushan, B. (2021). An internet of health things-driven deep learning framework for detection and classification of skin cancer using transfer learning. *Transactions on Emerging Telecommunications Technologies, 32*(7), e3963.

25. Muhammad, A. N., Aseere, A. M., Chiroma, H., Shah, H., Gital, A. Y., & Hashem, I. A. T. (2021). Deep learning application in smart cities: Recent development, taxonomy, challenges and research prospects. *Neural Computing and Applications, 33*(7), 2973–3009.
26. Goodfellow, I., Bengio, Y., & Courville, A. (2016). *Deep learning.* MIT Press. https://doi.org/10.4258/hir.2016.22.4
27. Hochreiter, S., Bengio, Y., Frasconi, P., & Schmidhuber, J. (2001). Gradient flow in recurrent nets: The difficulty of learning longterm dependencies. In S. C. Kremer & J. F. Kolen (Eds.), *A field guide to dynamical recurrent neural networks* (pp. 1–15). IEEE Press.
28. Khan, Z., Anjum, A., & Kiani, S. L. (2013). Cloud based big data analytics for smart future cities. In *2013 IEEE/ACM 6th international conference on utility and cloud computing,* pp. 381–386. https://doi.org/10.1109/ucc.2013.77
29. François-Lavet, V., Henderson, P., Islam, R., Bellemare, M. G., & Pineau, J. (2018). An introduction to deep reinforcement learning. *Found Trends Machine Learning, 11*(3–4), 219–354.
30. Sung, W.-T., & Chang, K.-Y. (2013). Evidence-based multi-sensor information fusion for remote health care systems. *Sensors and Actuators A: Physical, 204,* 1–19.
31. Fortino, G., Galzarano, S., Gravina, R., & Li, W. (2015). A framework for collaborative computing and multi-sensor data fusion in body sensor networks. *Information Fusion, 22,* 50–70.
32. Fuster-Garcia, E., Bresó, A., Martínez-Miranda, J., Rosell-Ferrer, J., Matheson, C., & García-Gómez, J. M. (2015). Fusing actigraphy signals for outpatient monitoring. *Information Fusion, 23,* 69–80.
33. Idrees, A. K., Harb, H., Jaber, A., Zahwe, O., & Abou Taam, M. (2017). Adaptive distributed energy-saving data gathering technique for wireless sensor networks. In *2017 IEEE 13th international conference on wireless and mobile computing, networking and communications (WiMob)* (pp. 55–62). IEEE.
34. Ciuonzo, D., Papa, G., Romano, G., Salvo Rossi, P., & Willett, P. (2013). One-bit decentralized detection with a Rao test for multisensor fusion. *IEEE Signal Processing Letters, 20*(9), 861–864. arXiv:1306.6141.

Chapter 10
Smart Intelligent System for Cervix Cancer Image Classification Using Google Cloud Platform

P. Subashini, T. T. Dhivyaprabha, M. Krishnaveni, and M. B. Jennyfer Susan

Abstract Smart healthcare system provides clinical care condition become more intelligence. It is developed using diverse sort of information technology components which include cloud computing, big data, Internet of Things (IoT), wearable devices, software application, image analysis, Artificial Intelligence (AI) algorithms and sensors. It penetrates into the multi-faceted aspects related to offering a rich set of medical services, effective tools for disease diagnosis, health monitoring, information pooling of patient records, identifying medical patterns, clinical decision making, forecasting medical trends or complications, drug discovery, recommend medical practices, delivering rehabilitation therapy, personalized and patient centric medication. The evolution of digital technologies, intelligent systems and smart devices empowered healthcare supports sustainable smart city development. In this work, a smart intelligent system is proposed for the staging classification of cervical cancer images by applying Automated Machine Learning (AutoML) using Google Cloud Platform (GCP). The description of the proposed system pipeline is given as follows. (1) Real time cervical cancer images from EVA digital colposcopy are collected from Kaggle site. These raw datasets are utilized to construct the proposed system, (2) The different stages of cervical cancer images are prepared, labelled and then uploaded into GCP environment, (3) A smart intelligent system is constructed using AutoML framework to categorize the stages of cervical cancer, and (4) The developed model is uploaded, stored and deployed in vertex Artificial Intelligence (vertex AI) platform to evaluate its accuracy. The outcome of this study demon-

P. Subashini · M. Krishnaveni · M. B. Jennyfer Susan
Department of Computer Science, Centre for Machine Learning and Intelligence,
Avinashilingam Institute for Home Science and Higher Education for Women,
Coimbatore, Tamil Nadu, India
e-mail: subashini_cs@avinuty.ac.in; krishnaveni_cs@avinuty.ac.in;
19phcsf008@avinuty.ac.in

T. T. Dhivyaprabha (✉)
Centre for Machine Learning and Intelligence, Avinashilingam Institute for Home Science
and Higher Education for Women, Coimbatore, Tamil Nadu, India

M. A. Ahad et al. (eds.), *Enabling Technologies for Effective Planning and Management in Sustainable Smart Cities*, https://doi.org/10.1007/978-3-031-22922-0_10

245

strates that the proposed system assists physicians to diagnose the stages of cervical cancer with minimal efforts and lesser time. It is significantly beneficial to healthcare professionals to arrive at clinical decisions without the involvement of taking biopsy and earlier detection of precancerous lesions.

Keywords AutoML · Cervical cancer · GCP · Smart healthcare · Vertex AI

10.1 Introduction

Data and digital technologies used in smart cities help the public to facilitate advanced infrastructure, offer security and privacy concerns, safer communication to make better decisions, and improve the quality of living. Smart city development includes the social, economic institutional and physical infrastructure of the people and cities. Smart city technologies employed to grasp current conditions, predict future changes, enhance city services, and provide suggestions for the unsolved problems [1]. The vital essentials for the development of smart cities are Internet of Things (IoT) devices, user interfaces (UI), software solutions and communication networks. IoT sensors devices help in the collection of data, and directly store them the cloud or servers. The use of data analytics (DA) to connect these devices facilitates the combining of the physical and digital city situation, which in turn helps in enhancing the efficiency of the public and private sector, providing economic growth and improvising resident lifestyle [2]. Smart cities include the development of infrastructure and services for government, citizens, building construction, energy, infrastructure, technology, mobility and healthcare as shown in Fig. 10.1.

The smart healthcare system contributes to the development and growth of smart cities [3]. The traditional healthcare is unable to address everyone's needs due to the tremendous rise of the human population. The medical services are inaccessible and expensive to people, despite having of excellent infrastructure and cutting-edge technologies. The advantage of employing healthcare enables people to get better treatment by rapidly accessing medical facilities, clinical and medical record maintenance and diagnosis tools. The smart healthcare system is applied to a variety of scenarios like smart homes, community health centres and smart hospitals. It helps in tracking the abnormal behavior of the patients, disease prevention, diagnosis and treatment, clinical decision-making, hospital management, prescription recommendation, rehabilitation, and postmarking surveillance [4]. The smart health uses are projected in Fig. 10.2.

The participants like doctors and patients, hospitals, and research institutions are involved in the smart healthcare system. Smart technologies are the major aspect that is employed for the development of smart healthcare system. Patients can use wearable smart devices to keep track of their health, use virtual assistants to seek medical care, and use remote residences to implement the remote services. To aid and improve diagnosis, clinicians can use a number of sophisticated clinical decision support systems. They can also handle medical data with the use of an

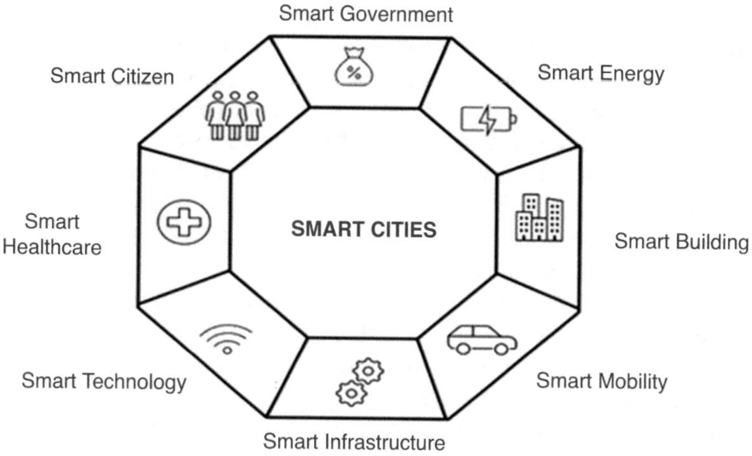

Fig. 10.1 Diamond chart representation depicting the development of smart cities

Fig. 10.2 Smart healthcare system

integrated information platform that includes tools like the Management System, Telecommunication Networks (PACS), Digital Analysis, Electronic Healthcare Record, and a surgical robot for precision surgery. According to hospital perceptions, RFID technology is utilised in hospitals to manage employee and patient resources, and the distribution network in the medical fields with integrated management platforms helps in collecting resources and supports in decision-making. Patients' experiences are now enhanced by the use of mobile medical platforms. Techniques like machine learning can be utilised instead of traditional drug screening at scientific research centres, and big data can be leveraged to find suitable individuals [5]. Smart healthcare may significantly lower the cost and risk of medical treatments while also promoting regional exchanges, pushing the advancement of telemedicine and self-service medical treatment, and finally making individualised medical services widespread.

According to Grand View Research's recent analysis, the worldwide smart healthcare sector is expected to reach USD 225.54 billion by 2022. Over the projected period, rapid technological improvements in healthcare shows that the information technology is expected to be the key driving factor in the worldwide smart healthcare market. It is predicted to increase as more inventory management solutions, such as RFID KanBan and RFID smart cabinets, with reduced costs and proper logistical management. Smart syringes, smart pills and smart bandages are predicted to increase the platform for future market growth by allowing remote monitoring of patients, aiding in the diagnosis of gastrointestinal illnesses, reduction of infection spreading, and remote monitoring of the healing processes [6]. In 2019, it is expected to reach around USD 143.6 billion which in turn would increase the compound annual growth rate (CAGR) of 16.2% during the period 2020–2027. The rise in mHealth adoption, government efforts to digitise healthcare, and the prevalence of chronic diseases are all projected to increase demand for smart healthcare systems. According to the United Healthcare Consumer Sentiment Survey, around 37.0% of Americans relied on the mobile application for health-related consultations in 2019 [7]. The smart healthcare system has enhanced patient safety, decreased healthcare costs, made healthcare services more accessible, and increased the healthcare operational efficiency.

The smart healthcare system plays a key role in cancer diagnosis and in monitoring the cancer patient. According to the International Agency for Research on Cancer, 18.1 million new cases of cancer were reported in the year 2018, with more than nine million deaths [8]. Above all types of cancer, cervical cancer is the highest reported in women with higher mortality and incidence rate. In the year 2020, the World Health Organization (WHO) report stated that 3, 42,000 deaths are caused by cervical cancer [9]. According to the report, the mortality rate of cervical cancer is highly seen in low and middle-income countries (LMIC). It is caused by the Human Papilloma Virus (HPV) infection which shows viral cytopathic changes on the membrane of the cervical region. Cervical Intraepithelial Neoplasm (CIN) is graded as CIN1, CIN2 and CIN3 with the extent of abnormal proliferation on the lower epithelium region of the cervical images. The CIN1 is also known as the low-grade squamous intraepithelial lesion (LSIL) covering a small portion of the epithelium with neoplasm. The CIN2 and CIN3 come under the category of High-grade squamous intraepithelial lesion (HSIL) which covers two-thirds of the epithelium with cancer cells [10]. The diagnosis of cervical cancer is based on its grading that determines stage classification. It is viewed as a challenging task in the medical field. It depends on the acetowhite portion of the captured cervical images. A highly experienced physician is required for the analysis and classification of cervical cancer images. It is a great challenge to the avail the services of experts all the time and it is a time-consuming process. Due to the development of smart technology in the recent scenarios, these problems can be reduced by applying machine learning and deep learning algorithms for the diagnosis of cervical cancer images. A gap exists between developing algorithms for medical image analysis and clinical approaches practiced in hospitals. It occurs due to enormous reasons such as, tests are done with synthetic datasets, lack of communication between developers and physicians, evaluations being conducted with few dataset complexity, need of software infrastructure for deployment, technical expertise and so on. These practical difficulties involved in the deployment of AI-based application in the healthcare domain is overcome by introducing AutoML algorithm for developing intelligent clinical application using GCP. In this work, cervical cancer images are procured using highly advanced MobileODT devices.

Smart healthcare is connected with the cloud-based platform which helps in storing, processing and networking capabilities over the cloud [11]. It provides the Application Programming Interface (API) in which the resources are accessed by the user through the programmatic remote access Google Cloud Platform (GCP) which is the most important and rapidly growing cloud API provided by the cloud market [12]. The Google Cloud Platform (GCP) was launched in the year 2008 and made available to general customers in the year 2011. It can provide updates every week and can provide the user to access information anywhere in the world. Google Cloud Platform provides services like computing, storing and networking, and is also used in the fields like big data, machine learning and the internet of things (IoT). It provides a quick collaboration with multiple users to access the project at a time that is stored in the GCP and provides public cloud computing resources and services [13].

Vision AI is the concept that helps machine learning to understand the images and it works similar to human vision. It involves image classification, image recognition and image analysis. Google Cloud Platform play a major role in machine learning and provides the services like Google AutoML Vision API and the Google Vision API which are used for the classification and analysis of the images in the GCP platform. Google Vision API is the pre-defined model trained for the identification of the object and analysis of the images. But Google AutoML Vision API is the supervised learning method that helps in the classification of the images based on labels defined on the images [14]. Google Cloud AutoML was initiated in January 2018 as a Machine Learning Tool for development of a machine learning model. Initially, developing a traditional machine learning model requires sufficient time and coding skills [15]. AutoML decreases the coding skill and time consumption in the development of machine-learning models [16, 17]. It is also used in the training and evaluation of deep learning models without any coding knowledge and neural networks for image classification and recognition. AutoML beta version was provided to the public during the Google Cloud NEXT Conference organized in the year 2018. It was defined as the state-of-the-art neural network which is used to train and classify the images. AutoML was released by various vendors like Amazon, SageMaker, and IBM Waston Studio, but the first publicly available AutoML is provided by the Google Platform on a free trial basis. Automated machine learning (AutoML) with neural networks is applied in various applications like image recognition, object identification, image generation and semantic segmentation. It provides features for training data, deployment model and Google cloud server. The dataset was selected and labelled based on its attribute for the classification process and imported into AutoML. It trained and deployed the data and predicted the output and stored data in the google cloud server [18].

Advantages of GCP and AutoML in the classification of cervical:

1. AutoML helps the non-technical and medical community to work with machine learning without any domain knowledge,
2. It reduces the demand for physician experts, and it will act as a tool for the classification of cervical cancer as CIN1, CIN2 and CIN3,
3. AutoML of the Google cloud platform is connected with the google cloud storage which is accessed through the authentication process. Hence it protects medical data from theft,
4. AutoML transfers the data automatically to the training stage and searches for the best neural network architecture to train the model and helps in the better classification of cervical cancer, and
5. It reduces the computational time and provides faster results with higher accuracy of prediction.

The utilization of AutoML greatly improves healthcare outcomes, reduce healthcare costs and helps in the developing clinical support in cancer diagnosis.

The following is the chapter's structure: Sect. 10.2 examines relevant studies for the creation of smart healthcare apps employing the Internet of Things (IoT), Machine Learning, Google Cloud Platforms (GCP), Computer Vision, and their merits and drawbacks in the medical domains. The proposed methodology for grading-based classification of cervical cancer images is discussed in Sect. 10.3. Section 10.4 outlines the suggested methodology's results and analysis, and finally, the paper's conclusion and future works are presented in Sect. 10.5.

10.2 Related Works

The medical services are using the IoT, Machine learning and GCP for further improvising the smart healthcare system. In this section, discuss the smart healthcare application using IoT, machine learning, vision AI and GCP is analysed.

10.2.1   *Smart Healthcare Using the Internet of Things (IoT)*

The Internet of Things (IoT) has demonstrated its ability to connect a variety of medical technologies along with healthcare professionals to deliver maximum medical services at a remote location. The related paper of the smart healthcare system using the IoT is presented in Table 10.1.

Table 10.1 Related paper of the smart healthcare system using IoT

Authors	Hardware Components	Hardware Components/Dataset/Metrics	Description
Islam et al. [19]	Introduced a smart healthcare system for patient monitoring and room condition of the patient	Hardware components: ESP32 Processor and sensors like Body Temperature, Heart Beat sensor, Co2 Room temperature Dataset: Real time dataset Metrics: Error rate value	The proposed method tracks the patient monitoring system with an error rate of 1.58 for room humidity, 0.81% for body temperature, 4.05% for heart rate data collection
Durga et al. [20]	Proposed a new approach for the forgery detection in medical images	Hardware components: Temperature sensors, Body movement sensors, Heart beat sensors, Spo2 sensors, Eye Blink Sensors, Arduino IDE, Embedded C	On comparing the existing method, the proposed method achieved an accuracy of 84.3% in detecting image forgery
Khan et al. [21]	Introduced the medical image encryption for data protection	Dataset: SPIEAAPM Lung CT and MedPix Dataset Metrics: Number of Pixels Change Rate, Uniform Average Change Intensity	The proposed approach is assessed, and the number of pixel change rate is 99.99%, and the uniform average change intensity value is 33.32%
Hao et al. [22]	Proposed the smart connected electronic gastroscopy (SCEG) system for screening gastroscopy	Hardware components: EGmodule, CCD camera, EVMS module, Cloud service, AR glasses Methods: AlexNet, GoogleLeNet, VGGNet, Adaboost based MCNN Metrics: Sensitivity, Specificity, Miss-diagnoses rate, Misdiagnosis rate	Based on the analysis, AdaBoost – based MCNN method give the higher specificity and sensitivity rate of 79.62% and 66.93% respectively
Imran et al. [23]	Presented an IoT based automated system for the screening and classification of pneumonia from the X-ray images	Dataset: DI COVID-chest X-Ray dataset. Metrics: Accuracy	The proposed method gives the classification accuracy of 97% in the classification and screening of X-ray images

(continued)

Table 10.1 (continued)

Authors	Hardware Components	Hardware Components/Dataset/Metrics	Description
Mohammad et al. [24]	Proposed a smart monitoring system using IoT for the COVID-19 patients	Hardware component: Arduino Uno, Temperature sensor, SpO_2 Pulse Sensor, Node MCU Wireless Module, Bluetooth module, LCD display, Buck converter, Lithium battery, Lithium battery protector, Battery adapter, Wire set Switch Dataset: Real time dataset	The proposed method is tested on five human subjects. The oxygen level and pulse are monitored. It is a small and easily portable device to any location
Bhardwaj et al. [25]	Proposed an IoT based system to monitor the COVID-19 patients	Hardware component: Analog to digital convertor, Power Supply, Display Unit, Cloud server Dataset: Real time dataset Metrics: Relative Error percentage	Based on the qualitative analysis, the proposed method is tested on the five users and it accurately identifies the oxygen level, temperature and pulse rate of the human body
Onasanya et al. [26]	Proposed the IoT/WSN technology for providing the healthcare solution to the existing treatment	Hardware component: WSN Sensor, Smart Device, WSN routing	The proposed methods are compared in the qualitative analysis. Based on the analysis the proposed method are helps in tracking the patient location and in supporting the cancer services. But it lacks in the security purpose
Zulfiqar et al. [27]	A study for the medical service for the under-reserved and rural areas of the Pakistan	Smart healthcare application	The application helps in providing the medical access to the entire rural region and helps to maintain the good relationship between the doctor and patients
Ankur et al. [28]	Proposed the PSO approach in the IoT framework for the physiological sensor data fusion calculation	Hardware component: Electroencephalography sensor, Pulse Sensors, Body Temperature Sensors Methods: Genetic Algorithm and Particle Swarm Optimization	The proposed method improvised than 4.6% from the existing method of genetic algorithm optimum selection model
Hesham et al. [29]	Proposed the secure based data collection from the patient using secured IoT communication system	Hardware components: Sensors, Zigbee, RFID tag Mobile phone sensing, WSW measurement nodes Methods: Fuzzy Logic Metrics: Sensor peak measurement, Multimodal measurement	The proposed method takes less than 9 s for transferring the data and obtained the entropy value of 2.25J/K

(continued)

Table 10.1 (continued)

Authors	Hardware Components	Hardware Components/Dataset/Metrics	Description
Site et al. [30]	Proposed distributed framework for fast access of the data in the smart healthcare system	Methods: Block chain network, Database management system	The processing time and delay time is calculated for the 200 number of transactions. The processing time is 73 s with average delay of 3.3 s
Annamalai et al. [31]	Introduced a smart pillbox includes a programme that allows medical clients to choose the pill size and dosage for their patients	Hardware component: LCD screen, communication number sensors, Raspberry Pi 3, Wi-Fi module and cloud server Methods: Augmented Data Recognition (ADR) algorithm Dataset: UCI dataset. Metrics: Adaptive data rate, Time complexity	Based on the comparison analysis, the Bruce force attack and web-based attacks are calculated and obtained the value of 87% and 82% respectively. The time complexity of the proposed method is reduced to 1.3 s for the 100 locations
Jeong et al. [32]	Introduced the iotHEALTHCARE system for the monitoring the patient and diagnosis for the early detection of health condition	Methods: Machine learning, Greedy strategy	The iotHEALTHCARE product helps in improvising the healthcare system and also helps in analyzing, collecting and exchanging medical data
Khamparia et al. [33]	An Internet of Health and Things (IoHT) framework based on transfer learning technique was proposed for the classification of skin lesion cancer	Methods: e VGG19, Inception V3, ResNet50, and SqueezeNet. Dataset: Benign and malignant skin lesions were acquired from International Skin Imaging Collaboration (ISIC) image archive. Metrics: Precision, Recall, F1-score and Accuracy	The proposed framework achieves 99.60% classification accuracy when compared to conventional methods. It assists clinicians to remotely access patient images to diagnose and conduct classification
Azad et al. [34]	A hybrid framework was developed using Synthetic Minority Oversampling Technique, Genetic Algorithm and Decision Tree (PMSGD) for the categorization of diabetes mellitus disease	Dataset: Pima Indians Diabetes Database (PIDD). Metrics: Classification Accuracy (CA), Classification Error (CE), Precision, Recall (sensitivity), measure (FM) and Area_ Under_ROC (AUROC)	This clinical decision support system produces excellent classification results of 82.1256% and outperforms on a different data split up

(continued)

Table 10.1 (continued)

Authors	Hardware Components	Hardware Components/Dataset/Metrics	Description
Deepanshu Bajaj et al. [35]	A comprehensive investigation has done on evolving ideas, advancement and confronting approaches involved in the implementation of healthcare industry 4.0	Methods: Internet of Things (IoT), Bigdata, Blockchain technology, Machine Learning and Information and Communication Technology (ICT)	This study recommended that the emerging smart technologies upgrades and modernizing medical sectors (e-Health) include infrastructure, clinical data schemas, representation, architecture and frameworks for patient data management and wellbeing physiological parameters
Goyal et al. [36]	A study was conducted to examine healthcare-based Internet of Things (IoT) technologies for clinical information confidentiality, data augmentation and maintenance	Methods: Big data, Cloud computing, smart healthcare devices and IoT	The detailed analysis of this work showed that the current wearable technologies, medical gadgets, information and communication technology empowers medical sectors and provides pathways to a greater height

10.2.2 Smart Healthcare Using Machine Learning

Similar to IoT technologies, machine learning also plays a vital role in the development of smart health care. It is used to automate the diagnosis and detection process in the medical field. The uses of machine learning in the smart healthcare system. Table 10.2 shows the application of machine learning in the smart healthcare system to automate processes.

10.2.3 Smart Healthcare Using Vision AI

Computer vision involves some of the tasks like object identification, image categorization and segmentation. The recent advancements of vision AI are image classification and object identification which helps in medical image analysis. Several types of research in dermatology, radiology and pathology have shown encouraging results in challenging medical diagnostics tasks. Deep learning technologies could help doctors by providing second opinions and highlighting problematic regions in images. The related paper on the smart healthcare system using computer vision is presented in Table 10.3.

Table 10.2 Related paper of the smart healthcare system using machine learning

Authors	Objective	Methods/Dataset/Metrics	Outcome of the study
Ahmed et al. [37]	Proposed the forgery detection system in medical image using support vector machine	Methods: Wiener-filter, multi resolution regression filter, support-vector-machine Dataset: DDSM database images Metrics: Accuracy	The proposed approach was put to test and found to be 98% accurate for natural photographs and 84.3% accurate for medical images
Mahmoud et al. [38]	Presented a machine learning approach to identify the tumors in the MRI brain images	Methods: Neural Network classifier, Decision tree classifier, Feature Extraction Dataset: KG hospital database (MRI Images) Metrics: Accuracy, Recall, Precision, F-Measure Value	Based on analyzing the machine learning approach the MRI images after preprocessing and trained with neural network classification algorithm gives the accurate detection of 66% for the tumors
Konstantina et al. [39]	A review on the supervised machine learning approaches for the cancer progression	Methods: Support Vector Machines, Artificial Neural Networks Bayesian Networks and Decision Trees Metrics: Accuracy	The integration of multidimensional heterogeneous data is paired with the application of multiple strategies for feature selection and classification, which can assist in providing promising tools for inference in the cancer domain
Mehmood et al. [40]	Proposed an approach called CervDetect to evaluate the risk elements that lead to the formation of malignant cervical formation. The CervDetect is combined with random forest and shallow neural networks for the identification of Cervical Cancer	Methods: CervDetect, Random Forest Dataset: The University of California's database Metrics: Accuracy, Mean Squared Error, False Positive Rate and False Negative Rate	CervDetect enhances the detection rate substantially. It had a 93.6% accuracy, 0.07111 MSE error, 6.4% false positive rate, and 100% false negative rate
Kadir et al. [41]	Proposed a lungs prediction approach and to highlight the strength and weakness of the approaches	Methods: Support vector machine, Convolution Neural Network Dataset: LIDC-IDRI dataset Metrics: AUC points	The proposed method helps in the prediction and classification of lung cancer on the CT images with the performance accuracy of 90%

(continued)

Table 10.2 (continued)

Authors	Objective	Methods/Dataset/Metrics	Outcome of the study
Elngar et al. [42]	Proposed to construct a Mobile Android Application with the machine learning and deep learning algorithm for the prediction of skin illnesses	Method: Support vector machine, Convolutional neural network, and android application Source:Beni-Suef University Hospital, Cairo University Hospital Metrics: Detection Rate	The skin diseases like Eczema detected with the detection rate of 100%, Melanoma with the detection rate of 100%, Psoriasis with the detection rate of 80%, Onychosis detected with the detection rate of 70%, Acne diseases with the detection rate of 80%, and Corn with the detection rate of 90%
Wei et al. [43]	Proposed a support vector machine for the identification of three type skin diseases	Methods: The grey-level co-occurrence matrix, Support Vector Machine Metrics:Recognition rate in percentage	Recognition rate for the identification of skin cancer using support vector machine reaches the accuracy of reach to 90%
Hatem [44]	Proposed the K-nearest neighbour method for the identification and classification of skin lesions	Method: Image acquisition, threshold segmentation, statistical feature extraction and KNN classifier Dataset: Real time dataset Metrics: Accuracy	KNN identifies the skin lesion with the accuracy of 98% in classifying skin lesions with less efficient time
Zhang and Liu [45]	Proposed support vector machine for automating cervical cancer detection in multispectral microscopic thin PAP smear images	Method: Background segmentation and normalization for preprocessing, Feature extraction for pixel classification and region detection Dataset: multispectral PAP smear image database Metrics: True positive rate and false positive rate	The experiment result given higher accuracy in pixel-level classification and from 40 images obtains the true positive rate of 98%
Pandey and Prabha [46]	Proposed framework to predict the early stages of heart disease using the machine learning algorithm	Hardware component: Heart beat sensor ML algorithm: Naïve Bayes Decision tree K Nearest neighbour classifier Random forest classifier Metrics: Accuracy	Based on the comparison analysis of the machine learning algorithm the support vector machine identifies the heart diseases with an accuracy of 86%

(continued)

Table 10.2 (continued)

Authors	Objective	Methods/Dataset/Metrics	Outcome of the study
Nusaibah and Turgay [47]	Comparison analysis of the decision tree algorithm that is suitable for breast cancer classification	Methods: J48 method, Function Tree, Random Forest Tree, AD Alternating Decision Tree, Decision stump and Best First Dataset: UCI Machine Learning Repository Metrics: True positive rate, false positive rate, execution time, Precision, Recall, F-Measure, ROC curve, Accuracy	Based on the comparison analysis the function tree algorithm gives the higher precision rate 97.7%. From the decision tree the best suitable method for breast cancer classification is function tree algorithm
Verma et al. [48]	Proposed a Transparent Breast Cancer Management System with P-Rules that uses a decision tree and neural network to identify the primary risk factors for breast cancer	Methods: Rule generation, pruning and neural network Dataset: UCI repository	This system identifies the risk factor responsible for breast cancer and the proposed method prevent the breast cancer in the rate of 94.56%
Thohir et al. [49]	Proposed a support vector machine for the identification of cervical cancer	Method: GLCM, SVM Metrics: Accuracy, Specificity, Sensitivity	The proposed method identifies the cervical cancer at the accuracy of 90%. It helps the clinician for the automatic identification of cervical cancer
Zorkafli et al. [50]	Proposed a Hybrid Radial Basis Function along with the genetic algorithm to improvise the detection rate in the cervical cancer	Method: Hybrid multi-layered perceptron and Genetic algorithm Source: Hospital UniversitiSains Malaysia Metrics: Accuracy, Specificity, Sensitivity	Based on the comparison analysis of the machine learning method, Hybrid multi-layered perceptron and Genetic algorithm gives an accuracy of 74.85%
Priyanka and Suvarna [51]	Proposed a feature selection method using f advanced fuzzy based technique and trained in KNN and Neural network for the cervical cancer classification	Methods: Statistical feature extraction, K nearest neighbors, artificial neural network Metrics: Accuracy	Based on the comparison analysis the K nearest neighbor obtained an accuracy of 88.04%

(continued)

Table 10.2 (continued)

Authors	Objective	Methods/Dataset/Metrics	Outcome of the study
Sonam Mehta et al. [52]	A review on the recent advancement and applications of artificial intelligence techniques available for smart city developments	Methods: Information and Communication Technology (ICT), Deep Learning (DL), Artificial Intelligence (AI) and Machine Learning (ML)	It demonstrated that AI techniques provides solutions to various domain include smart transportation system, energy consumption, green environment, healthcare, security and financial transactions
Rao et al. [53]	A pretrained model was developed using ensemble learning approach for breast cancer classification	Method: Resnet, Mobilenet and Densenet Dataset: BreakHis	It yields 98.5% training accuracy and 89% of test accuracy on 8-class classification and achieves 99.1% and 98% train and test accuracy on 2-class classification

Table 10.3 Related paper on the smart healthcare system using computer vision

Author	Objective	Methods/Metrics/Dataset	Outcome of study
Yunchao et al. [54]	Review on the computer vision and deep learning application for the diagnosis of breast cancer	Methods: Convolution neural network and traditional machine learning method survey	Convolutional neural network technology helps in locating and classifying the lesion region in breast ultrasound image in faster and efficient way
Shen et al. [55]	The comparison analysis of the deep learning algorithm for the detection of breast cancer	Methods: Resnet - Resnet, Resnet-VGG, VGG-VGG, VGG-Resnet Dataset: INbreast dataset Metrics: Sensitivity, specificity, AUC curve, Accuracy	The single model achieved the AUC value of 0.91 and similarly the four models averaging achieved the AUC value of 0.95 for the detection of breast cancer
Shen et al. [56]	The Generative Adversarial Network is used for the reconstruction of the human brain activity images	Methods: Generative Adversarial Network Dataset: fMRI dataset Metrics: Loss function, Structural similarity index measure	GAN method constructs the brain images with the Pearson correlation value of 69.3% and 56.9% by Structural similarity index measure
Sathesh [57]	Proposed the IoT based system with the computer vision for the management system in the healthcare system	Methods: Primary artificial intelligence screening layers, Cloud layers, Multi Algorithm Service, Adaptive Wavelet Sampling Metrics: Execution time, Throughput	The proposed method is tested with the 100 data request. The execution time for the data request is 15 ms The throughput is 90% with the power consumption value of 25 joules

(continued)

Table 10.3 (continued)

Author	Objective	Methods/Metrics/ Dataset	Outcome of study
Ranjbarzadeh et al. [58]	Proposed the Cascade Convolutional Neural Network for the brain tumor segmentation for the MRI multi modalities brain images	Methods: Distance wise attention module, Cascade CNN model Dataset: BRATS 2018 dataset Metrics: Dice score, Sensitivity, HAUSDORFF	The proposed method achieves a mean value for the tumor, tumor enhancement and tumor core with the dice scores value of 0.9203, 0.9113 and 0.8726 respectively
Hussain et al. [59]	Comparison analysis of the machine learning method which is suitable for the classification of liver tumor from the CT dataset	Methods: J48, Random Forest, Logistic Model Tree, Random Tree Source: Nishter Medical University Metrics: Precision, Recall, F-Measure, ROC curve	Based on the comparison analysis the random forest and random tree gives the higher accuracy for the tumor classification with the accuracy value of 97.48% and 97.08% value respectively
Zhang et al. [60]	Designed new convolutional neural network architecture for the classification of fatty liver on B-mode ultrasonic images	Methods: Convolutional neural network with and without skip connection Dataset: Sensitivity and specificity Metrics: Accuracy, Sensitivity and Specificity	The proposed CNN architecture classifies the fatty liver images with an accuracy of 90%, Specificity value of 92% and Sensitivity value of 81%
Shaikh et al. [61]	Proposed the CAD system for the detection of liver cancer using the computer vision techniques	Methods: Artificial neural network and support vector machine Dataset: Github and Kaggle Metrics: ROC curve, Confusion matrix	The proposed method is implemented and evaluated and obtained the accuracy of 92.67% for the liver cancer detection and grading
Liu et al. [62]	Review on computer vision methods in bioprinting bone research	Methods: Convolutional neural network, Data augmentation	Based on the analysis, the computer vision helps the bioprinting developers to provide higher accuracy and automatic identification of the default in the bone images
Lin et al. [63]	Proposed the automated diagnosis of bone metastases for the tuned parameter of DenseNet model	Methods: The VGG, ResNet, and DenseNet with tuned parameters Metrics: Accuracy, precision, recall, specificity, F-1 score and AUC, respectively	The proposed method achieves accuracy of 98.07%, precision value of 99%, recall value of 98.30%, specificity value of 98.90%, F-1 score value of 98.02% and AUC value of 99.33%

(continued)

Table 10.3 (continued)

Author	Objective	Methods/Metrics/Dataset	Outcome of study
Leelavathy et al. [64]	Proposed the hybrid approach with the combination of the deep learning and machine learning approach for the skin diseases detection	Methods: Convolutional Neural network, Feature extraction	The skin types diseases are predicted with the accuracy value of 98.58%
Patnaik et al. [65]	The comparison of various deep learning methods for the identification of skin diseases	Methods: Inception V3, Inception Resnet V2, Mobile Net Metrics: Precision, Recall, F1-Score	Based on the comparison analysis, the Inception V3 model gives the higher accuracy value of 79.07% for the identification of skin diseases
Chandran et al. [66]	Proposed the CYENET for the grading of cervical cancer	Methods: Vgg19 and Colposcopy Ensemble Network (CYGNET) Dataset: Kaggle Metrics: Sensitivity, Specificity, Kappa score	The proposed method performs higher than the VGG 19. The sensitivity, specificity and kappa value of the proposed method is 92.4%, 96.2% and 88% respectively

10.2.4   Smart Healthcare Using GCP

The google cloud platform plays an import in the medical image analysis. In this section discuss related paper of the smart healthcare system using the google cloud platform in Table 10.4.

10.2.5   Clinical Methods and Practices for Cervical Cancer Under a Smart Healthcare System

Cervical cancer is a malignant epithelial tumor that is formed in the lower region of the uterus. It is sexually transmitted and caused by HPV. The other external factors like smoking, early sex, multiple sex partners and overconsumption of child control pills are the cause of cervical cancer. There are various screening approaches applied for the diagnosis of cervical cancer as shown in Fig. 10.3. This disease is curable when it is diagnosed at its initial stages [74].

Table 10.4 Related paper of the smart healthcare system using google cloud platform

Author	Objective	Methods/Metrics/Dataset	Outcome of the study
Faes et al. [67]	Provided a feasibility study on the automated deep learning method with no coding for the healthcare professionals	Methods: AutoML Cloud Vision API Dataset: Retinal fundus images, optical coherence tomography images, skin lesions and both paediatric and adult chest x-ray images Metrics: Sensitivity, Specificity	Binary classification on each dataset the specificity value ranges from 73.3% to 97.0%. The specificity for the multi-classification ranges from 67% to 100%
Ekaba [68]	The classification of the pneumonia and normal Xray images using AutoML	Methods: GoogleAutoML Dataset: Kaggle Metrics: Precision, Recall	The classification obtains the precision rate of 96.66% and recall 96.65%
Tian et al. [5]	A review on smart healthcare system on several medical fields	Methods: Smart hospitals, virtual assistant, Assisting drug research	The technology and regularization are the important concept in smart healthcare system
Ka et al. [69]	Comparative study on traditional machine learning models, convolutional neural network models, and AutoML models for the classification of breast lesion on ultrasound images	Methods: Random Forest, Convolutional Neural Network, AutoML. Metrics: Specificity, Sensitivity, Accuracy, F1 Score, AUCPR	The traditional machine learning gives the accuracy of 90%, the convolutional neural network gives the accuracy of 91% and AutoML vision gives the accuracy of 86%. The AutoML almost reaches the accuracy of the CNN and Machine learning model It will help the clinician to classify the breast lesion with no coding experience
Dong et al. [70]	Proposed the machine learning called Transformer-based AutoML (T-AutoML) for the lesion segmentation on 3D Medical images	Method: Transfer AutoML Dataset: ImageNet dataset Metrics: Dice score	The dice score is evaluated for the proposed method using the lesion and liver images. The lesion segmentation identifies with the average dice score of 76.50% and liver segmentation identifies with the average dice score of 86.60%

(continued)

Table 10.4 (continued)

Author	Objective	Methods/Metrics/ Dataset	Outcome of the study
Hussain et al. [71]	The AutoML is employed for faster diagnosis of the COVID-19 in the X-ray images	Method: Google Cloud AutoML Metrics: Sensitivity, Specificity, Accuracy, Precision, Recall	AutoML gives the accuracy of 98.41% for the binary and multi-classification process
Harikrishnan et al. [72]	The Neural Architecture Search model is trained using the retina images for the prediction of diabetic retinopathy from retina images	Method: AutoML Dataset: EyePACS dataset Metrics: Training accuracy and Validation accuracy	The trained model predicts the diabetic retinopathy from retina images. With the validation accuracy of 85% and testing accuracy of 82%
Abhinav [73]	The AutoML is used identification of lungs infection on the X-ray images	Method: Google Cloud AutoML Dataset: Kaggle Metrics: Precision, Recall	The prediction of the lung infection obtains the precision and recall value of 100%

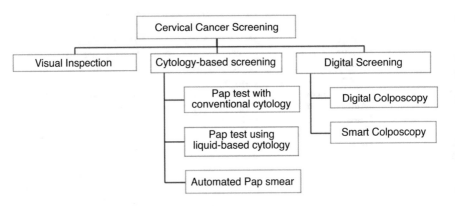

Fig. 10.3 Hierarchical representation for cervical cancer screening

10.2.5.1 Visual Inspection

The World Health Organization recommends Visual Inspection with Acetic Acid (VIA) as a screening tool for early-stage cervical cancer in developing countries. The cervical region is swapped with 3–5% of the acetic acid and visualized through the naked eyes. The acetic acid application covert the squamous epithelium to appear as pink color, columnar epithelium appears as a red color and lesion region as the acetowhite region on the cervical tissues. The whitening process is visible for a few minutes and helps in the subjective differentiation of dysplastic and normal tissue [75]. Visual inspection is an appropriate cervical cancer screening procedure that appears to be efficient and cost-effective in detecting high-level abnormalities.

But the application of the acid solution is highly sensitive and irritates the cervical region. The false-positive rate for the visual inspection is higher which can lead to over-treatment of cervical cancer [76].

10.2.5.2 Cytology Based Screening

By implementing a high-quality screening programme, cervical cancer prevalence and death have been reduced. The cytology-based screening procedures are carried out with a high-quality laboratory infrastructure. The different types of cytology methods are analysed as follows: [77]

10.2.5.2.1 Pap Test with Conventional Cytology

Traditional cytology has been used over the world for almost 50 years. The cell is gently removed from the ectocervix and endocervix using a spatula or brush and prepared for the respective smears. The physician will examine the smears under the microscope for the identification of abnormalities. In most of the developing nations, this approach is routinely used to screen for cervical cancer, although the test is highly specific and false-negative rates in cytology-based programs have always been a source of concern. The malignant cells are diagnosed as normal cells and lead to the higher false positive rate. Due to large range of variation of the test results, it is necessary to repeat the test at regular period to achieve programmatic efficacy [78].

10.2.5.2.2 Pap Test Using Liquid-Based Cytology

Liquid Based Cytology (LBC) collects tissue cells in the same way as the conventional Pap method. But instead of a spatula, a brush is used to collect the cancer cells. The brush's head collects the tissue region and drops into a small pot of liquid containing a preservation solution. The sample is filtered or processed in the cytology lab to eliminate blood and debris and the cells are transferred to the slides called monolayers. The cost of this method is higher than the traditional cytology and it requires additional equipment for the screening process. Based on National Health Service (NHS) study, the smear process is repeated with 1–2% along with liquid-based cytology [79]. The meta-analysis of the result obtained from pap with LBC has no difference in sensitivity from the traditional method [80].

10.2.5.2.3 Automated Pap Smear

Automated Pap testing (AutoPap and AutoCyte Screen) aims to eliminate errors by evaluating Pap smear slides using computerized analysis. The slide is examined and scored using an algorithm to determine the abnormality present with AutoPap. The algorithm considers visual properties like cell shape and optical density to detect abnormalities in the cervical tissues [81]. For cases that have been flagged as anomalous by the cytologist or the computer rating, a manual evaluation is conducted.

10.2.5.3 Digital Screening

Digital screening is an advanced method introduced for screening cervical cancer. There are two types of digital screening procedures, namely, digital colposcopy and smart colposcopy.

10.2.5.3.1 Digital Colposcopy

Colposcopy is a visual inspection process used to diagnose cervical cancer after an abnormal cervical cancer screening test. It is a binocular microscope with a strong light source that is used for enlarged visual inspection of the uterine cervix to aid in the diagnosis of cervical region. Positive screening tests are the most prevalent reason for a referral to colposcopy [82]. It helps in examining the two major areas namely, squamocolumnar junction (SCJ) and the transformation zone of the cervix region. The SCJ is located between the squamous epithelium and columnar epithelium of the cervical region which is located in the external cervical region. The cervix is inspected with the colposcopy after applying 3–5% of acetic acid solution. The acid solution dehydrates cells after 30–90 s causing the affected region to turn into a white region. This method helps in screening the cervical region without touching or affecting the cervical portion. As the device is too large it is not easily portable to any location and requires high expenses for screening.

10.2.5.3.2 Smart Colposcopy

Eva system is also called as a smart colposcope which is a recent technological method developed by the MobileODT company [83]. It is a portable AI-based handheld device and easy to use which reaches many countries to organize the camps. Israeli Digital Health FemTech company proudly announced that smart colposcope method of Visual screening AI technology enables to organize a massive cervical cancer screening project. The screening project was supported by the government of Israel in the Dominican Republic in the year 2021. EVA Visual screening smart technology screened 9000 women and decided to expand the program to cover another 50,000 women around the world. The reliable fast and portable device helps to screen high number of patients and produces clinical results with the promising accuracy [84]. In July 2018, China's Health and Gynecologic Cancers Research Foundation planned a screening campaign with the help of a charity. The screening camp was conducted for 6 days, and, 4000 women participated from which 3886 women got screened for HPV test and 168 women had undergone colposcopy screening using EVA System and 40 women received on-site treatment for dysplasia [85]. The descriptive analysis on the development of smart healthcare in the various domain are illustrated in this section and comparative observations are depicted in Table 10.5.

Table 10.5 Inferential analysis on the evolution of smart healthcare systems in different domains

S.No.	Domain	Inferences
1.	IoT	Storage: The medical records collected are manually stored in the cloud server IoT is highly used inpatient monitoring but not suitable for diseases like cancers Blockchain is used for storage, but a very large amount of data cannot be stored
2.	Machine Learning	Domain Knowledge: Medical experts are not convenient for working with the coding and machine learning models To develop the machine learning model, medical experts should have domain knowledge Time complexity: Building up the best machine learning model that fits the classification is a time-consuming process Storage: The medical data collected are analyzed in the local system and there is no storage or data protection provided in the traditional machine learning
3.	Vision AI	Domain Knowledge: Similar to the machine learning, Vision AI is a vast topic and requires more to obtain the domain knowledge and the construction of deep learning models is a challenging task Time complexity: To identify the best fit model in the Vision AI for classification requires more coding and implementation time Storage: The medical data collected are analyzed in the local system and there is no storage or data protection provided in the traditional machine learning
4.	GCP	Domain Knowledge: There is no specific domain knowledge to work with the google cloud platform. To work with the GCP AutoML the only knowledge required is to set the input data It does not require any coding skills to work with AutoMl because it is a completely code-free platform Time complexity: Requires less implementation time Storage: The input data and the processed results are directly stored in the google cloud platform which can be accessed through authentication process

(continued)

Table 10.5 (continued)

S.No.	Domain	Inferences

5.	Clinical Methods	Visual Inspection
		  The initial screening process requires more time and a less costly method
		  But this method causes substantial irritation and bleeding making women panic and refuses to take the screening process
		Liquid-Based Cytology
		  The liquid-based cytology screening in the laboratory setting for screening is not highly convenient for conducting the camp screening process
		  The false positive rate is higher in the liquid-based cytology method and it's a high-cost traditional method for screening the cervical cancer
		  For this method a small portion of tissue is taken for analysis. It may cause bleeding and irritation in the cervical region
		Digital colposcopy
		  It is a non-invasive method that uses the focus lens to directly view the cervical portion. As the traditional colposcopy is not portable, the smart colposcopy has been introduced
		  It is small and portable and is highly used for screening camps in the tribal and rural regions of developing countries
		  It minimizes the human resource, cost of screening, and pain-free procedure, which encourages women to participate in screening

10.3 Proposed Methodology

Cervical cancer is among the leading gynecologic malignancies among women worldwide. The incidence of cervical cancer and mortality rate is high in the developing countries, especially in the remote/rural areas were poor clinical facility available. It is caused due to various factors such as lack of awareness, low income, living in the interior locations, lack of medical infrastructure, funding sources, socio-economic status, illiteracy, cultural beliefs and ignorance in attending awareness programmes and screening test. There are various screening approaches that exist for cervical cancer screening such as Cervical biopsy, Loop Electrosurgical Excision Procedure (LEEP), Pap smear, Visual inspection, Liquid based cytology, Digital colposcopy, and Smart colposcopy. Among these, the widely used screening approaches are questionnaires, cervical cytology and smart colposcopy. In the questionnaire, demographic information, literacy level, socioeconomic status and awareness about the cervical cancer and treatment are collected from the participants. It is observed that questionnaires section was largely conducted in several screening camps. Many women exhibited involuntary hesitation to share their personal information during the programme. The next widely used method is the Pap smear. It is also known as gold standard method which is utilised for cervical cancer screening. In this approach, a sample tissue is collected from patients and it is examined under the microscope. Most women hesitate to get screened due to its invasive and painful procedure. To overcome these barriers, MobileODT EVA system is the smart colposcopy device. It is an alternative advanced screening approach that helps to screens the cervix region without much pain. It captures cervix images and is stored in cloud. It acts as a clinical decision support system in which annotation can be added along with input images. The real time cervix images acquired using

MobileODT EVA system are used in this study which is collected from Kaggle site. It is employed to construct the proposed intelligent system using AutoML algorithm that classify cervical cancer images into three stages, namely, Type 1, Type 2 and Type 3. It assists clinicians to diagnose cervix cancer stages with minimal efforts and lesser time. This model is significantly beneficial to physicians to take clinical decisions namely, need of taking biopsy and identify the precancerous lesions efficiently. It is also helpful to the patients to avoid stress, phobia and pain during cervix examination. The implementation procedure of vertex AI, a Google Cloud unified platform that is employed to construct a cervical cancer stages classification system is briefly described in this section. It is explicated in two dimensions which include mathematical procedures of AutoML and workflow of AutoML model.

10.3.1 Mathematical Background

The mathematical notations employed to construct an Auto ML model for the classification of cervical cancer stages are described in this section [86]. Consider a search space P consisting of distinct elements, p, such as, $p \in P$. It is divided into two blocks for training and validation, namely, P1 and P2. The aim of AutoML model is to find the best samples, P*, such that:

$$P^* = \frac{argmin}{p \in P} \frac{1}{K} \sum_{i=1}^{M} L\left(P, P1_{train}^{(i)}, P2_{train}^{(i)}\right) \qquad (10.1)$$

where,

$\left\{ P1_{train}^{(1)}, P2_{valid}^{(K)} \right\}$ P1 and P2 denotes the training set and validation set obtained in K-fold cross validation.

The loss of a pipeline P is calculated using a formula is given in Eq. 10.2.

$$L\left(P, P1_{train}^{(i)}, P2_{valid}^{(i)}\right) \qquad (10.2)$$

The generic syntax of AutoML is given as follows [87].

```
def Setup ( ):
    p2 = 0.001           // Init learning rate
def Predict ( ):                // t0 = features
    p1 = dot(t0, t1)     // Apply weights
def Learn ( ):                  // t0 = features; p0 = label
    p3 = p0 - p1         // Compute error
    p4 = p3 * p2         // Applying learning rate
    t2 = t0 * p4         // Compute gradients
    t1 = t1 + t2         // Update weights
```

The pseudocode representation of AutoML algorithm to construct a cervix cancer stages classification model is given as follows [88]. It is developed as a virtual memory that consists of scalar, vector and matrix variables. Image samples consist of features (F) sequence which are encoded as a matrix (m). Input values are represented as scalar (s) and output are stored in vectors (v).

Pseudocode: AutoML
def Evaluate (Initialization, Prediction, Learning, Training, Validation):

> *Initialization:*
>
>> Setting up platform, instance, region and zone, bucket, storage class, access control, encryption key settings, and training method.
>
> *Setup():*
>
>> Cervix cancer image dataset and annotation file to describe the dataset.
>> for (a, b) in P1: // training phase
>>
>>> t0 = a // a and b define the input and output variables
>>> Prediction () // Allows input variables for prediction
>>> s1 = Normalization (s1) // Normalize the prediction
>>> s0 = b // b is allowed to mapping and learning the input variables
>>> Learning() // Execution of learning instructions
>>
>> sum_loss() = 0.0
>> for (a,b) in P2: // validation phase
>> t0 = a
>> Prediction() // Only prediction is allowed here. No learning is done here.
>>
>>> s1 = Normalization (s1) // Normalize the prediction
>>> sum_loss += Loss (b, s1)
>>
>> mean_loss = sum_loss / len(validation)

return mean_loss

The pseudocode of a AutoML model development is analysed as follows. It consists of three main components, namely, Setup, Predict and Learn and involves two processes, namely, training phase and validation phase. It produces mean loss for every execution cycle of algorithm. Dataset are randomly split into training samples and validation samples. The prediction range of $(-\infty, \infty)$ is normalized to $(0, 1)$ through a soft-max activation function to attain a multi-label classification. In this study, cervical cancer dataset and annotation file are uploaded in the GCP environment. Instance and bucket creation, platform, region and zone settings, storage class, access control, key settings and training method are initialised to configure the model. Learning the input and output variables are carried out in this training phase. Then, it is segmented into training phase and testing phase for the model evaluation. Based on the knowledge gained in the training phase, the developed model predicts cervical cancer stages as output variables (Type 1, Type 2 and Type 3).

10.3.2   Workflow of AutoML Model

Google Cloud Platform (GCP) offers a rich set of resources, such as computers, hard disk drives, Virtual Machines (VMs), computing, services and infrastructure contained in Google data centres around the globe. Google Cloud console offers a Vertex AI that brings AutoML and AI Platform together into a unified API, client library and user interface [89]. The skeleton of AutoML pipeline is depicted in Fig. 10.4.

The dataset is loaded into a customized AutoML workflow model which is utilized for a model training. Once a model gives better results, then it is deployed as endpoint in GCP to make predictions. It automatically generates API in Python and JSON file that can be used to access the model anywhere in the world without being depending on platform, environment, infrastructure and hardware settings. The vertex AI pipeline applied to develop a custom machine learning workflow is shown in Fig. 10.5. It is utilized to construct a cervical cancer classification system in this study.

Data Ingestion   It is the foremost step in the development of an intelligent system. This step loads raw dataset into the pipeline which is also termed as data preparation or data readiness. It involves two sub-tasks, namely, data collection and data pooling. Cervix cancer images procured using MobileODT EVA system are collected from Kaggle site [90]. This repository consists of three different types of cervical images, namely, Type 1, Type 2 and Type 3 from normal (pre-cancerous stage to advanced cancerous stage). The acquired cervical cancer images are pooled into a folder which is used to develop an intelligent system. The sample screenshot of data ingestion stage process is presented in Fig. 10.6.

Data Preprocess   The next step is the conversion of raw dataset into a customized machine learning workflow understandable form. In addition to cervical cancer images, supplementary information is also incorporated into a pipeline that enables

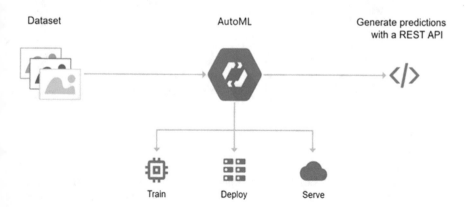

Fig. 10.4 Workflow of AutoML

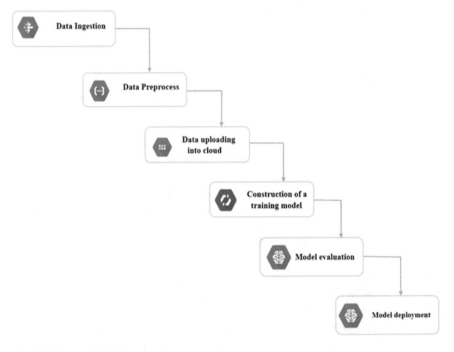

Fig. 10.5 Vertex AI pipeline workflow

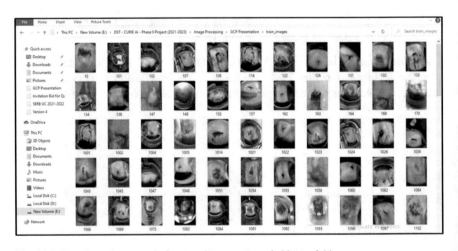

Fig. 10.6 Data ingestion - cervical cancer images are pooled into a folder

machine learning workflow to understand and learn the input values. Data labelling task that provides annotation to cervix image dataset is done in this step. The three stages of cervix cancer image files are labelled as 1, 2 and 3 and stored in a comma separated value file format to generate a labelled data. Henceforth, cervical images and labelled data are upload into GCP environment.

Data Uploading into Cloud Once the training data (cervical images) and labelled data (csv file) are refined and finalized, the next step is to upload the aforementioned images and data into GCP environment. It consists of four steps, namely, production selection, creation of new instance, bucket creation and uploading files into cloud. As a first step, the user has to choose the required products and resources in GCP console page. In this page, AI platform is selected, then new instance is created which is available under notebooks menu in AI platform dashboard. Cervical cancer stages classification system is coded in Python programming language. So, new instance is created in Python 3 custom container in GCP. Moreover, the user-defined instance (ccautomlmodel) name, region (asia-southeast1(Singapore)) and zone (asia-southeast1) are also selected to create an open Jupyter Lab Notebook.Next step is to create cloud storage for uploading original images and annotation file. Cloud storage is selected under navigation menu. A user-defined new bucket is created under browser menu. storage location, storage class, access control and advanced settings are also configured to create a bucket. The final step is to upload cervical images and annotation file into a cloud storage bucket.

Construction of a Training Model An intelligent system is developed to classify cervical cancer images into three stages, namely, Type 1, Type 2 and Type 3. There are three tasks performed to develop a customized training model. That is, AutoML model type is selected to construct a model, uploading cervical image samples and importing annotation file from cloud storage to do a mapping from data samples to annotation. Vertex AI container has chosen from navigation menu, in which, dataset option and region are selected to construct a vertex AI model. Once the uploaded cervix cancer images are imported in vertex AI platform, it is visualized in Browse section. Figure 10.7 shows that distinct number of datasets that belong to the category of labelled data and unlabelled data.

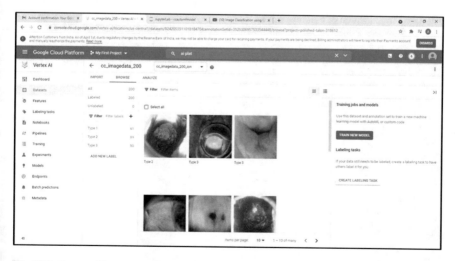

Fig. 10.7 Imported image samples are visualized in browse section

Various properties, such as, annotation, objective, items, created, last updated, region and encryption type of input samples are given in Analyze section. The following task focus on the construction of a customized training model using AutoML code. It is composed of three steps, such as, initialization of training method, model details and compute and pricing. Dataset (cervical images), annotation set (labelled data), objective (multi-label image classification) and deployment option (AutoML) are defined in training method. A user-defined model name (cc_image_data_demo) and data split up (randomly assigned) are setting up in model details. The number of nodes (eight) required to train a new model is declared in compute and pricing field. Lastly, training pipeline is successfully created in vertex AI. It is portrayed in Figs. 10.8 and 10.9. The evaluation approach of a new training model and deployment options are deliberated in the next section.

Fig. 10.8 Initialization of training method

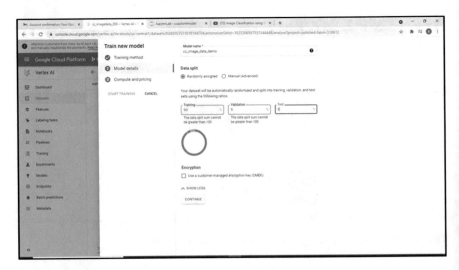

Fig. 10.9 Setting up of data split in model details 4

10.4   Experimental Observations

The validation of a developed AutoML model for the classification of cervix cancer images is conducted to do a better investigation of this work. The pipeline of Vertex AI model evaluation is depicted in Fig. 10.10.

10.4.1   Model Evaluation

A customized training model constructed for the classification of cervix cancer stages is validated to conduct a better investigation of this study. Evaluate option available under Models are selected from vertex AI menu which is utilized to visually analyze the classification accuracy of a training model. Figure 10.11 portrays the total number of values labelled by training model (cc_image_data_demo) as Type 1, Type 2 and Type 3. It shows the precision-recall curve graph and precision-recall by threshold graph. It is a bias-variance tradeoff graph that represents average precision, precision, recall, model created date, total images, training imageset, validation image samples and test images. The mathematical formulas used to calculate precision and recall are given in Eqs. (10.3) and (10.4) [91].

$$Precision = \frac{True\ Positive(TP)}{True\ Positive(TP) + False\ Positive} \tag{10.3}$$

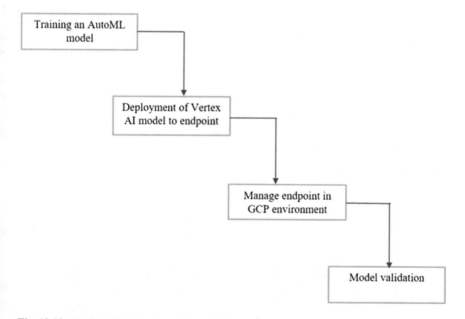

Fig. 10.10 Pipeline of vertex AI model validation

Fig. 10.11 Evaluation of a new training pipeline

Fig. 10.12 Confusion matrix plotted for a training pipeline

$$Recall = \frac{True\ Positive(TP)}{True\ Positive(TP) + False\ Negative} \tag{10.4}$$

The confusion matrix generated in Fig. 10.12 illustrates that the correctly classified class labels of Type 1, Type 2 and Type 3 are highlighted in blue color and the probably classified labels of Type 1, Type 2 and Type 3 are shown in gray color. The examined results demonstrate that classification accuracy of a developed model suffers due to small volume of data. As an initial step, 200 cervical cancer image samples are utilized to construct a model. It can be further improved by accumulating the huge volume of cervical cancer images for a model training that enables to attain better accuracy.

10.4.2   Model Deployment

A training model is deployed as endpoint in GCP environment that allows users to access the intelligent cervical cancer stages classification system in an online mode. It consists of two steps, such as, defining endpoint and model settings. A user-defined endpoint name (cc_model_deploy) is created in defining endpoint and the number of nodes (one) are required to compute for a model training is defined in model settings. Once endpoint is successfully deployed, sample request API is created in both REST and PYTHON codes are automatically generated that can be accessible anywhere and any point.

10.4.3   Model Testing

The deployed endpoint is evaluated using test images to measure the performance of an intelligent system. For instance, cervical image of Type 1 is used for testing purpose and the obtained result is shown in Fig. 10.13. It illustrates that the numerical proportion of test image is highly correlates with category of Type 1 rather than Type 2 and Type 3. It reveals that the developed system is able to produce better possible outcomes.

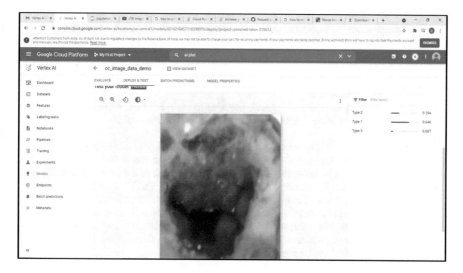

Fig. 10.13 Validation of a deployed endpoint

10.5   Conclusion and Future Works

In this research, an intelligent cervical cancer stages classification system is developed using AutoML codes in Google cloud platform. It is constructed by employing the real time cervical images and the observed results demonstrate its efficacy. The primary benefits of the smart intelligent system are its simplicity, that is, ease to build a customized machine learning model with less efforts, minimal time, does not require coding expertise, storage and experimental set up to build a system. The most important things that need to be considered to develop a reliable and robust model, are, it requires a highly qualitative and large volume of data, budget settings (number of nodes required to compute a training model) and maintenance expenditure (it incurs cost when a training model is deployed as endpoint in GCP). The proposed system is greatly beneficial to clinicians for patient remote monitoring, and patients who are surviving in inadequate healthcare infrastructures and lack of clinicians to get frequent medical treatments/suggestions. It enables physicians to access, visualize and investigate cervix images and quickly suggest medical treatments that helps to reduce cervical cancer incidence and mortality rate of women, especially those who are living in the remote/rural locations. This study can be extended to include a large volume of cervix cancer image datasets to improve the classification accuracy and then deploy the developed intelligent system in a real-time environment to measure its efficiency.

Acknowledgements   The authors express deep gratitude to the Centre for Machine Learning and Intelligence funded by the Department of Science and Technology (DST) under the scheme of DST-CURIE (AI) for supporting and sharing the resource for this research work.

References

1. Gade, D. S., & Aithal, P. S. (2022). ICT and digital technology-based solutions for smart city challenges and opportunities. *International Journal of Applied Engineering and Management Letters, 6*(1), 1–21.
2. Smart City. In *TechTarget*. https://www.techtarget.com/iotagenda/definition/smart-city/. Accessed on 27 Mar 2022.
3. AI-powered smart healthcare in smart cities. In *Research Topic*. https://www.frontiersin. org/research-topics/21020/ai-powered-smart-healthcare-in-smart-cities/. Accessed on 27 Mar 2022.
4. Sundaravadivel, P. E., Kougianos, S. P., & Mohanty, G. M. K. (2018). Everything you wanted to know about smart health care: Evaluating the different technologies and components of the Internet of Things for better health. *IEEE Consumer Electronics Magazine, 7*(1), 18–28.
5. Tian, S., Yang, W., Le, G., Jehane, M., Wang, P., Huang, W., & Ye, Z. (2019). Smart healthcare: Making medical care more intelligent. *Global Health Journal, 3*(3), 62–65.
6. Smart healthcare market detailed analysis by product, region, and forecasts to 2022: Grand view research Inc. In *abnews wire*. https://www.abnewswire.com/pressreleases/smart-healthcare-market-detailed-analysis-by-product-region-and-forecasts-to-2022-grand-view-research-inc_422379.html/. Accessed on 27 Mar 2022.

7. Companies in smart healthcare products market collaborate with health stakeholders to reduce burden of chronic diseases, global valuation to expand at 8.8% from 2019 to 2027: TMR. In *CISION PR Newswire*.https://www.prnewswire.com/news-releases/companies-in-smart-healthcare-products-market-collaborate-with-health-stakeholders-to-reduce-burden-of-chronic-diseases-global-valuation-to-expand-at-8-8-from-2019-to-2027-tmr-301325980.html/. Accessed on 27 Mar 2022.
8. Troiani, T., Napolitano, S., Terminiello, M., Vitiello, P. P., Ciardiello, F., Martinelli, E., Fenza, G., Orciuoli, F. J., & Romanelli, L. (2022). Enabling smart environment for monitoring cancer patients therapy through OncoSmart. *Journal of Smart Environments and Green Computing, 1*(4), 189–201.
9. World Health Organization. (2022). Cervical cancer. In *WHO Newsroom*.https://www.who.int/news-room/fact-sheets/detail/cervical-cancer/. Accessed on 29 Mar 2022.
10. Cho, B. J., Kim, J. W., Park, J., Kwon, G. Y., Hong, M., Jang, S. H., Bang, H., Kim, G., & Park, S. T. (2022). Automated diagnosis of cervical intraepithelial neoplasia in histology images via deep learning. *Diagnostics, 12*(2), 1–15.
11. Ekaba, B. (2019). *Building machine learning and deep learning models on Google Cloud Platform a comprehensive guide for beginners.* Apress.
12. Challita, S., Zalila, F., Gourdin, C., & Merle, P. (2018). A precise model for Google Cloud Platform. In *6th IEEE International Conference on Cloud Engineering (IC2E), Orlando, FL, USA*, pp. 177–183.
13. Anand, D., Manish, K., & Vikram, C. (2020). Hands-On artificial intelligence on Google Cloud Platform: Build intelligent applications powered by TensorFlow, Cloud AutoML, BigQuery, and Dialogflow, Packt.
14. AutoML Vision Beginner's guide. In *Google Cloud*. https://cloud.google.com/vision/automl/docs/beginners-guide/. Accessed on 27 Mar 2022.
15. Eduonix. A brief introduction to AutoML. In *Towards Data Science*. https://blog.eduonix.com/artificialintelligence/brief-introduction-automl/. Accessed 27 Mar 2022.
16. Brownlee, J. Automated Machine Learning (AutoML) libraries for Python. In *Python Machine Learning*. https://machinelearningmastery.com/automl-libraries-for-python/. Accessed on 27 Mar 2022.
17. Dinsmore, T. Automated machine learning: A short history. In *Datarobot*. https://www.datarobot.com/blog/automatedmachine-learning-short-history/. Accessed on 27 Mar 2022.
18. Automated Machine Learning (AutoML). In *TechTarget*. https://www.techtarget.com/searchenterpriseai/definition/automated-machine-learning-AutoML/. Accessed on 27 Mar 2022.
19. Islam, M. M., Rahaman, A., & Islam, M. R. (2020). Development of smart healthcare monitoring system in IoT environment. *SN Computer Science, 1*(3), 1–12.
20. Durga, K. S., Krishnamurthy, R., Srinivas, K. N. H., Sarveswara, R. T. D. N. S. S., & Amiri, I. S. (2019). IoT-based health monitoring system using BeagleBone Black with optical sensor. *Journal of Optical Communication, 40*, 1–7.
21. Khan, J., Li, J., Haq, A., Parveen, S., Khan, G., Shahid, M., Monday, H., Ullah, S., & Ruinan, S. (2019). Medical image encryption into smart healthcare IOT system. In *International Computer Conference on Wavelet Active Media Technology and Information Processing, Chengdu, China*, pp. 378–382.
22. Hao, W., Ding, S., Wu, D., Zhang, Y., & Yang, S. (2018). Smart connected electronic gastroscope system for gastric cancer screening using multi-column convolutional neural networks. *International Journal of Production Research, 57*(21), 1–12.
23. Imran, A., Jeon, G., & Chehri, A. (2021). An IoT-enabled smart healthcare system for screening of COVID-19 with multi layers features fusion and selection. *Computing, 103*(6), 1233–1254.
24. Mohammed, M. K., Mehnaz, S., Shaha, A., Nayem, M., & Bourouis, S. (2021). IoT-based smart health monitoring system for COVID-19 patients. *Computational and Mathematical Methods in Medicine, 2021*, 1–11.
25. Bhardwaj, V., Joshi, R., & Gaur, A. M. (2022). IoT-based smart health monitoring system for COVID-19. *SN Computer Science, 3*(2), 1–11.

26. Onasanya, A., & Elshakankiri, M. (2021). Smart integrated IoT healthcare system for cancer care. *Wireless Networks, 27*(6), 4297–4312.
27. Zulfiqar, A. S., Yasir, A. S., & Zulfikar, A. M. (2021). Adoption of IoT-based smart healthcare: An empirical analysis in the context of Pakistan. *Journal of Hunan University Natural Sciences, 48*(9), 143–153.
28. Ankur, G., Hoshiyar, S., Shivkant, K., & Rijwan, K. (2021). IoT based cloud network for smart healthcare using optimization algorithm. *Informatics in Medicine Unlocked, 27*(2021), 1–8.
29. Hesham, A., El, Z., & Mustafa, M. H. (2021). Secure IoT communications for smart healthcare monitoring system. *Internet of Things, 13*, 2021.
30. Sita, R., Meetali, C., Aman, K., & Alex, K. (2021). IoT equipped intelligent distributed framework for smart healthcare systems. *Networking and Internet Architecture*, abs/2110.04997, 1–29.
31. Annamalai, M., Mary, J., & Nithya, M. (2021). Smart IOT based healthcare monitoring and decision-making system using augmented data recognition algorithm. *Turkish Journal of Computer and Mathematics Education, 12*(11), 1971–1979.
32. Jeong, J., Han, O., & You, Y. (2016). A design characteristics of smart healthcare system as the IoT application. *Indian Journal of Science and Technology, 9*(37), 1–8.
33. Khamparia, A., Singh, P. K., Rani, P., Samanta, D., Khanna, A., & Bhushan, B. (2020). An internet of health things-driven deep learning framework for detection and classification of skin cancer using transfer learning. *Transactions on Emerging Telecommunications Technology, 32*(7), 1–11.
34. Azad, C., Bhushan, B., & Sharma, R. (2021). Prediction model using SMOTE, genetic algorithm and decision tree (PMSGD) for classification of diabetes mellitus. *Multimedia Systems, 27*(3).
35. Deepanshu, B., Bharat, B., & Divya, Y. (2021). Healthcare 4.0: An insight of architecture, security requirements, pillars and applications. *Biomedical Data Mining for Information Retrieval: Methodologies, Techniques and Applications*, 103–130.
36. Goyal, S., Sharma, N., Bhushan, B., Shankar, A., & Sagayam, M. (2021). IoT enabled technology in secured healthcare: Applications, challenges and future directions. *Cognitive Internet of Medical Things for Smart Healthcare, 311*, 25–48.
37. Ahmed, G., Muhammad, G., Amin, S. U., & Gupta, B. (2018). Medical image forgery detection for smart healthcare. *IEEE Communications Magazine, 56*(4), 33–37.
38. Mahmoud, A., Husari, G., Darwish, O., & Alabed, A. (2012). Machine learning approach for brain tumor detection. In *3rd international conference on information and communication systems, Tokyo Japan.*
39. Konstantina, K. T. P., Exarchos, K. P., Exarchos, M. V., Karamouzis, D. I., & Fotiadis, D. I. (2015). Machine learning applications in cancer prognosis and prediction. *Computational and Structural Biotechnology Journal, 13*(2015), 8–17.
40. Mehmood, M., Rizwan, M., Gregus, M., & Abbas, S. (2021). Machine learning assisted cervical cancer detection. *Frontiers in Public Health, 9*, 1–14.
41. Kadir, T., & Gleeson, F. (2018). Lung cancer prediction using machine learning and advanced imaging techniques. *Translational Lung Cancer Research, 7*(3), 304–312.
42. Elngar, A. A., Kumar, R., Hayat, A., & Churi, P. Intelligent system for skin disease prediction using machine learning. *Journal of Physics: Conference Series, 2021, 1998*(2021), 1–15.
43. Wei, L. S., Gan, Q., & Ji, T. (2018). Skin disease recognition method based on image color and texture features. *Computational and Mathematical Methods in Medicine, 2018*, 1–10.
44. Hatem, M. Q. (2022). Skin lesion classification system using a K-nearest neighbor algorithm. *Visual Computing for Industry, Biomedicine, and Art, 5*(1), 1–10.
45. Zhang, J., & Liu, Y. (2004). Cervical cancer detection using SVM based feature screening. In *Advanced data mining and applications, Paris, France*, pp. 873–880.
46. Pandey, H., & Prabha, S. (2020). Smart health monitoring system using IOT and machine learning techniques. In *2020 Sixth International Conference on Bio Signals, Images and Instrumentation (ICBSII), Chennai, India*, pp. 1–4.

47. Nusaibah, K. A. S., & Turgay, I. (2017). Classifying breast cancer by using decision tree algorithms. In *Proceedings of the 6th international conference on software and computer applications, Bangkok, Thailand*, pp. 144–148.

48. Verma, A. K., Chakraborty, M., & Biswas, S. K. (2021). Breast cancer management system using decision tree and neural network. *SN Computer Science, 2*(234), 1–15.

49. Thohir, M., Foeady, A. Z., Novitasari, D. C. R., Arifin, A. Z., Phiadelvira, B. Y., & Asyhar, A. H. (2020). Classification of colposcopy data using GLCM-SVM on cervical cancer. In *2020 international conference on artificial intelligence in information and communication, Fukuoka, Japan*, pp. 373–378.

50. Zorkafli, M. F., Osman, M. K., Isa, I. S., Ahmad, F., & Sulaiman, S. N. (2019). Classification of cervical cancer using hybrid multi-layered perceptron network trained by genetic algorithm. *Procedia Computer Science, 163*(2019), 494–501.

51. Priyanka, K. M., & Suvarna, N. (2017). Machine learning technique for detection of cervical cancer using k-NN and artificial neural network. *International Journal of Emerging Trends & Technology in Computer Science, 6*(4), 145–149.

52. Mehta, S., Bhushan, B., & Kumar, R. (2022). Machine learning approaches for smart city applications: Emergence, challenges and opportunities. *Recent Advances in Internet of Things and Machine Learning, 215*, 147–163.

53. Rao, P. P. M., Singh, S. K., Khamparia, A., Bhushan, B., & Podder, P. (2022). Multi-class breast cancer classification using ensemble of pretrained models and transfer learning. *Current Medical Imaging, 18*(4), 409–416.

54. Yunchao, G., & Jiayao, Y. (2019). Application of computer vision and deep learning in breast cancer assisted diagnosis. In *Proceedings of the 3rd international conference on machine learning and soft computing, New York, United States*, pp. 189–191.

55. Shen, L., Margolies, L. R., & Rothstei, J. H. (2019). Deep learning to improve breast cancer detection on screening mammography. *Scientific Reports, 9*(2019), 1–12.

56. Shen, G., Dwivedi, K., Majima, K., Horikawa, T., & Kamitani, Y. (2019). End-to-end deep image reconstruction from human brain activity. *Frontiers in Computational Neuroscience, 13*(21), 1–11.

57. Sathesh, A. (2020). Computer vision on IOT based patient preference management system. *Journal of Trends in Computer Science and Smart Technology, 2*(2), 68–77.

58. Ranjbarzadeh, R., Bagherian, K. A., Jafarzadeh, G. S., Anari, S., Naseri, M., & Bendechache, M. (2021). Brain tumor segmentation based on deep learning and an attention mechanism using MRI multi-modalities brain images. *Scientific Reports, 11*(1), 1–18.

59. Hussain, M., Saher, N., & Qadri, S. (2022). Computer vision approach for liver tumor classification using CT dataset. *Applied Artificial Intelligence, 36*, 1–23.

60. Zhang, L. H., Zhu, T., & Yang. (2019). Deep Neural Networks for fatty liver ultrasound images classification. In *2019 Chinese Control and Decision Conference (CCDC)*, pp. 4641–4646.

61. Shaikh, I. T., & Kadam, V. K. (2021). Liver cancer detection and grading using efficient computer vision techniques. *Annals of the Romanian Society for Cell Biology, 25*(2), 1740–1755.

62. Liu, C., Wang, L., & Lu, W. (2022). Computer vision-aided bioprinting for bone research. *Bone Research, 10*(21), 1–14.

63. Lin, Q., Li, T., & Cao, C. (2021). Deep learning based automated diagnosis of bone metastases with SPECT thoracic bone images. *Scientific Reports, 11*, 4223.

64. Leelavathy, S., Jaichandran, R., Shobana, R., Vasudevan, S. S., & Prasad, N. (2020). Skin disease detection using computer vision and machine learning technique. *European Journal of Molecular & Clinical Medicine, 7*(4), 2999–3003.

65. Patnaik, S. K., Sidhu, M. S., Gehlot, Y., Sharma, B., & Muthu, P. (2018). Automated skin disease identification using deep learning algorithm. *Biomedical and Pharmacology Journal, 11*(3), 1429–1436.

66. Chandran, V., Sumithra, M. G., Karthick, A., George, T., Deivakani, M., Elakkiya, B., Subramaniam, U., & Manoharan, S. (2021). Diagnosis of cervical cancer based on ensemble deep learning network using colposcopy images. *BioMed Research International, 2021*, 1–15.

67. Faes, L., Wagner, S. K., Fu, D. J., Liu, X., Korot, E., Ledsam, J. R., Back, T., Chopra, R., Pontikos, N., Kern, C., Moraes, G., Schmid, M. K., Sim, D., Balaskas, K., Bachmann, L. M., Denniston, A. K., & Keane, P. A. (2019). Automated deep learning design for medical image classification by health-care professionals with no coding experience: A feasibility study. *The Lancet Digital Health, 1*, 232–242.
68. Ekaba, B. (2019). Google Cloud AutoML vision for medical image classification. In *Towards Data Science*. https://towardsdatascience.com/google-cloud-automl-vision-for-medical-image-classification-76dfbf12a77e/. Accessed 27 Mar 2022.
69. Ka, W. W., Wong, C. H., Ip, H. F., Fan, D., Yuen, P. L., Fong, H. Y., & Ying, M. (2021). Evaluation of the performance of traditional machine learning algorithms, convolutional neural network and AutoML Vision in ultrasound breast lesions classification: A comparative study. *Quantitative Imaging in Medicine and Surgery, 11*, 1381–1393.
70. Dong, Y., Andriy, M., Xiaosong, W., Ziyue, X., Holger, R., & Roth, D. X. (2021). T-AutoML: Automated machine learning for lesion segmentation using transformers in 3D medical imaging. *IEEE/CVF International Conference on Computer Vision (ICCV)*, 3942–3954.
71. Hussain, S. I., & Ruza, N. (2022). Automated deep learning of COVID-19 and pneumonia detection using Google AutoML. *Intelligent Automation and Soft Computing, 31*, 1143–1156.
72. Harikrishnan, Vijarania, M., & Gambhir, A. (2020). Diabetic retinopathy identification using autoML. *Computational Intelligence and Its Applications in Healthcare*, 175–188.
73. Singh, A. (2021). Identifying lung infection using AutoML. In *Medium*. https://abhinav-singh.medium.com/identifying-lung-infection-using-automl/. Accessed 29 Mar 2022.
74. Basic Information About Cervical cancer. Centers for Diseases Control and Prevention. https://www.cdc.gov/cancer/cervical/basic_info/. Accessed 27 Mar 2022.
75. Poli, U. R., Bidinger, P. D., & Gowrishankar, S. (2015). Visual Inspection with Acetic Acid (VIA) screening program: 7 years' experience in early detection of cervical cancer and pre-cancers in rural South India. *Indian Journal of Community Medicine: Official Publication of Indian Association of Preventive & Social Medicine, 40*(3), 203–207.
76. Pothisuwan, M. (2011). Visual inspection with acetic acid for detection of high grade lesion in atypical squamous cells and low grade squamous intraepithelial lesions from cervical Pap smear. *Journal of Gynecologic Oncology, 22*(3), 145–151.
77. Mishra, G., Shastri, S., & Pimple, S. (2011). An overview of prevention and early detection of cervical cancers. *Indian Journal of Medical and Paediatric Oncology, 32*, 125.
78. Sankaranarayanan, R., Thara, S., Sharma, A., Roy, C., Shastri, S., & Mahé, C. (2004). Accuracy of conventional cytology: Results from a multicentre screening study in India. *Journal of Medical Screening, 11*(2), 77–84.
79. Fielder, H. (2003). Cervical screening Wales. Liquid based cytology – Pilot project. In *Project Report*. http://www.cancerscreening.nhs.uk/cervical/lbc.html/. Accessed 29 Mar 2022.
80. Arbyn, M., Bergeron, C., Klinkhamer, P., Martin-Hirsch, P., Siebers, A. G., & Bulten, J. (2008). Liquid compared with conventional cervical cytology: A systematic review and meta-analysis. *Obstetrics and Gynecology Clinics of North America, 111*, 167–177.
81. Nuovo, J., Melnikow, J., & Howell, L. P. (2001). New tests for cervical cancer screening. *American Family Physician, 64*(5), 780–786.
82. Sellors, J. W., & Sankaranarayanan, R. (2003). *Colposcopy and treatment of cervical intraepithelial neoplasia: A beginner's manual*. International Agency for Research on Cancer.
83. MobileODT [online]. Available at: https://www.mobileodt.com/. Accessed 15 May 2021.
84. Prnewswire.com. Israeli FemTech Company MobileODT, Engaged in Large Scale Government Cervical Cancer Screening Project. Available from: https://www.prnewswire.com/news-releases/israeli-femtech-company-mobileodt-engaged-in-large-scale-government-cervical-cancer-screening-project-301256186.html. Accessed 17 Oct 2021.
85. Mobileodt.com. Cervical cancer screening in China: MobileODT takes part in the largest ever self-swab HPV study. Available from: https://www.mobileodt.com/blog/cervical-cancer-screening-in-china-largest-ever-self-swab-hpv-study/. Accessed 17 Oct 2021.

86. Medium.com. A brief overview of Automatic Machine Learning solutions (AutoML). Available from: https://medium.com/hackernoon/a-brief-overview-of-automatic-machine-learning-solutions-automl. Accessed 17 Oct 2021.
87. Towardsdatascience.com. AutoML-Zero. Available from: https://towardsdatascience.com/automl-zero-b2e06517094. Accessed 17 Oct 2021.
88. Esteban, R., Chen, L., David, R. S., & Quoc, V. L. (2020). AutoML-Zero: Evolving machine learning algorithms from scratch. In *Proceedings of the 37th international conference on machine learning*, pp. 1–23.
89. Google Cloud AutoML [Online]. Available at: https://cloud.google.com/automl/. Accessed 10 June 2022.
90. Intel &MobileODT cervical cancer screening [online]. Available at: https://www.kaggle.com/competitions/intel-mobileodt-cervical-cancer-screening/overview. Accessed 15 May 2021.
91. Precision vs. Recall – An intuitive guide for every machine learning person [online]. Available at: https://www.analyticsvidhya.com/blog/2020/09/precision-recall-machine-learning/. Accessed 5 May 2021.

Chapter 11
IoT and an Intelligent Cloud-Based Framework to Build a Smart City Traffic Management System

Saroja Kumar Rout (ID)**, Bibhuprasad Sahu, Pradyumna Kumar Mohapatra** (ID)**, Sachi Nandan Mohanty** (ID)**, and Ashish K. Sharma** (ID)

Abstract Congestion is a major issue in all metropolitan cities, particularly in urban areas. Using smart technologies, Cities may be extraordinary and can be transformed into "smart cities". The Internet of Things (IoT) is a new paradigm in computing that seems to have the capacity to enhance impact in smart city implementation. For smart cities, IoT and cloud-based road traffic technologies are proposed in this article. The overarching goal is to use cloud computing to resolve some of the IoT's present issues and limits to create upgraded solutions for smarter cities. With the combination of IoT and cloud computing, smart cities will be able to generate novel and enhanced facilities by utilizing large amounts of data saved in the cloud and analyzing it in real-time. This study proposes a method for real-time traffic control that combines the Internet of Things (IoT) and data analytics. After analyzing sensor data, the device controller uses a traffic management algorithm to set the Wi-Fi module to collect data from traffic signals and transfers it to a cloud server. The proposed system will forecast the likelihood of at the intersection, there

S. K. Rout (✉)
Department of Information Technology, Vardhaman College of Engineering (Autonomous), Hyderabad, India

B. Sahu
Department of Artificial Intelligence and Data Science, Vardhaman College of Engineering, Hyderabad, India

P. K. Mohapatra
Department of Electronics & Communication Engineering, Vedang Institute of Technology, Bhubaneswar, Odisha, India

S. N. Mohanty
School of Computer Science & Engineering (SCOPE), VIT-AP University, Amaravati, Andhra Pradesh, India

A. K. Sharma
Department of Computer Science Engineering, Bajaj Institute of Technology (BIT), Wardha, India

© The Author(s), under exclusive license to Springer Nature Switzerland AG 2023
M. A. Ahad et al. (eds.), *Enabling Technologies for Effective Planning and Management in Sustainable Smart Cities*, https://doi.org/10.1007/978-3-031-22922-0_11

283

is a lot of traffic. If an emergency vehicle is not available or identified, the intersection is given priority, with a longer signal length.

Keywords Cloud · IoT · Architecture · Sensors · Wi-Fi system · Smart traffic

11.1 Introduction

A considerable number of people are migrating to urban areas and predicted that by 2030, With over 60% of worldwide people will live in cities 2050 [1, 2]. Cities all over the world are confronting numerous problems and issues as a result of the rapid growth of the urban population. This circumstance has increased the urgency of finding better solutions to the problems. ICF (Intelligent Community Forum) has developed the Smart 21 community, which yearly announces several cities with high scores in five areas evaluated by the neighborhoods (Broadband access, a skilled workforce, digital inclusiveness, innovation, marketing, and advocacy are all examples.) A smart city is a dynamic and constantly growing urban, complex, and distributed system in nature. Complex systems, such as the nervous system or societies, are examples of complex systems. The overall behaviors of the system are determined by these individual behaviors. The trend toward smart cities also renders them vulnerable to new computerization technologies that could be integrated into services that already have infrastructure [3]. From sociological, technological, and urban aspects, smart cities are defined [4–6]. Smart cities, according to the definition given in [7], include boosting the city's computerization in numerous other areas such as both to enhance quality and economic expansion.

The Internet of Things (IoT) uses modern ubiquitous communication methods to bring the digital world into the physical world. Many commonplace items, such as networked cellphones and tablets, have distinct traits and are also linked to the Web. The Internet of Things (IoT) focuses on the configuration, operation, and connectivity of "Internet of Gadgets" or "Things" that have never been connected to the Internet, thermostats, for example, electrical equipment, appliances, utility meters, medical gadgets, cameras, and other sensors are all examples of sensors [8]. The IoT ushers in a new era of Internet-connected endpoint possibilities. IoT applications can be found in a variety of industries, including homes, cities, the ecosystem, energy sources, retail, transit, industrial, agro, and healthcare. Experts estimate that by 2025, The Internet of Things will have an $11 trillion annual hidden impact, which is comparable to 11% of the global GDP [9]. By 2035, it is estimated that users will have installed a total of 1 trillion IoT devices [10]. More than merely connecting items to the internet is at the heart of the IoT. The IoT enables these gadgets to exchange information while accomplishing a critical task for a basic human or machine purpose. To obtain useful pieces of information and/or its users, as well as the surroundings and activities, Currently, IoT data makes up the vast majority will be cloud servers that are used to save and process data. Cloud computing systems are highly scalable and may be scaled up or down promptly "pay-per-use" model, reducing the cost of developing the required analytics application. Existing data analytics techniques can handle the massive amounts of data processing in a managed cloud network, on the other hand, falling short of the standards for the reasons listed below [11]. A number of innovative and real-life applications are being developed as a result of the exponential growth of Internet of Things (IoT) devices. A resource-constrained fixed node or a mobile node is used by IoT to support such applications [12].

(a) Cloud providers (CPs) aspire to create data centers in faraway locations with low-cost resources to lower cloud service running expenditures since cloud servers positioned far from sensing nodes struggle to analyze real-time data for connection applications. The physical distance between servers increases the time it takes for data to be transmitted. This is inefficient for time-sensitive applications, which frequently have milliseconds or even microsecond data transmission delays. Whenever sensors on oil refineries sense a pressure shift in oil extraction, for example, rapid action is required to avoid disaster by automatically shutting down pumps.

(b) The volume of data generated by IoT continues to grow, causing the cloud to become significantly overburdened. IoT technology is a cloud-based system that incorporates a range of sensing, identification, communication, networking, and data management devices. It is inefficient to send massive amounts of data generated by millions of IoT devices [13] for storage and analysis to the cloud. This could cause network bandwidth to be overburdened, as well as place a strain on the data center [14]. The study's major purpose is to employ IoT to create an intelligent traffic system. In addition, the proposed approach is more user-friendly than existing alternatives.

11.1.1 Problem Statements

Traffic congestion and delays are caused by the lack of an effective emergency vehicle traffic management system, which replaces the flawed and inefficient manual method. Using a smart city-like traffic control service, this research evaluates the feasibility of implementing a scientific testbed in the cloud. Establishing stateful data-driven IoT services at a scalable scale with real-time limits.

The rest of the paper is organized as follows: The literature reviews are discussed in Sect. 11.2. The suggested system's architecture is described in Sect. 11.3, and the mathematical model of the system also the system's result analysis and methodology are represented in Sects. 11.4 and 11.5. Finally, the study's findings and future directions are presented in the final part.

11.2 Related Works

In our modern-day, the urban population is rapidly rising, which has a significant impact on daily living, particularly transportation. For the rapidly growing population, Cities in rising countries such as Delhi, Dhaka, and many others continue to adopt the old vehicle management technique. According to a report published by the United Nations, around 55% of the world's majority population lives in cities in 2018, with the rate of increase in Asia and Africa expected to reach 90% by 2050. According to recent research, Japan, which holds one of the top ITS [Intelligent Transportation System] jobs, collects real-time data using two ways, which helps to reduce congestion. One method is to implant sensors in roadside barriers, while another is to use smartphones [16].

In such parts of India, to ease traffic congestion, MATLAB, KEIL (Microcontroller coding)-based devices, and surveillance cameras are used [19]. Because the system was difficult to deploy and expensive, some provinces now employ detection of the shortest route and infrared to sensors evaluate traffic density. Temperature and humidity, however, affect the IR sensor. As a result, the result obtained by the IR sensor was not correct. The density of traffic in Pakistan is measured using cameras and sensors. Pakistan regulates traffic signaling based on the data gathered by the sensors. A smoke sensor was also utilized to identify an emergency scenario, such as a fire accident [20]. Rain and fog can wreak havoc on the camera's sensitivity. It's also not economical. In Nepal, 35 traffic crossings use wireless traffic data and CCTV live video. To avoid traffic congestion, the system may modify signal policies and divert traffic [21].

Swathi and her colleagues demonstrated a traffic control scheduling system that determines the shortest and least crowded route. To get information on the density of traffic, sensors are used, which are powered by solar and battery power. As an object approached, sensors continued to transmit infrared light, and assess traffic density, they studied the reflected light from the vehicle. The readings may vary if the temperature and humidity alter [22]. Al-Sakran et al. created a system whose main goals had been to use sensors as well as RFIDs to recognize cars and evaluate their location, then send the information to a central control unit for further processing via a wireless link [23] (Table 11.1).

11.3 Proposed System

Sensors are used in the proposed model described in Fig. 11.1, video surveillance, and RFID tags are placed on the roadside to regulate traffic on road networks. The proposed system (shown in Fig. 11.1) uses sensors, video surveillance, and RFID tags placed on the roadside to regulate traffic on road networks users can also use it to predict traffic congestion on a certain road. There are three layers to the system.

Table 11.1 Different existing approaches

Objectives	S/w / H/w requirements	Techniques	Findings
Compared with the population trend in the biggest urban centers, examine the global trend in the population [15]	Urban population data.	Cellular automata have also been widely used to simulate and predict possible urban development.	By 2050, the proportion of people living in urban areas will reach 68%, up from 55% today The population of urban areas will reach 2.5 billion by 2050
Controlling the traffic on the roads [16]	Sensors, smartphone cameras, traffic light poles, and high-end processors. Sensors like GPS, accelerometer, proximity, Gyro meter, microphone, and camera	ITS techniques, use of sensors like GPS, microphone, WI-Fi, and camera in smartphones can be used to predict the traffic conditions and arrival time of the vehicle at the destination.	Real-time traffic information Route guidance / navigation systems Traffic operations centers Real-time traffic status
Traffic management system (TMS) using SS network in an SMC context [17].	Machine learning, artificial neural network, computer vision, sensors	Mitigating the traffic concern issues by implementing TMS using the SS network. Android app that can monitor the live traffic load / jam during the journey and help the TMS Model to take the best route or decision of changing routes live	Adapted the shape-based detection Focused on its most prominent part, smart transportation
Location information of sensor nodes [18]	Sensors, GPS	Distributed technique for localization of sensor nodes using a few mobile anchor nodes using RSSI.	Mobile anchor nodes provide better accuracy as compared to static anchor nodes for sensor node localization.
A smart traffic control technique for smart cities [19].	The web camera, sensors	Image processing, using Canny Edge detection technique	Smart traffic control technique for smart cities that can be implemented by using image processing Reducing delay time in the traffic lane.

(continued)

Table 11.1 (continued)

Objectives	S/w / H/w requirements	Techniques	Findings
Smart traffic control framework [20]	IoT devise, Cloud computing, s server, storage, sensors	Microcontroller-based IoT technique is used for prediction.	Track the number of vehicles and the traffic congestion at the intersections on a road and rerouting will be done based on the traffic density on the lanes of a road
Using IoT, traffic can be effectively controlled and compared in real-time [21].	Raspberry Pi, Python programming, light emitting diode, ultrasonic sensor/hall effect sensor, radio waves transmitter, radio signal detector	The sensor collects data on the real-time density of vehicles present on the road, and this is the underlying philosophy behind controlling the timing of traffic lights based on current traffic conditions. The data from the sensors are collected and stored in the cloud.	This smart traffic management system can significantly reduce the waiting time and travel time of passengers and emergency vehicles can move without obstructions or barriers, thereby reducing pollution.

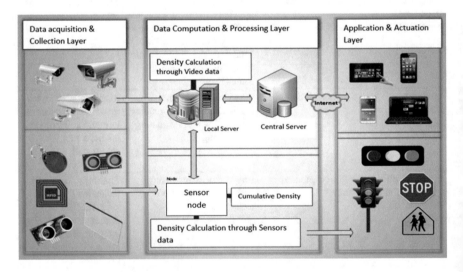

Fig. 11.1 The model of the smart road traffic system

(1) Layer for data capture and gathering.
(2) The layer of Selection and Data Analysis
(3) A layer of Actuation and Utilization.

11.3.1 Layer for Data Capture and Gathering

To identify traffic in the current state of the art, researchers have used ultrasonic waves, RFIDs, video monitoring, and laser beams. All of these sources are good candidates for the proposed system. They include surveillance cameras, ultrasonic sensors, RFIDs, smoke detectors, and flame sensors. Surveillance cameras are the most often used source for detecting road traffic in this field because of their efficiency and ease of maintenance [25–28]. The blob identification method [28] is used on the video stream at the local server because of its speed and noise reduction capabilities. Following traffic detection, a local server sends the density determined by image processing to the required microcontroller.

This technology uses ultrasonic sensors in addition to cameras to improve precision. Sensors are an important component for identifying traffic density in numerous traffic management system applications represented in [24]. It works out the distance by sending out a sound wave at a specific frequency and listening to the reply. This inexpensive sensor can detect distances ranging from 2 to 400 cm [29]. The system uses the formula below to compute the distance.

$$Distance = \left(\frac{(a \times b)}{2} \right) \tag{11.1}$$

where 'a' is represented as sound speed and 'b' defines as the time taken

Figure 11.2 shows IOT-based traffic management, which describes how easy it is to identify a path for an emergency in an ambulance, as well as how traffic violators are identified and transferred to the police. To compute the traffic density, As indicated in Fig. 11.3, three pairs of sensors are embedded on a chord side of a section at a particular distance. The readings of each sensor are either 1 or 0. At the node level, density is calculated by combining the signals from all of the sensors put along that particular road.

$$\sum_{i=1}^{3} (Si) = s_i + s_{i+1} + s_{i+2} \tag{11.2}$$

The pair of ultrasonic sensors is signified as S. The statuses of the sensors are shown in Table 11.2, and the results are as follows:

Where S1, S2, S3 are sensors and C1, C2, C3 are different conditions. Also, L, M, and H are represented as High, Low, and Medium traffic density. The microcontroller uses Table 11.3 to determine cumulative density after receiving data using sensors, as well as video from a local server.

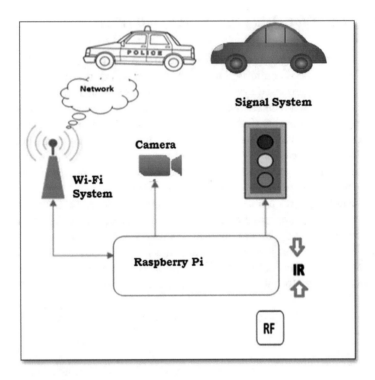

Fig. 11.2 The proposed smart road traffic system

11.3.2   The Layer of Selection and Data Analysis

Based on the present situation, the system regulates traffic flow. In the beginning, respectively traffic signal takes a predetermined time in seconds when there is typical traffic on the road. Each signal goes green for a few seconds, but the other signals at an intersection remain red until all traffic signals have completed their turns. Because the traffic ratio is increasing day by day, our current fixed-time signal control system is not performing properly in this circumstance. The density-based traffic control module must be able to dynamically assign lanes at their times based on traffic density. After Step 1, when the traffic capacity is increased and flow fluctuates, the algorithm calculates the level of density using Table 11.2. A traffic light's time is modified based on the volume of traffic. It is also subjected to the algorithm's traffic control techniques.

Algorithm 1: Traffic Management Algorithm
Phase 1: When there is no emergency vehicle in sight

1. if (TD == H)   //Traffic Density = TD
2. if (RI == Yes)   //Rush Interval = RI
3. Time = $((\alpha \times e^x \times \sin\theta) + \beta) + y$

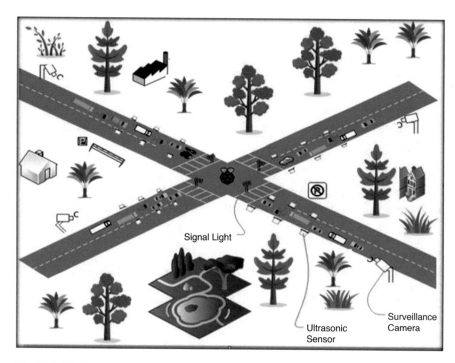

Fig. 11.3 Wireless sensor network in the road traffic system

Table 11.2 Ultrasonic sensors measure shows traffic density

Condition/Sensors	S1	S2	S3	Status
C1	1	0	0	L
C2	1	1	0	M
C3	1	1	1	H

Table 11.3 Cumulative density

Instances	Sensor's result	Camera's result	Traffic density
I1	H	H	H
I2	H	M	H
I3	H	L	M
I4	M	H	H
I5	M	M	M
I6	M	L	M
I7	L	H	M
I8	L	M	M
I9	L	L	L

4. else
5. Time = $(\alpha \times e^x \times \sin\theta) + (\cos\theta \times y) + \beta$
6. else if (RI = =Yes)
7. Time = $(\alpha \times e^x \times \sin\theta) + y$
8. else
9. Time = α

Phase 2: RFID tags are activated when an emergency vehicle is detected.

1. While (vehicle Exits = = True)
2. Time! = 0

Algorithms 2: Vehicle Counter Algorithm
1. Assume that the objects identified by the IR Sensors are automobiles.
2. int $\eta = 0$;   # η is counter
3. int O_1 = false;   // O_1 is hit object
4. int V_1;
5. Step 1: Read the sensor's value (V_1). If a car is spotted, the sensor outputs 0; otherwise, it outputs 1.
6. Step 2: If val == 0, O_1 = false then increment the counter and set O_1 = true.
7. else if val == 1, O_1 = true
8. then set O_1 = false.
9. Step 3: Go to step 1

11.3.3   The Layer of Actuation and Utilization

This layer explains the duration of a green signal from node to traffic light, as well as daily, weekly, monthly, and yearly data to a centralized server's web application for smart traffic control system administration. To begin, the technology uses the regression tree methodology it analyses data recorded on the server-side of a local server to estimate rush intervals, and it communicates this information to the centralized server every day (after 24 h). In the system, a rush interval is specified as thirty minutes. This report is again shown on a user interface connected to a centralized server that manages a smart traffic management system and displays graphs of rush intervals for roadways on a daily, weekly, and monthly basis. Monthly, and yearly basis. Future road design and resource management will benefit from this graphical data.

Second, the server notifies the relevant information to the microcontroller, together once the actuation module recognizes the rush interval, the route id is used. The length of the green signal is adjusted by the decision-making module to the associated traffic signal after receiving the rush interval notification. In today's society, lost time is pricey, and time equals money, knowing the traffic conditions on a given road before traveling on that road is essential, which can be done with the help of a smartphone app. In addition, if smoke or fire is detected on the road, this system can handle the situation. The system uses a mobile application to notify the appropriate department in the region, flame sensors detected a roadside fire, while smoke sensors detected significant smoke in the system.

11.3.4 Component Description of Proposed System

11.3.4.1 HC-SR04 Ultrasonic Sensors

The sensor head of the HC-ultrasonic SR04 creates an ultrasonic pulse and detects the reflected wave from the target. The distance to the target is calculated using the period between emission and reception. Ultrasonic sensors HCSR04 are utilized in this system to assess traffic density on roadways at a frequency of 40 kHz, with a detection range of 2 cm to 400 cm [30].

11.3.4.2 Arduino Mega 2560 Controller

The Arduino Mega 2560 is a microcontroller with 16 analog inputs, 54 digital input/output pins, four UARTs, a 16 MHz crystal oscillator, an ICSP connector, a USB connection, a reset button, and a power jack. It is based on the ATmega2560-family [31].

11.3.4.3 RFID Sensor Module

The TMF RC-522 RFID module recognizes and tracks tags attached to goods using electromagnetic fields. By scanning a person's RFID tag with a non-contact card reader chip that is low-cost and tiny in size, this device detects a signal violation.

11.3.4.4 ESP8266 Wi-Fi Module

The ESP8266 Wi-Fi Module, which is based on TCP/IP, has powerful enough processing capabilities to allow it to be combined with sensors while operating with minimal load. On the server side, the system under control was also used to convey real-time data [32].

11.3.4.5 LED Signal

When IoT devices and sensors are connected to a lighting system, additional capabilities can be provided with a simple user interface. A timer is used to control the traffic LED signals light.

11.3.4.6   IR Sensor

An infrared sensor is an electrical device that uses infrared light to detect environmental features. An infrared sensor can both detect motion and measure the temperature of an object. Almost everything emits some form of infrared heat radiation. These are infrared radiations that are invisible to the naked eye but may be detected by an infrared sensor. The number of vehicles on the route is counted using an infrared sensor.

11.3.5   Software

IoT analytics develops channels for plotting real-time graphs by analyzing real-time traffic data. The Arduino programming language was used to create this work. The data from the sensors is sent with the help of the ESP8266 Wi-Fi module to the server, which is controlled by a microcontroller. Sensor data is stored in a server database for later processing. The Arduino IDE is used to burn the uploaded system code, which is user-friendly and trustworthy. The Traffic Wallet mobile app was created with Android Studio. The proposed Signal prototype model is shown in Fig. 11.4.

11.4   Mathematical Modelling of Systems

This section introduces the suggested smart traffic light system mathematical modelling. Vehicle velocity, vehicle position, and the cost function, all expressed as ordered pairs, dominate the system. The speed of approaching vehicles at the intersection is defined as

$$Ve_i(t) = \left[Ve_i'(t), Ve_i''(t) \right] \tag{11.3}$$

where $Ve_i'(t)$ is the rear endpoint and $Ve_i''(t)$ is the front endpoint

$$Ve_i'(t) = \min\left\{ Ve_i'(t-1) + 1, E_i(t), Ve_{max}'(t) \right\} \tag{11.4}$$

$$Ve_i''(t) = \max\left\{ Ve_i''(t-1) + 1, E_i'(t), Ve_{max}''(t) \right\} \tag{11.5}$$

where,

$Ve_i'''(t-1)$ is the rear endpoint/At step t, the position of the vehicle it's the front end

$E_i'(t)$ is at time step (t), in front of the vehicle (i) there are several empty cells

$Ve_{max}'''(t-1)$ is the rear end/front end maximum vehicle i at the time step t

The vehicles' location,

Fig. 11.4 Proposed prototype model of traffic lights signal module

$hv_i(t) = [hv_i'(t), hv_i''(t)]$ are updated concerning the vehicle's speed:

$$h_i'(t+1) = h_i'(t) + Ve_i'(t) \tag{11.6}$$

$$h_i''(t+1) = h_i''(t) + Ve_i''(t) \tag{11.7}$$

where,

$h_i'^{/''}(t+1)$ is the predicted rear endpoint/At step $t + 1$, the position of vehicle i's front end.

$h_i'^{/''}(t)$ is the current rear endpoint/At step t, the position of vehicle i's front end.

The cost of alternative control actions is determined using a cost function, and choose and perform the control action that has the lowest cost. The cost is expressed in time delay intervals.

$c(\alpha) = \left[c(\alpha)', c(\alpha)'' \right]$ and it is derived by:

$$c'(\alpha) = \min\left\{ \sum_i \sum_i n_i'(t), \sum_i \sum_i n_i''(t) \right\} \tag{11.8}$$

where,

$$n_i'(t) = \begin{cases} 1, Ve_i'(t) = 0, \\ 0, otherwise \end{cases}$$

$$n_i^{''}(t) = \begin{cases} 1, Ve_i^{''}(t) = 0, \\ 0, otherwise \end{cases}$$

11.5 Results and Discussion

The wireless sensor nodes, which are made up of sensors, are the system's first and most important component. The sensors interact with the physical world, such as the presence or absence of cars, and the data from the sensors is sent to the central microcontroller by the local server. This system involves in each direction, the 4×2 sensor nodes array. This denotes four tiers of traffic and two lanes in each direction. Ultrasonic sensors provide information based on a vehicle's proximity. The sensor nodes send data to a central microcontroller stationed at each intersection at predetermined intervals. The signal is received by the microcontroller, which calculates which road and which lane should be used based on traffic density. The Microcontroller's computed data is then sent to a local server via Wi-Fi and cloud connections. The data acquired by the controller is used by the controller to execute Intelligent Traffic Routing. The fundamental goal of this system is to acquire information from moving cars via WSN to provide them with a clear path to their destinations, and traffic signals should alter automatically to offer these cars a clear path.

The design was constructed to demonstrate the applicability of our suggested strategy. The suggested algorithm's efficiency was tested using real-world traffic data in a series of experiments. Vehicle detection was utilized to track and calculate traffic density, as seen in Fig. 11.4. When a road's traffic density surpasses a predetermined level, Until the situation on the road returns to normal, the system suspends normal activities and displays the green signal. Data was sent to the cloud, as well as a local and central server, in a real-time system.

In addition, as discussed in Sect. 11.3, a traffic update interface was created to allow authorities to make real-time and long-term decisions about traffic. Figure 11.5 depicts statistical traffic data, such as the vehicles passing on a certain road during a given time.

Methodologies, the traffic lights inside this system are LEDs, and the vehicle tracking sensor is an ultrasonic sensor. These blocks are physically connected to the microcontroller. Based on the distances measured by the ultrasonic sensor and the time between those measurements, the Microcontroller calculates the number of cars on the street of the intersection it is monitoring. A traffic light controller is a microcontroller that receives sensor data and switches between green, yellow, and red traffic lights. The microcontroller communicates the number of cars to the local server every minute. The serial port on the microcontroller is used for this communication. The data is exchanged between the local server and the cloud server to be able to predict changes in traffic signal timing, this information is transmitted through Wi-Fi. The cloud server, in particular, uses an equation to compute the time interval of LEDs required for smooth traffic flow based on the data collected (number of cars). After that, the estimated time is compared to the current LEDs' actual time. The server then makes a choice. The green time will be increased if the computed time is less than the current true green time; else, it will be decreased.

11.5.1   Different Lanes and Signal View

LANE 1 has a green signal and is currently open in Pt. – 1, LANE 4 has a yellow signal and is ready to go, however, LANE 2 and LANE 3 are blocked. Because the number of vehicles in LANE 3 exceeds the threshold value, the route leading to LANE 2 of Pt. – 1 is blocked in Pt. – 2. As a result, they are rerouted through different lanes. (Assume the present intersection is point 1 and the previous intersection is point 2.) Figure 11.5 depicts a comprehensive view of the lane (Figs. 11.6, 11.7 and 11.8).

Lane 1 has a green signal, while the other lanes have a red signal.
Lane 2 is open with a green signal, while the remaining lanes are closed with a red
    signal in the diagram above
Lane 3 has a green light, while the other lanes have a red signal, and Lane 4 will
    receive a green signal automatically.

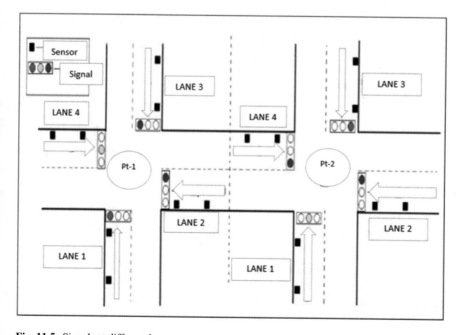

Fig. 11.5 Signals at different lanes

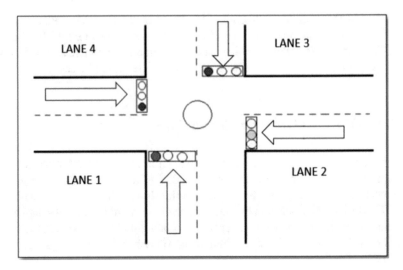

Fig. 11.6 Signal at lane 1

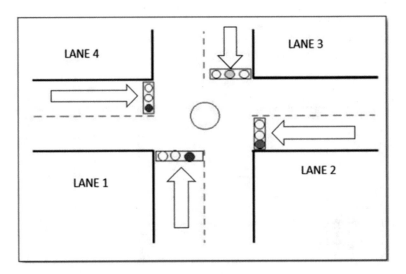

Fig. 11.7 Signal at lane 2

11.5.2 Sequence Diagram of Signal Control System (Fig. 11.9)

The suggested system improves time-based monitoring and hence offers various advantages over the current technique, including fewer accidents, cheaper fuel costs, and remote controllability, to name a few. The proposed technology is designed to manage traffic congestion and keep track of the number of vehicles on the route. The system administrator has access to the local server and can utilize it to keep the system up to date.

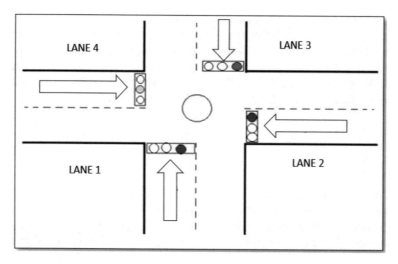

Fig. 11.8 Signal at lane 3

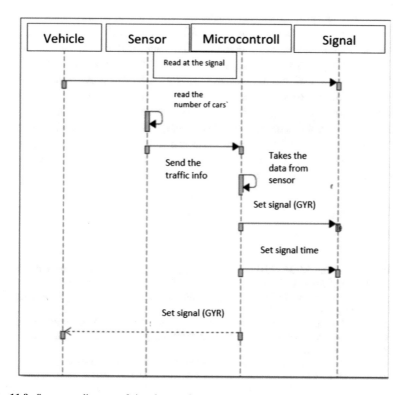

Fig. 11.9 Sequence diagram of signal control system

A real-time traffic monitoring system based on ultrasonic sensors can detect traffic density on highways. When there is a lot of frequency, it is a green path, and when the density is low, it is red. The technology may also detect users who break the rules and determine whether or not their license has expired. The system can immediately take action against such a guilty person by issuing a fine. The data was transferred to and stored on a cloud server for further analysis.

11.6 Conclusion

The Smart Traffic Management System was made possible by merging various IoT hardware components. The Internet of Things (IoT) is being used to improve traffic flow by giving each traffic light changing timings based on the number of vehicles on the route. To successfully deal with traffic congestion and conduct re-routing at road crossings, the Smart Traffic Management System is used. This study offers a practical solution for the fast-growing traffic flow, in major urban areas, which is increasing every day, and current traffic management systems have some difficulties in successfully controlling current traffic. A smart traffic management system is introduced that uses the most up-to-date traffic management technique to improve the efficiency and effectiveness of road traffic control. It communicates with the local server to adjust signal timing automatically based on traffic density on the specific roadside, allowing it to better regulate traffic flow than ever before. Because the system continues to work even if a central or local server crashes, the decentralized technique optimizes and boosts efficiency. In the event of a catastrophe, the centralized server notifies the nearest fire brigade, ensuring human safety as soon as possible. A user can also find out how much traffic is expected on a particular road, saving time spent stuck in traffic. Higher authorities can use the technology to help with road design, which helps with resource optimization.

References

1. Alli, A. A., & Alam, M. M. (2019). SecOFF-FCIoT: Machine learning based secure offloading in Fog-Cloud of things for smart city applications. *Internet of Things, 7*, 100070.
2. https://www.intelligentcommunity.org/index.php?submenu=Awards&src=gendocs&ref=Smart21&category=Events
3. Yigitcanlar, T., Desouza, K. C., Butler, L., & Roozkhosh, F. (2020). Contributions and risks of artificial intelligence (AI) in building smarter cities: Insights from a systematic review of the literature. *Energies, 13*(6), 1473.
4. Raj, E. F. I., Appadurai, M., Darwin, S., & Rani, E. F. I. (2022). Internet of Things (IoT) for sustainable smart cities. In *Internet of things* (pp. 163–188). CRC Press.
5. T.C.G on behalf of the Global eSustainability Initiative. (2010). *The ICT behind cities of the future*. SMART 2020.

6. Al-Turjman, F., Zahmatkesh, H., & Shahroze, R. (2022). An overview of security and privacy in smart cities' IoT communications. *Transactions on Emerging Telecommunications Technologies, 33*(3), e3677.
7. Tzioutziou, A., & Xenidis, Y. (2021). A study on the integration of resilience and smart city concepts in urban systems. *Infrastructures, 6*(2), 24.
8. Zeeshan, K., Hämäläinen, T., & Neittaanmäki, P. (2022). Internet of things for sustainable smart education: An overview. *Sustainability, 14*(7), 4293.
9. Bhushan, B., Sahoo, C., Sinha, P., & Khamparia, A. (2021). Unification of Blockchain and Internet of Things (BIoT): Requirements, working model, challenges and future directions. *Wireless Networks, 27*(1), 55–90.
10. Arora, A., Kaur, A., Bhushan, B., & Saini, H. (2019). *Security concerns and future trends of internet of things* (Vol. 1, pp. 891–896). 2019 2nd International Conference on Intelligent Computing, Instrumentation and Control Technologies (ICICICT), IEEE.
11. Elhadad, A., Alanazi, F., Taloba, A. I., & Abozeid, A. (2022). Fog computing service in the healthcare monitoring system for managing the real-time notification. *Journal of Healthcare Engineering, 2022*, 1–11.
12. Mangla, M., Kumar, A., Mehta, V., Bhushan, M., & Mohanty, S. N. (Eds.). (2022). *Real-life applications of the internet of things: Challenges, applications, and advances.* CRC Press.
13. Paranjothi, A., Khan, M. S., Zeadally, S., Pawar, A., & Hicks, D. (2019). GSTR: Secure multi-hop message dissemination in connected vehicles using social trust model. *Internet of Things, 7*, 1–16.
14. Rout, S. K., Rath, A. K., & Bhagabati, C. (2017). Energy efficient dynamic node localization technique in wireless sensor networks. *Indian Journal of Science and Technology, 10*(15), 1–8.
15. U. News. (2018, May 16). *"68% of the world population projected to live in urban areas by 2050, says UN,"* ed. New York – USA
16. Singh, G., Bansal, D., & Sofat, S. (2014). Intelligent transportation system for developing countries – A survey. *International Journal of Computer Applications, 85*, 34–38.
17. Jain, S., Kumar, A., & Priyadharshini, M. (2019). Smart city: Traffic management system using smart sensor network. *Journal of Physics: Conference Series, 1362*(1), 012129. IOP Publishing.
18. Rout, S. K., Mehta, A., Swain, A. R., Rath, A. K., & Lenka, M. R. (2015). Algorithm aspects of dynamic coordination of beacons in localization of wireless sensor networks. In *2015 IEEE International Conference on Computer Graphics, Vision and Information Security (CGVIS)* (pp. 157–162). IEEE.
19. Bhardwaj, V., Rasamsetti, Y., & Valsan, V. (2022). Traffic control system for Smart City using image processing. In *AI and IoT for Smart City applications* (pp. 83–99). Springer.
20. Singha, H., Nath, K. K., Basumatary, B., & Swargiary, J. (2019). *Smart traffic management system using Internet of Things (IoT).* PhD diss., Central Institute of Technology.
21. Varshney, T., Sharma, N., Kaushik, I., & Bhushan, B. (2019). Architectural model of security threats & their countermeasures in IoT. In *2019 International Conference on Computing, Communication, and Intelligent Systems (ICCCIS)* (pp. 424–429). IEEE.
22. Swathi, K., Sivanagaraju, V., Manikanta, A. K. S., & Kumar, S. D. (2016). Traffic density control and accident indicator using WSN. *Traffic, 2*(4), 2455–3778.
23. Al-Sakran, H. O. (2015). Intelligent traffic information system based on the integration of Internet of Things and Agent technology. *International Journal of Advanced Computer Science and Applications (IJACSA), 6*(2), 37–43.
24. Rout, S. K., Rath, A. K., & Rout, B. R. (2016). Efficient energy utilization and node localization in dynamic DV-hop algorithm for wireless sensor networks. *Indian Journal of Science and Technology, 9*, 30.
25. Nidhi, A. S., & Agrawal, D. (2015). Intelligent real time traffic controller using image processing – A survey. *International Journal of Science and Research (IJSR) ISSN (Online), 4*(4), 2319–7064.

26. Pandit, V., Doshi, J., Mehta, D., Mhatre, A., & Janardhan, A. (2014). Smart traffic control system using image processing. *International Journal of Emerging Trends & Technology in Computer Science (IJETTCS), 3*(1), 2278–6856.
27. Sukhadia, A., Upadhyay, K., Gundeti, M., Shah, S., & Shah, M. (2020). Optimization of smart traffic governance system using artificial intelligence. *Augmented Human Research, 5*(1), 1–14.
28. Mehboob, F., Abbas, M., Jiang, R., Tahir, M. A., Al-Maadeed, S., & Bouridane, A. (2016). Automated vehicle density estimation from raw surveillance videos. In *2016 SAI Computing Conference (SAI)* (pp. 1024–1030). IEEE.
29. Mahalank, S. N., Malagund, K. B., & Banakar, R. M. (2016, March). Device to device interaction analysis in IoT based smart traffic management system: An experimental approach. In *2016 Symposium on Colossal Data Analysis and Networking (CDAN)* (pp. 1–6). IEEE.
30. Electronic Wings. (2018). Ultrasonic Module HC-SR04. [Online]. Available: http://www.electronicwings.com/sensorsmodules/ultrasonic-module-hc-sr04. Accessed 23 Sep 2018.
31. ARDUINO MEGA 2560 REV3. (2018). [Online]. Available: https://store.arduino.cc/usa/arduino-mega-2560-rev3. Accessed 23 Sep 2018
32. Sethi, R., Bhushan, B., Sharma, N., Kumar, R., & Kaushik, I. (2021). Applicability of industrial IoT in diversified sectors: Evolution, applications and challenges. In *Multimedia Technologies in the Internet of Things Environment* (pp. 45–67). Springer.

Chapter 12
Emersion and Immersion of Technology in the Development of Smart Cities: A Bibliometric Analysis

Manisha Gupta, Bhawna Choudhary, and Deergha Sharma

Abstract The emergence and immersion of technology are essential for creating smart cities. Therefore, technology is vital in developing sustainable, smart, and resilient cities. Using cutting-edge technologies like cloud computing, blockchain, and artificial intelligence, the concept of a "smart city" envisions a future in which smart gadgets execute various applications with minimal resource consumption. The study uses bibliometric analysis using software R studio and package biblioshiny. The study incorporates publications from the Scopus database from the last few years using keywords like smart cities, technology, Information Communication Technology, Artificial Intelligence, and digitalization. The study is an attempt to answer questions. Firstly, what are the literature characteristics produced during the last two years? Secondly, to identify the most relevant keywords related to technology were highlighted by different researchers in their study about smart cities, and lastly, to create a path that can illustrate the emerging and immersing technologies in developing smart cities. The study's findings would be purposeful for the agencies developing technology to develop sustainable smart cities.

Keywords Smart cities · Technology · Bibliometric · Biblioshiny · ICT

12.1 Introduction

The investigation of the relationship between information technologies and communication technologies and the urbanized ecosystem has been continuously studied since 1992 with the concern for "smart city" in the academic and industrial

M. Gupta (✉) · B. Choudhary
School of Business Studies, Sharda University, Greater Noida, India
e-mail: Manisha.Gupta1@sharda.ac.in; Bhawna.choudhary@sharda.ac.in

D. Sharma
NorthCap University, Gurugram, Haryana, India

research domain. An incredible increase in this area of research related to smart cities and related publications has been seen in recent years [1]. Citizens of a "smart city" might benefit from instantaneous, collaborative, and smart services due to the integration of advanced processes such as advance monitoring, sensing, communication, and control technology [2]. The definition of the smart city is *"a smart city is that part of urban place where technology based solutions are applicable in all works of life new technologies and innovation are applied to make the processes sustainable and develop high quality of life."* The smart city is essentially an idea. Practitioners and academics are still grappling with how to define it clearly and consistently. An easy way to explain what constitutes a "smart city" is to say that it is a place where old networks and services have been modernized to be more adaptable, efficient, and long-lasting by integrating digital and information technologies. Living in a smart city has several advantages, including being more environmentally friendly, safer, quicker, and more familiar. A smart city comprises several elements, including smart technology, smart infrastructure, smart transportation, smart energy, and smart medical care. These factors contribute to the intelligence and effectiveness of cities. Through the use of information and communication technology, it is possible to construct smart cities, Information communication Technology (ICT). Big data (BD), an emerging technology paradigm strongly tied to the Internet of Things (IoT), makes smart cities more responsive and efficient.

Smart cities are able to give the best level of services to its residents, which can improve the overall quality of life in a variety of spheres, including medical care, public transportation, educational possibilities, and the amount of energy that is consumed. The idea of a "smart city" is just in its infancy as far as urban planning is concerned, and despite the exciting possibilities it offers, there are an increasing number of safety concerns associated with it. Blockchain technology is the tools that are being imbibed to play a large part in the cocreation of smart cities. Blockchain technology's many desired properties, including audibility, transparency, immutability, and decentralization, make it an ideal candidate for this role [3]. The structure of a smart city is made up of multiple layers, the first of which is the perception layer, followed by the network layer, and then the application layer. If implemented correctly, these layers have the potential to make the world of the future more appreciable and measurable, more interconnected and interoperable, and more intelligent [4].

There have been many publications in the form of articles and research studies. Still, the researchers failed to define smart cities clearly and could not give an appropriate definition of smart cities [5]. ICT, which stands for information and communication technology, is a reoccurring element in depictions of smart cities. This technology acts as a catalyst to facilitate the growth of cities, enhance municipal services, and broaden stakeholder access to data. Rapidly emerging smart cities worldwide are city-wide investments in information and communications technology with the goals of fostering technological innovation, assisting in the development of new industries, bolstering the economy, preserving an enhanced quality of life and sustainable ecosystem [6].

This exploratory study intends to present a detailed picture of what transpired throughout the last decade of research studies on smart cities. It leads to an improved understanding of the beginnings and progressive expansion of this rapidly expanding study issue and its conceptual structure about the technologies that have emerged as the framer for creating the infrastructure of smart cities. The study tries to investigate and answer the following research questions.

- An overview of the literature produced during the last few years about smart cities and the technologies associated with smart city development.
- What are the key countries and organizations contributing to researching smart cities?
- What keywords have been dominatingly used globally in research studies related to smart cities?
- Is there an interpretation of the smart-city notion that has emerged due to their Research study investigation?
- To study the immersion of the smart city concept globally.

To investigate the aforementioned research issue, the current research makes use of bibliometric analysis carried out with the 'Biblioshiny' package that is included with R studio. The purpose of this article is to identify major actors who contribute to the intellectual foundation of the study area at all levels, from the most comprehensive to narrow, specifically from the country level down to the individual Author and paper level. Simultaneously, the current research study examines the evolution of significant technologies associated with smart cities. The entire chapter is organized into sections, namely the literature review. The review of the literature section deals with an elaboration of past literature published in the domain of smart city technologies. The data collection and research methodology further highlight the research design adopted for the current study. The analysis section describes literature published globally, annual scientific production, Bradford's law analysis, journal ranking, core and most cites article analysis, and word cloud analysis to highlight the key themes emerging in smart city technologies.

12.2   Literature Review

The current literature review highlights the conceptual attributes of a smart city and how technological interventions have enhanced the existence of a smart city. Smarter Cities are metropolitan areas, particularly the urban area with a high population density, to maximize the operation of city services by utilizing operational data, data resulting from congestion in traffic, the consumption of electricity per household data, and incidents related to public safety. The basic notions are Intelligent, instrumented, and networked. When data is collected from real-world sources in real-time, it is referred to as Instrumented. Interconnected refers to incorporating these data into computing platforms and exchanging such data among the many city services. This strategy makes it possible for city services to be adapted to the actions of residents, which in turn makes it possible to make the most efficient use of the available physical infrastructure and resources. Some examples include keeping track of the amount of energy and water consumption with the help of sensors and developing technologies to control the wastage [7]. The ability to aggregate and abstract heterogeneous resources according to tailored thing-like semantics enables the Things as a Service paradigm, or more accurately, a "Cloud of Things." In Future Internet efforts, sensor networks will play a more significant role, particularly in creating smarter cities. More intelligent sensors will be the peripheral aspects of a future ICT environment that is more complicated [8]. There is a requirement of multidimensional components to underpinning the smart city concept and the most prominent factors for a successful smart city effort are determined in this study; the strategic alignment with the three possible dimensions of smart city namely technology, people and institution the authors suggested strategic principles aligned with the three primary dimensions (technology, people, and institutions) of smart city [9]. The transformation of smart cities from traditional to most modern technology driven can only be possible with the help of Information Communication Technology (ICT). This will help improve public services, efficiency, and sustainability in various fields related to future urban environments. These fields include transportation and mobility, management of supply chains, consumption of natural resources, public services, citizen engagement, business centres with high added value, and government, amongst others [10]. Technology is indeed is regarded as the lifeline of smart city initiatives because it can significantly impact other factors like people, governance, and the economy [11]. Big data is unquestionably enhancing our understanding of the functioning of smart cities. Big data technology not only enhances the knowledge of how smart cities function but also provides certain creative and innovative platforms for social interaction [12]. The equipping of cities with digital devices and infrastructure that produce "big data," also known as "smart cities." According to advocates of smart cities, such data makes it possible to study urban life and new forms of metropolitan government in real-time. It also provides the raw material for imagining and putting into practice cities that are more efficient, sustainable, competitive, productive, open, and transparent [13]. The creation of all-inclusive, standardized, and shareable geographic data models will have the accessibility of utility networks as their primary goal. Every day, the construction activities for utility networks like energy supply, household drinking water, cooking gas, sewage and irrigation, and telecom communication networks need to be meticulously supervised to ensure that the enormous amounts of resources and labour that are involved are utilized to their full potential [14]. An essential purpose of smart cities is to meet the needs of residents economically and efficiently. It is anticipated and most evident that with an increase in technological interventions, there would be major offering in the services which would witness the improved quality, cost reduction, and decrease in adverse environmental impacts; These services would include electronic enabled banking services, commerce facility, and intelligent transport traffic management system. Apart from these services, the government will focus on public administration, safety, and civil protection [15]. The development of the most cutting-edge examples of smart cities is now within reach thanks to the most recent and inventive applications of information and communication technology [16]. In today's world, the goal of smart cities is to effectively manage all aspects of city life, including increasing urbanisation, preserving a green environment, reducing energy consumption, and improving residents' lifestyles. The goal of this approach is to give individuals a greater capacity for effectively adapting to and making use of all of the latest developments in information and communication technology (ICT). The primary goal is to enhance the fundamental infrastructure of the cities so that residents can enjoy an improved standard of living. Tools and technology like machine learning (ML) algorithms, Deep Reinforcement Learning (DRL), and Artificial Intelligence (AI) are the key components for the creation of smart cities [17]. The rapid increase in the global population, in combination with the ongoing process of urbanization, poses a threat to the cities' ability to maintain their status as economically and ecologically viable places to live. To this end, the idea of a "Smart City" has been floated, which refers to a municipality that makes strategic use of current information and communications technology (ICT) to develop a more environmentally friendly urban environment and enhance the quality of life for its residents. Nevertheless, there are increasing concerns regarding safety in smart cities. Because of its advantageous characteristics, such as audibility, transparency, immutability, and decentralization, blockchain technology is a powerful tool that can effectively address the challenges outlined [18].

12.2.1 Smart Cities Concepts

A smart city is one that is technologically enabled, connected, and adaptable to address the environmental, social, and economic challenges of the twenty-first century. Within the context of a "smart city," "advanced technologies" and "intelligent networks" are the essential enablers that make it possible for the city to operate efficiently. Real-time interoperability is essential for key aspects of the ecosystem that makes up a smart city, such as the city's extensive physical infrastructure and the electronic services provided by the local government [19]. Many generations of technology, each of which developed in their own way and at their own pace, have contributed to the evolution of city infrastructure. The use of contemporary digital technologies presents the possibility of striking a healthy equilibrium between the social, environmental, and economic opportunities that will be made available through the planning, design, and construction of smart cities. Initiatives that rely on technology to create cities that are more integrated, sustainable, informed, and managed are referred to as "smart cities." Other names for smart cities include intelligent cities and knowledge cities [20]. Blockchain technology for municipal management, as well as overall process efficiency optimization and integration, with the goal of creating smarter and more sustainable cities [21]. The technologies that are relatively new, which refers to as a recommendation for the implementation in a city to constitute it as a smart city these are, Drones, the Internet of Things

(IoT), clouds, software as a service (SaaS), big data, 3D scanning, wearable technologies, virtual and augmented realities (VR and AR), artificial intelligence (AI), and robotics. Hence these can be stated as emerging technologies [22]. When the components such as social, environmental, and economic development when are integrated via devolved procedures for the purpose of manging assets, resources and urban system processes in real time, a city is said to be smart [23].

12.3 Data Collection and Research Methodology

For analysis, the database was Scopus timeline restricted from 2010 to 2022. The search query to acquire extensive data was limited to the following terms' Smart cities', 'sustainable cities,' 'technologies, and 'Digitalization,' all singular and plural versions were considered. The final search query resulted in 3326 publications relating to smart cities, digitalization, and emerging technologies for smart cities.

In contemporary academic research, the application of bibliometrics is a vital tool and the R-tool for comprehensive science mapping analysis. Several topics have received more attention due to the expanding body of literature and its relative longevity. Biblioshiny is a program that may be used in an environment that uses R. It is designed for users who are not proficient in programming. It offers various customization options, including detecting sources, published documents, the Authors who contributed to the relevant study, conceptual framework depending on the theme deducted, social and network structure creation, etc. [24].

12.4 Analysis

The present section has recapitulated literature pertaining to 'smart city, a discussion on scientific annual production, briefing on Bradford's Law and core article analysis and application of thematic analysis for preparing thematic map and word cloud.

12.4.1 Description of Literature Published Globally

The table below (Table 12.1) demonstrates the description related to the literature on 'smart city' characteristics that the study initially grasps before proceeding with the investigation. It was eventually discovered in 2000 publications that contained 5862 author keywords between 2020 and 2022. Thus, 8846 authors contributed to the creation of these works.

Table 12.1 Important and relevant Information about the dataset used

Description	Result
Timespan	2020:2022
Sources from journals, books, etc.	811
Total documents extracted	2000
Publication (per year Avg)	1.13
Avg citations (documents)	6.654
Avg citations every year per document	2.679
References	182,245
Appearance (ID) keywords plus	7115
Appearance (DE) Author's keywords	5862
Total authors contributions	8846

Source: Author self-calculated by Vos viewer

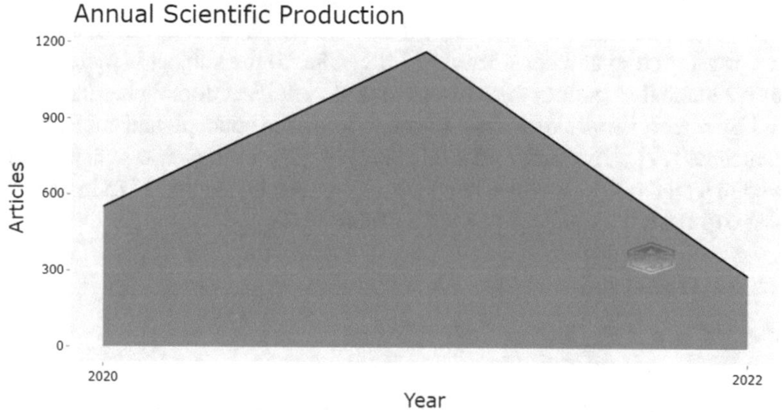

Fig. 12.1 Annual scientific production. (Source: Author self-calculated by Vos viewer)

12.4.2 Scientific Annual Production

The literature published (Fig. 12.1) on the smart city with related keywords like digitalization, sustainable city, and technologies for smart cities. The data and the graphical representation showcase that the maximum literature production was from 2020 to 2022. There has been a peak in 2021 for the literature on the topic, with the average annual publication output for 2021 being 1165. Further, in the year 2020, the publication score was 551, and in the year 2022, which is at the initial months of 2022, the average publication was 284.

Triple analysis of the Scopus database extracted from 2020 to 2022, describe a relation between the Author's keywords (left credentials), Country of publication (middle credentials), and Affiliation or origin institution (Right credentials). The Triple analysis shows that the United Kingdom collaborates with most affiliated institutions on the study theme, namely smart cities. Countries like Iran, the USA, and India have also contributed significantly to studying smart city domain.

12.4.3   Bradford's Law Analysis

A law that describes declining returns and scattering is known as Bradford's Law of Scattering. In 1948, Bradford came up with the idea. Bradford stated that there are limited productive journals for subject areas he also further mentioned that a greater number of more middling producers, and a larger number with continuously diminishing production." Bradford is credited with developing the notion." [25] For every particular topic or subject area, the top most (also known as Zone 1 or core) indicates the most randomly mentioned journals in the literature associated with that subject and that are, as a result, most likely to be of highest interest to academics working in the discipline. The journals with an average number of citations are included in the middle third (Zone 2). At the same time, the long tail of articles that are never referred to and considered of little value to the subject is included in the tail or we name it as bottom third (Zone 3) [26]. A subject domain has been characterized by researchers using lexical concept, semantic concept, and subject scattering concepts [27]., The Bradford's law analysis [28] in this case, when executed, showed in a total of 812 journals in which 25 journals lie in zone 1 175 in zone 2 and the rest 614 from the category of zone 3 (Table 12.2).

12.4.4   Core Article Analysis Globally

On analysing the top 15 most cited article globally related to topics in smart city, sustainable city, and technology associated with smart city evolution. The top-cited article stated that substantial technological advancements had converted several manual jobs and processes where humans had reached their physical limits since the Industrial Revolution. In a broad spectrum of industrial, intellectual, and social applications, artificial intelligence (AI) has the same disruptive potential. As the new AI technological age progresses, recent advancements in algorithmic machine learning and autonomous decision-making open up new avenues for innovation [29]. further, the second most cited article also demonstrated the there is an important relationship between Artificial intelligence and sustainable development goals. The advent of Artificial Intelligence and its growth has increasingly impacted the globally stated Sustainable Development Goals [30].

Table 12.2   Based on Bradford's Law the journal ranking

Source	Ranking	Frequency	Cumulative frequency	Zone
Sustainability (Switzerland)	1	202	202	Zone 1
Energies	2	57	259	Zone 1
Journal of cleaner production	3	48	307	Zone 1
Technological forecasting and social change	4	37	344	Zone 1
Applied sciences (Switzerland)	5	35	379	Zone 1
Acm international conference proceeding series	6	25	404	Zone 1
Lecture notes in networks and systems	7	25	429	Zone 1
E3s web of conferences	8	22	451	Zone 1
IEEE access	9	20	471	Zone 1
Journal of business research	10	17	488	Zone 1
Sensors	11	15	503	Zone 1
Sustainable cities and society	12	15	518	Zone 1
Technology in society	13	15	533	Zone 1
Environmental science and pollution research	14	14	547	Zone 1
Research for development	15	14	561	Zone 1
Energy research and social science	16	13	574	Zone 1
Renewable and sustainable energy reviews	18	13	600	Zone 1
Electronics (Switzerland)	19	11	659	Zone 1
Energy policy	20	11	670	Zone 1
The smart and sustainable built environment	21	11	681	Zone 2

Source: Author self-calculated by Vos viewer

12.4.5   Thematic Analysis Using Thematic Map and Word Cloud

Co-word analysis creates keyword clusters. They are regarded as themes, the density (y-axis) and centrality (X-axis) of which can be utilized for categorizing refrains and demonstrating it using a two-dimensional graphic. A thematic map is a highly innate figure that enables us to investigate topics as per the quadrant in which they lie, as follows: (1) In the upper -right window motor themes are located, (2) fundamental themes are located in the lower-right quadrant, (3) In the lower left corner quadrant if we see it clearly shows the emerging or vanishing themes, and (4) extraordinarily specialized or niche themes are located in the upper-left quadrant [31].

Figure 12.2 represents the thematic graph for the data set used in the study; as per the relevance degree of centrality, the themes that emerged as the important ones are the smart city, sustainable development, sustainability, and industry. The overall effect of the theme can be stated by analysing the density. As per Fig. 12.2, the

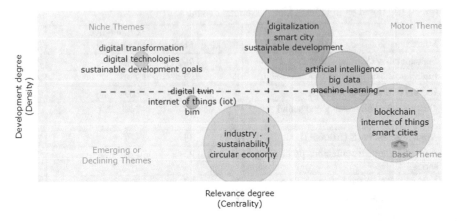

Fig. 12.2 Thematic map analysis. (Source: Author self-calculated by Vos viewer)

themes related to sustainability, smart city, circular technology, and emerging tech-nologies are pretty prevalent. As the thematic map analysis draws themes and sub-themes, the quadrant first represents the motor theme, showing a development momentum. The quadrant second, named as niche theme, showcases research topics that are well established but are relevantly niche as a topic to be researched in the concerned area of study. Quadrant third is related to the emerging themes in the concerned research domain, and quadrant four specifies the basic theme of the data-set, which refers to the primary research domain of the concerned study.

Table 12.3 demonstrates the cluster, theme, and the important keywords associ-ated with the cluster. As per the analysis, the emerging themes that have been reported are sustainability, circular economy, big data analytics, and smart manufac-turing [32]. The basic theme as per the analysis is the Internet of things, blockchain, smart cities Information communication Technologies [33]. The analysis's niche themes comprise digital transformation, sustainable development goals, and digital technologies [34].

Technology is a critical driving force in the quest for sustainability and the implementation of smart city operations. Technology has allowed us to digitize all of our daily tasks. Technology also makes it possible to provide services in elec-tronic commerce, banking services, education, entertainment, big data analysis, smart vehicles, and energy-efficient household equipment, among others [35]. The emerging technologies associated with smart city development are notified in the cluster and theme analysis Table 12.3 above.

Table 12.3 Cluster, theme, and keywords of thematic analysis

Cluster	Theme	Keywords associated with cluster
Industry Sustainability Circular economy	Emerging theme	Industry4.0, sustainability, circular economy, big data analytics, digital technologies, smart manufacturing
Blockchain Internet of things Smart cities	Basic theme	Blockchain, Internet of things, smart cities, digitalization, IoT, ICT, supply chain management
Artificial intelligence Big data Machine learning	Motor theme	Artificial intelligence, big data, machine learning, smart grid, energy efficacy, digitalization, deep learning
Digitalization Smart city Sustainable development	Motor theme	Digitalization, smart city, sustainable development, innovation, technology- governance
Digital twin Internet of things BIM	Emerging theme	Digital twin, internet of things, cybersecurity, virtual reality, artificial intelligence, augmented reality.
Digital transformation Digital technologies SDGs	Niche theme	Digital transformation, digital technologies, sustainable development goals

Source: Author self-calculated by Vos viewer

12.4.6 Word Cloud

Visual representations of word frequency are known as "word clouds." The larger the word appears in the resulting graphic, the more frequently it appears in the analysed text. In recent years, word clouds have become increasingly popular as an easy way to highlight the main points in a piece of writing [36]. The content of the Author's keywords has been visualized with the use of these tools and represented in Fig. 12.3.

The word cloud analysis of the Author's keyword shown in (Fig. 12.3) highlights the term like smart city, innovation, sustainability, Internet of things, artificial intelligence automation, digitalization, circular economy, and many more are the main keywords on which the majority of literature have been published in the past couple of years globally.

Creating a smart city is a novel idea. Smart cities can be built thanks to the rapid advancement of new technology. However, as the review of the literature demonstrates [37] the rapid advancement in technology has made the concept of a smart city evolve and adaptive to a large extent. Figure 12.4 illustrates the emerging technology-related words that have been documented by authors globally, which are an integral part of developing a smart city. These are undoubtedly industry 4.0, which is part of smart manufacturing, artificial intelligence, and blockchain

Fig. 12.3 Word cloud representing Author's Keywords. (Source-Author self-calculated by Vos viewer)

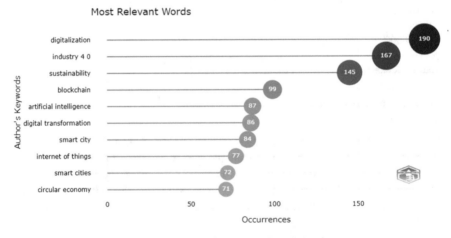

Fig. 12.4 Frequency of Author's keyword. (Source: Author self-calculated by Vos viewer)

technology. The technology behind blockchain is one of the many promising technologies that can provide many valuable services to the people who utilize them. It is an immutable, programmable digital register primarily intended for digital currencies like Bitcoin. It aims to record virtual assets with some value, and it was designed to do so [38]. Cities are increasingly reliant on specialized technologies to address difficulties relating to society, environment, morphology, and many other relevant topics. This possibility is given a great deal of support by the recently developed idea of smart cities, which stimulates the incorporation of sensors and Big Data using the Internet of Things (IoT) [39]. The recent influx of data carries new economic prospects and new opportunities for the planning and administration of urban areas. While the processing of large amounts of data using artificial intelligence (AI) has the potential to make significant contributions to the urban fabric, the sustainability and liveability components of the problem must not be ignored in favour of the technological ones [40]. Recent advances in digital technology are making it possible for cities to go through transformations that will streamline intelligent services and introduce new products. The process of living, working, collaborating, and communicating for people and other stakeholders have been significantly altered due to digitization. This transformative change is intertwined with all information systems and procedures vital to providing services. Despite this, however, the digital transition opens up possibilities for the development of smart cities. The management of data integration and complexity is still difficult for municipal governments [41].

12.5 Conclusion

Based on articles 2000 retrieved from the Scopus database, the current study attempts bibliometric study to review the literature published in technology support for developing smart cities. Based on the analysis using bibiloshiny as the tool to perform bibliometrics, some of the valuable conclusions in this study are as follows.

Firstly, the descriptive statistics of the study demonstrate that the technologies in smart cities are the emerging area in which the researchers are showing interest in publications and witness the topic as the emerging topic of research. There have been leading publications in the area in the year 2021. As per the analysis done using Bradford's law, 812 journals were extracted from the dataset used in the study, out of which 25 journals lie in the category of zone 1, which clearly shows that these journals can be considered as the highest interested journals for the academicians to publish their work, among these the top five journals that can be of highest interest to researchers are namely Sustainability, Energies, Journal of cleaner production, Technological forecasting and Social change and applied sciences.

Secondly, the triple analysis shows that the United Kingdom has initiated collaborations for research efforts in smart cities and technologies related to the development of smart cities. Lastly, the study elaborates the emerging themes such as Industry4.0, sustainability, circular economy, big data analytics, digital technologies, smart manufacturing, Digital twin, Internet of Things, cybersecurity, virtual reality, Artificial intelligence, and augmented reality.

This study is an initial attempt to analyse smart city technology's theoretical underpinning, influential elements, and conceptual framework. This research gives contemporary academics and policymakers complete and up to date knowledge. The findings of this study are beneficial to researchers in that they help them better comprehend the topic at hand and identify important papers. In conjunction with the compelling research themes, it elucidates and makes proposals to investigate pertinent theories and practices further.

12.6 Limitations of the Study

The study demonstrates significant limitations majorly due to the fact that just one database source was used in the study namely Scopus. Even though the known fact is that Scopus is the largest known database there are still many journals which are not included in its database. Many journals are entirely neglected and not considered. Further as we are aware the no search query is error-free we cannot neglect this fact and state that the future scope of the study is much more as the keywords which were restricted to this study were namely digital transformation, sustainability, artificial intelligence, and smart cities.

References

1. Mora, L., Bolici, R., & Deakin, M. (2017). The first two decades of smart-city research: A bibliometric analysis. *Journal of Urban Technology, 24*(1), 3–27.
2. He, X., Wang, K., Huang, H., & Liu, B. (2018). QoE-driven big data architecture for Smart City. *IEEE Communications Magazine, 56*, 88–93.
3. Bhushan, B., Khamparia, A., Sagayam, K. M., Sharma, S. K., Ahad, M. A., & Debnath, N. C. (2020). Blockchain for smart cities: A review of architectures, integration trends and future research directions. *Sustainable Cities and Society, 61*, 102360.
4. Su, K., Li, J., & Fu, H. (2011). Smart city and the applications. In *2011 international conference on electronics, communications and control (ICECC)* (pp. 1028–1031). IEEE.
5. Albino, V., Berardi, U., & Dangelico, R. M. (2015). Smart cities: Definitions dimensions performance and initiatives. *Journal of Urban Technology, 22*, 1.
6. Chou, W., Lam, T., & Chan, R. (2018). *Super smart city happier society with higher quality.* Deloitte.
7. Harrison, C., Eckman, B., Hamilton, R., Hartswick, P., Kalagnanam, J., Paraszczak, J., & Williams, P. (2010). Foundations for smarter cities. *IBM Journal of Research and Development, 54*(4), 1–16.
8. Mitton, N., Papavassiliou, S., Puliafito, A., & Trivedi, K. S. (2012). Combining Cloud and sensors in a smart city environment. *EURASIP Journal on Wireless Communications and Networking, 2012*(1), 1–10.
9. Manchanda, C., Sharma, N., Rathi, R., Bhushan, B., & Grover, M. (2020). *Neoteric security and privacy sanctuary technologies in smart cities.* 2020 IEEE 9th International Conference on Communication Systems and Network Technologies (CSNT). https://doi.org/10.1109/csnt48778.2020.9115780
10. Pellicer, S., Santa, G., Bleda, A. L., Maestre, R., Jara, A. J., & Skarmeta, A. G. (2013). A global perspective of smart cities: A survey. In *2013 Seventh International Conference on Innovative Mobile and Internet Services in Ubiquitous Computing* (pp. 439–444). IEEE.
11. Chourabi, H., Nam, T., Walker, S., Gil-Garcia, J. R., Mellouli, S., Nahon, K., et al. (2012). Understanding smart cities: An integrative framework. In *2012 45th Hawaii international conference on system sciences* (pp. 2289–2297). IEEE.
12. Batty, M. (2013). Big data, smart cities and city planning. *Dialogues in Human Geography, 3*(3), 274–279.
13. Kitchin, R. (2014). The real-time city? Big data and smart urbanism. *Geo Journal, 79*(1), 1–14.
14. Al-Hader, M., Rodzi, A., Sharif, A. R., & Ahmad, N. (2009). Smart city components architecture. In *2009 International Conference on Computational Intelligence, Modelling and Simulation* (pp. 93–97). IEEE.

15. Cimmino, A., Pecorella, T., Fantacci, R., Granelli, F., Rahman, T. F., Sacchi, C., et al. (2014). The role of small cell technology in future smart city applications. *Transactions on Emerging Telecommunications Technologies, 25*(1), 11–20.
16. Haque, A. B., Bhushan, B., & Dhiman, G. (2022). Conceptualizing smart city applications: Requirements, architecture, security issues, and emerging trends. *Expert Systems, 39*(5), e12753.
17. Mehta, S., Bhushan, B., & Kumar, R. (2022). Machine learning approaches for Smart City applications: Emergence, challenges and opportunities. *Recent Advances in Internet of Things and Machine Learning*, 147–163.
18. Bhowmik, T., Bhadwaj, A., Kumar, A., & Bhushan, B. (2022). Machine learning and deep learning models for privacy management and data analysis in smart cites. In V. E. Balas, V. K. Solanki, & R. Kumar (Eds.), *Recent advances in internet of things and machine learning. Intelligent systems reference library* (Vol. 215). Springer. https://doi.org/10.1007/978-3-030-90119-6_13
19. Rathore, M. M., Paul, A., Ahmad, A., Chilamkurti, N., Hong, W. H., & Seo, H. (2018). Real-time secure communication for Smart City in high-speed big data environment. *Future Generation Computer Systems, 83*, 638–652.
20. Johnson, P. A., Robinson, P. J., & Philpot, S. (2020). Type, tweet, tap, and pass: How smart city technology is creating a transactional citizen. *Government Information Quarterly, 37*(1), 101414.
21. Haque, A. K. M. B., Bhushan, B., Hasan, M., & Zihad, M. M. (2022). Revolutionizing the industrial internet of things using blockchain: An unified approach. In V. E. Balas, V. K. Solanki, & R. Kumar (Eds.), *Recent advances in internet of things and machine learning. Intelligent systems reference library* (Vol. 215). Springer. https://doi.org/10.1007/978-3-030-90119-6_5
22. Ullah, F., Sepasgozar, S. M., & Wang, C. (2018). A systematic review of smart real estate technology: Drivers of, and barriers to, the use of digital disruptive technologies and online platforms. *Sustainability, 10*(9), 3142.
23. Abosaq, N. H. (2019). Impact of privacy issues on smart city services in a model smart city. *International Journal of Advanced Computer Science and Applications, 10*(2).
24. Aria, M., & Cuccurullo, C. (2017). Bibliometrix: An R-tool for comprehensive science mapping analysis. *Journal of Informetrics, 11*(4), 959–975.
25. Nash-Stewart, C. E., Kruesi, L. M., & Del Mar, C. B. (2012 Apr). Does Bradford's law of scattering predict the size of the literature in cochrane reviews? *Journal of the Medical Library Association, 100*(2), 135–138.
26. Potter, J. (2010). Mapping the literature of occupational therapy: An update. *Journal of the Medical Library Association, 98*(3), 235–242.
27. Hjørland, B., & Nicolaisen, J. (2005). Bradford's Law of Scattering: ambiguities in the concept of "subject". In F. Crestani & I. Ruthven (Eds.), *Context: nature, impact, and role: 5th International Conference on Conceptions of Library and Information Sciences* (pp. 96–106). Springer. Lecture Notes in Computer Science, v.3507.
28. Heine, M. (1998). Bradford ranking conventions and their application to a growing literature. *Journal of Documentation, 54*(3), 303–331.
29. Dwivedi, Y. K., Hughes, L., Ismagilova, E., Aarts, G., Coombs, C., Crick, T., et al. (2021). Artificial Intelligence (AI): Multidisciplinary perspectives on emerging challenges, opportunities, and agenda for research, practice and policy. *International Journal of Information Management, 57*, 101994.
30. Vinuesa, R., Azizpour, H., Leite, I., Balaam, M., Dignum, V., Domisch, S., et al. (2020). The role of artificial intelligence in achieving the sustainable development goals. *Nature Communications, 11*(1), 1–10.
31. Cobo, M. J., López-Herrera, A. G., Herrera-Viedma, E., & Herrera, F. (2011). An approach for detecting, quantifying, and visualizing the evolution of a research field: A practical application to the Fuzzy Sets Theory field. *Journal of Informetrics, 5*(1), 146–166.
32. Nižetić, S., Ocłoń, P., & Tsoutsos, T. (2022). Progress in smart and sustainable technologies. *Journal of Cleaner Production, 130450*, 130450.

33. Malik, P., Singh, R., Gehlot, A., Akram, S. V., & Das, P. K. (2022). *Village 4.0: Digitalization of village with smart internet of things technologies* (p. 107938). Computers & Industrial Engineering.
34. Busulwa, R., Pickering, M., & Mao, I. (2022). Digital transformation and hospitality management competencies: Toward an integrative framework. *International Journal of Hospitality Management, 102*, 103132.
35. Gupta, M. (2023). Sustainable urban development of smart cities in India-a systematic literature review. *Sustainability, Agri, Food and Environmental Research, 12*(1).
36. Atenstaedt, R. (2012). Word cloud analysis of the BJGP. *The British Journal of General Practice: The Journal of the Royal College of General Practitioners, 62*(596), 148.
37. Winkowska, J., Szpilko, D., & Pejić, S. (2019). Smart city concept in the light of the literature review. *Engineering Management in Production and Services, 11*(2), 70–86.
38. Hakak, S., Khan, W. Z., Gilkar, G. A., Imran, M., & Guizani, N. (2020). Securing smart cities through blockchain technology: Architecture, requirements, and challenges. *IEEE Network, 34*(1), 8–14.
39. Goyal, S., Sharma, N., Bhushan, B., Shankar, A., & Sagayam, M. (2020). *Iot enabled technology in secured healthcare: Applications, challenges and future directions* (pp. 25–48). Cognitive Internet of Medical Things for Smart Healthcare. https://doi.org/10.1007/978-3-030-55833-8_2
40. Allam, Z., & Dhunny, Z. A. (2019). On big data, artificial intelligence and smart cities. *Cities, 89*, 80–91.
41. Anthony, J. B. (2021). Managing digital transformation of smart cities through enterprise architecture – A review and research agenda. *Enterprise Information Systems, 15*(3), 299–331.

Chapter 13
Examining Social Media, Citizen Engagement and Risk Communication: A Smart City Perspective

Tamanna Dalwai, Menila James, Nujood Al Haddabi, William Webster, Abdullah Mohammed Alshukaili, and Arockiasamy Soosaimanickam

Abstract Governments around the world have had a varied response to social media adoption to communicate and engage their citizens. For the official purpose, social media has been used to create awareness of policies, ongoing projects, and new and other important public announcements. The smart city concept is predominantly based on the technology implementation that is expected to create sustainable economic development and improved quality of life. Oman 2040 strategy has aimed to achieve Smart Cities as a national ambition. During the pandemic, social media became an invaluable tool for the direct transmission of important information directed toward saving lives. This chapter aims to investigate the communication strategies and level of citizen engagement during COVID-19, through the Ministry of Health (MoH) Twitter posts in Oman. It also examines the risk communication strategies by MoH. The social media posts are analysed for the pandemic's initial six-month period in Oman which began on 24th February 2020. A total of 1722 COVID-19-related tweets were analysed. The content analysis of the tweets suggested the MOH preferred to use the push strategy of communication during the COVID-19 period. The tweets were predominantly communicating the

T. Dalwai (✉)
Department of Business and Accounting, Muscat College, Muscat, Oman
e-mail: tamanna@muscatcollege.edu.om

M. James
Department of Computing, Muscat College, Muscat, Oman
e-mail: menilajames@muscatcollege.edu.om

N. Al Haddabi
Independent Researcher, Muscat, Oman

W. Webster
University of Stirling, Stirling, UK
e-mail: william.webster@stir.ac.uk

A. M. Alshukaili · A. Soosaimanickam
University of Nizwa, Nizwa, Oman
e-mail: a.alshukaili@unizwa.edu.om; arockiasamy@unizwa.edu.om

risk related to the pandemic. This study is expected to benefit the governments, health agencies, community and researchers as it provides insights on citizen engagement and risk communication strategies.

Keywords E-participation · Social media · Twitter · Oman · COVID-19 · Risk

13.1 Introduction

Citizen engagement is very vital in developing successful smart cities as it permits governments to respond to the requirements of the dynamic environments and take decisions in the best of public interest. Smart cities are known to offer innovative solutions that boost the day-to-day affairs of their citizens through the use of Information and Communication Technology (ICT) in the healthcare, transportation, energy consumption and education sectors [1, 2]. The rising urban thickness is expected to have significant levels of contamination, higher gridlock and social osmosis. It is a major contributing factor to smart city development [3]. Social media offers powerful platforms for smart city governments to connect, engage and associate with citizens, especially in crisis management [4]. Citizen engagement is predominant in crisis management, as it enhances the society's capacity to effectively mitigate the various phases of the emergency. Enlisting citizen trust and cooperation is one of the major roles of the government's risk mitigation process during a health crisis [5]. The government's social media platforms play an important role in participating the public to combat the pandemic such as COVID-19. Previous public health risks and the COVID-19 pandemic share a lot of common features with other calamities, for instance, a high level of uncertainty, unexpected rapid, misinformation, economic inflation, new political regulation, development and short triggering events. The need for online engagement for the government is a part of risk management to provide trusted information about crisis stages, raise awareness and promote behavioural changes, rumour control, and cultivate information security behaviour against scams. Furthermore, the potential of social media platforms to spread information faster is the main advantage of using them during public health crises [6].

According to Górska et al. [7], in a situation of emergency or a disruptive environment, communication is crucial for protecting and ensuring the safety of citizens and it became a priority to ensure that reliable information is available for citizens to protect themselves. However, the online engagement for government organisations during a health crisis is not only limited to obtaining information but also extends to participation in the decision-making process. According to studies based on communication strategies, in order to have an effective government management, it is important to involve citizens in decision-making with reference to matters relating to the development of their local governments and communities [8, 9]. The use of social media in health crisis management such as the COVID-19 pandemic allows governments to receive feedback from citizens.

COVID-19 had a multi-level impact on society's lives, including social, political, and environmental, and a massive effect was on the communication strategies between government and the public. Previous studies on crisis communications found that most governments in the past failed to find ways to communicate with citizens during a crisis. However, we are in the information technology revolution, which is the right opportunity to develop communication strategies before and after a crisis. Furthermore, local governments in many countries found social media platforms the right ways to communicate with a citizen during COVID-19 [6, 7, 10]. Facebook, Twitter and YouTube are possibly the most common social media platforms appropriate for LGs to engage with the citizens and spread information. In some countries, Twitter is used to approach the citizen while Facebook has been used in other areas [6].

According to Górska et al. [7], there are three strategies used by the government to engage during COVID-19. These strategies are classified on the basis of content, language, and tone of posts shared by the cities. The tweets or posts were bifurcated in three major categories that include: Business as usual (Usual), We are great! Just observe (Great), and We are in this together (Together). The descriptive statistics of the study show that the "Together" strategy involving the networking tactics of communication was the predominant strategy in COVID-19 posts across all social media platforms. Thus, using the model proposed by Górska et al. [9], this study examines the communication strategies observed by the Sultanate of Oman's Ministry of Health (MoH) Twitter account. In addition, this chapter explores the tweets from the risk management strategies perspective advocated by [11].

The research makes vital contributions to the extant literature about government communication on the pandemic. The case of Oman's Ministry of Health (MoH) serves as how public institution applies strategies for engagingly communicating with the public during the pandemic. The government applied the push strategy of communication whereby most of its tweets were classified in the "We are great! Just observe" category. Media-rich tools such as the use of videos were more prevalent in the first few months of the crisis, and it was followed by more hashtags in the following months. Citizen engagement measured by the number of likes was high in the initial few months of the pandemic. Thus, the use of the selected communication strategy may be seen as successful in the initial months when the unknown related to the pandemic was much higher. The study also contributes to the risk management strategies adopted by the MoH. As expected, the communication strategies focused more on the risks, followed by the efficacy related to the pandemic. From a smart city perspective, effective risk management strategies will augment the reliability of the government and diffuse any public fears.

The remainder of the chapter is presented as follows: Sect. 13.2 discusses an overview of the literature review; Sect. 13.3 presents the methodology adopted by the study; Sect. 13.4 presents the results and discussions related to the tweets classifications in terms of communication and risk management and lastly, Sect. 13.5 concludes with recommendations and limitations of the study.

13.2 Literature Review

Citizen engagement is critical for the establishment and achievement of a modern city. Citizens are no more viewed to be passive technology and service consumers only but are expected to serve an extended role of an active contributor to ideas [12]. Social media serves to be an effective communication tool in a period of crisis for the citizens and governments. This section reviews the prior studies related to the smart cities' framework, risk management and government responses to the pandemic.

13.2.1 Smart City: Characteristics and Pillars

Smart cities are those that have well-established connections of ICT, physical, social and business infrastructure [13]. Intelligence from the perspective of smart cities refers to the ability or technique to make informed decisions.

Bhushan et al. [14] described a smart city as an interplay of four important characteristics that include: sustainability, smartness, urbanization and quality of life. The sustainability element is built upon certain key attributes that address social issues, infrastructure and governance, environment, health and economics in smart city. Smartness is associated with the improvement of social, economic and environmental benchmarks. Quality of life is measured through the financial and emotional well-being of its citizens. Whereas urbanization is the outcome of rural transformation achieved through improvement in the infrastructural, economical, technological and governing attributes.

Additionally, a smart city is based on four major themes or pillars that consist of: physical, institutional, social and economic infrastructure [14]. Physical infrastructure through smart energy, building renovation, green urban planning, and green buildings ensures resource sustainability and smooth city operations. Institutional infrastructure is an integration of national, civic, public and private organisations that contributes to the enhancement of smart city governance. The social infrastructure consists of human capital, quality of life and intellectual capital and contributes to the sustainability of a smart city. Economic infrastructure ensures the growth of the economy and leads to job creation by enhancing e-business and e-commerce. This chapter seeks to contribute to the social and institutional infrastructure that enhances smart city governance. Citizen engagement is a key attribute for decision-making and easy governance. This requires effective government communication strategies which are addressed through the social infrastructure. Table 13.1 summarizes the studies related to social media usage during the pandemic. The findings report no consistent application or usage of social media by the local government. While it was noted by several studies as an important tool for better preparedness for COVID-19, some also reported its misusage due to misinformation.

Table 13.1 Summary of studies addressing the use of social media for crisis management

Authors	Year	Findings
Selerio et al. [15]	2022	Social media was important for public health policy development, monitoring and controlling misinformation, and managing citizen behaviour and response.
Gorska et al. [7]	2022	Social media was used by the local government for managing pandemic-related crisis communication. Specifically for Poland, the together communication strategy was applied.
Young et al. [16]	2022	Social media was an important surveillance method for COVID-19 health policy compliance.
Abbas et al. [17]	2021	Excessive usage of social media contributed to providing emotional, informational and peer support.
Gesser-Edelsburg [18]	2021	The research argued that there exist discrepancies in health and risk communication in the existing literature. The article recommended engaging the public on social media for encouraging informed decision-making.
Vraga and Bode [19]	2021	The use of correct infographics supported in reducing social media misperceptions about science-related COVID-19 prevention strategies but did not affect misperceptions regarding COVID-19 prevention itself.
Malecki et al. [20]	2021	The risk communication strategy should have certain key features that involve careful planning, treating the stakeholders as partners, ensuring transparency and honesty, demonstrate empathy in communication, and continuously evaluate and revisit the strategies.
Bridgman et al. [21]	2020	More misinformation was communicated through social media such as twitter whereas the inverse applied to news media.
Zhou et al. [22]	2021	Social media supported the communication of accurate information about the pandemic and facilitated the public to move to the next normal.
Camilleri [23]	2021	The institutions and organisations should accept the need to embed digital and social media for pandemic-related information and risk management plans.

13.2.2 Online Engagement and Risk Management

According to studies on crisis management, emergency communications have been comprised of two broad categories, risk communication, and crisis communication. Crisis communication attempts to address the crisis by collecting, processing and disseminating information [24]. Risk communication on the other hand is involved in identifying health related risks and persuade stakeholders to adopt medically proven strategies [25]. The primary concern of risk communication is to find out the likelihood of probable harm and identify and communicate methods to reduce the harm. Additionally, the impetus of risk communication was primarily found in the health communication domain [26].

The usage of social media platforms has been remarkably increasing in times of acute crisis, and many health organizations use social media platforms to interact and foster public participation to facilitate decision-making during the crisis. However, the government's online engagement has not been only in the public health sector but in many crises, for instance, tornados, earthquakes, and extremist attacks. In recent years, online engagement played a significant role for local governments and World Health Organization (WHO) to communicate critical health-related information to the stakeholders. Furthermore, social network tools have been accelerating the dissemination of information about the risk as evidenced by the 2009 H1N1 influenza epidemic [26]. The related literature on emergency communication highlights the importance of online engagement to the government organisation during periods of broader risk events and public health crisis [11]. One of the risk management practices done during the COVID-19 pandemic by governments worldwide is having an efficient and effective risk communication practice on social media platforms such as Twitter, including the use of tweets that promote self-efficacy.

According to Slavik et al. [11], one way to measure online engagement and examine the type of communication is through Twitter accounts. Twitter uses tools such as the number of retweets (sharing the tweet on Twitter or other platforms), likes (number of times users agreed with a tweet), and replies (comments on a particular tweet). Furthermore, retweets are considered to be an effective tool for measuring online engagement. The research studies have highlighted that strategies such as hashtags, URLs, and user mentions can improve online engagement on the various social media accounts of the government, especially (Twitter and Facebook) during COVID-19, thus engaging citizens in the risk management approaches and decision-making [6]. Pang et al. [6] investigated public engagement during COVID-19 in Macao by exploring the social media posts on the government Facebook account. The posts derived from the Macao SAR government Facebook data regarding online engagement have been classified into 7 categories which include plans and measures, public health messages, rumour control, latest news, appreciations, community resilience, and press conference. The online engagement was frequently updated during different stages of the pandemic.

The risk communication coding used by Slavik et al. [11] to determine and understand the risk management strategies. These tweets were categorised into six exclusive coding variables that were classified as corrective, risk, efficacy, concern, uncertainty, and experts. Tweets that were amended to remove incorrect information about the COVID-19 pandemic or aimed to control misinformation spread were classified as corrective. Tweets were classified as "risk" if they included information that would likely assist the reader form an opinion on the risks of contracting COVID-19 or experiencing health complications due to COVID-19. Moreover, the tweet category "risk" includes tweets pertaining information on absolute risks, relative risks and high-risk population identification. The tweets that demonstrated the ability of an individual or community to implement an action or activity and resulted in improvement of health or reduced COVID-19 related hard was classified as efficacy. Tweets acknowledging the fears, worries, or anxiety related to the COVID-19 pandemic were mentioned as a "concern". Tweets that communicated the collaboration or agreement with individuals, health organisations or knowledgeable experts were terms as experts.

13.2.3   Government Social Media and COVID-19

Social media role has been vital in connecting individuals and providing an update on the latest news about COVID-19. Social media empowered the citizens in addressing social issues to a great extent during lockdowns related to COVID-19 [8]. The primary medium used by the governments to spread information and provide awareness about COVID-19 was social media platforms. Research studies prove that the use of social media in crisis time is an accurate decision to minimize loss and reach the majority of citizens. In order to minimize losses and to provide information most efficiently, the government institutions utilize social media platforms to update and share important information about the general public's situation [8]. During the COVID19 crisis management, the social media accounts of the government became the major source of communication of critical information to all main stakeholders that included citizens, hospital staff, government officials, and non-governmental associations, which even helped to minimize the loss and reduce anxiety and confusion [7, 8]. Government organizations have noticeably activated their social accounts during the COVID-19 to manage the risk, update news and reports, control rumours and distribute donations among the affected citizens. For several countries, social media accounts publicized government activities and became a new channel for connecting and serving the population. In crisis management, especially during a public health crisis, every single piece of information become valid to stakeholders [27].

According to Broniatowski et al. [28], significant attention has been dedicated to deciding the reliability of the information provided on social media platforms regarding the COVID-19 pandemic. Furthermore, in health crisis management, there is a high probability of conveying misinformation to the citizens about the illness, vaccines, and political situation, and there are no particular reasons behind that. Research on governmental social media platforms found that even though there is a vast amount of information available about COVID-19, it was difficult to rate the reliability of the source of information. The percentage of local government-sponsored propaganda increased among the non-credible or less credible sources suggesting that the pandemic may also be used for political purposes and advantages. However, the research studies highlighted that government around the world efficiently use social media platforms to provide information to citizens and the global public. Social media acts as a bridge between governments and citizens in disseminating timely information in fighting the pandemic. Thus, social media has proven to be quite useful and effective for the world during the Covid19 outbreak, enabling governmental organizations and the World Health Organization (WHO) to constantly update citizens about rumours and misinformation [8].

The recent COVID-19 pandemic demonstrated that it required quick responses and fast decision making which is how prior public health crises were handled [7]. Studies have proven that citizen e-participation through government social media platforms has led to a new form of democratization that enables citizens to engage in the decision-making process related to the development of their local governments and communities. In crisis management, citizen involvement in decision-making reduces the risk, controls misinformation and obtains the normal life of communities [7]. The increase of public engagement in governmental social media enables the citizens to engage in the decision-making process through sharing ideas, feedback, and complaints on policy implementation and provision of government services [12].

According to public administration research, a primary concern for the local government is the citizen's trust and worldwide government officials have been constantly worried about its decline and are continually working towards attaining their citizens' trust [8]. The increase in trust in local government is positively correlated to public engagement [29]. In addition, there are factors affecting government trust e.g., perception of government institutes' transparency, citizen's socio-psychological features, and achievements of the government. Government institution trust is an important determinant in calming down the public during a crisis. However, the research studies highlighted the relationship between citizens' trust in government on civic engagement through government social media accounts (GSMAs) during COVID-19. The element of trust in government moderated the relationship between citizen participation in GSMAs and online civic management, such that the higher the trust, the stronger the relationship and vice versa. The researchers found that governments and crisis management cells used GSMAs to reach citizens and gain high trust and engagement. The trust in government has positively translated through citizens' civic behaviour during COVID-19. For example, governments were successful in providing awareness to the citizens on the importance of social distancing, usage of masks, washing hands, as well as to rigorously comply with the government instructions and rules [8, 30, 31].

13.3   Methodology and Data

13.3.1   Data Collection

The data for this study was collected from the "Ministry of Health" Twitter account. The tweets were extracted for the period, 23rd August 2019 to 24th August 2020, resulting in a total of 2945 posts. Oman reported its first COVID-19 case on 24th February 2020. Thus, using this as a mid-point period, the tweets before and during the pandemic are collected for six months each. During the pandemic period (24th February to 24th August 2020), there were a total of 2017 posts. Before the pandemic, 928 tweets were published by the MoH. For each tweet information was captured on content, number of likes, number of reposts, and number of comments. The media type was determined by analysing the posts for URLs of pictures and videos uploaded.

13.3.2 Inter-Coder Reliability and Data Analysis

Two undergraduate students were employed to code the tweets which were mostly in Arabic. The students were given the training to familiarise themselves with the coding norms. To ensure the inter-reliability, 15% of sample tweets were randomly and independently coded. The Kappa value for the categories was above 0.90. The results confirmed high inter-reliabilities and thus were acceptable.

13.3.3 Coding

The tweets were coded for two major categories, communication, and risk management strategy. All the tweets published after the first reported case of COVID-19 were coded for three communication strategies adopted by Gorska et al. [7]: Business as usual (Usual), We are great! Just observe (Great) and We are in this together (Together). This was similar to Mergel's [32] communication strategy whereby the usual strategy was similar to pull; the great strategy was closer to push, and together was similar to networking. The tweets which were specific to Covid-related information were coded for risk management strategy. There were 6 nonmutually exclusive coding variables: corrective, risk, efficacy, concern, uncertainty and experts.

13.4 Results and Discussion

Figure 13.1 presents the usage of the media-rich tools in the first six months after the announcement of COVID-19 cases in the Sultanate of Oman. A total of 2017 tweets were posted in the six months after the first case of COVID-19 was detected in the Sultanate of Oman. The tweets published were consistent across the months. May was the highest usage of photos, videos or hashtags in comparison to the other months. The usage of photos across the months ranged from 11% to 17%. This similar usage was noticed for videos and hashtags as well in the tweets.

Figure 13.2 presents a graphical overview of the citizen engagement that was evoked through the tweets during the pandemic. The initial few months (March to May 2020) saw an average of 12% likes for the tweets. The replies and retweets were considerably less. This analysis highlights the limitations in the engagement of the citizens with the Twitter handle of MOH. While the news of the pandemic was fairly new and with a lot of unknowns, citizen engagement did not see a similar response.

Table 13.2 presents the descriptive statistics of COVID-19-related tweets specifically. The 2017 tweets over six months during the pandemic had a mix of related and non-related COVID-19 tweets. Using content analysis, the COVID-19-related

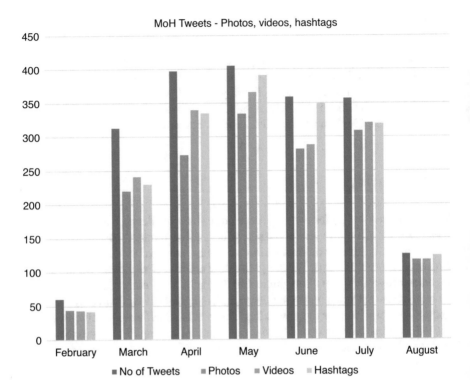

Fig. 13.1 Month-wise tweets engagement using media-rich tools during COVID-19. (Source: Authors)

tweets were specifically identified and coded for the different communications strategies of: "Business as usual", "We are great just observer", and "We are in this together". These three strategies reflected Mergel's [32] push, pull and networking strategies respectively. A total of 1722 COVID-19-related tweets were identified in 2017 which reflects an emphasis of 85% on the pandemic. The communication statistics adopted by the MOH was about 70% on "We are great just observe". This strategy reflected the MOHs push strategy. This is a consistent approach that resonates with the social media usage of the Royal Oman Police in Oman [4]. Poland's government in comparison focused more on the push strategy. It may be argued that while MOH is a government-owned institution, it wanted to build more confidence in its citizens during the pandemic by adopting a push strategy and showcasing the efforts in dealing with the same. The highest average likes were given for the "We are great just observe" strategy followed by tweets related to "Business as usual". This suggests that the citizen was also expecting to receive such forms of communication. The average retweets were highest when the tweets were in the category of "We are in this together".

Table 13.3 presents the risk management strategies adopted in its tweets related to the pandemic. Most of the tweets were either adopting risk communication

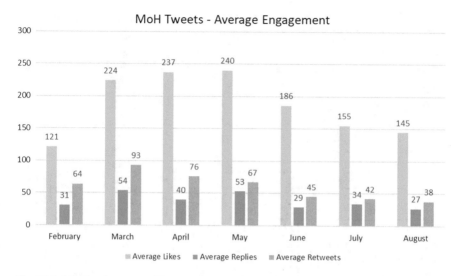

Fig. 13.2 Month-wise tweets citizen engagement during COVID-19. (Source: Authors)

Table 13.2 Descriptive statistics of COVID-19-related tweets with different communication strategies

Variable	Business as usual			We are great just observe			We are in this together		
	Obs	Mean	Max	Obs	Mean	Max	Obs	Mean	Max
nlikes	91	190.35	1845	1212	212.73	2654	419	182.45	1731
nreplies	91	20.1	313	1212	54.5	1603	419	21.95	487
nretweets	91	48.96	644	1212	63.37	695	419	71.29	1255
photos	91	0.76	1	1212	0.79	1	419	0.74	1
video	91	0.82	1	1212	0.84	1	419	0.87	1
hashtags	91	0.91	1	1212	0.91	1	419	0.97	1

strategies or varying between efficacy and corrective strategies. As this was an early stage in the pandemic, it was expected that the government would communicate the risks associated to COVID-19. This attracted the highest average engagement in terms of likes, replies and retweets. Concerns related to the pandemic were followed with the next highest engagement with the public. The use of hashtags was more predominant for efficacy or expert-related risk communication strategies. Retweets were lowest for tweets that communicated some form of uncertainty which also reflected citizen responsibility.

Table 13.4 presents Pearson's correlation between the communication strategies, citizen engagement and media richness tool. The push strategy represented by "Business as Usual" is significantly and positively correlated to the usage of hashtags. The "We are great just observe" communication strategy is significantly and negatively related to all the citizen engagement representatives and media richness tools. This suggests that as the MOH tweeted more from a push strategy perspective the citizen engagement reduced. Additionally, increased usage of this

Table 13.3 Descriptive statistics of COVID-19-related tweets with different risk strategies

Variable	Corrective			Risk			Efficacy		
	Obs	Mean	Max	Obs	Mean	Max	Obs	Mean	Max
nlikes	201	160.04	1104	964	229.48	2654	378	172.27	1096
nreplies	201	19.96	448	964	64.04	1603	378	18.96	253
nretweets	201	67.36	581	964	68.75	695	378	58.61	553
photos	201	0.74	1	964	0.84	1	378	0.7	1
video	201	0.81	1	964	0.89	1	378	0.83	1
hashtags	201	0.87	1	964	0.93	1	378	0.95	1
Variable	Concern			Uncertain			Expert		
	Obs	Mean	Max	Obs	Mean	Max	Obs	Mean	Max
nlikes	91	202.54	1731	36	129.33	585	52	192.6	1096
nreplies	91	29.29	487	36	13.28	129	52	19.77	216
nretweets	91	61.98	1255	36	32.83	175	52	45.13	280
photos	91	0.51	1	36	0.72	1	52	0.81	1
video	91	0.6	1	36	0.78	1	52	0.85	1
hashtags	91	0.89	1	36	0.78	1	52	0.96	1

Table 13.4 Correlation of communication strategies with citizen engagement and media richness tools

Variables	Business as Usual	We are great just observe	We are in this together
nlikes	0.03	−0.082***	0.119**
nreplies	−0.02	−0.100***	0.04
nretweets	−0.08	−0.121***	0.05
photos	0.14	−0.160***	−0.05
video	0.1	−0.142***	−0.02
hashtags	0.296***	−0.03	−0.01

*** $p < 0.01$, ** $p < 0.05$, * $p < 0.1$

strategy led to less use of photos and videos. The networking strategy of "We are in this together" is as per expectation significantly and positively related to the citizen engagement expressed through the number of likes.

Table 13.5 presents the correlation between the risk management strategies, citizen engagement and media richness tools. None of the risk communication strategies was significantly related to citizen engagement except for "concern". This as per expectation evoked a smaller number of likes as the tweets focused more on concern-related communication. Efficacy and concern were significantly and positively related to the usage of photos. The usage of videos and hashtags reduced with the increase in tweets related to risks.

Table 13.5 Correlation of risk management strategies with citizen engagement and media richness tools

Variables	Corrective	Risk	Efficacy	Concern	Uncertain	Expert
nlikes	−0.04	−0.01	−0.01	−0.187*	−0.06	−0.08
nreplies	−0.02	−0.04	0.07	−0.14	0.07	−0.12
nretweets	−0.07	−0.02	−0.04	−0.13	−0.07	−0.11
photos	0.05	−0.063*	0.141***	0.177*	0.2	−0.283**
video	0.05	−0.068**	0.04	0.232**	0.25	−0.22
hashtags	0.140**	−0.091***	0.02	0.08	0.296*	−0.04

$***p < 0.01, **p < 0.05, *p < 0.1$

13.5 Conclusion

This study examined the tweets posted by the Ministry of Health during the early period of the pandemic from 24th February to 24th August 2022. The tweets were analysed to identify the prominent communication strategy adopted by the MOH and how it is associated with citizen engagement and media richness tools. The study concluded that MOH adopted the push strategy of communication in the early crisis stages. Similarly, during the early stages, the MOH tweets were also classified for risk management communication techniques. The MOH tweets were predominantly on communicating the risks related to the pandemic.

This study offers some useful practical implications for the MOH Twitter account management. There can be a clearer understanding of the crisis management cycle. As the MOH adopted heavily the push strategy through its tweets, it would be a good initiative to engage equally in a networking strategy. This would enhance citizen engagement and in times of crisis ease compliance with the government initiatives. As suggested by Soyata et al. [33], effective government communication during times of crisis especially at an early stage would protect and ensure citizen safety.

The research suffers from certain limitations. The study focused exclusively on the Twitter account of the MOH of Oman. Though the study can be generalised to other Twitter accounts of other governmental agencies within Oman, future research can cover more Twitter accounts to have wider applicability to the GCC region. Citizen engagement is measured in terms of likes, retweets or replies but combined their usage may be put to a different use. The tone of the tweets was not examined in this research and thus it can be taken up for future study.

Acknowledgments The research leading to these results has received funding from The Research Council (TRC) of the Sultanate of Oman under the Block Funding Program. TRC Block Funding Agreement No [BFP/RGP/ICT/18/172].

References

1. Manchanda, C., Sharma, N., Rathi, R., Bhushan, B., & Grover, M. (2020). Neoteric security and privacy sanctuary technologies in smart cities. *2020 IEEE 9th International Conference on Communication Systems and Network Technologies (CSNT), 2020*(10–12), 236–241.
2. Madaan, G., Bhushan, B., & Kumar, R. (2021). Blockchain-based cyberthreat mitigation systems for smart vehicles and industrial automation. In R. Kumar, R. Sharma, & P. K. Pattnaik (Eds.), *Multimedia technologies in the Internet of Things environment* (pp. 13–32). Springer Singapore.
3. Haque, A. K. M. B., Bhushan, B., & Dhiman, G. (2022). Conceptualizing smart city applications: Requirements, architecture, security issues, and emerging trends. *Expert Systems, 39*(5), e12753.
4. Dalwai, T., James, M., Webster, W., Alshukaili, A. M., & Soosaimanickam, A. (2020). An investigation of citizen's e-participation within Oman's police department Facebook page. In H. Santos, G. V. Pereira, M. Budde, S. F. Lopes, & P. Nikolic (Eds.), (pp. 236–248). Springer International Publishing.
5. Yang, Y., Deng, W., Zhang, Y., & Mao, Z. (2021). Promoting public engagement during the COVID-19 crisis: How effective is the Wuhan local government's information release? *International Journal of Environmental Research and Public Health, 18*(1), 118.
6. Pang, P. C., Cai, Q., Jiang, W., & Chan, K. S. (2021). Engagement of government social media on Facebook during the COVID-19 pandemic in Macao. *International Journal of Environmental Research and Public Health, 18*(7), 3508.
7. Górska, A., Dobija, D., Grossi, G., & Staniszewska, Z. (2022). Getting through COVID-19 together: Understanding local governments' social media communication. *Cities, 121*, 103453.
8. Islm, T., Meng, H., Pitafi, A. H., Ullah Zafar, A., Sheikh, Z., Shujaat Mubarik, M., & Liang, X. (2021). Why DO citizens engage in government social media accounts during COVID-19 pandemic? A comparative study. *Telematics and Informatics, 62*, 101619.
9. Sathish, R., Manikandan, R., Priscila, S. S., Sara, B. V., & Mahaveerakannan, R. (2020). A report on the impact of information technology and social media on Covid–19. *ICISS 2020*, 224–230. 3–5 Dec 2020.
10. Tang, Z., Miller, A. S., Zhou, Z., & Warkentin, M. (2021). Does government social media promote users' information security behavior towards COVID-19 scams? Cultivation effects and protective motivations. *Government Information Quarterly, 38*(2), 101572.
11. Slavik, C. E., Buttle, C., Sturrock, S. L., Darlington, J. C., & Yiannakoulias, N. (2021). Examining tweet content and engagement of Canadian public health agencies and decision makers during COVID-19: Mixed methods analysis. *Journal of Medical Internet Research, 23*(3), e24883.
12. Trencher, G. (2019). Towards the smart city 2.0: Empirical evidence of using smartness as a tool for tackling social challenges. *Technological Forecasting and Social Change, 142*, 117–128.
13. Mehta, S., Bhushan, B., & Kumar, R. (2022). Machine learning approaches for Smart City applications: Emergence, challenges and opportunities. In V. E. Balas, V. K. Solanki, & R. Kumar (Eds.), *Recent advances in internet of things and machine learning: Real-world applications* (pp. 147–163). Springer International Publishing.
14. Bhushan, B., Khamparia, A., Sagayam, K. M., Sharma, S. K., Ahad, M. A., & Debnath, N. C. (2020). Blockchain for smart cities: A review of architectures, integration trends and future research directions. *Sustainable Cities and Society, 61*, 102360.
15. Selerio, E., Caladcad, J. A., Catamco, M. R., Capinpin, E. M., & Ocampo, L. (2022). Emergency preparedness during the COVID-19 pandemic: Modelling the roles of social media with fuzzy DEMATEL and analytic network process. *Socio-Economic Planning Sciences, 82*, 101217.
16. Young, S. D., Zhang, Q., Zeng, D. D., Zhan, Y., & Cumberland, W. (2022). Social media images as an emerging tool to monitor adherence to COVID-19 public health guidelines: Content analysis. *Journal of Medical Internet Research, 24*(3), e24787.

17. Abbas, J. A.-O., Wang, D. A.-O., Su, Z. A.-O., & Ziapour, A. A.-O. (2021). The role of social media in the advent of COVID-19 pandemic: Crisis management, mental health challenges and implications. *Risk Management and Healthcare Policy, 14*, 1917–1932. (1179–1594 (Print)).
18. Gesser-Edelsburg, A. A.-O. (2021). How to make health and risk communication on social media more "social" during COVID-19. *Risk Management and Healthcare Policy, 14*, 3523. (1179–1594 (Print)).
19. Vraga Ek Fau-Bode, L., & Bode, L. (2021). Addressing COVID-19 misinformation on social media preemptively and responsively. *Emerging Infectious Diseases, 27*, 396. (1080–6059 (Electronic)).
20. Malecki, K. M. C., Keating, J. A., & Safdar, N. (2021). Crisis communication and public perception of COVID-19 risk in the era of social media. *Clinical Infectious Diseases, 72*(4), 697–702.
21. Bridgman, A., Merkley, E., Loewen, P. J., Owen, T., Ruths, D., Teichmann, L., & Zhilin, O. (2020). The causes and consequences of COVID-19 misperceptions: Understanding the role of news and social media. *Harvard Kennedy School Misinformation Review, 1*(3), 118.
22. Zhou, Y., Draghici, A., Abbas, J., Mubeen, R., Boatca, M. E., & Salam, M. A. (2021). *Social media efficacy in crisis management: Effectiveness of non-pharmaceutical interventions to manage COVID-19 challenges.* Frontiers in Psychiatry. (1664–0640 (Print)).
23. Camilleri, M. A. (2021). *Strategic dialogic communication through digital media during COVID-19 crisis. Strategic corporate communication in the digital age.* Emerald Publishing Limited.
24. Coombs, W. T., & Holladay, S. J. (2011). *The handbook of crisis communication.* John Wiley & Sons.
25. Reynolds, B. W., & Seeger, M. (2005). Crisis and emergency risk communication as an integrative model. *Journal of Health Communication, 10*(1), 43–55.
26. Hagen, L., Neely, S., Scharf, R., & Keller, T. E. (2020). Social media use for crisis and emergency risk communications during the Zika health crisis. *Digital Government: Research and Practice, 1*(2), Article 13.
27. Haro-de-Rosario, A., Sáez-Martín, A., & del Carmen Caba-Pérez, M. (2016). Using social media to enhance citizen engagement with local government: Twitter or Facebook? *New Media & Society, 20*(1), 29–49.
28. Broniatowski, D. A., Kerchner, D., Farooq, F., Huang, X., Jamison, A. M., Dredze, M., & Quinn, S. C. (2020). The covid-19 social media infodemic reflects uncertainty and state-sponsored propaganda. *arXiv preprint arXiv:2007.09682, 3*(2).
29. Lee, G., & Kwak, Y. H. (2012). An open government maturity model for social media-based public engagement. *Government Information Quarterly, 29*(4), 492–503.
30. Alnasser, A. H. A., Al-Tawfiq, J. A., Al Kalif, M. S. H., Alobaysi, A. M. A., Al Mubarak, M. H. M., Alturki, H. N. H., Alharbi, A. A. A., Albahrani, R. S. S., Sultan, S. A., & AlHamad, A. R. N. (2020). The positive impact of social media on the level of COVID-19 awareness in Saudi Arabia: A web-based cross-sectional survey. *Le Infezioni in Medicina, 28*(4), 545–550.
31. Wang, S., Schraagen, M., Sang, E.T.K., & Dastani, M. (2020). 14 July. *Public sentiment on governmental COVID-19 measures in Dutch social media.* EMNLP 2020 Workshop NLP-COVID Submission https://openreview.net/forum?id=37zyB5yuPXi. Accessed 14 July 2022.
32. Mergel, I. (2013). A framework for interpreting social media interactions in the public sector. *Government Information Quarterly, 30*(4), 327–334.
33. Soyata, T., Habibzadeh, H., Ekenna, C., Nussbaum, B., & Lozano, J. (2019). Smart city in crisis: Technology and policy concerns. *Sustainable Cities and Society, 50*, 101566.

Chapter 14
5G and 6G Technologies for Smart City

Sonia Chhabra, Manpreet Kaur Aiden, Shweta Mayor Sabharwal, and Mustafa Al-Asadi

Abstract A smart city is one in which data is collected using multiple electrical and sensor systems. Smart cities work on information & communication technology to improve customer experience by focusing on convenience, reliability, and security. Mobile wireless communication's 5g technology (5G) brings up a whole new universe of possibilities. Everyone and everything are connected through a communication network. 5G will have a significant economic impact and civilizations, since it will provide the requisite communication infrastructure for a variety of smart devices applications for the city. Cities might use 5G technologies to save commuting times, enhance public safety, and save money on their smart grids. The 6G revolution will test how we communicate and regulate billions of pieces in our digital future, from macro to micro to nano. 6G would enhance health systems, transport, logistics, safety, privacy, and more, in addition to enabling lightning-fast connectivity. 6G detects large amounts of data at breakneck speeds, computes, maintains, and displays it to humans. The purpose of this research is to look into 5G and 6G technologies and how they might affect the development of smart, perceptive, and intellectual cities.

Keywords Smart Cities · 5G and 6G technologies · ICT

S. Chhabra (✉) · M. K. Aiden · S. M. Sabharwal
Computer Science and Engineering, Sharda University, Greater Noida, Uttar Pradesh, India
e-mail: Manpreet.aiden@sharda.ac.in; shweta.sabharwal@sharda.ac.in

M. Al-Asadi
Faculty of Engineering and Natural Sciences, Computer Engineering Department, KTO
Karatay University (KTO Karatay Üniversitesi), Konya, Turkey
e-mail: bilgi@karatay.edu.tr

© The Author(s), under exclusive license to Springer Nature Switzerland AG 2023
M. A. Ahad et al. (eds.), *Enabling Technologies for Effective Planning and Management in Sustainable Smart Cities*, https://doi.org/10.1007/978-3-031-22922-0_14

14.1 Introduction

With the introduction of analogue mobile networks in the 1980s, radio technology has experienced a rapid & multidirectional evolution. Following that, digital wireless systems have been on a constant endeavour to meet human needs (1G...4G, 5G and now 6G) [1]. The deployment of 5G is still in its early stages, and many of us are still trying to wrap our minds around it. With the rapid advancement of technology, we are now hearing about a new thing called 6G technology. While no technology is now available, several ideas about just how 6G communication might look are beginning to emerge.

This chapter presents evolution of mobile communications and 5G and 6G technology emphasizing on its characteristics. Furthermore, new technologies related to 5g and 6g, Enabler of Smart City Technologies, Services and Applications. We also layout the challenges and future of technologies.

Mobile network operators have already started to build the necessary infrastructure in a number of American cities, indicating that 5G development is well under way [2]. The use of relatively new technologies, such as the use of new aspect blocks in higher frequency ranges, extensive outdoor small cell deployment, a nonterrestrial SATCOM infrastructure, massive MIMO (mMIMO) base stations, as well as the compaction of macro-cells and the wireless backhaul network, is necessary to achieve the 5G key performance indicators (KPIs) that were initially set in 2015 within the IMT-2020.

Near instant connectivity is anticipated to be attained with 6G connectivity, which is only a stepping stone, to support future, bandwidth-hungry processes with three-dimensional media, artificial intelligence (AI)/machine learning (ML), wearable technology, autonomous vehicles, commuting realistic devices, sensing, and 3D mapping [3]. This leads to a question that When will 6G be made available and what exactly is 6G? Rest of the chapter aims to offer a basic response by contrasting the two cellular network generations and discussing into detail about the 6G future vision and its supporting technologies.

14.2 The Evolution of Mobile Communications

Telecommunication makes use of loads of Wi-Fi and stressed-out strategies and mediums to allow statistics verbal exchange over an extended distance among the two or greater nodes in a network. The telecommunications revolutions, mainly Wi-Fi cellular verbal exchange, have advanced substantially over successive generations. This stage is marked each through manner of technical implementation of a selected standard, which includes new techniques and skills that set it apart from preceding generations [4].

14.2.1 0 Generation

Moving from stressed to Wi-Fi verbal exchange turned into a chief step forward that turned into to begin with dubbed cellular radio telephone, however as new Wi-Fi generations emerged, it turned into dubbed precellular or 0G pioneers. In the 1940s, Motorola & Bell Systems co-based 0g, Push-to-communicate turned unutilized with the aid of using 0g. It turned into later up to date to Mobile Telephone Service, IMTS (), and AMTs (), that supplied complete duplex talents and elevated speech quality. Telephones have been a long way too big to be carried in an ordinary manner [5]. The antennas, sanders, and transceivers have been located at the returned of the automobile, at the same time as the smart phone turned into installed at the front. Later, an extra available briefcase version turned into developed. It appears not going that everybody could be capable of use it.

14.2.2 1 Generation

In 1979, the primary technology of cell communications changed into established, permitting absolutely each person to have get right of entry to Wi-Fi technology. In the fall, worldwide roaming changed into launched, permitting human beings in numerous nations to speak wirelessly. Signals modulated in 1G may be digitally or analogy modulated [6]. Information changed into transferred thru analogue alerts in 1g. This changed into constrained to handiest voice conversations at a pinnacle variety of 2.4 Kbps and a frequency of 150 MHz, ensuing in excessive insurance and additionally immoderate latency and strength usage. The vocal fine changed into likewise unsatisfactory. It is probably transported in a traditional manner.

14.2.3 2 Generation

In 1991, the second one technology of cell telecommunications, which includes GSM, turned into introduced (Global System for Mobile communication). Instead of analogue modulation, 2G hired virtual modulation. For multiplexing, it used TDMA AND CDMA, for time department a couple of access & code department multiplexes. It had a 900 MHz frequency. It enabled the addition of SMS to voice calls, subsequently enhancing name quality [7]. If a molecular telecall smartphone desires to speak facts to some other molecular telecall smartphone, it needs to ship facts to a BTS that is controlled through a BSC that is a better tier within side the GSM network. MSC, which turned into in fee of the whole network, turned into in fee of all BSC.

14.2.4   3 Generation

In 1998, 3G became delivered with the intention of improving community pace. WCDMA-UMTS became the primary 3G standard. CDMA & packet switching have been hired within side the first version, with 3 important frequency bands of 850, 1900, and 2100 MHZ [7]. Although WCDMA became primarily based totally at GSM and UMTS became a brand standard. The pace ranged from 384 Kbps to 2 Mbps, relying at the movement. People in 3G did not pay for time, however for records transferred. It later launched extra standards, HSPA and HSPA+.

14.2.5   4 Generation

The 4th technology of cell technology, regularly referred to as LTE, became advanced via way of means of the International Telecommunication Union (ITU) in 2004 and commercially commercialized in 2009. LTE and WiMAX are the 2 principal standards. LTE makes use of OFDMAMIMO and is absolutely packet switched thru IP. It functions a velocity variety of 100Mbps to 1Gbps and a frequency variety of two to eight GHz. Data transmission has end up quicker due to the low latency velocity. Mobile networks have end up the fundamental and maximum generally used communications technology, with tons extra over 9.5 billion connections [8]. Mobile networks, on the alternative hand, are utilized broadly speaking via way of means of humans; they may be additionally utilized by a number of different gadgets that make net of Things (IoT). Over the following decade, billions of IoTs are anticipated to be globally related, forming brand-new disbursed surroundings called the net of Everything (IoE). The large interconnectedness of human beings and matters will bring about a large growth in information flow, placing a pressure on present day Wi-Fi cell conversation systems. As a result, enterprise and lecturers are focusing their interest on organizing the specs for such 5th technology (5G) of cell Wi-Fi conversation, fueled via way of means of remarkable boom within side the range of gadgets related, cell information traffic, in addition to the boundaries of 4G technology. Over a thousand towns within side the globe has populations from over 500,000 human beings, whilst towns are domestic to almost 55% of the world's population that is predicted to climb to 68%. With the elevated migration amongst human beings to city areas, new problems emerge, which require towns to address. This is what has caused worldwide endeavors to apply technical improvements to make the metropolis extra sustainable. These tasks searching for to make towns clever, offers manner to the Smart City idea. By dealing with public sources and stressing comfort, maintenance, and sustainability, clever towns try to enhance provider quality. The Internet of Things (IoT) is certainly a conversation version which lets in regular matters to hook up with every different over the Internet. Manufacturers, healthcare, power & application administration, car and public transportation, and numerous different industries use the IoT paradigm [9]. The Internet of Things will sell numerous programs in an effort to deliver new offerings to human beings, businesses, and authority's agencies. Moreover, making use of the IoT idea to a city putting is of unique relevance because it meets the requirement for plenty government to undertake ICT-primarily based totally answers in authorities' affairs management, ensuing within side the realization of so Smart City idea. Smart towns, connected industries, and related homes have been the pinnacle 3 IoT tasks in 2018, as according to IoT Analytics. Furthermore, the global clever metropolis marketplace is anticipated to upward thrust at an annual boom rate of 14.8 percentage from $410.eight billion via way of means of 2021 to $820.7 billion in 2025.

14.2.6 5 Generation

It turned into deliberate to be delivered in 2020 and employs a radio broadcasting preferred as Air interface. Instead of FTD, it employs time department duplexing, allocating one slot upstream for each 3 downlinks. It has a better pace and potential than 4G, helps interactive multimedia and audio streaming, and is greater electricity efficient. This generation will be thoroughly covered in Sect. 14.3.

14.2.7 6 Generation

The 6th era well-known for Wi-Fi communications era permitting mobile records networks is presently in development. To revolutionize 6G, a hundred trillion gadgets are deliberate to be constructed and related to the net with the aid of using the stop of 2030. As a result, a 1000-fold fee lower might be required to provide a long-time period clever society. Section 14.4 will go in-depth on this generation.

14.3   Fifth-Generation Technology

Fifth-generation technology, often known as "beyond 2020 connectivity," will be the next major step in the evolution of global telecommunications. It has already proven to be beneficial in a number of regions throughout the world. The three main aspects of 5G networks are enhanced broadband Internet, super duper low bandwidth telecom services, and huge machine-type interactions [10]. The 4G technology that preceded 5G has some limitations in terms of data transfer capabilities, with download speeds limited to 100 Bits/s. 5G technology, on the other hand, is evolving toward more complicated and smart uses of technology. 5G is a network system that relies heavily on communication.

Furthermore, 5G can indeed be dynamically customized to guarantee that the relevant control layer is used by a specific application. Many different organizations will be able to adopt 5G technology because of the high-speed data transport it provides. 5G technology incorporates rigorous latency standards of ≤1 m for time-sensitive applications. For non-time-sensitive applications, it also includes lower latency constraints. Furthermore, 5G could be employed in a variety of situations where strict process controls and consequently great network reliability are necessary. Alternatively, network dependability can be relaxed for services that are not process-sensitive.

5G technology can potentially be applied in situations where massive amounts of data must be analyzed in real time. The software can be requisitioned in situations when only limited amounts of data need to be processed. IoT has evolved into the most important 5G applications, with applications in a wide range of industries and sectors. Its popularity has skyrocketed in the last several years. According to Gartner, there could be as more than 24 billion Devices connected to the internet by December 2020. As the Internet of Things develops, a growing number of locations for accessing data through the network (via Internet) will be necessary. The development of the Internet of Things has been aided in great part by centralized data storage (like the cloud). Users, on the other hand, frequently have no understanding how the information they've given just on system is used, making it a black box [11].

Experts are debating advantages of utilizing Internet of Things mainly various applications, such as connected autos and smart metering. This would allow IoT to be employed in a range of business operations across a wide range of vertical industries, including manufacturing and raw material production. In the future, 5G will pave the way for novel Smart City applications. Furthermore, a growing number of products will indeed be able to access the internet anywhere at time. This would make it easier to combine diverse vertical apps.

Technological advancements will underpin the 5G network, which will revolutionize the core of communication networks. By delivering entirely new network architecture, 5G will allow a variety of application possibilities. Emerging improvements like such AI in addition to multi-get right of entry to Edge Computing, and the idea of community reducing in addition to software solution technology such as Software-Defined Networking in addition to Network Function Virtualization, will play a crucial function in making immersive preference alternatives and ubiquitous. MEC is a crucial factor for programs that require close to-real-time processing and decision-making. MEC reduces community latency via way of means of permitting records to be analyzed close to its source. SDN is certainly a networking version which permits networks to be designed, while NFV implements many styles of hardware-primarily based totally networking gadgets as software program times the usage of virtualization technologies. In evaluation to 4G, 5G might manage 10 and one hundred instances greater information charges and connected gadgets. Furthermore, 5G will supply near-entire availability and geographic coverage, in addition to more suitable safety and privacy [12].

Moreover, 5G will make use of ten drastically much less power even as additionally doubling tool battery life. Radio access, massive Multiple Input Multiple Output, hybrid densification, coding or decoding, in addition to Millimeter Wave (mm Wave) are all vital technology for 5G era deployment. The look at does now no longer crosses into super element approximately the technology in use via way of means of 5G. In 2035, the 5G fee chain is predicted to generate $12.three trillion in items and offerings in the course of all industries, assisting as much as 22 million employment. 5G gives the foundation for an effective enterprise, clever era, and novel conversation methods. In addition, 5G will function that of the conversation community for specific clever town vertical businesses' IoT infrastructure. 5G will meet the desires of an extensive variety of enterprise verticals, like power, clinical offerings, manufacturing, enjoyment and media, automotive, and public transportation, to say a few.

The part of community cutting becomes created to satisfy the diverse provider desires of vertical industry. Slice is a collection of logical configured community capabilities that fulfill precise packages or enterprise models' conversation provider requirements. Figure 14.1 indicates how community slices are categorized into wonderful classes primarily based totally at the summary of traits of each the offerings they facilitate.

The third Generation Partnership Project has recognized 4 classes of community slices [13]:

Enhanced Mobile Broadband: One such slice kind has more records speeds and necessities for higher coverage.

Massive Internet of Things: One such slice kind has quite a few gadgets packed right into a tiny space. Low-cost, low-strength gadgets that switch little records packets, inclusive of IoT in clever cities, are examples of mIoT applications. Other enterprise institutions seek advice from this variety of offerings as Massive Machine Type Telecommunications (mMTC).

Critical Communications (uRLLC): One such slice approach is likewise called ultra-dependable extraordinarily low latency conversation. This is usually used to assist gadgets with strict latency in addition to reliability necessities.

V2X conversation (automobile-to-everything): This slice kind enables conversation among the automobile and the surroundings.

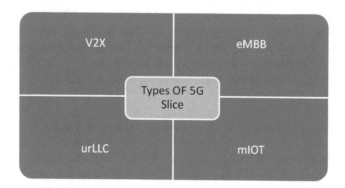

Fig. 14.1 5G supports a variety of slice types

14.3.1   Characteristics of the 5G Communication Technology

This section focusses on different characteristics of 5G technology with comparative analysis.

14.3.1.1   Improved Network Efficiency

Users could have got right of entry to ultra-excessive switch rates, ultra-low latencies, ultra-dependable offerings, ultra-excessive connectivity, ultra-excessive site visitors density, and ultra-excessive mobility over 5G networks [14]. It will even enhance spectral performance for networks, reducing community offerings and protection charges at the same time as additionally enhancing community electricity performance.

14.3.1.2   Adaptive Network Operations

Intelligent sensing & decision-making competencies could be drastically multiplied way to 5G technology. The progressive answers of 5G technology, such as such real-time notion and the cap potential to examine person characteristics (including preferences, geographical area, community context, and terminal status), will in large part help groups in growing technological answers which could assure that records community capabilities in addition to sources are deployed efficiently.

14.3.1.3   The Flexibility of Network Functions Is Greater

The evolution of 5G networks is closely encouraged via way of means of person feedback. It is accordingly created to fulfill the wishes of cell net customers in addition to the wishes of IoT enterprises. In phrases of get right of entry to networks, 5G eras will permit each plug-and-play and self-organizing base-station networks [15]. This will permit for the introduction of a light-weight community gets right of entry to topology, make sure the gadget is easy to apply it and maintain. In phrases of center networks, the growing new community offerings using packet-center networks could be remodeled and streamlined to decide whether or not the gadget and processing features are optimal, and community manage is adaptable.

14.3.1.4   Network Ecology Is More Environmentally Friendly

Vertical corporations and rising enterprise ecologies could be enabled with the aid of using 5G networks that allows you to offer a higher user-pleasant & open community to satisfy their needs. Third events could be given with this type of bendy deployment carrier with the aid of using increasing in addition to beginning up community capabilities [16]. The purpose is to make it less difficult to connect to third-celebration apps in a pleasant manner. Through 5G networks, custom designed offerings may bc introduced on-demand. Furthermore, enterprise networks can be improved, new environments may be created, and community carrier fee may be increased.

14.3.1.5 Comparison of Reliabilities

In business automated manipulate systems, the facts switch method is in particular dependable. Wired conversation systems, which include Ethernet, hubs, and switches, were round for a long term and feature proven to be pretty reliable. Channel estimation generation is used to include verification statistics in 5G networks. The 5G generation also can stumble on any facts this is misplaced after transmission and check whether or not any facts that has been brought is incorrect. The trouble can be robotically rectified in such circumstances.

14.3.1.6 Expense Comparison

The facts factors in 5G communications networks are extraordinarily adaptable, because of this that they may be without problems modified and tweaked. There aren't any pipelines to embed or shaky bridges to build, and no wires to lie. This saves quite a few cash ultimately on networking wiring, installation, building, and maintenance [17]. Furthermore, due to the 5G gadget's tremendous flexibility, it could be altered at any factor at some stage in the improvement procedure to satisfy converting web website online conditions. The gadget is adaptable sufficient to reply to adjustments in call for or demanding situations bobbing up from inter-career conflicts. During the development procedure, no subterranean pipelines or bridges are necessary, and no state-of-the-art wiring paintings are required. Because challenge fees are drastically reduced, the manner is simple, adaptable, and cost-effective.

14.3.1.7 Comparative Analysis of Safety

An unauthorized user must first connect to the physical line before joining to the community using the community card if they want to connect to a stressed-out community. The community's identification verification process must then be successfully ended. A firewall is set up on the frazzled community to provide boom machine security.

14.4   Sixth Generation Technology

Despite the truth that 5G has but to be officially deployed, specialists are actually focusing at the 6G communiqué generation. Future cell networks are anticipated with a purpose to manage plenty of unknown IoT services, because of this that community architectures and capabilities need to be capable of adapt to continuously converting carrier functions and requirements [18]. As a result, the destiny community has to then be smart first, able to getting to know and adapting to the traits of carrier on its own. It has to additionally be open so the structure and capability can be without problems changed as modifications occur. Each node needs to make contributions to the introduction of a smart in addition to open 6G community. A great quantity of communiqué has to be to be had at every node. Assets for compute and caching to facilitate smart self-evolution and operations in 6G, the information charge will quadruple. Fifty instances quicker than the quickest Fifth Generation community of a 10th of the latency the latency that is a ten-fold variety of devices, is one hundred instances greater reliable 6G can have the cap potential to connect. Everything needs to be integrated, inclusive of diverse generation and applications. It may even control the Internet of Things with holographic, haptic, space, and underwater assistance. Examples include the Internet of Everything, the Internet of Nano-Things, and the Internet of Bodies.

In connected drones and robots, those IoT gadgets will allow stronger offerings such as clever traffic, environmental tracking and control, digital reality (VR)/digital navigating, telemedicine, virtual sensing, excessive definition (HD), in addition to complete HD video transmission. For worldwide coverage, 6G will also cope with satellite TV for pc networks. Telecommunication satellite TV for pc networks, navigation satellite TV for pc networks, and Earth imaging satellite TV for pc networks are the 3 forms of satellite TV for pc networks. The 6G net can be an exceptionally speedy Wi-Fi community that makes use of an aggregate of radio & fiber optics technology. In a 6G community, line-of-sight transport means that net velocity is unaffected through the variety among your commercial enterprise and the exchange. There are 3 foremost drivers of 6G: coverage lead (authorities' position), tech-push (technical breakthroughs), and in want of (societal requirement). For the 6G promotion, the above 3 drivers will travel & carry out a supplementary position with one another. The information from afar is a part of a coverage initiative to deal with social troubles and decorate lifeless pool. In phrases of the technological push, the authorities simply launched the 6th GRND plan, and a few governments have given a proposed 60 regular lives inside of white papers and Research &Development proposals. Based on those, we introduce the 6th life, wherein human beings and a huge variety of exceptionally self sufficient and wise machines coexist in bodily and virtual space [19].

The first essential characteristic of bodily vicinity is a totally immersive provider that connects real-global studies to humans, such as progressed tactile feedback. The 2nd characteristic is that automatic structures engage with human beings with severe precision and speed. We'll divide 6g era in 4 categories. The first is non-cell topology with elevated coverage. It encompasses satellite, airborne, and unmanned aerial vehicles (UAVs). It may have a more variety and mobility so that you can make certain higher connectivity & provider continuity. One of the essential revolutions within side the destiny technology could be new spectrum & antenna era. Sensing and communiqué inside terrorist ranges, in addition to Meta substances and wise provider, are all feasible alternatives for ultra-dependable communiqué. A candidate will be unfastened area optical in addition to line-of-sight memo. Medium get admission to era will be progressed with the aid of using sensing statistics concerning localization and propagation [20]. When the cell gadgets ship and accumulate records, the 0.33 is certainly a local AI with linked intelligence. The records could be divided for tool or cloud computing earlier than flowing into community and MEC. We can automate the real-time optimization of allocation of reasserts from molecular sensing to MEC manner to the entire AI. The radio get right of entry to generation is the very last but now not least.

In 6g, we can also envision three most important provider scenarios. They are ultra-broadband, big IoT with zero energy, and massive broadband URLLC. In a 6G world, we count on a developing name for this huge broadband quad LLC with low energy usage. Another giant problem is the improvement of latest get entry to technology consisting of such channel coding, modulating multiplexes, waveforms, and completes duplex. The goals, in addition to the technological necessities and preferred features that we agree with are required in 6g, encompass minimum complexity, low processing latency, and occasional energy consumption. The six number one overall performance metrics encompass revel in for users, statistics rate, excessive bit rate, three-D connection density, dependability, air latency, spectrum efficiency, and electricity efficiency. We additionally keep in mind prolonged overall performance metrics for allowing technology, along with three-D insurance and mobility, three-D localization precision, and architectural and carrier cease-to-cease latency and synchrony [21]. The key views appear to be open computerized real-time quality energy utilization, absolutely immersive disbursed infrastructure empowering real-time interplay amongst bodily and virtual worlds, and absolutely immersive disbursed infrastructure empowering real-time interplay amongst bodily and virtual worlds.

Now that we've moved on from societal issues, trustworthiness has a lot of desirable qualities. Each social issue will have to be defined of individuals, households, cities, and countries. Because education disparity occurs from the individual's standpoint, resulting in large income polarization, we should also incorporate issues on extended cyberspace. From a national perspective, the education inequality gap across regions is widening in health and welfare. Some people are merely hoping for a faster version of 5G. Self-driving cars, for example, benefit from 6G. It allows you to see dangers in a matter of seconds, and your affiliation will not be jeopardized in any way [22, 23]. It aids in the connection of an automobile to another automobile located a mile away. Self-driving automobiles will avoid traffic jams by collaborating with other cars and ensuring that no one is ever stranded in a traffic jam by receiving notifications about it (Fig. 14.2).

Fig. 14.2 Breaking down 6G technology into its basic components

14.5 Emerging Technologies of 5G and 6G

The creation of 5g networks has already started in a few components of the sector and is anticipated to be completed through the stop of 2021. However, with the growing needs for automation and records measurement, the modern functionality is anticipated to expire of thoughts through 2030. If we evaluate know-how in 2010 with anticipated call for in 2030, we are able to assume worldwide cellular penetration to growth through seven-hundred instances [24]. As a result, scientists have already commenced strolling on 6g; it is expected to extrude the digital world. We are evolving towards a totally networked society in which several civic and human duties are device-controlled with the help of smart machines and approaches. 6g ought to provide a canvas on which advanced approaches and interfaces might in all likelihood feature with minimal human interaction. Artificial intelligence, digital reality, more device functionality, large statistics rate, notably reliable low latency networks, huge device type communications, and accelerated records protection and consumer revel in are only a few of the predominant technology that might be deployed on 6g converting networks. Other associated technology encompasses clever wearable gadgets, area and underground communication, clinical implants, self-using vehicles, and drones. An unflappable switch of statistics of up to ten GBPS could be required for digital reality-primarily based totally devices. It is envisioned that the 6g device-pushed Wi-Fi belongings could be 1,000 instances greater cost-powerful as compared to 5g. All can result in well-design society that observes & protects the environment, in addition to catastrophe mitigation and management. Allow us to have a look at the thrilling opportunities in a short manner. The following technology could stand up in reaction to the advent of 6G:

14.5.1   Brain Computer Interface

Humans controlling machines with their brains can also additionally sound like something out of a technology fiction film, however its miles turning into a fact way to mind laptop interfaces. Understanding this rising generation now will make it simpler to install vicinity powerful rules earlier than BCI turns into a manner of life [25]. BCI generation permits a person's focus and an outside tool to communicate, changing indicators and information. It offers people the capacity to at once manipulate and manipulate machines without the want for bodily restraints. Wearable headsets, embedded gadgets, and frame implants are all examples of cordless mind – laptop interface (BCI) applications. By utilizing BCI technologies, the human mind could be capable of interface with outside equipment, with a purpose to then examine and interpret the records. 6g can aid the float of records from the 5 human senses, permitting customers to transport via the surroundings in a neat and far-flung manner. Wireless BCI generation, in keeping with virtualization generation, will permit customers to connect to their very own environment in addition to different human beings including via a slew of separate gadgets – wearables, 'clever frame' implants, in addition to gadgets embedded within the world – in an upcoming 6G surroundings, bearing in mind absolutely one-of-a-kind and richer kinds of connectivity [25]. Tactual communications, which simulate touch & notions associated with the computing, wherein a tool can also additionally discover and accurately reply to the user's feelings the usage of sensors, microphones, cameras, and code logic, are examples of increase generation of this type.

14.5.2   Artificial Intelligence -AI

Machine getting to know and deep getting to know strategies provide significant capacity for addressing strength performance problems within side the inexperienced 6G destiny. Deep getting to know, federated getting to know, and reinforcement getting to know are examples of AI procedures that would be used to plan, develop, and refine 6G structure and networks orchestration in a cost-powerful way [26]. AI will tame complexity of the community for the making plans and layout of 6G air interfaces with the aid of using getting to know the complex community topology and unique approached site visitor's patterns. Smart cities, clever grids, driverless vehicles, and business automation are only a few of the diversified, various 6G sanctionative packages that could make AI extra far-attaining and crucial in strength savings. On both hand, AI and system getting to know procedures regularly necessitate a massive quantity of computing and communication. This ought to pose a large trouble in phrases of designing and imposing strength-green system getting to know algorithms for destiny 6G systems. One benefit is Sixth Generation's Gb-degree transmission fee may doubtlessly give in a first-rate paradigm shift for Artificial Intelligence, with allotted system getting to know & facet intelligence getting used to advantage omnipresent AI. Artificial intelligence might allow machines to assume intelligently, permitting a massive quantity of strategies to run within side the historical past with minimum human intervention. This can be beneficial in a number of domains, consisting of rule of regulation in addition to monitoring. The easy conveyance of information can be altered and advanced with the aid of using AI. Meta-materials, clever networks, unbiased and self wireless networks, and in-constructed device studying will all help it succeed. Remote surgical approaches have emerged as viable within side the health-care zone because of the reality to using robots and artificial intelligence. As a result, the confluence of AI with 6G guarantees to resolve the trouble of community complexity and pave the manner for an extra sustainable and green environment [27]. However, confined studies or analytic efforts were performed, and there is little research at the strength-performance implications of the confluence of 6G and AI. The demanding situations of tailoring AI on apprehensive nodes and always operating closer to an inexperienced 6G, in addition to the way 6G networks will allow AI, continue to be unsolved. This Special Issue (SI) brings collectively academia and enterprise lecturers to look at latest improvements and accomplishments in AI and 6G integration layouts and optimization.

14.5.3   The Internet of Everything in Industry (IIoE)

Despite the truth that the 5G transportable tool can be capable of aid loads of IoT offerings, it can now no longer be capable of absolutely meet the wishes and necessities of IoE new packages. As a result, 6G cellular answers are defined to paintings across the barriers of the 5G Wi-Fi infrastructure. IoE-primarily based totally clever offerings necessitate 6G Wi-Fi communications and are constituted of 4 foundations: data, things, humans, in addition to techniques which can be intelligently related. It describes a global in which billions of objects are embedded with sensors to distinguish length and affirm their u. s. a. of affairs. Furthermore, IOE is a concept that focuses the IoT's importance on machine-to-machine (M2M) connections to create a greater today's machine that includes people and strategies that communicate at some point of publicly or privately networks using proprietary and/or great protocols. Sensors tools, higher cellular devices, gadget gaining knowledge of (ML) systems, interfaces for far flung home equipment to gadget gaining knowledge of systems, and numerous sorts of dispensed smart gadget-pushed hardware are all examples of IoE packages. The Industrial Control System (ICS), that's in detail connected to humans' lives, is important to the increase of the IIoE, as its protection influences the complete IIoE. ICS being related to the internet and is consequently unsecured in cyberspace. Intrusion detection systems (IDS) are becoming loads of interest as a manner to shield those precious assets. There are not any 6GIIoE architectures within side the literature [28]. This paper argues for such resource of a 5-layer format for the GIIoE ecosystem, further to the developments for you to guide the improvement of the following technology infrastructure. CII is the fusion of 6G, IoE, and one of a kind growing relevant generation that ensures new potentialities, opportunities, offerings, and immersive character reviews through presenting associated clever industrial programs inclusive of doing in reality factories (CIF), associated clever transport offerings (CIT), associated clever cities (CIC), related clever robots and drones (CIRD), related clever food and beverage (CIFB), associated smart food and beverage (CIFB), associated smart food and beverage (CIFB), related clever food and beverage (CIFB), associated clever The CIIW is supposed to revolutionize endowing digitization in the direction of personalization for each kind of alternate to develop huge edges, based completely on the 6G connection vision, with 6GIIoE programs.

14.5.4 Block Chain

To meet the desires of growing services and programs, which consist of multigigabit transmission rates, extra precision and authenticity, sub-1 ms latency, and pervasive association for the Internet of Everything, the sixth-era (6G) connectivity should offer higher and further inexperienced average overall performance than in advance eras (IoE). However, given the dearth of spectrum resources, cost-effective beneficial aid planning and distribution are critical to achieving all of these lofty goals [29]. The block chain is one era that might help with all of this. The block chain has nowadays attained an especially essential function because of its inherent qualities, it really is exceptionally essential to the 6G network similarly to extraordinary networks. To be greater explicit, the block chain's incorporation in 6G will urge the network to show and manage beneficial aid usage and distribution with maximum efficiency. By presenting holograms connectivity for industrial use-instances such far off renovation or large-scale networking of business production instrumentation, it'd additionally permit many programs and carrier alternatives that encapsulate business programs for anything past Industry 4.0. Furthermore, it permits for non-stop environmental tracking via way of means of taking into account decentralized cooperative environmental sensing programs to be carried out on a global scale the use of 6G. Healthcare optimization and the implementation of clever fitness gadgets have turn out to be an increasing number of vital globally, and as a result, 5G networks should pass one step similarly to remedy current challenges. Without a centralized truthful 0.33 party, user-managed privateers and secure statistics garage ought to be feasible with block chains.

14.5.5   Extended Reality (XR)

Extended reality will benefit greatly from 5G, but we won't see anything genuinely remarkable until 6G. The function of intelligent networks in hosting extended reality resources, on the other hand, is of particular importance. When these technologies are coupled, they have the potential to create extremely powerful XR applications. Multisensory experiences, telemedicine, and implants are just a few of the possibilities. In 6g, we're moving away from battery-powered devices and toward network-powered gadgets that are fueled remotely and intelligently, eliminating the need for battery packs [30].

Extended fact, or XR, can be constructed and commercially available in pretty some generation, at the side of virtual, enhanced, and blended fact. It will often be a virtual fact revel in created through manner of approach of computers. XR is essentially a hybrid of the real and virtual worlds; computer video games can provide a 3D revel in that can be used to beautify advanced vice, simulation, and pretty some extraordinary applications. Extended fact (XR) has numerous untapped potentials, and it's far all because of wireless generation's gift limits. That's one of the primary reasons why proponents are so obsessed on 5G and beyond. Audio-seen sensors, radar gps, and length systems are all predicted to be used in self-driving vehicles. UAVs can also be used considerably to help navy intelligence, agriculture, law enforcement, product delivery, aerial photography, and disaster management. While plenty folks count on that 5G ought to finally make XR viable, we take into account that 6G may be required to absolutely make the maximum its capabilities. Nonetheless, as new generation develop, extended fact needs to preserve to beautify in terms of power and capabilities.

14.5.6   Wireless Communication with Tera-Hertz Support

Despite the cost-effective deployment of 5th wireless connections using developing millimeter-wave (mm Wave) spectrum, the selection for higher statistics costs persists. Higher frequencies within side the terahertz (THz) region (0.1–10 THz) is probably halfway to often happening wireless communications for beyond-5G or sixth generation (6G) networks, steady with this opinion. THz frequencies, in particular, promise to provide sufficient spectrum, statistics costs exceeding a hundred gigabits consistent with second (Gbps), inexperienced connectivity, denser networks, and specifically constant and real communications [31]. By allowing the superiority of nano sensors, THz statistics length permits nano devices to modify within side the soma every suited and some distance flung commands. THz generation turned into indexed as one of the 4 number one and maximum vital analytical fields that might have a preserve on society large than the Internet itself via way of means of the US Defense Advanced Research Projects Agency in 2014. Similarly, the United States National Research Council and the Semiconductor Research Consortium particular THz as one of the 4 maximum critical additives of the following IT revolution (SRC).

14.6 5G: Smart Cities' Technology Enabler

IoT is speedy turning into one of the maximum crucial packages for 5G. The relevance of 5G networks as simply an enabler of this method is developing as humans end up extra privy to the transformative have an impact on that IoT might also additionally have on a town's infrastructure. The Internet of Things (IoT) is being mentioned past packages like related automobiles and clever meters to consist of the whole huge variety of procedures inside vertical enterprise sectors such as manufacturing, utilities, and uncooked fabric processing. 5G will open up new possibilities for Smart City packages within side the future. 5G will permit increasingly more gadgets to hook up with the net no matter their vicinity or time, taking into account extra integration among vertical packages [32].

14.6.1 Drivers of Smart City Demand

Even alevins though 5G era enhancement is conceivable, the selection to include its miles primarily based totally at the call for the improved in addition to new offerings enabled, in addition to their use and socio-monetary benefits [33]. The call for and utilization of cellular community offerings through town citizens, town authorities, and town organizations are the primary drivers of multiplied cellular visitors within side the town.

14.6.1.1 Drivers of City Governance

The number one aim of town authorities is to make certain the health of its residents through imparting suitable offerings inclusive of power, water, gas, and sanitation in a well timed and cost-powerful manner. Revenue from software provider departments can certainly be multiplied through optimizing operators ought to make certain that sources aren't wasted. Residents' productiveness may be raised through enhancing the town's roadways and transportation infrastructure, ensuing in multiplied tax revenues [34].

14.6.1.2 Residents' Drivers with Inside the City

The primary requirements of town citizens consist of dependable software materials inclusive of water, power, gas, sanitary facilities, and an amazing transportation gadget with assured private protection and safety. Beyond that, citizens would really like to have a higher nice of existence each at domestic.

14.6.1.3 Drivers of the City Business

Entrepreneurs with inside the town need to look new possibilities get up from the upgrading of current offerings or the advent of latest ones. This may appeal to investments whilst additionally imparting process opportunities for locals. Due to the aforementioned need for drivers, there will likely be an increase in cellular connections and data usage, as well as the use of over-the-top (OTT) offers and cellular packages for data, as everyone may be obliged to become digitally connected [35].

Next-generation verbal exchange & entertainment – Online media for the Smart Home era and security/surveillance requirements. According to Cisco, foreign Internet video traffic will make up 80% of all client internet activity by 2021. The extensive style of more youthful people may rise, especially in developing global places such India and Brazil. The so-called "Digital Natives" is probably immoderate-name for video & immoderate-tempo verbal exchange company developers. Video communications is probably in immoderate name for real-time protection inclusive of video surveillance at homes, streets, and offices [36].

The real nature of offerings might necessitate extraordinarily excessive communiqué provider reliability. For a few mission-crucial offerings, there may be no downtime at all. As an end result, call for "constantly on" cellular offerings becomes the standard.

Increased mobility improves enterprise productiveness through using humans from any tool from any place. Citizen's productiveness rose because of this. As an end result, there might be a preference for people for you to paintings from anywhere, at any time, on any tool.

To aid the brand-new offerings and enhance current ones, however there's a want for growing Cloud adoption.

14.6.2 5G: Enabler of Smart City Technologies

Along with improved traits, as said within side the preceding section, 5G is nicely positioned to fulfill the Smart City's wishes. The following 5G traits are vital for Smart Cities to permit large-scale IOT adoption [37]:

14.6.2.1 Device Interoperability

Device Interoperability serving a large boom within side the range of gadgets linked to Wi-Fi networks, inclusive of sensors, cameras, actuators, and so on. These are vital at homes, streets, site visitor's intersections, and public regions inclusive of bus stops, teach stations, and airports, amongst different places. This will assist Smart Cities meet their wishes for Smart Traffic Systems, Home Automation, Public Safety, privacy & Surveillance. To allow each add and down load of video wealthy offerings over Wi-Fi networks, in addition to large facts quantities, very vast bandwidth is vital. This is made feasible through 5G [38].

14.6.2.2 Ultra-Low Latency

Ultra-low latency is vital for improved consumer experiences, inclusive of the shipping of 3-d visuals and holograms, in addition to programs like self-riding cars. This want is supported via way of means of 5G's low latency of the much less than 1 mS.

14.6.2.3 5G's 'constantly on' connectivity

5G's 'constantly on' connectivity helps offerings in excessive-mobility conditions like vehicles and excessive-velocity trains, in addition to offerings that require ultra-excessive reliability, inclusive of driverless cars & site visitors tracking. To assist a sophisticated site visitors tracking and manipulate machine and driverless cars, 100% insurance is likewise vital. Many fitness offerings additionally require a "constantly ON" feature due to the fact an electricity loss may be fatal [39].

14.6.2.4 Energy Conservation

Energy Conservation with sure cell broadband system requires staying of all of the time while some switch on intermittently, the widespread upward push in related gadgets that make up with a completely fashioned IoT is predicted to call for higher electricity performance than presently attainable. The extraordinarily scalable and context-conscious nature of 5G networks may accommodate the extensive variety of IoT and different Smart City programs; every with its personal set of prices, mobility, latency, community stability, and resilience wish.

14.7   5G Enables Smart City Services and Applications

The following are some clever metropolis sports and offerings that 5G can allow or deliver greater efficiently.

14.7.1   Smart Homes Residents

Smart Homes Residents wishes have to be met each outside and inside the residence so as for a Smart Home to be successful. Remote tracking and manipulate of houses for safety, surveillance, and control of kids and the aged are the various necessities. It calls for a home gateway device that accepts a whole lot of technology as inputs, combines them, and interacts with the crucial tracking device. Remote domestic safety tracking and manipulate, in addition to far off manipulate of family gadget inclusive of heaters, refrigerators, lighting fixtures structures, and water sprinklers, are examples of Smart Home applications. Households are in all likelihood to turn out to be tremendous statistics turbines and providers of records. Residents' wishes have to be met each outside and inside the residence so as for a Smart Home to be successful. Remote tracking and manipulate of houses for safety, surveillance, and control of kids and the aged are the various necessities. It calls for a home gateway device that accepts a whole lot of technology as inputs, combines them, and interacts with the crucial tracking device. Remote domestic safety tracking and manipulate, in addition to far off manipulate of family gadget inclusive of heaters, refrigerators, lighting fixtures structures, and water sprinklers, are examples of Smart Home applications [40]. Households are in all likelihood to turn out to be tremendous statistics turbines and providers of records. The expectation can be for a full-period video to be downloaded and performed instantly, which might be made viable via way of means of 5G. 5G's substantial tool connectivity, speedy speeds, and ultra-low latency features permit for a huge variety of applications.

14.7.2   Smart Education

The conventional academic version is challenged via way of means of the cap potential to examine at any time and from any location. It's viable that it is now not only a classroom-primarily based totally approaches. Network-primarily based totally answers and connectivity becomes important infrastructure. Massive Open Online Courses (MOOCs) becomes the same old as connectivity improves. Students ought to be capable of choose their favored path from a listing of global players. Also, there may be a want to present extremely good schooling to people with disabilities who're not able to tour. In a related society, the bulk of households will certainly be capable of display and take part of their kid's getting to know technique in actual time. With era allowing virtual & augmented truth elements, the limitations of bodily lecture rooms can be lifted, and schooling becomes virtual [41]. The following functionalities are enabled via way of means of 5G's speedy speeds and ultra-low latency, paving the door for clever schooling.

14.7.3 Smart Health

The following are a number of the 5G residences a good way to help the Healthcare use case:

Device Connections and Bandwidth-To accommodate excessive massive datasets and a developing range of wirelessly related gadgets, inclusive of fitness tracking, customer electronics, and sensors

Low Latency (Ultra-Low Latency)- For far off surgical operation applications.

Constant Internet Access- With ultra-excessive dependability necessities for far off surgical operation, affected person care, and tracking, in addition to making sure that new far off fitness offerings are to be had all through metropolitan, regional, and rural regions [42]

Telemedicine through audio and video conference-Sensitive metrics has to be analyzed in actual time and straight away pronounced to the doctor. To manipulate diabetes, asthma, and cardiac problems, far off tracking of parameters inclusive of blood pressure, coronary heart rate, blood sugar, and ECG is viable.

Telesurgery (far off surgical operation)- Local paramedics/surgeons can be educated to adopt urgent/precise operations beneath neath the course of distant (even international) specialists who can be tracking every operation in actual time.

3-D mind imaging- Enable speedy records retrieval of Client EMRs stored in networked gadgets and the cloud statistics garage in emergency conditions inclusive of injuries, which could keep lives. These facts can be used effectively through manner of method of paramedics in ambulances and/or doctors in emergency rooms in hospitals to preserve lives. The next natural step is to implant microchips and sensors into our bodies, at which component the body becomes absolutely interwoven into to the surround networked ecosystem.

14.7.4 Smart Transportation Systems

By establishing close by warning systems via vehicular communications, street accidents can be considerably reduced. Approaching automobiles at intersections supply caution messages to the opposite automobiles traversing that intersection, whilst departing cars can alert different motors that they intend to go away the highway. Automatic braking on every occasion the auto detects an obstruction will in all likelihood decrease the quantity of rear-stop collisions via way of means of a sizeable amount.

Some of the functions of 5G-enabled cars encompass [43]:

Passenger infotainment that calls for massive capability and mobility on the equal time.

Automobiles with integrated motive force useful resource structures that use three-D imagery and sensors.

Vehicles capable of come across life-threatening activities inclusive of collisions in the automobile's attain and different risky avenue situations.

Augmented reality interfaces detect objects in the dark and tell the driver about their whereabouts and motions by superimposing records over what they view through the front window.

Self-using or remotely managed cars that take fee of all using sports, require ultra-dependable and extraordinarily brief verbal exchange among self-using automobiles in addition to among automobiles with infrastructure. This is possible way to 5G's ultra-low latencies and extremely good reliability. According to a survey via way of means of 4G Americas, international call for related automobiles is rising. In 2013, best kind of 7% of automobiles had been deployed with connectivity functions. In 2020, international automobile income is predicted to be over ninety-two million, with sixty-nine million of these having connectivity functions, or kind of 75% of all automobiles added globally [44].

Vehicle-to-Vehicle (V2V) communications is a Wi-Fi community wherein automobiles ship every different message with records approximately their sports. These records might encompass such things as speed, location, tour course, braking, in addition to lack of stability. Connected Vehicles may be enabled with 5G era, which has a low latency potential. Vehicle-to-Infrastructure (V2I) communications is a Wi-Fi community wherein automobiles ship messages to roadside infrastructure or satellites with records approximately their whereabouts. These records might encompass such things as speed, location, tour course, braking, or lack of stability. 5G era, with its low latency potential, can allow this form of verbal exchange. Individual automobile status (– for example, position, speed, acceleration, and so on.) or occasion records (– for example, site visitors' congestion, ice avenue, fog, etc.) may be communicated to close by cars or to a middle location (base station, back) wherein it is able to had been amassed after which dispensed to different cars to utilize. This can help drivers keep away from collisions at junctions and while converting lanes.

14.7.5   Surveillance Systems and Smart Safety

Smart metropolis governance performs an important function in making sure inhabitants' protection and safety. Theft, riots, and terrorism may want to pose a safety hazard. This can bring about the lack of people's life and feature a bad effect on residents' social lives [45]. Real-time video tracking and emergency reaction ought to be to be had in clever cities. Traffic surveillance cameras hooked up all through the metropolis ought to allow for clearer viewing and recording of site visitor's situations and incidents. Video tracking at ATMs, banks, jewelry stores, and secluded highways, amongst different places, is important for citizens' protection. In a Smart City, 5G will permit actual-time video surveillance to be mixed with get entry to specific places. N within side the midst of a throng

14.7.6   Smart Power

Smart grid era permits for precise, actual-time dimension of power intake and disruptions. Further low-fee tool connections are probably to be had with 5G, making an allowance for thorough insurance of the power device. By integrating disconnected power gadgets into the grid, a massive range of disconnected power gadgets may be monitored & controlled in actual-time, permitting correct forecast of strength intake. This may want to assist with load balancing and probably decrease power charges for houses [46]. Outages may be rectified rapidly, saving downtime. Because the plethora of sensors and gadgets in the road can display human beings or cars in actual time and dim public illumination if there aren't any pedestrians or automobiles in the road, 5G may want to allow Smart Street Lighting.

14.8   Smart Cities and the Economic Implications of 5G

Smart City Solutions used to strength grid control and car site visitors control may save and profit many billions of greenbacks with the aid of using decreasing electricity consumption, gas consumption, and electricity usage. Cities may use 5G technology to keep commuting instances, enhance public safety, and keep cash on their clever grids [47]. Small molecular networks could be used to construct 5G networks, which could have 10–a hundred instances the wide variety of antenna positions as 3G/4G networks. These cells could now no longer best deliver the excessive speeds and capacities of 5G; however, they could additionally help the growing variety of gadgets so that it will be linked to the destiny community. Telecom agencies are expected to invest $275 billion growing 5G infrastructure, which may bring about the advent of three million new jobs and a $500 billion growth in GDP. Many jobs could be created with the aid of using the approaching 5G community infrastructure. Governments must inspire the deployment of recent 5G infrastructure, due to the fact there could be a circulate far from conventional massive telecom towers and in the direction of small molecular websites positioned on lamp posts and software poles. This may want to necessitate a change within side the present-day permission manner and rate structures. According to a study carried out both with the aid of using New Policy Center, each shift from one era cellular communiqué to some other affords a slew of recent process possibilities in set up and deployment, in addition to different offerings enabled with the aid of using that era. The GDP could advantage due to this.

14.9 Vision 6G

Additionally, we can emphasize important features from the systems' perspective in the center, including enhanced service overlaying for all machines and people worldwide and local AI for all offerings networks and devices. 6g will join intelligence within side the bodily international via accelerated coverage, in addition to open community layout within side the virtual international, blending this fashion within side the actual international [48]. Figure 14.3 shows the 6G foundations and accompanying analytical tools.

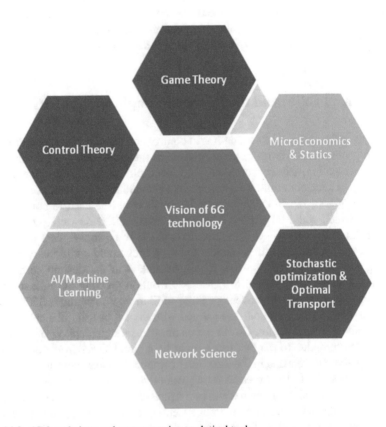

Fig. 14.3 6G foundations and accompanying analytical tools

14.9.1   Intelligent Personal Edge

This software consists of augmented projection interfaces and bodily to cyber fusing fitness analytics services, amongst different functions. The fundamental technology could be customized AI, projection interfaces using cross-provider architectures, and Wi-Fi multi-get right of entry to connectivity.

14.9.2   Sensor to AI Fusion

Ambient sensor intelligence, scanning fitness signs, and clever garments and surroundings are only some of the functions [49]. Machine gaining knowledge of, laptop security, edges analytics sensor fusion, and block chain could be required for those functions.

14.9.3   Super-Functional Components

Multidimensional layout technology mixed with digital components and side analytics within side the use of practical substances. On-the-fly configuration, product gamification, IoT, and hologram UIs may be required for the ones.

14.9.4   Smart Materials

For it to be practically effective, 3D IoT format and augmented sensing are required. Printed electronics and reusable materials are the examples.

14.9.5   Mobility as each a Service

This may want to growth mobility through manner of approach of which incorporates extra appropriate object and infrastructure connectivity, self enough safety management, and logistical assistance. Wireless multi-radio connectivity, streaming analytics, multi-object IoT, and facet computing must all be regarded conditions for the project [50].

14.9.6 Smart City Services

These include AI observing & catering services, town logistics management, sentient safety and comfort, and plenty extra. Highly scalable systems, AI, IoT, and cyber security may be required for the maximum suitable execution of these services.

14.9.7 Personalized Surfaces

Contextual applications combining posted electronics, IoT, AI, and wireless services. Prerequisites for the one's talents include consent management, context processing, facet computing, and smart ground era.

14.9.8 Multi-object Monitoring

This app may want to have programmable IoT relationships, edge connectivity, and sensing networks, among exclusive things. The critical era for their operation will include consent management, swarm analytics, cyber-security, and block chain [51].

14.9.9 Bio-Cybernetic Identity

This includes identity-critical company designs; device studying based totally mostly on sensing, and accepts as true with distribution. Context analysis, device studying, cyber-identity, and biometrics may be required for this software.

14.9.10 Autonomous Port

This 6G software could consist of human beings and merchandise logistics, swarm-primarily based totally operations, and collaborative mobility. Wireless IoT, community interoperability, information styles analytics, and streaming analytics could all be required for those capabilities to run well [52].

14.9.11 Smart displays

Augmented substances that may be programmed. The fundamental factors could be context-conscious content material introduction and preference-primarily based totally person experiences. Multi-channel connection, published electronics, context-unfastened IoT, and clever surfaces will all play a substantial role.

14.10 Challenges

Providing up with one Tbps every person has to be one of the number one problem in 6G analysis. The use of the spectrum within side the terahertz area might necessitate its company primarily based totally on soaking up and mirrored image qualities. Aside from the technical ones, extra key overall performance indicators (KPIs) are required. This is probably in phrases of the SDGs of worldwide organizations, which cannot be left out because of essential global concerns. In addition, the enlarged spectrum in the direction of terahertz might also additionally make it less difficult to mix communications with novel programs which include three-D imaging and sensing [53]. To reap 1 Tbps, an entire paradigm shift for transceiver structure and computing is required. Semiconductors, optics, and exchange related substances ought to all advantage from this environment. The 6G community desired to stable in opposition to attacks. Wherever privateer's safety and clean marketplace norms are essential drivers, era can allow know-how marketplaces. In order to grow to be a success community platform, the 6G community would really like to have the Associate in nursing stepped forward paradigm for safety and privateers.

14.11 Conclusions

The reason of Smart Cities' 'Integrated Vision' is to beautify citizens' first-rate of life in a long-term manner. To be a success, there must be incredible coordination a number of the numerous multi-stakeholders within side the Smart City eco-system. Today's 3G/4G wireless era can't obtain the interactive elements crucial for the Smart City concept, which consist of reliability, low delay, device energy efficiency, and etc.

5G is needed for the manipulate of IoT, which finally ends up within side the fame quo of Smart City packages and consequently serves as an enabler for the Smart City goal. 5G will be part of billions of topics, which consist of cars, home appliances, device, and wearable era, to wireless networks. Smart City era which consists of networked sensors and data can be used by forward-thinking municipalities to in reality provide close by services greater efficiently and efficiently. As a result, 5G will beautify the "Internet of Things," allowing Smart Cities to grow. For the effective implementation of Smart Cities, 5G will interrupt rate chains and create new opportunities on such a remarkable scale. 5G should open up new possibilities in Smart City packages via growing jobs because of non-public network infrastructure development similarly to the today's packages it enables. It would possibly result in increased monetary growth, raising the city's annual GDP. 5G networks have the cap potential to free up the maximum cap potential of Smart Cities, resulting in new employment and enterprises. Smart Cities with 5G connectivity can boost monetary development on the identical time as moreover improving services and life first-rate for all residents.

Although the opportunity of 6G is fantastically exciting, scientists anywhere within side the worldwide might also additionally have to overcome a few annoying conditions internal next 5–10 years. Due to big associated with notably better, the trendiest multiple channel models are being pushed to be built in order to overcome the issue of frequency dispersion. It is probably appropriate to create new modulation or cryptography strategies. Similarly, immoderate energy & frequencies can motive health problems. Compatible device may be required to be created in an effort to permit AR and XR. Integrating of terrestrial satellites and mobile networks into a single wireless link will also be required in advance than 6g services can be launched. 6g can be part of cell phone gadgets which is probably utilized in robotics, artificial intelligence, virtual reality actual cities, drones, and exceptional packages. To provide failsafe cyber protection, new protection solutions with modern cryptographic strategies may be required. The internet of the whole thing should have the network intelligence needed to be part of everyone, statistics processes, and physical topics proper right into a single system.

References

1. Chen, H., Yuan, L., & Jing, G. (2020). 5G boosting smart cities development. In *2nd international conference on artificial intelligence and advanced manufacture (AIAM)*. https://doi.org/10.1109/AIAM50918.2020.00038
2. Kim, J., Jang, S., Jee, D., Ko, E., Choi, S. H., & Han, M. K. (2020). 5G based smart city convergence service platform for data sharing. In *International conference on information and communication technology convergence (ICTC)*. https://doi.org/10.1109/ICTC49870.2020.9289155
3. Gang, L. (2020). Research on the measurement of the construction level and development strategy of Yiyang Smart city based on principal component analysis. In *International conference on intelligent transportation, big data & smart city (ICITBS)*. https://doi.org/10.1109/ICITBS49701.2020.00044.
4. Anwar, A., Ijaz-ul-Haq, Saeed, N., & Saadati, P. (2021). Smart parking: Novel framework of secure smart parking solution using 5G technology. In *IEEE international smart cities conference (ISC2)*. https://doi.org/10.1109/ISC253183.2021.9562776
5. Sharma, M., Choudhary, N., Ahuja, R., & Malhotra, S. (2021). A compact multiband 2x2 MIMO antenna For 5G 28GHz/38GHz IoT and smart city applications. In *International conference on computing, communication and green engineering (CCGE)*. https://doi.org/10.1109/CCGE50943.2021.9776458

6. Mehta, S., Bhushan, B., & Kumar, R. (2022). Machine learning approaches for smart city applications: Emergence, challenges and opportunities. In V. E. Balas, V. K. Solanki, & R. Kumar (Eds.), *Recent advances in Internet of Things and machine learning* (Intelligent systems reference library) (Vol. 215). Springer. https://doi.org/10.1007/978-3-030-90119-6_12

7. Yang, J., Kwon, Y., & Kim, D. (2021). Regional smart city development focus: The South Korean national strategic smart city program. *IEEE Access*. https://doi.org/10.1109/ACCESS.2020.3047139

8. Li, C., Yang, H., Bao, B., Guo, H., Jiang, Y., & Zhang, J. (2020). Spearman correlation coefficient abnormal behavior monitoring technology based on RNN in 5G network for smart city. *International Wireless Communications and Mobile Computing (IWCMC)*. https://doi.org/10.1109/IWCMC48107.2020.9148469

9. El-Dessouki, I., & Saeed, N. (2021). Smart grid integration into smart cities. In *IEEE international smart cities conference (ISC2)*. https://doi.org/10.1109/ISC253183.2021.9562769.

10. Rusti, B., Stefanescu, H., Iordache, M., Ghenta, J., Brezeanu, C., & Patachia, C. (2019). Deploying smart city components for 5G network slicing. In *European conference on networks and communications (EuCNC)*. https://doi.org/10.1109/EuCNC.2019.8802054

11. Haque, A. K., Bhushan, B., & Dhiman, G. (2021). Conceptualizing smart city applications: Requirements, architecture, security issues, and emerging trends. *Expert Systems*. https://doi.org/10.1111/exsy.12753

12. Arif Khan, M. (2019). Fog computing in 5G enabled smart cities: Conceptual framework, overview and challenges. In *IEEE international smart cities conference (ISC2)*. https://doi.org/10.1109/ISC246665.2019.9071695

13. Shehab, M. J., Kassem, I., Kutty, A. A., Kucukvar, M., Onat, N., & Khattab, T. (2022). 5G networks towards smart and sustainable cities: A review of recent developments, applications and future perspectives. *IEEE Access*. https://doi.org/10.1109/ACCESS.2021.3139436

14. Joshi, H., & Joshi, S. (2022). A decision support framework to conceptualize the impact of 5G on smart city ecosystem. In *International conference on decision aid sciences and applications (DASA)*. https://doi.org/10.1109/DASA54658.2022.9765185

15. Tealab, M., Hassebo, A., Dabour, A., & Abdel Aziz, M. (2020). Smart cities digital transformation and 5G – ICT architecture. In *11th IEEE annual ubiquitous computing, electronics & mobile communication conference (UEMCON)*. https://doi.org/10.1109/UEMCON51285.2020.9298156

16. Al Ridhawi, I., Aloqaily, M., Boukerche, A., & Jararweh, Y. (2021). Enabling intelligent IoCV services at the edge for 5G networks and beyond. *IEEE Transactions on Intelligent Transportation Systems*. https://doi.org/10.1109/TITS.2021.3053095

17. Ibrahim, K., & Sadkhan, S. B. (2021). Radio access network techniques beyond 5G network: A brief overview. In *International conference on advanced computer applications (ACA)*. https://doi.org/10.1109/ACA52198.2021.9626804

18. Fourati, H., Maaloul, R., & Chaari, L. (2020). A survey of 5G network systems: Challenges and machine learning approaches. *International Journal of Machine Learning and Cybernetics*, 385–431.

19. Jamil, S. U., Arif Khan, M., & Sabih ur Rehman (2020). Intelligent task off-loading and resource allocation for 6G smart city environment. In *IEEE 45th conference on local computer networks (LCN)*. https://doi.org/10.1109/LCN48667.2020.9314819

20. Petrović, N., Al-Azzoni, I., & Blank, J. (2021). Model-driven multi-objective optimization approach to 6G network planning. In *15th international conference on advanced technologies, systems and services in telecommunications (TELSIKS)*. https://doi.org/10.1109/TELSIKS52058.2021.9606345

21. Malik, A., & Bhushan, B. (2022). Challenges, standards, and solutions for secure and intelligent 5G Internet of Things (IoT) Scenarios. In *Smart and sustainable approaches for optimizing performance of wireless networks: Real-time applications* (pp. 139–165). Wiley. https://doi.org/10.1002/9781119682554.ch7

22. Lee, Y. L., Qin, D., Wang, L.-C., & Sim, G. H. (2021). 6G massive radio access networks: Key applications, requirements and challenges. *IEEE Open Journal of Vehicular Technology.* https://doi.org/10.1109/OJVT.2020.3044569

23. Kamruzzaman, M. M. (2021). New opportunities, challenges, and applications of edge-AI for connected healthcare in smart cities. In *IEEE Globecom workshops (GC Wkshps).* https://doi.org/10.1109/GCWkshps52748.2021.9682055.

24. Shehab, M., Khattab, T., Kucukvar, M., & Trinchero, D. (2022). The role of 5G/6G networks in building sustainable and energy-efficient smart cities. In *IEEE 7th international energy conference (ENERGYCON).* https://doi.org/10.1109/ENERGYCON53164.2022.9830364

25. Osorio, D. P. M., Ahmad, I., Sánchez, J. D. V., Gurtov, A., Scholliers, J., Kutila, M., & Porambage, P. (2022). Towards 6G-enabled Internet of vehicles: Security and privacy. *IEEE Open Journal of the Communications Society.* https://doi.org/10.1109/OJCOMS.2022.3143098

26. Bhowmik, T., Bhadwaj, A., Kumar, A., & Bhushan, B. (2022). Machine learning and deep learning models for privacy management and data analysis in smart cites. In V. E. Balas, V. K. Solanki, & R. Kumar (Eds.), *Recent advances in Internet of Things and machine learning* (Intelligent systems reference library) (Vol. 215). Springer. https://doi.org/10.1007/978-3-030-90119-6_13

27. Lopez, M. A., Barbosa, G. N. N., & Mattos, D. M. F. (2022). New barriers on 6G networking: An exploratory study on the security, privacy and opportunities for aerial networks. In *1st international conference on 6G networking (6GNet).* https://doi.org/10.1109/6GNet54646.2022.9830402

28. Li, H., Shi, D. C., Zhou, R., Liao, D., Zhang, M., & Zhou, Y. (2021). Distributed trust evaluation mechanism of LEO satellites for 6G network. In *IEEE 23rd international conference on high performance computing & communications; 7th international conference on data science & systems; 19th international conference on smart city; 7th international conference on dependability in sensor, cloud & big data systems & application (HPCC/DSS/SmartCity/DependSys).* https://doi.org/10.1109/HPCC-DSS-SmartCity-DependSys53884.2021.00132

29. Le, T.-V., Lu, C.-F., Hsu, C.-L., Do, T. K., Chou, Y.-F., & Wei, W.-C. (2022). A Novel Three-Factor Authentication Protocol for Multiple Service Providers in 6G-Aided Intelligent Healthcare Systems. *IEEE Access.* https://doi.org/10.1109/ACCESS.2022.3158756

30. Hewa, T., Gür, G., Kalla, A., Ylianttila, M., Bracken, A., & Liyanage, M. (2020). The role of blockchain in 6G: Challenges, opportunities and research directions. In *2nd 6G wireless summit (6G SUMMIT).* https://doi.org/10.1109/6GSUMMIT49458.2020.9083784

31. Mittal, V., Tyagi, A., & Bhushan, B. (2020). Smart surveillance systems with edge intelligence: convergence of deep learning and edge computing. *SSRN Electronic Journal.* https://doi.org/10.2139/ssrn.3599865

32. Chen, N., & Okada, M. (2021). Toward 6G Internet of Things and the convergence with RoF system. *IEEE Internet of Things Journal.* https://doi.org/10.1109/JIOT.2020.3047613

33. Feng, Z., Wei, Z., Chen, X., Yang, H., Zhang, Q., & Zhang, P. (2021). Joint communication, sensing, and computation enabled 6G intelligent machine system. *IEEE Network.* https://doi.org/10.1109/MNET.121.2100320

34. Ahammed, T. B., & Patgiri, R. (2020). 6G and AI: The emergence of future forefront technology. *Advanced Communication Technologies and Signal Processing (ACTS).* https://doi.org/10.1109/ACTS49415.2020.9350396

35. Gupta, A., Fernando, X., & Das, O. (2021). Reliability and availability modeling techniques in 6G IoT networks: A taxonomy and survey. *International Wireless Communications and Mobile Computing (IWCMC).* https://doi.org/10.1109/IWCMC51323.2021.9498628

36. Vaezi, M., Azari, A., Khosravirad, S. R., Shirvanimoghaddam, M., Azari, M. M., Chasaki, D., & Popovski, P. (2022). Cellular, wide-area, and non-terrestrial IoT: A survey on 5G advances and the road toward 6G. *IEEE Communication Surveys and Tutorials.* https://doi.org/10.1109/COMST.2022.3151028

37. Mohsan, S. A. H., Mazinani, A., Malik, W., Othman, I. Y. N. Q. H., Amjad, H., & Mahmood, A. (2020). 6G: Envisioning the key technologies, applications and challenges. *International Journal of Advanced Computer Science and Applications (IJACSA), 11*(9), 2020.

38. Ullah, Z., et al. (2020). Applications of artificial intelligence and machine learning in smart cities. *Computer Communications, 154*, 313–323.
39. Del Rio, D. D. F., et al. (2020). Critically reviewing smart home technology applications and business models in Europe. *Energy Policy, 144*, 111631.
40. Daissaoui, A., et al. (2020). IoT and big data analytics for smart buildings: A survey. *Procedia Computer Science, 170*, 161–168.
41. Saxena, S., Bhushan, B., & Ahad, M. A. (2021). Blockchain based solutions to secure IoT: Background, integration trends and a way forward. *Journal of Network and Computer Applications*, 103050. https://doi.org/10.1016/j.jnca.2021.103050
42. Lafioune, N., & St-Jacque, M. (2020). Towards the creation of a searchable 3D smart city model. *Innovation & Management Review, 17*(3), 285–305.
43. Adreani, L., Colombo, C., Fanfani, M., Nesi, P., Pantaleo, G., & Pisanu, R. (2022). Rendering 3D city for smart city digital twin. In *IEEE international conference on smart computing (SMARTCOMP)*. https://doi.org/10.1109/SMARTCOMP55677.2022.00046
44. Gang, L. (2020). Research on the measurement of the construction level and development strategy of Yiyang Smart City based on principal component analysis. In *International conference on intelligent transportation, big data & smart city (ICITBS)*. https://doi.org/10.1109/ICITBS49701.2020.00044
45. He, Q. (2021). Smart city network security evaluation system. In *International conference on intelligent transportation, big data & smart city (ICITBS)*. https://doi.org/10.1109/ICITBS53129.2021.00070
46. Gao, D., Wu, J., & Niu, L. (2021). A method for comprehensive ability assessment of smart city construction from the perspective of big data. In *International Conference on Intelligent Transportation, Big Data & Smart City (ICITBS)*. https://doi.org/10.1109/ICITBS53129.2021.00021
47. Heck, G. C., Hexsel, R., Gomes, V. B., Lantorno, L., Junior, L. L., & Tiago. (2021). SantanaGRID-CITY: A framework to share smart grids communication with smart city applications. In *IEEE International Smart Cities Conference (ISC2)*. https://doi.org/10.1109/ISC253183.2021.9562794
48. Häring, T., Ahmadiahangar, R., Rosin, A., Korõtko, T., & Biechl, H. (2020). Accuracy analysis of selected time series and machine learning methods for smart cities based on Estonian electricity consumption forecast. In *IEEE 14th international conference on Compatibility, Power Electronics and Power Engineering (CPE-POWERENG)*. https://doi.org/10.1109/CPE-POWERENG48600.2020.9161690
49. Manchanda, C., Sharma, N., Rathi, R., Bhushan, B., & Grover, M. (2020). Neoteric security and privacy sanctuary technologies in smart cities. In *2020 IEEE 9th international conference on Communication Systems and Network Technologies (CSNT)*. https://doi.org/10.1109/csnt48778.2020.9115780
50. Astrain, J. J., Falcone, F., Lopez-Martin, A. J., Sanchis, P., Villadangos, J., & Matias, I. R. (2022). Monitoring of electric buses within an urban smart city environment. *IEEE Sensors Journal*. https://doi.org/10.1109/JSEN.2021.3077846
51. Mohanty, S. P., Thapliyal, H., & Bajpai, R. (2021). Consumer technologies for smart cities to smart villages. In *IEEE International Conference on Consumer Electronics (ICCE)*. https://doi.org/10.1109/ICCE50685.2021.9427601
52. He, H. (2020). Research on the application of electronic technology of Internet of Things in smart city. In *International Conference on Intelligent Transportation, Big Data & Smart City (ICITBS)*. https://doi.org/10.1109/ICITBS49701.2020.0009
53. Hajam, S. S., & Sofi, S. A. (2021). IoT-Fog architectures in smart city applications: A survey. *China Communications*. https://doi.org/10.23919/JCC.2021.11.009

Chapter 15
Software Defined Virtual Clustering-Based Content Distribution Mechanism in VNDN

Anu Sharma (ID), Deepanshu Garg (ID), Shilpi Mittal (ID), and Rasmeet Singh Bali (ID)

Abstract Vehicular named data networking is supporting various kinds of content-oriented applications. The inherent feature of in-network caching in Named Data Networks helps in an efficient delivery of the content and provides a better communication in vehicular network. However, the vehicles are moving with varying speed, due to which the process of content distribution becomes challenging. Furthermore, these problems can be overcome by integrating NDN with vehicular ad-hoc network. To provide support in this direction, we propose a Software Defined Virtual Clustering Scheme for Vehicular Named Data Networks, which provide a flexible environment for accessing any type of content to a moving vehicle at its present location. In the proposed model, various virtual clusters are formed based on different content type and all these clusters are controlled by a central SDN Controller. Content distribution mechanism has been developed for inter cluster communication to provide nonnative cluster information to the consumer. The simulation results show that most of the vehicles can acquire the requested content and can significantly improves the performance of the network.

Keywords Vehicular network · Named data network · Virtual clusters · Software defined networks · SDN controller · Content distribution

A. Sharma · D. Garg · R. S. Bali
Department of CSE, Chandigarh University, Mohali, Punjab, India

S. Mittal (✉)
University Institute of Computing, Chandigarh University, Mohali, Punjab, India

© The Author(s), under exclusive license to Springer Nature Switzerland AG 2023
M. A. Ahad et al. (eds.), *Enabling Technologies for Effective Planning and Management in Sustainable Smart Cities*, https://doi.org/10.1007/978-3-031-22922-0_15

367

15.1   Introduction

These days the prime aim of smart cities is to change the life of people by excelling in numerous areas such as safe environment, stability and economic growth. There are several factors like development of technologies, intelligent transportation and motivation to wards ease in an individual's life style which are the prime responsible factors for this conventional growth. Intelligent Transportation System (ITS) is one of the key parameters in the growth of these cities. On the other hand, Vehicle ad-hoc Networks (VANETs) is showing its progress and playing a vital role in ITS and supporting various needs of smart cities in terms of faster data delivery and communication. There as on behind this achievement is integration of traditional VANETs with various technologies such as Software Defined Networks (SDN) [1], Internet of Things (IOT) [2], Fog Computing [3], Edge Computing [4] etc. The integration of VANETs with SDN has built a new communication system which has resulted in heterogeneous, programmable and large-scale networking. The integration of these two technologies is named as Software Defined Vehicular Networks (SDVN) [5, 6]. SDVN is a software enable networking mechanism in which the whole infrastructure is divided into layered architecture with centralized controller. This layered architecture comprises of application, control and data layer. This architecture provides a paradigm that differentiates the control plane from the data plane. The data plane includes data forwarding elements such as routers and switches. In the control plane of SDN, the controller is placed to manage and handle the entire network. Open-flow controller work on the control layer of SDVN. This provides a broader vision of the network which ultimately helps in the managing the tasks. The application and data layer are served by the central layer by using the north and south bound interfaces. On the application layer different applications and policies are designed for data communication. In SDVNs, delivery model is based on IP, where point-to-point connection takes place during data transmission which may leads to issues of unstable connection between vehicles during high mobility [5]. To overcome this issue an alternative type of network architecture came up as a solution which is known as Information Centric Networks [7]. Among the various types of Content Centric Network, the most well-managed network architecture chosen is called Named Data Networks (NDN) [8]. NDN focuses on content distribution by utilizing the content names rather than addresses. It provides the requested content from any of the nearby node regardless of the location of the producer. NDN's communication process includes two types of packets for communication such as Interest packets (IP) and Data Packets (DP) [9]. The named consumer node sends an Interest to the network and the named producer revert with the requested Data as shown in Fig. 15.1. Each node of NDN maintains three data structures such as Content Store (CS), Pending Interest Table (PIT) and Forwarding Information Base (FIB). The forwarding daemon of NDN includes the Interest forwarding process. A consumer sends an Interest in the network. When a node receives the same, it performs a looks up function on the data in its CS. On look up hit, the Data is sent back to the consumer. In case of a miss, the Interest is checked against the PIT

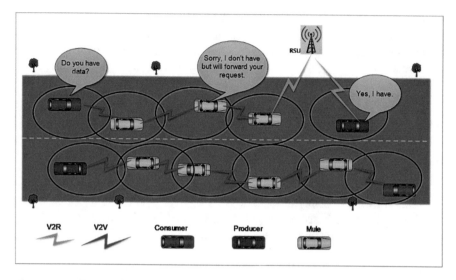

Fig. 15.1 NDN communication architecture

entries. On encountering an entry in PIT, the Interest is discarded. In case of a look up miss in PIT, the entry of the Interest is made in PIT and further forward it to the next hop by looking at the FIB. In the delivery phase, whenever a node encounters Data it checks whether an entry with the same name exists in PIT. In case the match is not found, the packet is discarded and if the match exists, the node multicasts the DP to all incoming interfaces and the PIT entry is discarded after satisfying the request [10]. The same communication process can be a beneficial to ben turn in the field of vehicular networks. Thus, a lot of research is gaining its Interest in vehicular named data networking [11] which makes NDN as a communication architecture for VANETs. This combination of SDVN with NDN provides a better network management [12], avoidance of transmission interference, reduced delay and supports cooperative data dissemination.

15.1.1 Data Dissemination in SDV

The data dissemination in SDVN supported NDN networks can be performed efficiently with the help of clustering [13–15]. These clusters can be formed based on various parameters such as relative mobility patterns of vehicles, trajectories, locations, speed and a search for a specific Interest. Through clustering long term connections can be created within vehicle which would help in fast delivering the content and also reduce number of re-transmissions [16]. In our proposed mechanism, for an efficient content distribution caused by high mobility vehicles, NDN supported software defined virtual clustering-based content distribution (SD-VCCD) mechanism in VANETs is proposed. Here, virtual cluster are created based on the particular request generated by the moving vehicles, which would contain the information of those vehicles only, who will be the part of communication for that particular Interest. These clusters will be managed by the centralized SDN controller.

15.1.2   Contributions

The main contribution of the work focus on the following:

(a) To identify the producer node, creation of chain like structure for a particular request by broadcasting IP request.
(b) A virtual cluster-based technique is used to divide the vehicles into different clusters. The formation of clusters is done on the basis of particular Interest packet request.
(c) In the designed scheme, the SDN act as a static cluster head which further manages all the clusters and communication occur between vehicles efficiently.
(d) According to experiment results, the scheme helps in improving the data management and transmission for high-speed vehicles.

15.1.3   Chapter Organization

Rest of this chapter is organized as follows. Section 15.2 describes related work and Sect. 15.3 presents the proposed system mode land network architecture of SD-VCCD for vehicular NDN. Section 15.4 states the proposed work while Sect. 15.5 presents an analysis of the results, followed by the conclusion of the presented scheme.

15.2   Literature Review

This article deals with the content distribution by using SDN with V-NDN to achieve effective distribution of content via virtual clustering in vehicular network. Therefore, this section contains are view of important work related to content distribution in NDN, V-NDN, SDN and clustering in vehicular networks.

15.2.1 Named Data Networking

Jacobson et al. [17] proposed a blueprint of NDN architecture along with highlight-ing the importance of retrieval of content by their names for a generic CCN. The blueprint focused on different aspects related to content-oriented data forwarding. Zhang et al. [8] extended the generic CCN architecture and conceptualized NDN as an alternative network architecture and implemented one of the preliminary ver-sions of Information Centric Network. Zhang et al. [18] described the vision towards the new architecture based on Content Centric Networking called Named Data Networking. The main components along with the various operations has been briefed inside. The design of NDN along with the development status and various research challenges are also presented. Yi et al. [19] proposed the design of NDN's adaptive forwarding and explained various benefits derived from the forwarding process. The design focused on the effective utilization of Data and Interest packets so as to achieve high performance and resilience in an NDN network.

15.2.2 Vehicular Named Data Networking

Wang et al. [20] proposed an IP-based vehicular Content-Centric networking frame-work by focusing on addressing technique. The framework used address-Centric unicast instead of the Content-Centric broadcast for effective communication. The proposed framework achieves a better content acquisition, success rate and reduce the cost for the same. Duarte et al. [21] proposed a distributed framework for Vehicular Named Data Networking (V-NDN) communications called MobiVNDN. Its main focus was to reduce the effect of communication perfor-mance overheads caused by mobility and wireless communications in V-NDN. It also addressed several other issues including broadcast storm, redundancy, reverse path partitioning, network partitions, and content source mobility.

Araujo et al. [22] presented a test bed for evaluating various applications of IT Sin V-NDN. The proposed test bed allows bidirectional communication and inte-grates the NDN stack as well as network forwarding daemon code. The test bed integrates key components such as set of codes, models, functionalities, and tech-nologies to improve functionality of V-NDN. Grassi et al. [23] proposed a network architecture for V-NDN and applied designed to address challenges present in tradi-tional VANETs. The architecture uses NDN based naming scheme that decouples the communication process, so that data can be efficiently retrieved from the any one of the nearby interfaces. This architecture increases the performance of the system by exploiting the key parameters of V-NDN.

15.2.3 Software Defined Network

Alowish et al. [24] proposed VANET architecture with two different technologies such as SDN and NDN. The NDN is used to resolve the issues related to IP addressing and SDN is used for the global view of the network. A policy-based bi-fold classifier is used for segregation of Interest packets for effective data delivery. This architecture is evaluated in terms of specific Interest packet parameters such as Interest satisfaction rate, Interest satisfaction delay, forwarder Interest packets, average hop count, and scalability in software defined networking-controlled V-NDN. Ahmed et al. [25] proposed an architecture which combines the functionalities of SDN and vehicular networks for the retrieval of required content via NDN. Various components of proposed architecture such as SDN controller, Caching, Content Naming, Intelligent Forwarding, Push-Based Forwarding, Intrinsic Data Security, Congestion Control, Topology Indicator, Content prefix manager and State Information are discussed in detail. The SDN and NDN enabled Vehicular Networks along with their similarities are also analyzed. Arslan et al. [26] proposed a broadcast storm avoidance mechanism (BSAM) for SDN and NDN-based VANET. All the IPs and DPs are cached at the controller site. However, caching huge number of packets in the controller leads to delay.

15.2.4 Clustering in V-NDN

Wang et al. [27] proposed a novel V-NDN framework to increase the stability of backbone topology through a cluster-chain scheme by fulfilling consumers request by following uni-cast mode to acquire data from the nearest provider. The framework is evaluated on the basis of various parameters such as speed, transmission radius and rounds. A reduced acquisition delay, success rate of data retrieval along with the low network cost is achieved. Fan et al. [28] proposed a solution for the broadcast storm by a broadcast storm mitigation strategy based on hierarchical hybrid network architecture integrated with distributed data named cluster. The scheme introduced a real-time route update algorithm, which updates the local interface node on the basis of named set of data received from the vehicles. The local interface node further updates the data at the local cluster and FIB. The strategy aims to mitigate the effect of broadcast storm thereby improving the communication efficiency among the vehicles. Hou et al. [29] proposed a DP Back-haul Prediction Method based on clustering. The method focused on the problem of reverse path breakage for DPs caused by high mobility of vehicles. A routing mechanism based on Back-haul prediction was produced. This method establishes cluster routing based on the structure of clusters and further the target road-side unit is predicted which improves the inter-cluster performance. The scheme achieved a reduced average delay and packet loss ratio in the vehicle-to-infrastructure communication in urban scenarios. Ardakani et al. [30] proposed a Cluster-based routing protocol called CNN. It uses the hamming distance technique to form clusters and the network transmissions are handled based on named data networking. Hybrid communication along with Dedicated Short-Range Communication has been used for intra-cluster link establishment and inter-cluster transmissions. The protocol shows an improvement in various parameters such as, average end-to-end delay, path length, data delivery ratio, and total transmitted traffic. Siddiqa et al. [31] proposed a vehicular-Content Centric network which adopts in- network caching to satisfy the requests. Further, to address the problem of broadcast storm a multi-head nomination clustering scheme was proposed. The scheme forwards the hello packet header to access the information about the vehicle from the cluster. A proposed cluster information table (CIT) is used to store the information regarding the nominated heads. The road-side unit nominates the new head on the basis of CIT entries which finally eliminating the broadcasting storm effect on disruptive communication links gives vehicle to focus on the problem of broadcast storm. The scheme helped in increasing the successful communication rate, decreases the communication delay, and ensures a high cache success ratio on an increasing number of vehicles. Sampath et al. [32] proposed a position-based adaptive clustering model to solve the issues regarding frequent cluster formation. The cluster formation was performed using the trajectory as the main parameter. The model provides an improvement in various parameters such as packet delivery ratio, mean delay, cache hit rate and mean hop distance. Huang et al. [33] proposed cluster-based cooperative caching approach with mobility prediction in V-NDN. The cluster formation was done on the basis of mobility pattern of vehicles by using the concept of mobility predictors. The approach classifies the cached data content into most and least popular data based on request frequency for increasing the cache resource utilization. A cache placement and transmission schemes is also proposed. This approach provides a stable and are liable delivery of data among the vehicles and simultaneously increasing the performance of the system. The above discussed schemes and approaches are use full for various types of scenarios. These schemes include clustering to increase the performance of the network. However, there is still a gap for efficient communication within a high-speed vehicular network. The high-speed networks need a better scheme as the high mobility causes the break in the connection, which will result in packet loss and ultimately decreases the efficiency of the network.

To evaluate the effectiveness of above protocols a comparative analysis of the reviewed NDN based schemes has also been done. Table 15.1 depicts this analysis in terms of clustering techniques used for content distribution with respect to named data networks.

Table 15.1 Comparative evaluation of NDN based clustering schemes

Paper Ref.15	CH selection	Evaluation parameters			NDN Characteristics		Scenario		Communication mode	
		Packet loss ratio	Delay	Cache hit ratio	Routing	Caching	Urban	Highway	Uni-cast	Broadcast
[20]	NA	✗	✓	✓	✓	✗	✓	✓	✗	✓
[22]	NA	✓	✓	✓	✓	✗	✓	✗	✗	✓
[23]	NA	✓	✗	✓	✓	✓	✗	✓	✗	✓
[27]	Link duration time	✗	✓	✗	✓	✗	✓	✗	✓	✗
[28]	NA	✓	✗	✗	✗	✓	✓	✗	✗	✓
[29]	Middle node	✓	✓	✗	✓	✓	✓	✗	✗	✓
[30]	Maximum connectivity	✗	✓	✗	✓	✗	✓	✗	✓	✗
[31]	Cluster information table	✗	✓	✓	✓	✓	✗	✓	✗	✓
[32]	Relative velocity	✓	✓	✓	✗	✓	✗	✓	✗	✓
[33]	Relative velocity	✗	✓	✓	✗	✓	✓	✗	✗	✓

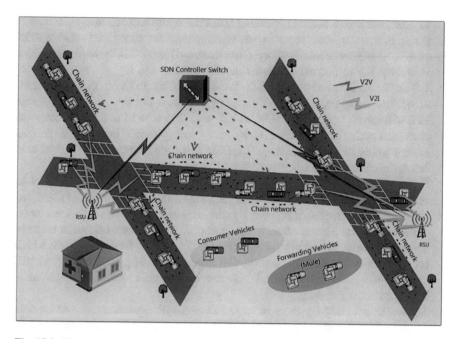

Fig. 15.2 Virtual cluster based chain structure for VNDN

15.3   System Model

The aim of the proposed system model is to deliver the content from the producer to the consumer in an efficient way. To achieve the desired level of communication a virtual cluster-based content distribution scheme is designed. In the proposed scheme the whole infrastructure is supervised by SDN controller as shown in Fig. 15.2. In this figure, the content distribution between the vehicles is done by utilizing NDN network forwarding daemon strategy. In this type of network, the request for content is generated by the vehicle and the generated request is fulfilled by any of the nearby vehicle irrespective of the producer of the content. The generated content can be bifurcated and stored in the virtual clusters. These clusters are formed on the basis of types of content such as safety alerts, entertainment and education. In this individual virtual clusters are created for each content type. These virtual clusters are further connected and controlled by the SDN controller. In case the requested content is not available with the neighboring vehicle, the Interest packet request will be broadcast to the next and previous hop until the producer node is not found. The tasks performed by each component of the network are discussed below:

- V-NDN: The whole vehicular network is observed under NDN. In this each vehicle which is requesting for data will be named as consumer's node and it will raise an Interest packet. The vehicle who will provide the Data to fulfill the requirement of consumer node will be known as producer node.
- FIB: This is at able which is created at every node, the main components of FIB are name prefix and next hop. FIB can be filled in two ways self-learning and

routing protocol. It helps in breaking Interest looping and can freely use any/all paths. In our proposed scenario, we are creating centralized FIB table at SDN switch to support centralized communication. Due to this centralized FIB, it would be easy to find the consumer mobile node.

- PIT: It is also formed at every node. Each entry in the PIT comprises of Interest name, incoming interfaces and outgoing interfaces sending time. Centralized PIT will also be created at SDN *switch* SIDE. The role of this PIT is once the consumer node that will receive the data by using the PIT from the centralized table it would be updated one a CH vehicle that were the part of the FIB table to break the connection.
- CS: As we know each vehicle in our proposed network is supporting NDN so now each vehicle can perform caching in its content store to check the requested data by the consumer node whether that data is available or not in its content store.
- Virtual Clusters: Theses clusters are used over the vehicles that form a chain. There will be separate chain of vehicles for a particular request. Vehicle which are the part of a particular request will become part of virtual cluster. Virtual cluster will be updated periodically because each vehicle would add new vehicle for the searching of data.
- SDN- The role of SDN is to manage PIT and FIB tables centrally as its core functionality. It will work as supervisor of whole underlying network as it will control and manage the all activities taking place within the vehicles. Virtual cluster creation and updating, link establishment and dissolving, all these activities will be created and implemented by the centralized controller only.

As SDN works on layer architecture, all the above components are logically designed on the different layers of SDN as shown in Fig. 15.2. Here, VNDN will be on the physical layer and each VNDN would have their own CS, PIT and FIB table. In the control layer, there will be centralized SDN controller which will control the whole network. In the application layer each application such as virtual cluster creation, content distribution etc. will be designed. In the next section, the working scenario of proposed scenario with respect to network model is discussed in detail.

15.4 Network Model

In proposed network model, we are assuming each vehicle on the road is moving bidirectionally and supporting NDN. Therefore, each vehicle would have their own cache for content storage. These vehicles would also have FIB and PIT for storing data transmission records. Here, first the Interest packet request will be broadcast by consumer node and after that the request will be forwarded to the next node from hop-to-hop only in forward and backward direction until the producer is not found. This will create the one-to-one links between different nodes that would help in traversing of data from producer to consumer by using V2V communication only. To support this vehicular communication various policies are designed and implemented on the SDN application plane. By utilizing these policies, virtual cluster of the vehicles for each type of content is generated for a particular request and which

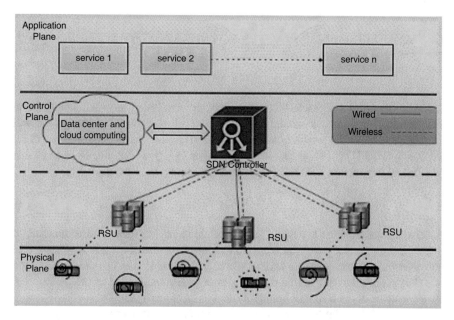

Fig. 15.3 Logical distribution of various components on SDVN layers

is updated periodically. The whole working scenario of proposed network model is classified into some steps. The first step is to create nomenclature for the request message and then the other steps involve Interest packet generation by the consumer node, nomenclature of message, updating of FIB table, virtual cluster creation and update, update of PIT table. All these steps are discussed in details as follows:

Interest packet generation: In this any V-NDN who requires data can generate an Interest Packet (IP) request and broadcast it to all neighboring vehicles as shown in Fig. 15.3. In this figure IP request is generated by the consumer node and it has been broadcast to all neighboring vehicles. Before broadcast nomenclature of the IP will be done which is described in next step.

Nomenclature Scheme: This nomenclature scheme is one of the policies which is designed at the application plane of SDN. By utilizing this scheme each IP packet would be given a unique name. This proposed naming scheme is used to name the data as well the vehicles. The data naming follows this format: /*<area>*/*<location>* /*<V_{id}>*/*<datatype>*. In this format, area explains the area from where the vehicle belongs to, location depicts the data at the origin, V_{id} is the reference Id of vehicle and lastly, domain specifies the category to which the type of data belongs to. The parameter area will be selected through the designed policy at the application layer of SDN. The parameter location can be calculated on the basis of the x and y coordinates. Let x and y are the coordinates that shows the location that is required to add in the naming component. Let c_i be a pairing function on which both the parts of the coordinates agreed upon. The coordinates are represented in decimal form of sequence of digits. These are aligned on the decimal points, and the leading zeroes are added until the same number of digits are achieved. If the decimal points are ignored, the resulting sequences will be in the form $x_1, x_2, x_3, \ldots,$ and $y_1, y_2, y_3, \ldots\ldots,$ y_n. Finally, $\forall c_i = 1, , n,$ calculate:

$$f(x_1, y_1) = \frac{1}{2}(x_1 + y_1)(x_1 + y_1 + 1) + y_1$$

(15.1)

$$c_i = f(x_i, y_i)$$

(15.2)

Every c_i becomes a separate NDN name component called location. The location can be added separately to the regular naming of the data. Here V_{id} denoted ask will be vehicle unique ID which is calculated based on the parameters such as 48 bit vehicle's OBU ID (OBU_{id}) and vehicle number (V_{Num}). Blockwise $\oplus$ operation is performed to generate k bitV_{id} of the vehicle as shown in below equation.

$$k = OBU_{id} \oplus V_{Num}$$

(15.3)

Lastly, the parameter data type can be classified on the basis of the domains to which the data belong to. The whole procedure of nomenclature is represented in the below algorithm. Suppose area in which IP is generated is Toronto and the type the data request is educational data. So, after implementing all the steps the final nomenclature of each IP will be represented as "/toronto/c_1/k/edu/".

Updating of FIB table: After broadcasting IP requests consumer node will update its FIB table with the ids of the vehicles to whom it had sent the IP request. Then the vehicles who has received the request from consumer node will check their content storage whether that data is available or not. If that data is not available with them then they will send the same request to its next hope only and this process will be continued until producer node is not found and would create a chain like structure.

Algorithm 15.1: Interest Packet Nomenclature

Input: Vehicle Coordinates (vx), OBU Id (OBUid),
vehicle numbe(**V***Num*)
Output: Nomenclature of IP
1: Begin
2: TransmitIP_{REQ}Message
3: Initiate Nomenclature Process
4: **if** (Unsuccessful) **then**
5:          return-1;
6: **else**
7:          return Vehicle area
8:          $f(x_1, y_1) = \frac{1}{2}(x_1 + y_1)(x_1 + y_1 + 1) + y_1$
9:          $c_i = (x_i, y_i)$
10:         return c_i;
11:         $k = OBU_{id} \oplus V_{Num}$
12:         return $V_{ID} = k$;
13:         return content type
14: **end if**
15: End

Virtual cluster creation: There would be assumed as on centralized FIB at the SDN side which would have entry of each vehicle which is part of the communication chain. The collection of these vehicles will be named as virtual cluster and each vehicle entry for that particular IP request will considered as cluster member. These cluster a managed by the SDN controller each new vehicle enter into the chain will become a part of the virtual cluster. Virtual cluster will be updated periodically to check the active chain members.

Updating of PIT table: PIT table is also managed by each vehicle. PIT entry in the table of cluster member will be pending until the producer is not found. Once the producer is found data will be move back to consumer node according to FIB table and PIT will also be updated for a particular IP request. For each pending entry P will be updated in the PIT table.

Data Transmission Stage: Once the producer node is found during chain creation process then data transmission will take place from producer to consumer. For this only those vehicles will be the part of communication whose entry is available is the virtual cluster. By utilizing those vehicular ids, through backtracking data will be transmitted to the consumer node. This procedure for backtracking will take place by using FIB table of each vehicle. After transmitting data each vehicle will update its PIT table also and once PIT status will be updated as successful that vehicle will be removed from virtual cluster. The process of data transmission from producer to consumer is shown in algorithm 15.2. Once the consumer is removed from the virtual cluster link dissolving process will take place which is describe in the next step.

Chain disconnection: Once the consumer has received the data it will be removed from the centralized FIB then PIT entry will be multicast to all vehicles who are the part of virtual cluster. After this all connection of the vehicles will be dissolved. The whole procedure for this V2V communication using NDN is described in algorithm 15.3.

Algorithm 15.2: Data Transmission from Producer to Consumer

Input: $Producer_{id}$
Output: Data Transmission Status
1:Begin
2: **if** (Producer Found==True)**then**
3:　　　　**while**(Consumer's PIT entry!=Successful)**do**
4:　　　　　　$backtrack V_{id} from FIB table$
5:　　　　　　transmit data
6:　　　　　　update PIT table
7:　　　　　　update virtual cluster
8:　　　　　　$update\ Producer_{id}=V_{id}$
9:　　　　**end while**
10: **else**
11:　　Chain Creation Process Continues
12: **end if**
13: End

Algorithm 15.3: Chain Rule Procedure

Input: g_{Code}, V_{id}
Output: Status Flag
1: Begin
2: Check Interest Packet Status
3: **if** Interest packet Status==True **then**
4:      IP Nomenclature
5:      **while** (Producer Status! = True) **do**
6:          broadcast IP request
7:          **for** each road segment **do**
8:              select chain leaf members
9:              Add leaf member to chain
10:             update chain status in virtual cluster
11:                 **for** (*each leaf node* $v=1toN$) **do** Check Content Store
12:                     **if** (Content status==True) **then**
13:                         transmit data
14:                     **else**
15:                         Update FIB table
16:                         Update PIT table
17:                         Update virtual cluster
18:                     **end if**
19:                 **end for**
20:             **end for**
21:         **end while**
22: End

15.5   Implementation and Result

To analyze the performance of SD-VCCD an urban roadside scenario has been considered, where the vehicles move along the different road segments. To implement this generated scenario ns-3 version 3.30.1 [34], with the ndnSIM [35] module version 2.0, are used which performs basic features of NDN. Ubuntu 18.04 has been used for testing and installing the entire environment. For incorporating the structure of VNDN into the simulated model, CS, PIT and FIB components of NDN as well as mobility has been considered. Table 15.2 shows various parameters along with description values which have been used for simulation. The maximum number of vehicular nodes used is 350 where each node is capable of acting as either a producer or a consumer. The Best route routing method has been used for creating the urban road side scenario in which the packets are directed by using the chaining scheme created in SD-VCCD. The number of Interest packets generated per second ranges from 10 to 35 packets, and the average packet size considered is 1024.

Table 15.2 Simulation parameters

Symbol name	Description
Parameter	Description value
Maximum number of nodes	350
Number of consumers nodes	350
Number of producers nodes	350
Routing method	Best route
Range of interest packets generated per second	10–35
Payload for data	1024
Vehicle speed	0–60 Km/h
Range of chaining cardinality	20–200

For simulating SD-VCCD, the term chaining carnality which defines the average number of vehicular within a chain has been considered. The value of chaining cardinality ranges between 20 and 200. The implemented urban roadside scenario works for Interest packets based on real-time content distribution between producers and consumer nodes. This scenario provides a logical representation of vehicles in NDN environment. To initiate content distribution, some consumer node raises an Interest over the network. As soon as the Interest packet arrives at the first installed NDN router in the network, the content is checked in its CS. In case the data is available in the CS, it is immediately forwarded back to the consumer node, otherwise PI and further FIB will be checked respectively. The raised Interest is forwarded in uni-cast mode within the chain. The chaining process generates a virtual cluster which is further attached to SDN controller and helps in providing the data thereby minimizing the look-up time. The performance of SD-VCCD is evaluated on basis of parameters such as Normalized Transmission Overhead and Throughput. The performance of proposed scheme is also compared on the basis of Average Delay and Interest Satisfaction Ratio with existing broadcast schemes such as Conventional VNDN (C-VNDN) and Distance Assisted Data Dissemination (DASB) [36] by considering two different simulation scenarios.

Figure 15.4 represents a static simulation scenario where a collection of vehicles tend to interact with each other directly. The scenario comprises of a partial snapshot representing vehicular nodes acting as producers and consumers.

Figure 15.5 shows the dynamic simulation scenario used for the evaluation of proposed scheme and represents a chaining process among the vehicular nodes, linking the producer with the consumer in a grid pattern.

Figure 15.6 shows the performance of the SD-VCCD in terms of Normalized Transmission Overhead. The figure depicts that as the Chaining Cardinality increases the Network Transmission Overhead decreases. The analysis shows that an increase in number of nodes results in decrease Network Transmission Overhead because the Interests will be satisfied by the increased range of chain. It shows that SD-VCCD has the least normalized transmission overhead, as the Interest has been satisfied by centralized SDN controller.

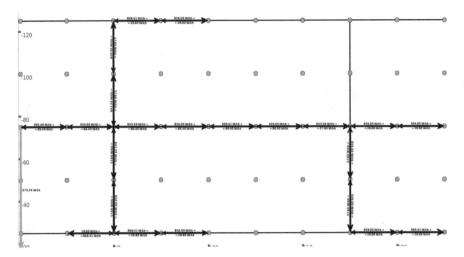

Fig. 15.4 Static scenario

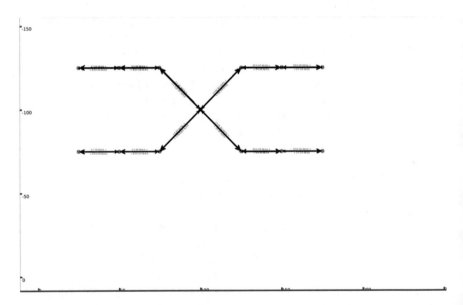

Fig. 15.5 Dynamic scenario

Figure 15.7 shows the Throughput for various number of nodes with respect to Simulation time. The behavior of the network shows that initially Throughput is at lower level but as the Simulation progresses, it increases gradually and reaches its saturation value. As the figure shows, increasing the number of nodes results in higher throughput value in SD-VCCD. This is due to the fact that the integrated SDN controller provides higher values for successful message delivery thereby improving the network throughput. To validate the performance of SD-VCCD, a comparative analysis has been performed with C-VNDN and DASB.

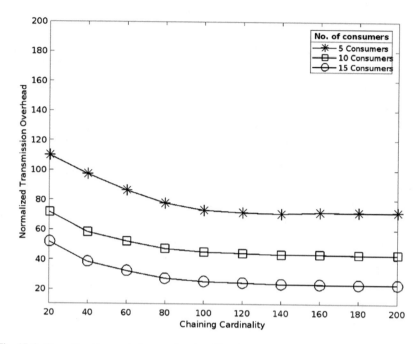

Fig. 15.6 Normalized transmission overhead vs Chaining cardinality

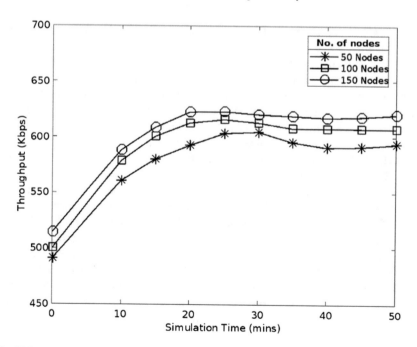

Fig. 15.7 Throughput (Kbps) vs Simulation time (mins)

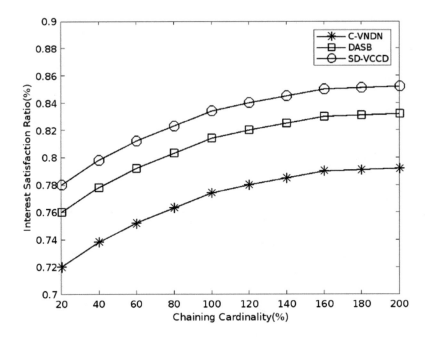

Fig. 15.8 Interest satisfaction ratio (%) vs Chaining cardinality (%)

Figure 15.8 depicts the performance of Interest Satisfaction Ratio of the above three schemes. It shows that average percentage of data received in response to the Interest is gradually increasing as the number of vehicles increases. The Interest Satisfaction Ratio of C-VNDN is lower than DASB and the SD-VCCD. The proposed scheme achieves the highest Interest Satisfaction Ratio as the Interest will be initially satisfied by all the neighboring vehicles with the help of NDN and in case the Interest is not present nearby it can be satisfied by the centralized SDN controller by forwarding it to the producer, which ultimately fits in with expectation.

Figure 15.9 shows the variation in average delay in terms of number of vehicles on the road. The value of average delay exhibits minor variations as the number of vehicles are increased. Initially the delay is a bit higher but with the increase in number of vehicles it decreases slightly ultimately attaining a constant value. The value of average delay is lower in case of SD-VCCD as compared to C-VNDN and DASB. This is due to the use of NDN based chaining structure resulting in the first nearby vehicle satisfying the Interest, resulting in lesser values of average delay of SD-VCCD. Thus, the obtained simulation results show that implementation of proposed chaining based virtual cluster in NDN results in effective content distribution of messages among vehicles travelling on an urban road. The use of high-capacity DPs also types of data within vehicles moving in the smart city.

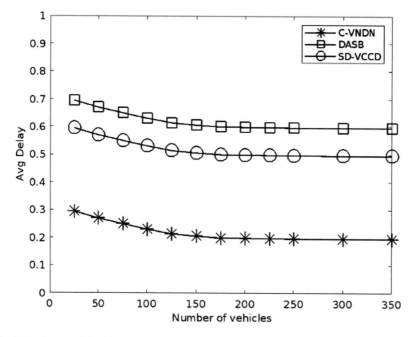

Fig. 15.9 Average delay(s) vs Number of vehicles

15.6 Conclusion

In this work, a virtual clustering-based content distribution scheme is presented that is based on a chain system built between vehicles for satisfying the consumer's request. The communication between nodes is achieved using Named Data Network that exploits its novel packet transmission characteristics for creating clusters as per the type of information. The whole model is controlled by a central SDN controller that manages the created chain network through a dynamic chain building procedure. The integration of SDN with Vehicular Named Data Network is especially useful for providing network support to intelligent applications in smart cities. The proposed scheme has been validated using ndnSim and obtained results indicate the satisfactory performance of SD-VCCD. Although still in its infancy, this scheme can be considered as a promising model that can be deployed with vehicular networks and provide effective network support for numerous vehicular applications in the future.

References

1. Ray, P. P., & Kumar, N. (2021). SDN/NFV architectures for edge-cloud oriented IoT: A systematic review. *Computer Communications, 169*, 129–153.
2. Laghari, A., Wu, K., Laghari, R. A., Ali, M., & Khan, A. A. (2021). A review and state of art of Internet of Things (IoT). *Archives of Computational Methods in Engineering*, 1–19.
3. Nayeri, Z. M., Ghafarian, T., & Javadi, B. (2021). Application placement in fog computing with AI approach: Taxonomy and a state-of-the-art survey. *Journal of Network and Computer Applications, 185*, 103078.
4. Mansouri, Y., & Babar, M. A. (2021). A review of edge computing: Features and resource virtualization. *Journal of Parallel and Distributed Computing, 150*, 155–183.
5. He, Z., Cao, J., & Liu, X. (2016). SDVN: Enabling rapid network innovation for heterogeneous vehicular communication. *IEEE Network, 30*(4), 10–15.
6. Garg, D., Garg, N., Bali, R. S., & Rawat, S.. (2022). SDVN-based smart data dissemination model for high-speed road networks. In *Software defined Internet of everything* (pp. 259–270). Springer.
7. Niari, K., Berangi, R., & Fathy, M. (2018). ECCN: An extended CCN architecture to improve data access in vehicular content-centric network. *The Journal of Supercomputing, 74*(1), 205–221.
8. Zhang, L., Estrin, D., Burke, J., Jacobson, V., Thornton, J. D., Smetters, D. K., Zhang, B., Tsudik, G., Massey, D., Papadopoulos, C., et al. (2010). Named data networking (ndn) project. *Relatório Técnico NDN-0001, Xerox Palo Alto Research Center-PARC, 157*, 158.
9. Dudeja, R. K., Bali, R. S., & Aujla, G. S. (2022). Secure and pervasive communication framework using named data networking for connected healthcare. *Computers and Electrical Engineering, 100*, 107806.
10. Li, Z., Xu, Y., Zhang, B., Yan, L., & Liu, K. (2018). Packet forwarding in named data networking requirements and survey of solutions. *IEEE Communication Surveys and Tutorials, 21*(2), 1950–1987.
11. Ahed, K., Benamar, M., Lahcen, A. A., & El Ouazzani, R. (2020). Forwarding strategies in vehicular named data networks: A survey. *Journal of King Saud University-Computer and Information Sciences*.
12. Dudeja, R. K., Singh, A., Bali, R. S., & Aujla, G. S. (2022). An optimal content indexing approach for named data networking in software-defined IoT system. *IET Smart Cities, 4*(1), 36–46.
13. Darabkh, K. A., Alkhader, B. Z., Ala'f, K., Jubair, F., & Abdel-Majeed, M. (2022). ICDRP-F-SDVN: An innovative cluster-based dual-phase routing protocol using fog computing and software-defined vehicular network. *Vehicular Communications*, 100453.
14. Garg, D., Kaur, A., Benslimane, A., Bali, R. S., Kumar, N., Tanwar, S., Rodrigues, J. J., & Obaidat, M. (2021). TRUCLU: Trust based clustering mechanism in software defined vehicular neworks. In *2021 IEEE global communications conference (GLOBECOM)* (pp. 1–6). IEEE.
15. Singh, P., Bali, R. S., Kumar, N., Das, A. K., Vinel, A., & Yang, L. T. (2018). Secure healthcare data dissemination using vehicle relay networks. *IEEE Internet of Things Journal, 5*(5), 3733–3746.
16. Bali, R. S., & Kumar, N. (2016). Secure clustering for efficient data dissemination in vehicular cyber–physical systems. *Future Generation Computer Systems, 56*, 476–492.
17. Jacobson, V., Smetters, D. K., Thornton, J. D., Plass, M. F., Briggs, N. H., & Braynard, R. L. (2009). Networking named content. In *Proceedings of the 5th international conference on Emerging networking experiments and technologies* (pp. 1–12).
18. Zhang, L., Afanasyev, A., Burke, J., Jacobson, V., Claffy, K., Crowley, P., Papadopoulos, C., Wang, L., & Zhang, B. (2014). Named data networking. *ACM SIGCOMM Computer Communication Review, 44*(3), 66–73.
19. Yi, A., Afanasyev, L., Wang, B. Z., & Zhang, L. (2012). Adaptive forwarding in named data networking. *ACM SIGCOMM Computer Communication Review, 42*(3), 62–67.

20. Wang, X., & Wang, X. (2018). Vehicular content-centric networking framework. *IEEE Systems Journal, 13*(1), 519–529.
21. Duarte, J. M., Braun, T., & Villas, L. A. (2019). MobiVNDN: A distributed framework to support mobility in vehicular named-data networking. *Ad Hoc Networks, 82*, 77–90.
22. Araujo, G. B., Peixoto, M. L., & Sampaio, L. N. (2021). NDN4IVC: A framework for simulating and testing of applications in vehicular named data networking. *arXiv preprint*, arXiv:2107.00715.
23. Grassi, G., Pesavento, D., Wang, L., Pau, G., Vuyyuru, R., Wakikawa, R., & Zhang, L. (2013). ACM hotmobile 2013 poster: Vehicular inter-networking via named data. *ACM SIGMOBILE Mobile Computing and Communications Review, 17*(3), 23–24.
24. Alowish, M., Shiraishi, Y., Takano, Y., Mohri, M., & Morii, M. (2020). A novel software-defined networking controlled vehicular named-data networking for trustworthy emergency data dissemination and content retrieval assisted by evolved interest packet. *International Journal of Distributed Sensor Networks, 16*(3), 1550147720909280.
25. Ahmed, S. H., Bouk, S. H., Kim, D., Rawat, D. B., & Song, H. (2017). Named data networking for software defined vehicular networks. *IEEE Communications Magazine, 55*(8), 60–66.
26. Arsalan, & Rehman, R. A. (2019). Distance-based scheme for broadcast storm mitigation in named software defined vehicular networks (NSDVN). In *2019 16th IEEE annual consumer communications & networking conference (CCNC)* (pp. 1–4). IEEE.
27. Wang, X., & Li, Y. (2019). Vehicular named data networking framework. *IEEE Transactions on Intelligent Transportation Systems, 21*(11), 4705–4714.
28. Fan, N., Li, C., Zhang, T., Duan, Z., Wang, Q., & Zhu, Y. (2020). BSMM: A broadcast storm mitigation model based on distributed data clusters and hybrid network architecture in vehicular named data network. *Journal of Physics: Conference Series, 1693*(1), 012029. IOP Publishing.
29. Hou, R., Zhou, S., Zheng, Y., Dong, M., Ota, K., Zeng, D., Luo, J., & Ma, M. (2021). Cluster routing-based data packet backhaul prediction method in vehicular named data networking. *IEEE Transactions on Network Science and Engineering, 8*(3), 2639–2650.
30. Ardakani, S. P., Kwong, C. F., Kar, P., Liu, Q., & Li, L. (2021). CNN: A cluster-based named data routing for vehicular networks. *IEEE Access, 9*, 159036–159047.
31. Siddiqa, M., Diyan, M. T. R., Khan, M. M., Saad, & Kim, D. (2021). Mitigating broadcasting storm using multihead nomination clustering in vehicular content centric networks. *Electronics, 10*(18), 2270.
32. Sampath, V., Karthik, S., & Sabitha, R. (2021). Position-based adaptive clustering model (PACM) for efficient data caching in vehicular named data networks (VNDN). *Wireless Personal Communications, 117*(4), 2955–2971.
33. Huang, W., Song, T., Yang, Y., & Zhang, Y. (2018). Cluster-based selective cooperative caching strategy in vehicular named data networking. In *2018 1st IEEE international conference on hot information-centric networking (HotICN)* (pp. 7–12). IEEE.
34. Carneiro, G. (2010, April). Ns-3: Network simulator 3. *UTM Lab Meeting, 20*, 4–5.
35. Afanasyev, I. Moiseenko, L., Zhang, et al. (2012). *ndnSIM: Ndn simulator for ns-3.*
36. Kuai, M., & Hong, X. Location-based deferred broadcast for ad-hoc named data networking. *Future Internet, 11*(6), 139–201.

Chapter 16
Sustainable Energy Usage in Urban and Rural Context-A Study

Sonali Vyas, Shaurya Gupta, and Vinod Kumar Shukla

Abstract Resourceful energy ingestion remains as the critical factor in terms of attainment of goals which are subjugated to sustainable enlargement besides actions which are directly associated directly with the conditions for a better atmosphere or surrounding. When considering the energy ingestion and its abstraction from varied sources, the scientists in addition to its innumerable commerce and industrialized use besides home user are considering innovative besides optimum clarifications for the purpose of upsurge efficiency and lessening the damaging after effects in terms of ingestion. All the emerging or emergent nations need to augment their renewable energy for future prospects. Effective usage of renewable sources has transformed the comprehensive policy of using fossil or coal energy to ecological renewable energy. Internet of Energy is becoming a crucial part of Internet of Things (IoT) by inculcating newer approaches with the help of adopting diverse atmospheres for energy consumptions as the energy in sensors are thereby constructing smart environments. With these kinds of sensor-based technologies, even the user behavior is also predicted as well as their behavioral outlines in terms of energy ingestion are acknowledged. However, there are many challenges like environmental changes use of information network, augmented energy expenses plus technological development. Assessment in terms of sustainable development challenges besides probable green development approaches will give feasible solutions, which are practically achievable in terms of implementation. Sustainable development significance valuation for urban metropolis will be an everlasting field in terms of development for researchers' and scientists and apparently, it is quite significant when considering the final conciliation during the enactment with administrators of city-scale expansion.

S. Vyas · S. Gupta (✉)
School of Computer Science, UPES, Dehradun, Uttarakhand, India

V. K. Shukla
School of Engineering and Architecture, Amity University, Dubai, UAE

Keywords Sustainability practices · Renewable energy · Energy efficacy · Energy management · Internet of energy · Ecological development

Abbreviations

IoT   Internet of Things
IT   Information Technology
EACS   Energy Administration Controller System
IoE   Internet of Energy
CO_2 Carbon di-oxide

16.1 Introduction

There are three mainstays when sustainable development is concerned and it is exemplified by manifold monetary, societal besides ecological objectives. Prioritizing amongst manifold objectives is always context and path dependent. Preceding approach and development which is centered on evidence-based research [1, 2] and has established the fact that the comparative prioritizing the goals relies on the comparative accomplishments in terms of study with respect to time and it may involve a municipal or region. Green development [3] addresses the goals in business, which supports the economic growth or social oriented growth objective. Little carbon emission can be taken in to consideration whenever green revolution is talked about as it includes the carbon release constituents, which directly affects the conservational concerns. While the considering the case of low carbon emission [4] it become quite important to classify its association with superior objective of sustainable development including the right approach in handling the evolutionary part in future prospects. While considering the database of a metropolis sector wise it gives a clear picture as in terms of a potential investment for green energy infrastructure, which again depends on overall competent expertise or technological deployment. Existing challenges in energy management act as a hindrance in achieving the optimal usage besides generation of energy in the most efficient and optimal way. Countryside or rural progress is also quite important in terms of commercial, societal besides ecological expansion of any state. There are varied potentials while considering the case in generation of sustainable income with the help of efficient and effective usage of accessible resources in a rural scenario. Technology-centered modernizations for accompanying income influence active rural participations along with keeping the environment in check. However, Internet of Things is making a momentous involvement regarding the expansion when considering the case of economic, societal besides environmental factors. Sustainability development in any field faces many technical, environmental and social challenges generally in the emerging countries. However, any low-cost technological implementation will be the finest situation in achieving sustainable development objectives. According to the United Nations, the rural population of India is 3.4 billion as of 2014 [4]. The populace of India existing in countryside was around 83.3 Crore as of 2016 [5]. In India, roughly 70% of people are living in countryside. Rural progress is indispensable when commercial, communal, and ecological progress of a nation is thought of. Rural advancement is achievable by the infrastructure development for social growth [6]. Quality of lifespan, occupation, well- being, cleanness, besides societal situation principally rests on nontoxic consumption of water besides efficient sanitation. Many have not comprehended the essential social and civil rights in case of social expansion [7]. However, there are numerous concerns while considering rural expansion at large [8]. While considering the current situation, government is providing adequate resources for countryside expansion, still many milestones are yet to be achieved. Most of the rural regions are very far from the urban boundaries and lacking in various facilities like transport and conveyance facility. It is because of these sorts of situation the individuals from rural background found it very difficult in selling their products or goods in market. Apart from that, they face emergency at times associated with their health, besides access to primary education for their wards. Current literateness rate for the age group of over seven and beyond in India in 2011 census was 82.14% for males plus 65.46% for females [9]. Edification plays an indispensable aspect in overall progress, which sturdily affects an entity's revenue generation possibility. Even joblessness stands as one of the major issues in rural or countryside India and because of this numerous people in their youth wander themselves to urban areas [10]. Fiscal aspects plus absences or lack of income generating chances in rural segment, nonexistence of existing arrangement causes serious migration of people to urban areas. Societal aspects comprise of healthiness, edification, besides finance, which too are noteworthy reasons for migration to urban or metropolis regions [10]. Digital commerce has changed the archetype from outmoded commerce to contemporary commerce by a large difference. Benefits and shortcomings of digital commerce plus digitization procedures are now a prime concern when considering edification, establishments besides corporations. Such digitized universal tools and sustainable green technologies assist executives in implementing their concepts in real. By innovative methods, they can estimate the future of their organization, market and life to transform it to a sustainable smart green life, towns and structures. Energy segment supports the financial prudence besides contributing straight away to quality of life, which is very important in terms of accomplishing sustainability. Currently, the mainstream energy possessions are derivative of fossil fuels like oil, coal thereby leading to ongoing reduction of energy possessions and developing of hostile conservational effects. Expansion besides disposition of uncontaminated, renewable energy is imperious while considering the monetary besides ecological awareness for any republic. Renewable energy plays a key role in fulfilling forthcoming energy essentials. Decisive objective lies in all the research work plus determinations put in for reducing energy ingesting while takin in account the wellbeing of customers keeping a tab on natural resources to move towards sustainable development besides conservational protection. Contemporary Internet expertise forms a dynamic network of energy, which helps in interconnecting of device and information exchange amongst them. Renewable energy for instance solar, wind, water, and biomass play a quite important role in sustainable development. As authors we have tried to focus on extensive conversation regarding the following points:

- The varied domain of sustainability i.e. Environmental, Social and Economical are being discussed which are quite necessary for sustainable development. The novel development must be feasible for the environment (eco-friendly), society and must be affordable by a large part of the population.
- The resources of sustainable energy are limited and it should be used wisely in terms of implementation to achieve a wider reach. Therefore, planning of sustainable energy resources is very crucial.
- It deliberates the association amongst Internet of Energy sources like smart power grid and their storage, generation apart from their users, i.e. smart meters, smart vehicles.
- There are many challenges, which needs to be addressed whilst, the efficient and effective management and usage of energy. The meeting of ISO standards, CO_2 emission are some of the challenges in effective and efficient energy management.

Section 16.2 deliberates literature review regarding sustainability, Sect. 16.3 discourses varied criteria in energy planning for sustainable development, Sect. 16.4 showcases energy management in a metropolitan context, whereas Sect. 16.5 briefs about challenges in energy management in terms of sustainability and lastly Sect. 16.6 concludes with conclusion and future scope.

16.2 Literature Review

The term sustainable development was primary cited in a report printed by WCED in the year 1987. According to the report, the sustainable development is well- defined as "development which is meeting the needs without negotiating the aptitude of forthcoming age group in terms of meeting needs." International Institute for Sustainable Development [11] labelled the perception of requirement and restraint. Development Education Program under World Bank Group clarifies as the perception of harmonizing amid societal, monetary besides atmosphere objectives [12, 13] although Sustainable Development Commission stated as central of complementary transformation plus consciousness of essentials with three domains of sustainability [14]. Global Development exploration epicenter permits harmonizing social needs apart from maintaining usual resources plus ecologies [15]. In the emerging world, IoT acts as an important portion in attaining sturdier in addition to sustainable expansion. IoT is achieving countless competence plus throughput improvements in industrial republics for the emergent ecosphere. The IoT has the marvelous chance for the social and economic advancement; overlooking the potential for larger and more important influence in emerging nations can be a huge mistake [16]. Emerging nations are perfect in terms of IoT revolution: the glitches observed by the emerging world can be varied and unknown areas to which IoT are quite applicable. Apart from it, IoT makes an important influence to expansion in societal, ecological, takin cultural aspects also in account [17]. In last few years, IoT projects arc bcing rapidly accepted in the devel oping world, for the purpose of sustainability achievement. Taking an instance, IoT applications are mounted for observing besides administration of energy, thereby upgrading varied access to power consumption and accordingly optimizing it [18, 19]. While considering the health segment, IoT is involved in observing of cold chain for vaccines, which needs implementation [20]. Water conservation stands as other seg ment which has immense prospects for IoT implementation, which focusses on endowment of water in terms of sanitary plus agriculture, and they are being devel oped and implemented in countryside zones of emerging republics [20]. IoT has implementation of disaster management situations in developing republics to handle natural catastrophes [21] like sensing tremors, surge in tidal wave. For the emerging republic, constraint in terms of resources leads to more economical solutions, which are operative in an emerging republic framework. Table 16.1 discourses some of the valuable research findings which are quite critical part of the literature review.

Sustainable growth planning necessitates settlement besides balancing associa tion amongst atmosphere, budget, plus humanity, which is showcased in Fig. 16.1.

The three purposes of sustainability are associated amongst themselves. For accomplishing the optimum resolution, these three verticals are considered alto gether [22].

16.3 Criteria in Energy Planning for Sustainable Development

Various procedures in three spheres of sustainability observes the presentation and impact while considering growth in terms of energy reserve. Each process is taken into account while keeping the energy reserve choice in mind. Righteous proce dures will continuously formulate as an important feature in terms of energy resource, besides will remain as constant choice of selection [23]. Authors in [24] designated comparable four main methods of sustainable development in energy expansion, which including monetary, administrative and recyclable usages. Capability, asset price, process and upkeep cost, CO_2 emanation, are amid inspira tions, being a part of energy planning process. The primary purpose of evaluating dissimilar substitutions comprising in terms of selection of an expansion track con sidering an energy sector contributing to sustainable growth of a nation. Sustainable expansion aspects were acknowledged because of matters catastrophe in energy segment of any republic or nation, counting the economic vertical (investment needs plus lack of local energy sources supplemented by a high prospective for green energy fabrication), social (price directive besides necessities about energy secu rity), and conservational or ecological (environmental sustainability), as well as technical (innovation in terms of energy system). The evaluation criteria for sustain able energy planning is being discussed in Table 16.2.

Table 16.1 Summary of literature review

Authors	Title	Findings
Drexhage, J., & Murphy, D. [11]	Sustainable development: from Brundtland to Rio 2012	It labeled the perception of requirements and restraints in terms of sustainability
Kantartzis, A., & Pollalis, S [12]	Sustainable Green Infrastructure Planning in Greece: Proposal for an Urban Greenway Network in the Greater Athens Metropolitan Area	Clarified the perception of societal apart from monetary benefits of adapting to sustainable development
Frappaolo, V [13]	Benefitting from Sustainable Development	Elucidated the discernment of societal apart from monetary benefits of adapting to sustainable development in terms of energy
Hák, T., Janoušková, S., & Moldan [14]	Sustainable Development Goals: A need for relevant indicators	Deliberated regarding three domains of sustainability
Robert, K. W., Parris, T. M., & Leiserowitz, A. A [15]	What is sustainable development? Goals, indicators, values, and practice.	Discussed global development exploration epicenter allowing social needs and resource management
Rahim, A. [16]	IoT and data analytics for developing countries from research to business transformation	Discussed IoT in collaboration with resource management
Barro, P. A., Degila, J., Zennaro, M., & Wamba, S. F. [17]	Towards smart and sustainable future cities based on Internet of things for developing countries	Conversed IoT in association with resource conservation
Garrity, J [18]	Harnessing the Internet of Things for global development	Discussed regarding energy optimization in case of energy management
Ramanathan, T., Ramanathan, N., Mohanty, J., Rehman, I. H., Graham, E. [19]	Wireless sensors linked to climate financing for globally affordable clean cooking. Nature Climate Change	Conferred regarding energy optimization in case of energy controlling
Bloom, D. E., Black, S., Salisbury, D., & Rappuoli, R [20]	Antimicrobial resistance and the role of Vaccines. Proceedings of the National Academy of Sciences	Deliberated regarding water conservation with respect to IoT device management
Zorn, M [21]	Natural disasters and less developed countries. In Nature, tourism and ethnicity as drivers of (de) marginalization	Deliberated regarding sanitary and agricultural concepts with respect to IoT operation

Energy stands as the critical and prime factor while considering varied prospects in terms of sustainable development. The rudimentary magnitudes of sustainability in case of energy production are ecologically, theoretically, economically and publically sustainable sources of energy resources which is quite dependable, tolerable besides reasonable in long term usage. Renewable, uncontaminated and cost operative sources of energy are always favored however regrettably none of the unconventional sources of energy are good enough in terms of meeting these loads

Fig. 16.1 Sustainability spheres. [22]

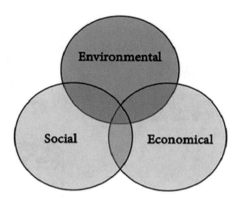

Table 16.2 Evaluation criteria for sustainable energy planning

Pointer	Norms
Technical	Energy fabrication capability
	Technological development
	Consistency
	Safety
Economical	Outlay cost
	Operation and maintenance cost
	Service life
	Reimbursement epoch
Environmental	Influence on ecology
	CO_2 emanation
Social	Communal assistances
	Societal adequacy

exclusively. Therefore, while determining the sustainable energy planning any tool which is strategic in nature can be considered for the overall development.

16.4 "Internet of Energy" Technology for Energy Management

Energy managing organization comprises relentless watching of oil distribution system, engendering elements, besides broadcast in addition to dissemination arrangements. Therefore, it means that significant data is accessible to sub divisions except the operation department. Information Technology protected Energy Administration and Controller System (EACS), which signifies a withdrawal from strategies factually, accompanying with energy administration systems. IT helps in integrating in terms of forecasting, observing and regulating power

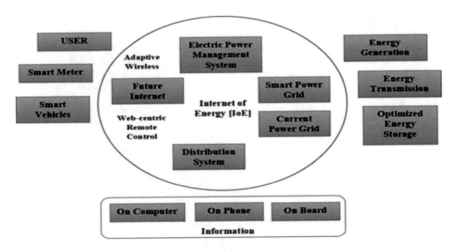

Fig. 16.2 Internet of energy architecture [25]

procedure and administration considering energy allotment amongst additional and dearth sections. The architecture of Internet of Energy is being showcased in Fig. 16.2. Management of energy in reducing functioning charge, minimalizing conservational impression besides upsurge in effectiveness is the prime goal. Since energy never noticed as "core" constituent of commercial commotion, a random tactic is charted. As and when the energy is supplied in small amount or in cases if energy charges increase, energy management turn out to be a chief emphasis. Operative managing of energy necessitates an administrative construction that uplifts the prominence of energy within the commercial sphere and defines the individuals, resources and planning to realize the anticipated output [25]. A business should have propagated an idea for effectively addressing any challenges. At times, plans must encounter constitutional requests and obey procedures very strictly, for instance like wellbeing plus safety, conservational administration. Considering such concerns, and cumulative levelling up of legislation and energy utilization, broadcasting techniques and the necessity of business competence ensures that facilities administrators must recognize that energy management requires comparable levels of possession plus accountability all over the association i.e., from top to bottom. In totaling, peoples should comprehend their role-play in decreasing pointless energy usage. The approach besides idea must need full sustenance at the official and operative level. The purpose must guarantee the approach is entrenched in the administrative policies and transforms the overall business as a whole. As the overall energy administration systems matures, besides developments, which will be focusing on the best solution for optimizing of energy completely [26]. Energy management is directly associated with scheduling, observing, besides regulating energy-associated progressions keeping in view the ultimate aim to reserve energy resources besides considering the factor of cost also in order of guarding the atmosphere. The applications of energy management approaches on varied systems, necessitates massive cost in the beginning, though by energy management it saves a lot of cost later. Though the annexation of numerous novel devices besides varied arrangements in terms of energy management declines the comprehensive constancy of systems. A major chunk of energy management system is very much recyclable, but considering the fact that they can be applied to a certain extent only. The equilibrium in between the energy ingestion besides generation should be taken care off to avoid any sort of disorder. Energy administration approaches necessitates enormous extent of energy storage systems for appropriate operational functioning, though their restricted capabilities make it quite problematic in efficient application in terms of energy administration approaches. Some of the smart energy management solutions are deliberated below [27]:

Smart Buildings: It involves the designing of buildings or structures energy wise and facilitating in terms of optimizing energy use besides facility administration. Connectivity in terms of heating, ventilating, besides air conditioning systems which is under strict monitoring and control, results in substantial energy saving. Smart Building can use JouleX design in terms of enabling IT departments to power-off devices in addition to computers distantly at any particular point of time as this software has the ability in waking up devices for upkeep work or turn off complete systems for the period of holiday or vacation. IP-centered physical access controls allows door access systems in receiving their power via Ethernet with the help of network switches and it lessens the cabling besides energy costs.

Smart Grids: It involves physical plant's generation besides dissemination of energy in addition to other substructures. A well-executed established smart grid may result in annual gain of 3–6% in in terms of grid efficiency.

Smart Meters: A foremost constituent of smart grids is Smart Meters as they help in identification of inadequacies besides reducing waste.

Any organization should be in close proximity with its customers with the help of varied system competences in order to attain a sustainable and modest IoT centered smart systems especially critical for companies facing monetary, environmental, and societal challenges [28]. In rapid product development lifecycles addressing to all budding digital technologies like big data analytics, smart mobile device, the IoT-centered smart systems have become extremely critical for enterprises and ultimately catering to the need of organizational sustainability. IoT-enabled smart system includes an integrated architecture of varied hardware and software constituents [29]. IoT involves variable ranks of communication networking substructure in terms of providing collaboration amongst gears besides persons to form a congregated space [30]. IoT-centered smart systems comprises of embedded hardware besides software components, subsystems and IoT empowers the comprehension of numerous devices for individual, corporate applications [31]. These systems also support in assortment besides distribution of user thoughts and understandings of varied services. Consequently, an IoT-centered smart system is authorized in terms of interaction amongst network constituents and services [32].

16.5 Challenges in Energy Management for Sustainability

Energy Management is important in minimizing energy costs in the industry, improving business performance and enabling the realization of energy/CO_2 reduction objectives [33]. The ISO 50001 – Energy Management offers an infrastructure for power management systems with the worldwide prototype of plan, do, check, act' which is often modified to accomplish enhancements in the world of engineering. Power consumption information is very important, but meters below costly prices are often not in the right place as the operating time and power consumption profile are not clear. How power management is commenced, and the responsibilities associated with roles can vary depending on the type of organization and the lifespan of the installation [34]. For energy to be successful, success must be a process- driven by a process of change that is based on technology that carefully evaluates how, where, why, and how energy is utilized. Vigilant monitoring and evaluation will recognize areas and chances for enhancement [35, 36]. Thereafter it is tough to understand and rectify data error in a place where the product will not be interrupted [37]. The issues of collecting and managing data are presented by the design of production models and machine outlines that form an idea of factory activities based on accessible data. A 2-D image of factory line processes making use of machine profiles with real data from sub-meters as an authentication of the finalized process model used as a warning of the rise of malfunctions [38]. As the cost of energy increases, concerns about the provision of durable energy and legal responsibilities for productions and climate transformation, there are many challenges related to energy management. The performance of energy management depends on the organization type and the installation process: large areas will possess duty holder with a definite part; some employers in small corporations take the role as more than one job among countless. The energy manager may turn off the lights where necessary, but the engineering manager needs the lights on for keeping the production process going. The facility executive wants a well-managed environment for all inhabitants to promote and provision production. There is a conflict of interest, but all processes require to be carried out together. Therefore, Ownership is the major issue, as who is responsible for Energy Management Problem? An organization must have a strategy to deal with the problem effectively. Legal responsibilities on health and safety, environmental management and chances are generated as per company procedures. Energy management requires the same level of proprietorship and accountability from higher to lower level [39]. Employees and visitor's requirement to comprehend their role in minimizing needless energy consumption. Effective energy management can be considered as process-based system that carefully evaluates where, what, why and how energy is consumed. Cautious investigation recognizes opportunities for development. A structure for energy management system utilizes the standard model of "Plan, Do, Check, Act", which is frequently improved to accomplish enhancements in the engineering area. However, no resolution is available: energy management systems must have suitable approaches and policies for using different types of equipment. A strategic direction is essential and agreements must be made on the processes that will utilize the resources efficiently keeping in mind the blend of technology and ecology [40].

16.6 Conclusion and Future Scope

Optimization of energy management and consumption is essential for ideal utilization of energy resources to fulfil the expectations of human society. Usually, the aim of an energy management system is to obtain, utilize, and produce energy in effective way. The energy sector and its amalgamation with information technology will pose important challenges and opportunities for industries and people in upcoming years. Previously, the electric power industry has never faced as significant challenges as it has in the past period of this era. Such challenges put straight influence on the process and control of electrical systems. Emerging technologies associated to microprocessors, communications, and computer that provide opportunities to embrace the issue. Rising energy utilization and many obstacles in its extraction, now facing many nations, have led scholars and customers, including businesses, industry and domestic segments, to explore novel and appropriate resolutions to upsurge production and reducing destructive impacts of consumptions. Amongst issues are resource depletion and renewable energy trends, environmental variations, and trends in the information systems network, rising electricity prices and technological advances. The outcome of the chapter demonstrates that IoE is able to detect heat, light, noise, heat and humidity in the environment, manage energy in smart environment, reduce carbon emissions, and protect from environmental indemnities. The analysis illustrates that the aim of sustainability is achievable only by facing major changes in the current power infrastructure. Recognizing renewable energy and seizing opportunities and managing energy establishes a renewable energy market and slowly builds a professional experience. The requirement to move into the future of sustainable energy through the widespread use of renewable energy will be a major challenge in Energy management. The utilization of the Internet for energy technologies applies to a variety of situations including the following, which can be considered a future course of study in terms of sustainable growth for any developing nation:

- Acknowledgement of Energy Sources.
- Alternate conducts of substituting renewable Energy Resources.
- Execution of Smart Energy Management System.
- Model Demonstration for the execution of Internet of Energy.
- Thoughtful structure of Internet of Things.
- Utilization of wireless sensor networks in Industry.
- Efficient utilization of energy-exhaustive materials.
- Augmented usage of renewable sources of energy.
- Well-organized manufacturing and usage of fuels.
- Replacement from high to low carbon or no carbon-based fuels.

Considering the above factors in case scenario of metropolitan and rural energy management system would be very useful as well as quite fruitful in achieving sustainable energy standard. As metropolitan and rural planning and development involves the efficient and orderly regulation of all activities, which would be quite helpful in the improvement of metropolitan and rural social, economic and environmental benefits keeping the ultimate aim of achieving sustainability in all aspects. Therefore, future work would involve attainment of optimization in terms of energy usage in a metropolitan as well as rural scenario keeping the economic growth also in consideration.

References

1. Roy, J., Chatterjee, B., & Basak, S. (2008). Towards a composite sustainability index: How are the states and union territories of India doing? *Indian Economic Review, 5*, 54–76.
2. Roy, J. (2014, March). Challenges and opportunities of sustainable low carbon green growth strategies for mega cities: A case study of Kolkata. In *2014 international conference and utility exhibition on green energy for sustainable development (ICUE)* (pp. 1–5). IEEE.
3. Grin, J., Rotmans, J., & Schot, J. (2010). *Transitions to sustainable development: New directions in the study of long-term transformative change.* Routledge.
4. Ritchie, H., & Roser, M. (2018). *Urbanization. Our world in data.*
5. Qiang, C. Z., Kuek, S. C., Dymond, A., & Esselaar, S. (2012). *Mobile applications for agriculture and rural development.*
6. Serban, O. (2015). Sustainable rural development in the knowledge age. *Quality-Access to Success, 16.*
7. Reese, H., Routray, P., Torondel, B., Sclar, G., Delea, M. G., Sinharoy, S. S., & Clasen, T. (2017). Design and rationale of a matched cohort study to assess the effectiveness of a combined household-level piped water and sanitation intervention in rural Odisha, India. *BMJ Open, 7*(3), e012719.
8. Van Dijk, H., Onguene, N. A., & Kuyper, T. W. (2003). Knowledge and utilization of edible mushrooms by local populations of the rain forest of South Cameroon. *Ambio: A Journal of the Human Environment, 32*(1), 19–23.
9. Chandramouli, C., & General, R. (2018). *Census of India 2011. Provisional population totals.* Government of India.
10. Sharma, A. (2007). The changing agricultural demography of India: Evidence from a rural youth perception survey. *International Journal of Rural Management, 3*(1), 27–41.
11. Drexhage, J., & Murphy, D. (2010). *Sustainable development: From Brundtland to Rio 2012* (pp. 9–13). United Nations Headquarters.
12. Kantartzis, A., & Pollalis, S. (2019). Sustainable green infrastructure planning in Greece: Proposal for an urban greenway network in the Greater Athens Metropolitan Area. In *Proceedings of the Fábos conference on landscape and greenway planning* (Vol. 6, No. 1, p. 45).
13. Frappaolo, V. (2017). Benefitting from sustainable development. *Sustainable Development Law & Policy, 17*(2), 6.
14. Hák, T., Janoušková, S., & Moldan, B. (2016). Sustainable Development Goals: A need for relevant indicators. *Ecological Indicators, 60*, 565–573.
15. Robert, K. W., Parris, T. M., & Leiserowitz, A. A. (2005). What is sustainable development? Goals, indicators, values, and practice. *Environment: Science and Policy for Sustainable Development, 47*(3), 8–21.

16. Rahim, A. (2017, September). IoT and data analytics for developing countries from research to business transformation. In *International conference on the economics of grids, clouds, systems, and services* (pp. 281–284). Springer.
17. Barro, P. A., Degila, J., Zennaro, M., & Wamba, S. F. (2018). Towards smart and sustainable future cities based on Internet of things for developing countries: What approach for Africa? *EAI Endorsed Transactions on Internet of Things, 4*(13).
18. Garrity, J. (2015). *Harnessing the Internet of Things for global development.* Available at SSRN 2588129.
19. Ramanathan, T., Ramanathan, N., Mohanty, J., Rehman, I. H., Graham, E., & Ramanathan, V. (2017). Wireless sensors linked to climate financing for globally affordable clean cooking. *Nature Climate Change, 7*(1), 44–47.
20. Bloom, D. E., Black, S., Salisbury, D., & Rappuoli, R. (2018). Antimicrobial resistance and the role of vaccines. *Proceedings of the National Academy of Sciences, 115*(51), 12868–12871.
21. Zorn, M. (2018). Natural disasters and less developed countries. In *Nature, tourism and ethnicity as drivers of (de) marginalization* (pp. 59–78). Springer.
22. Dagnaw, G. A., & Tsige, S. E. (2019). Impact of Internet of Thing in developing country: Systematic review. *Internet of Things and Cloud Computing, 7*(3), 65.
23. Wang, J. J., Jing, Y. Y., Zhang, C. F., & Zhao, J. H. (2009). Review on multi-criteria decision analysis aid in sustainable energy decision- making. *Renewable and Sustainable Energy Reviews, 13*(9), 2263–2278.
24. Mohamed, M. A. (2019). *A multicriteria decision aid approach for energy planning problems: The case of renewable energy option in Somalia.* Doctoral dissertation.
25. Mohammadian, H. D. (2019, April). IoE–A solution for energy management challenges. In *2019 IEEE global engineering education conference (EDUCON)* (pp. 1455–1461). IEEE.
26. Miglani, A., Kumar, N., Chamola, V., & Zeadally, S. (2020). Blockchain for Internet of Energy management: Review, solutions, and challenges. *Computer Communications, 151*, 395–418.
27. Shafik, W., Matinkhah, S. M., & Ghasemzadeh, M. (2020). Internet of things-based energy management, challenges, and solutions in smart cities. *Journal of Communications Technology, Electronics and Computer Science, 27*, 1–11.
28. Belli, L., Cilfone, A., Davoli, L., Ferrari, G., Adorni, P., Di Nocera, F., ... & Bertolotti, E. (2020). IoT-enabled smart sustainable cities: challenges and approaches. *Smart Cities, 3*(3), 1039–1071.
29. Abduljabbar, R. L., Liyanage, S., & Dia, H. (2021). The role of micro-mobility in shaping sustainable cities: A systematic literature review. *Transportation Research Part D: Transport and Environment, 92,* 102734.
30. Giles-Corti, B., Moudon, A. V., Lowe, M., Adlakha, D., Cerin, E., Boeing, G., ... & Sallis, J. F. (2022). Creating healthy and sustainable cities: what gets measured, gets done. *The Lancet Global Health, 10*(6), e782–e785.
31. Allam, Z., & Jones, D. S. (2021). Future (post-COVID) digital, smart and sustainable cities in the wake of 6G: Digital twins, immersive realities and new urban economies. *Land Use Policy, 101*, 105201.
32. Bibri, S. E., & Krogstie, J. (2020). Environmentally data-driven smart sustainable cities: Applied innovative solutions for energy efficiency, pollution reduction, and urban metabolism. *Energy Informatics, 3*(1), 1–59.
33. Kumari, A., Gupta, R., Tanwar, S., & Kumar, N. (2020). Blockchain and AI amalgamation for energy cloud management: Challenges, solutions, and future directions. *Journal of Parallel and Distributed Computing, 143*, 148–166.
34. Alam, M. S., & Arefifar, S. A. (2019). Energy management in power distribution systems: Review, classification, limitations and challenges. *IEEE Access, 7*, 92979–93001.
35. Gupta, S., & Vyas, S. (2021). IoT in green engineering transformation for smart cities. *Smart IoT for Research and Industry, 121.*
36. Arora, A., Kaur, A., Bhushan, B., & Saini, H. (2019, July). Security concerns and future trends of internet of things. In *2019 2nd international conference on intelligent computing, instrumentation and control technologies (ICICICT)* (Vol. 1, pp. 891–896). IEEE.

37. Bhushan, B., Sahoo, C., Sinha, P., & Khamparia, A. (2021). Unification of Blockchain and Internet of Things (BIoT): Requirements, working model, challenges and future directions. *Wireless Networks, 27*(1), 55–90.

38. Sethi, R., Bhushan, B., Sharma, N., Kumar, R., & Kaushik, I. (2021). Applicability of industrial IoT in diversified sectors: Evolution, applications and challenges. In *Multimedia technologies in the Internet of Things environment* (pp. 45–67). Springer.

39. Varshney, T., Sharma, N., Kaushik, I., & Bhushan, B. (2019, October). Architectural model of security threats & their countermeasures in IoT. In *2019 International conference on computing, communication, and intelligent systems (ICCCIS)* (pp. 424–429). IEEE.

40. Saxena, S., Bhushan, B., & Ahad, M. A. (2021). Blockchain based solutions to secure IoT: Background, integration trends and a way forward. *Journal of Network and Computer Applications, 181*, 103050.

Printed in the United States
by Baker & Taylor Publisher Services